ISLAMIC DEMOCRATIC DISCOURSE

GLOBAL ENCOUNTERS: STUDIES IN COMPARATIVE POLITICAL THEORY
Series Editor: Fred Dallmayr, University of Notre Dame

This series seeks to inaugurate a new field of inquiry and intellectual concern: that of comparative political theory as an inquiry proceeding not from the citadel of a global hegemony but through cross-cultural dialogue and critical interaction. By opening the discourse of political theory—today largely dominated by American and European intellectuals—to voices from across the global spectrum, we hope to contribute to a richer, multifaceted mode of theorizing as well as to a deeper, cross-cultural awareness of the requirements of global justice.

Gandhi, Freedom, and Self-Rule, edited by Anthony J. Parel

Race and Reconciliation in South Africa: A Multicultural Dialogue in Comparative Perspective, edited by William E. Van Vugt and G. Daan Cloete

Comparative Political Culture in the Age of Globalization: An Introductory Anthology, edited by Hwa Yol Jung

Conversations and Transformations: Toward a New Ethics of Self and Society, by Ananta Kumar Giri

Hinterlands and Horizons: Excursions in Search of Amity, by Margaret Chatterjee

New Approaches to Comparative Politics: Insights from Political Theory, edited by Jennifer S. Holmes

Comparative Political Philosophy: Studies under the Upas Tree, edited by Anthony J. Parel and Ronald C. Keith

Iran: Between Tradition and Modernity, edited by Ramin Jahanbegloo

Democratization and Identity: Regimes and Ethnicity in East and Southeast Asia, edited by Susan J. Henders

The Politics of Affective Relations: East Asia and Beyond, edited by Daniel Bell and Hahm Chaihark

From the Margins of Globalization: Critical Perspectives on Human Rights, edited by Neve Gordon

Imagining Brazil, edited by Jessé Souza and Valter Sinder

Islamic Democratic Discourse: Theory, Debates, and Philosophical Perspectives, edited by M. A. Muqtedar Khan

ISLAMIC DEMOCRATIC DISCOURSE

Theory, Debates, and Philosophical Perspectives

Edited by
M. A. Muqtedar Khan

LEXINGTON BOOKS

A division of
ROWMAN & LITTLEFIELD PUBLISHERS, INC.
Lanham • Boulder • New York • Toronto • Oxford

Some of the material in chapter 10 originally appeared as a journal article. This material is reprinted by permission from Marc Lynch, "Transnational Dialogue in an Age of Terror," *Global Society* 19, no. 1 (January 2005): 5–28.

LEXINGTON BOOKS

A division of Rowman & Littlefield Publishers, Inc.
A wholly owned subsidiary of The Rowman & Littlefield Publishing Group, Inc.
4501 Forbes Boulevard, Suite 200
Lanham, MD 20706

PO Box 317
Oxford
OX2 9RU, UK

British Library Cataloguing in Publication Information Available

Library of Congress Cataloging-in-Publication Data
Islamic democratic discourse : theory, debates, and philosophical
    perspectives / edited by M. A. Muqtedar Khan.
       p. cm. — (Global encounters)
    Includes bibliographical references and index.
    ISBN-13: 978-0-7391-0644-0 (cloth : alk. paper)
    ISBN-10: 0-7391-0644-9 (cloth : alk. paper)
    ISBN-13: 978-0-7391-0645-7 (pbk. : alk. paper)
    ISBN-10: 0-7391-0645-7 (pbk. : alk. paper)
    1. Islam and state.   2. Democracy—Religious aspects—Islam.
  3. Islam and politics.   I. Khan, M. A. Muqtedar.   II. Series.
  JC49.I7655 2006
  321.8—dc22   2005020654

Printed in the United States of America

♾ ™ The paper used in this publication meets the minimum requirements of American National Standard for Information Sciences—Permanence of Paper for Printed Library Materials, ANSI/NISO Z39.48–1992.

For John L. Esposito,
teacher, friend and mentor

Contents

Preface

We live in an age when the Muslim World is deeply engaged in the struggle to reconcile the existential realities of late modernity with its imagination of what an Islamic life means. What is really at stake is the re-understanding of the meaning of virtue and the good life in general and the meaning of good governance in particular.

After an extended period of external governance, the Muslim World became politically free but found itself often economically and culturally dependent on the West in its quest for self-governance and socio-political direction. The Muslim World has not succeeded in rescuing itself from historical cycles such as modernization, democratization and globalization, which are the global consequences of local Western developments. Thus even as the Muslim World became "free" from colonial patronage, it found its present and future hostage to structural conditions anchored in Western societies.

The Muslim World today is the most diverse in the forms of political systems it employs. It has traditional monarchies, constitutional monarchies, dictatorships, secular democracies, Islamic republics and some liberal democracies. Muslim polities vary vastly but the one issue in which they are all similar is their struggle to accommodate and/or contend with Islam and its growing role in the Muslim public sphere. Muslims have experimented enough. It is my strong and considered belief that the best solution for the political problems of the *Ummah* is the institutionalization of Islamic democracies.

This book seeks to explore the agonizing attempt by Muslim thinkers in the recent past and the present to discover an authentic formula for good and ethical self-governance. I am very proud to present a galaxy of intellectual stars who are either students of Islamic political thought or Muslim political philosophers in their own right, striving to shape Muslim understanding of Islamic democracy. I hope that this book will offer new direction and take the conversation on Islam and democracy many steps further.

Books are the jewels of civilization. They are not easy to produce and to partake in the development of one is always a blessing and special privilege. In putting this book together I had the honor of working with exceptional scholars from four continents and I am grateful for their intellectual fellowship.

I must make particular mention of Professor Asma Afsaruddin, who constantly motivated me and strongly supported this project. I owe Professor Fred Dallmayr an unrepayable debt for trusting me with such an important initiative. Thanks are also due to Serena Krombach of Lexington Books, who shepherded the production of the book.

I am grateful to the Center on Religion and Democracy at the University of Virginia, whose research grant supported part of this project. I owe thanks to Adrian College, whose summer research grants also helped support this endeavor. I also must recognize the Center for the Study of Islam & Democracy as a comrade-in-arms that seeks to realize in practice what scholars like me visualize in theory.

My wife and soulmate, Reshma, as always remains my biggest supporter and ally in everything that I attempt. Her love, her constant encouragement and support, and above all her understanding and appreciation for my life's mission are immeasurable and irreplaceable ingredients of my work. My children, Rumi and Ruhi, embody the innocence and beauty that reminds me constantly of what is human about humanity. My mother continues to support and pray for me and my brother remains a brother indeed. For all of them I am grateful.

This book is dedicated to John L. Esposito. I have known John for over a decade and in those years he has played the role of a teacher, a mentor, a friend, a guide and an intellectual father who has enriched and guided my development as a scholar and an intellectual. His most important contribution to me has been his example. His dedication to his work and his uncompromising moral politics even under adverse and critical circumstances are virtues that I struggle to emulate. I have learned a lot from him; I can never repay that debt. This book is for him in recognition of the special place he has in my life.

Finally, I cannot but marvel at my good fortune and reiterate how grateful I am to God for letting me live a life dedicated to the pursuit of knowledge. Nothing in my opinion can be more rewarding in the here and in the hereafter. Needless to say, I alone am responsible for all the limitations of this book.

M. A. Muqtedar Khan
September 2005
Newark, Delaware

Introduction

The Emergence of an Islamic Democratic Discourse

M. A. Muqtedar Khan

Rise to the Dawn of the People's Rule;
Erase all relics of the past you behold

—Allama Muhammad Iqbal[1]

He who says that democracy is disbelief; neither understands Islam,
nor democracy

—Sheikh Yusuf Al Qaradawi[2]

As the Muslim World became free from colonial domination, beginning in the first half of the twentieth century, it faced two significant challenges. First Muslims had to address the question, "How are we going to govern ourselves?" and second, "how are we going to face the new character of our times— modernity?" During the heydays of the global domination of European powers, modernity had stealthily invaded Asia and Africa and caught the natives completely unprepared, both in the intellectual as well as in the political context. Traditional epistemologies were not adequate to comprehend and negotiate the new realities of modernity and the forms of governments that still remained in the collective memory of Muslims were ill suited to the new social structures and much transformed and evolved societies that had emerged under colonial occupation.

Thus becoming free forced the Muslim World into a dual crisis of epistemology and politics—of theory and practice. Not only was there a challenge with regards to "how do we know what is the best form of government?" but also "how do we know that we know." It is not surprising therefore that today as the world at large focuses on the need for reform in the Muslim World, particularly the Arab World, two dominant themes have emerged; educational reform and the role of traditional educational institutions (*madrassahs*) and their compatibility with modernity, and political reform and the compatibility of tradition (Islam and Muslim culture) and modernity (Democracy).

Even after half a century the Muslim world has failed to produce a viable and appreciable model of self-governance. The frequent shifts in regime type, for example, in Pakistan, which oscillates between democracy and dictatorship is indicative of the unsettled nature of political structures in the Muslim World. Only nations that had tyrannical dictatorships and monarchies have enjoyed some degree of political stability, but without significant economic or human development. The level of disenchantment in the Muslim World today remains at such high levels that it is easily the most volatile region on the planet. Today the Muslim World boasts of a diversity of regime types, dictatorships and sham democracies in Egypt, Sudan and Tunisia, secular democracy in Turkey, monarchies in the Gulf, pluralist democracies in Bangladesh and Malaysia and an Islamic state in Iran (a sort of Theo-democracy), but it lacks stability and vitality that one now normally expects from thriving democracies in the first as well as the former Third World countries like the U.S., UK, and India.

Debating the Role of Islam in Muslim Polity

There is a growing consensus among experts and the masses alike that democratization will reduce the many problems of the Muslim World. Recent surveys have indicated that over 80% of Muslims would like to see their countries democratize.[3] Except for a rather radical brand of Islamists who reject any and every form of democracy in favor of a nebulous notion of an Islamic State/caliphate, most Islamists are now converging with secularists and moderate Muslims on the desirability of democracy. The only question that really needs to be settled is the role of Islam in the Muslim public sphere. Most Islamists will break from this emerging *Ijmaa* (consensus) if the preferred model of democracy was secular. The secularists and moderates are nervous about accepting Islam as a prominent basis for Islamic democracy fearing the implementation of medieval articulations of Islamic criminal codes. The issue of the role of women and the status of religious minorities is also a concern if the polity is completely theocratic as in Iran. But Muslims, regardless of their political persuasion do believe that Islam does have a lot of good to offer and must play a role in the public sphere. An illustrative example of this global debate among Muslims was played out in the discussions of interim laws for Iraq and Afghanistan as they democratize under the jurisdiction of U.S.'s occupying forces.

So far the Muslim world has not reached a consensus on the role of Islam and things Islamic—laws, clerics, scholars—in their polities. While in the Islamic State of Iran the masses are clamoring for more freedom and political and cultural liberalization, we are also witnessing extremists demanding greater Islamization in another Islamic State of Saudi Arabia. Islamists continue to demand more and more application of the *Sharia,* in places like Turkey and Pakistan, but in those same countries, we also see significant opposition to Islamists from secular authoritarian regimes that do enjoy sufficient support to prevent popular Islamic revolutions.

A quick survey of the political discourse of Muslims in the twentieth century also reveals similar trends and tensions; all culminating in the question, "what and how much role should Islam have in the public sphere?" Secularists, Islamists and Moderates have all advanced various conceptions of polities ranging from no role for Islam in politics (secularism *a la* Turkey) to imposition of Islamic law as the object of politics (Islamic Republic of Iran).[4] In this book we are not directly concerned with the ideas of either the secularists or the Islamists who both advocate mutually exclusive positions. We are more interested in the moderate discourse that seeks to find a place for Islam as well as democracy. The various essays in this book explore the contentious domain where freedom and faith, democracy and theology negotiate a mutually compatible future, and it is important to recognize that this is not a new initiative, but a continuation of a century-long search for an Islamic democracy.

Defining the Scope of Democracy in Muslim Polity

The early twentieth century saw many Muslim thinkers exploring the prospects of establishing an Islamic democracy. From 1910 to the 1930s Muhammad Iqbal the philosopher-poet *par excellence* of the subcontinent was already arguing that Islam was an egalitarian faith that had room for neither the clergy nor the aristocracy. Even as he rejected the imperialist tendencies of the British Empire, he continued to admire its democratic tendencies and argued that Muslims too must aspire for a similar egalitarian system. Like all contemporary Muslim democrats, Iqbal too recognized the importance of *Ijtihad* and argued for its democratization and institutionalization in a popular legislative assembly thereby bridging the theoretical gap between divine and popular sovereignty. Some superficial readers have misunderstood his critique of Western societies as rejection of democracy, but even they will concede that Iqbal was a strong advocate of freedom, individuality, equality and brotherhood, all necessary ingredients of liberal democracy. While he was a very early exponent of political reform and democratization of Muslim society, Iqbal was not the only thinker of his time who was discoursing an Islamic democracy.[5]

In 1942, H. K. Sherwani was writing about a "Quranic State," and finding a common Islamic political discourse extant for over 1200 years.[6] In 1944 Ilyas Ahmad expounded on the role of the social contract and the Islamic State. Ilyas Ahmad anticipated many of the contemporary debates by positing that civil society, like the Islamic state was to be based on social contracts. He deals explicitly with the various contracts, including the famous Constitution of Medina, to argue the civil democratic nature of Islam.[7] Charles Kurzman in his anthology on *Liberal Islam* provides an interesting collection of writings by Muslims on the compatibility of Islam and democratic governance. He includes, Muhammad Natsir who was writing in 1955 in Indonesia and was advocating democracy, S. M. Zafar who in 1980 wrote about Islam and a popular parliament in Pakistan, Mahdi Bazargan, an Iranian who argued the compatibility of religion and liberty in 1983, Humayun Kabir who in 1968 was making a case for religious pluralism, and Ali Bulac, a Turkish thinker who also argued that the Compact of Medina established the prophetic precedence for the Constitutional basis of an Islamic polity.[8]

Even hardcore Islamists who advocated an Islamic State that would *impose* the Islamic *Sharia* on its citizens (they prefer to use the term "implement") have actually either adopted or intuitively recommend democratic processes, including elections, in the Islamic State. Perhaps the only practical example of the idea of the Islamic State, the Iranian regime, is to some extent democratic, has elections and practices a degree of separation of powers. Maulana Maududi, the founder of *Jamaat-e-Islami* (Pakistan) and the father of the idea of divine sovereignty (*Al Hakimiyyah*) believed in democracy and called his Islamic state a *theodemocracy*. Syed Qutb, who is considered by some as a radical philosopher, also argued for the inclusion of democratic processes in the Islamic state.[9] Taqiuddin An-Nabhani, the founder of *Hizb-ut-Tahreer* and an advocate of a global Islamic Caliphate, also advocated elections and his ideal constitution looks like a pirated copy of the American constitution with cosmetic Islamization.[10] Lately Islamists like Rashid Ghannoushi (lives in the UK) of Tunisian Muslim Brotherhood (*an-Nahda*) and Yusuf al Qaradawi of the Egyptian Muslim Brotherhood (lives in Qatar) are acknowledging the compatibility and even desirability of democracy.[11] Even hardcore radicals such as Abid Ullah Jan of Pakistan (lives in Canada) who see democracy and Islamism in a zero-sum-game and have already announced the demise of democracy and the triumph of Islamism, too acknowledge that the positive qualities of democracy are included within Islam.[12]

Debating Islam and Democracy in the American Academy

The interest of the American Academy in the compatibility of Islam and Democracy is relatively new. It can be traced to an important article written by Bernard Lewis, "The Roots of Muslim Rage," published in *The Atlantic Monthly,* in September 1990, months after the fall of the Soviet Union.[13] This article sought to accomplish two strategic goals: identify Islamic resurgence as the next challenge/threat to the United States and the West after the collapse of the Soviet Empire, and it tried to establish freedom as the most significant difference between political Islam and the West. This article, and its last subheading—A Clash of Civilizations—launched the discourse of civilizational incompatibility and hostility, later on capitalized by Samuel Huntington, and presented to the American academy a strategic research agenda based on the assertion that contemporary Islamic resurgence was incompatible with freedom. He prompted the debate with subsequent articles arguing the incompatibility of Islam and liberal democracy. A more detailed discussion of the politics of this discourse can be found in my chapter in this book titled, "The Politics, Theory and Philosophy of Islamic Democracy."

While initially driven by strategic interests, the American academy quickly engaged the issues in its complexity. Two key questions started driving the theoretical and empirical study of Islam and democracy. The empirical studies sought to understand and explain the causes for the absence of democracy in the Muslim World even as Latin America and East Europe began to rapidly democratize in what is called the Third Wave of democracy. The second and more theoretical question continues to drive the discourse on the moral and philosophical compatibility of Islam and democracy.

The year 1992 witnessed some very interesting publications on the subject by a secular feminist Muslim woman from the east—Fatima Mernissi, an Islamic feminist woman from the West—Azizah al-Hibri, and an American government think tank—the United States Institute of Peace (USIP). Fatima Mernissi's *Islam and Democracy* was translated into English by Mary Jo Lakeland and became available to the American academy. The book is interesting in its style. It uses an anecdotal, story-telling style with occasional burst of analyses to construct a peculiar narrative that essentially tries to substantiate the Weberian distinction between the modern west and the traditional east. Mernissi's "Arab World" emerges as a closed, traditional and religious society unenlightened by western secular humanism; devoid of an appreciation for freedom, tolerance, and gender equality; afraid of democracy and things modern because they are seen as foreign. Mernissi equates her perception of Arab reality to Islam and alienates freedom and democracy from Islam. Her work, which does not meet the standards of rationality in Islamic theology, nor the rigor of political theory or the precision of sociological analyses, went a long way in making the case that democracy in the Arab World is absent because Islam and democracy are incompatible.[14]

It is interesting to see how two Muslim women came up with such contrasting positions on Islam and democracy at the same time. Azizah al-Hibri's long essay, "Islamic Constitutionalism and the Concept of Democracy," makes exactly the opposite case. Unlike Mernissi she does not try to explain the absence of democracy in the Muslim World. Her primary objective is to discuss the role of constitutionalism and Islamic law in an Islamic polity. She concludes that Islamic *Sharia* is compatible with democratic governance and is in its structure and form quite similar to the American constitution. She further argues that like the American constitution Islamic law too must be applied with popular consent. Al-Hibri's paper to this day remains one of the best-argued, extremely well documented cases for the compatibility of the Islamic *Sharia* to democratic form. Al-Hibri easily imagines an Islamic polity whose form is democratic and whose content is Islamic.[15]

For some unknown reason 1992 was a break through year for the discussion of Islam and Democracy in the American academy. Perhaps the sudden interest was sparked by the victory of Islamists in the Algerian elections. Besides al-Hibri and Mernissi, another woman Robin Wright too introduced the topic to the readers of *Foreign Affairs*; easily one of the most influential international political journals in the U.S.[16] It was in 1992 (May 15th), also that the United States Institute of Peace conducted its first seminar on Islam and Democracy and subsequently published a report.[17] The symposium included many prominent voices on the politics of the Middle East and concluded that while there were political and cultural hurdles to democratization, Islam and the resurgent political Islam were potential facilitators of democratization and not barriers.

In 1996 John Esposito and John Voll, two of the most prominent scholars of Islam and politics, published *Islam and Democracy*, a seminal work that settled the debate on the compatibility of Islamic values and democratic processes.[18] As far as the academy was concerned, Esposito and Voll had demonstrated in Islamic theory and by carefully charting political developments in the Muslim World that not only was Islam compatible with democracy but the rise of political Islam was in its own way a democratizing impetus. But policy makers remained skeptical of this position. The general media and the government remained under the influence of policy entrepreneurs who continued to argue that as long as Muslims adhered to Islamic values democracy would not take root in the Muslim Middle East.[19]

Islam, Democracy and Terror

After the attacks on the U.S. on September 11, 2001, the discussion on Islam and democracy has taken a new direction in American political and policy circles. Without delving into too much detail about the policy debates, it is enough to recall for this discussion that President George W. Bush simply assumed—in a *fatwa*-like fashion—that Islam and democracy are indeed compatible and it was now time for the rest of the world to expedite the democratization of the Muslim World. Washington is currently laboring under the assumption that terrorism by Muslims is a consequence of the absence of democracy and hence is determined to use democracy as an antidote to terror. Now that democracy in the Muslim World is also in U.S. national interest, there are very few who are willing to argue the incompatibility of Islam and democracy. There are, however, a few fanatical voices in the Muslim world that not only denounce democracy but also predict its demise everywhere.[20] In this new political context two books have been published on the subject of Islam and democracy. The first book is *Islam and Democracy in the Middle East,* a collection of essays published over the years in the *Journal of Democracy.*[21] The second, *Islam and the Challenge of Democracy,* is basically a long article by Khalid Abou El Fadl with very brief responses from a number of scholars, including the editor of this book.[22]

Islam and Democracy in the Middle East has several excellent chapters but since they have been written over a spread of years and over a wide variety of topics ranging from theoretical reflections on liberal Islam to the evaluation of the empirical progress of democratization, the book while rich in resources lacks cohesion. It however is an important book and provides a rich and broad perspective on the subject of Islam and democracy in the Muslim World.

Abou El Fadl's essay is interesting and provides insight into the compassionate and democratic dimension of Islam. His essay is well informed by medieval discourses but is completely unaware of the theoretical developments and discussions on Islam and democracy in the West as well as the Muslim World in the last hundred or so years. To an uninitiated reader it may appear as if the book is discovering the compatibility of Islam and democracy for the first time. I engage his essay in greater detail in my chapter "The Politics, Theory and Philosophy of Islamic Democracy" in this book and hence will be brief in my evaluation here. There are two things that stand out about El Fadl's essay: (1) it confuses jurisprudence for political philosophy and therefore one finds references to his own work on violence in the essay but there are no references to say Esposito and Voll's *Islam and Democracy* and (2) it is also completely uninformed by the vast discourse on Islam and democracy by Muslim thinkers. This is remarkable since El Fadl even ignores the work of fellow jurists such as al-Hibri's "Islamic Constitutionalism and the Concept of Democracy" in his reflections. This oversight essentially marginalizes the utility of *Islam and the Challenge of Democracy* to the cumulative development of an Islamic theory/discourse on democracy. The book however has an important element to it; it essentially is a book of endorsements as scholar after scholar reiterates optimistically the prospects of democracy in an Islamic milieu.

This Book and Its Challenge

This book attempts to accelerate the development of the gradually emerging philosophical and theological discourse on Islamic democratic theory. In this book political philosophers and theologians and students of political philosophy and theology come together to make a systematic effort to link contemporary Muslim ideas on Islam and democracy with classical Islamic theories and profound theological concepts and issues. Unlike most recent efforts which seek to either underscore or dispute the compatibility of Islam and democracy, this eclectic collection begins a comprehensive conversation on Islam's role in the public sphere, various Islamic concepts that can help define Islam's role in governance and most importantly opens new avenues to seriously build an authentic Islamic theory/theories of democracy.

The authors are working with several key fundamental assumptions. We assume that Islam and democracy are compatible; moreover we also believe that Islam in its revealed and its intellectual discourses (*aqli* and *naqli* sciences) already contains concepts and theories that can be developed into Islamic theories of democracy. We believe that perhaps it is possible to articulate multiple theories of Islamic democracy. While none of the chapters attempts to actually advance a specific architecture of an Islamic democratic theory, we are confident that there is much here that can fuel a healthy and productive discussion on the nature and character of Islamic democracy.

Tariq Ramadan and Asma Afsaruddin provide the intellectual histories of key Islamic political concepts. Ramadan whose work generally explores the areas of philosophy and Muslim identity examines critically the juristic concepts of *Ijtihad* and *Maslaha* and emphasizes their importance to the revival of Islamic thought. Afsaruddin's work essentially focuses on the key political concepts that have shaped the emergence of Islam political community and Islamic thought, particularly in the early and classical age. Here she examines the key concept of authority (*uli'l-amr*) and provides a genealogy of how the term gained several meanings over time and what that now means to the very idea of political authority in an Islamic polity.

Abdulaziz Sachedina and Tamara Sonn explore the historical and the potential role that Islam has played and can play in governance. Together they demonstrate how theologians and students of theology can illuminate the role of religion in the political sphere and contribute to the development of political theory and philosophy. Sonn delineates the constitutive role that Islam has played in the emergence of early forms of Islamic polity. Sachedina identifies Islamic sources that can refine that experience and allow Islam to play a central role in contemporary societies with particular sensitivity towards the need for inclusive and pluralistic political systems.

The next contributions are part of four chapters that examine diverse Muslim political theories. Osman Bakar discusses how Malaysia's diverse ethnic and plural constitution has interacted with its predominantly Islamic heritage to provide a unique model of Islamic democracy that is religiously and ethnically plural. Mahgoub El-Tigani Mahmoud and Carolyn Fluehr-Lobban explore how Sudanese scholars and thinkers have tried to bring Islam to the fore in their search for an authentic political system. Ali Paya elucidates the contemporary Shii political thought providing an insight into the Iranian approach to Islamization of governance. Özlem Denli provides an interesting analysis of how Ali Bulac, a prominent Turkish theorist, understood the early Islamic political experience as democratic and constitutional.

Marc Lynch critically examines the evolution of contemporary Muslim discourse in the area of political theory and philosophy. Lynch's article discusses and important element of the discourse on Islam and Discourse—the shadow of the power of the West. Today Muslims cannot indulge in any exercise of self-reflection and self-development without the involvement and intervention of the West and Western scholarship. Thus Lynch's argument that the dialogue continues even after September 11 is an important message and holds promise and hope for Muslim intellectuals and theorists seeking to define and redefine the contemporary role of Islam in Muslim and global society.

My chapter in this book explores the politics that underpins the theoretical discourse on Islam and democracy and then proceeds to evaluate the relative merits of philosophy, theology and jurisprudence in developing an authentic Islamic discourse on democracy. Finally Abdelwahab El-Affendi provides an enlightening discussion of how Muslims are presently engaging with the issue of Islam and democracy and Islamic democracy. His essay captures the efforts of contemporary Muslim thinkers to come to terms with the current challenges that Muslims face in devising good forms of governance while ensuring that Islam remains central in their lives.

Notes

1. Quoted in F. M. Mali, *Mohammad Iqbal: Muslim Political Thought—A Reconstruction* (Islamabad, Pakistan: Alhamra Publications, 2002), 21.

2. Quoted in *Ash-Sharq al-Awsat*, February 5, 1990. Also cited in the editorial by Mahbubur Rahman, "Islam and Democracy: Coming out of Misconceptions," *The Message International* (April/May 2002), 6.

3. See Siraj Mufti, "Muslims Love Democracy," *Muslim Democrat*, 4, 2 (July 2002), 1.

4. While considering the contemporary Iranian regime we must always remember that while Iran is today a theocracy of sorts struggling to balance freedom and religious imperatives, it experienced a full fledged constitutional revolution from 1905–1911, nearly three quarters of a century before the Islamic revolution. Iran's Islamic State is not an indication of a failure to modernize, but is an adamant expression of disenchantment with a modernity that allowed for monarchy. Iran's Islamic State is not just a failure of Iran to modernize fully, but is also a failure of modernity to satisfy its followers. For a review of Iran's constitutional revolution see Janet Afary, *The Iranian Constitutional Revolution* (New York: Columbia University Press, 1996). Bernard Lewis, who has harbored and trafficked extremely negative perceptions about Islam and Muslim societies writes about the Islamic Republic as follows "Even the Islamic Republic of Iran has a written constitution and an elected assembly . . ." in Bernard Lewis, "The Roots of Muslim Rage," 266, 3, *The Atlantic Monthly* (September 1990), 47–60. I am not trying to argue that the Islamic Republic of Iran is a good democracy, my point is even a state run by intolerant Mullahs cannot escape democratic processes and institutions.

5. See F. M. Mali, *Mohammad Iqbal: Muslim Political Thought—A Reconstruction*, 18–41. Also see Allama Muhammad Iqbal, *The Reconstruction of Religious Thought in Islam* (Lahore, Pakistan: Ashraf Printing Press, 1981). See also Robert D. Lee, *Overcoming Tradition and Modernity: The Search for Islamic Authenticity* (Boulder, CO: Westview Press, 1997), 71–74.

6. See H. K. Sherwani, *Studies in Muslim Political Thought and Administration* (Lahore, Pakistan: Sh. Muhammad Ashraf Publishers, 1942).

7. See Ilyas Ahmad, *The Social Contract and the Islamic State* (New Delhi, India: Kitab Bhavan, 1944).

8. See Muhammad Natsir, "The Indonesian Revolution: Harmony of Life! Freedom of Religion! Unity of Nation!," 59–66; S. M. Zafar, "Accountability, Parliament and Ijtihad," 67–72; Mahdi Bazargan, "Religion and Liberty," 73–84; Humayun Kabir, "Minorities in a Democracy," 145–154; Ali Bulac, "The Medina Document," 169–178. All these essays are included in Charles Kurzman (Ed.), *Liberal Islam: A Source Book* (New York, NY: Oxford University Press, 1998).

9. For an analysis of the democratic nature of Maududi and Qutb's Islamic State see, M. A. Muqtedar Khan, "First Islamic Society then Islamic State, But Democracy Now!," *The Diplomat*, 2 (November 1997), 48–51. Also see a comparison of John Locke and Syed Qutb in M. A. Muqtedar Khan, "Radical Islam, Liberal Islam," *Current History: A Journal of Contemporary World Affairs*, 102, 668 (December 2003), 417–421.

Also see M. A. Muqtedar Khan, "Syed Qutb—John Locke of the Islamic World?," *The Globalist* (July 28, 2003). On the World Wide Web: http://www.theglobalist.com/ DBWeb/printStoryId.aspx?StoryId=3324.

10. See Taqiuddin An-Nabhani, *The Islamic State* (Walnut, California, Islamic Cultural Workshop, 1996).

11. See Yusuf Al-Qaradawi, "Islam's Approach towards Democracy," *The Message International* (April/May 2002), 32–33. See John L. Esposito, "Practice and Theory" in Khalid Abou El Fadl, Joshua Cohen and Deborah Chasman (Eds.), *Islam and the Challenge of Democracy* (Princeton, NJ: Princeton University Press, 2004), 98–99. Also see M. A. Muqtedar Khan, "Second Generation Islamists and the Future of Islamic Movements," *Islamica*, 3, 1 (1999), 65–70.

12. See Abid Ullah Jan, *The End of Democracy* (Canada: Pragmatic Publishing, 2003).

13. Bernard Lewis, "The Roots of Muslim Rage," 266, 3, *The Atlantic Monthly* (September 1990), 47–60.

14. See Fatima Mernissi, *Islam and Democracy: Fear of the Modern World*, Trans. Mary Jo Lakeland (New York: Addison-Wesley Publishing Company, 1992).

15. Azizah al-Hibri, "Islamic Constitutionalism and the Concept of Democracy" (New York: American Muslim Foundation, 1992). This essay was also published in the *Case Western Reserve Journal of International Law*, 24, 1, in 1992.

16. See Robin Wright, "Islam, Democracy and the West," *Foreign Affairs* 71, 3 (Summer 1992), 131–147. Robin Wright has continued to explore the topic. See also Robin Wright, "Islam and Liberal Democracy: Two Visions of Reformation," *Journal of Democracy*, 7, 2 (April 1996), 64–76. Robin Wright has for over a decade continued to monitor the political as well as the intellectual development of the Islam and democracy issue.

17. See Timothy Sisk (Ed.), *Islam and Democracy: Religion, Politics, and Power in the Middle East* (Washington, DC: U.S. Institute of Peace, 1992). The institute also conducted another symposium on Islam and Democracy on June 18, 2002. The report on this convention can be found on the World Wide Web at: http://www.usip.org/ pubs/specialreports/sr93.pdf.

18. John L. Esposito and John O. Voll, *Islam and Democracy* (New York: Oxford University Press, 1996).

19. See M. A. Muqtedar Khan, "Policy Entrepreneurs: The Third Dimension of American Foreign Policy Culture," *Middle East Policy* (September 1997), 140–154.

20. For an example of this genre see Abid Ullah Jan, *The End of Democracy* (Canada: Pragmatic Publishing, 2003).

21. Larry Diamond, Marc F. Plattner, and Daniel Brumberg, eds., *Islam and Democracy in the Middle East* (Baltimore: Johns Hopkins University Press, 2003).

22. See Khalid Abou El Fadl, *Islam and the Challenge of Democracy* (Princeton, NJ: Princeton University Press, 2004).

CLASSICAL PERSPECTIVES ON ISLAM AND POLITICS

1

Ijtihad and Maslaha:
The Foundations of Governance

Tariq Ramadan

In the West, the idea of *Sharia* conjures up the darkest images of Islam: repression of women, physical punishments, and stoning among others. This negative association caused many Muslim intellectuals such concern that they do not even dare to mention the word for fear of arousing suspicion of all their work or frightening people by mere reference to the concept. This unnecessary apprehension is the result of confusion about the content and scope of *Sharia*. For, more than a mere penal code, *Sharia* is a global path, methodology and philosophy of life. Based on the Qur'an and the Sunna, it gives shape to a way of life: from performing daily prayers to fighting for social justice, from seeking knowledge to smiling, to respecting nature. *Sharia* is often confused with *Fiqh* and frequently the terms are used interchangeably. But while *Sharia* is the revealed and immutable path, *Fiqh* represents the product of human thought and elaboration on it; more precisely *Fiqh* is the state of juridical reflection reached by Muslim scholars at a certain time and in certain context in light of their study of the *Sharia*; and as such *Fiqh*, while remaining faithful to the function and purpose of *Sharia*, has to be dynamic, in constant elaboration since evolution is the defining character of our world.

To be faithful to the message of the Qur'an in no way means to confine oneself to a very restrictive and lazy reading of the two sources and the related scholarly commentaries of the great ulama of the past; to the contrary, faithfulness demands that one exerts all intellectual effort to provide solutions that are relevant to the social and political reality, and that is the true expression of our individual and collective intension to be genuine Muslims.

Among the tools listed by the classical ulama who specialised in the fundamentals of law and jurisprudence (*usul al-fiqh*), we find three basic notions that provide a way of making a connection between universal principles and social realities that change with the passage of time and cultures. A study shows that they present a significant degree of leeway for proposing new readings of the sources, finding new responses or thinking of innovative models of social and even economic organization. It is Muslim thinking that is stalled these days: the tools are available, and the work to be done is the double task of reading the sources and interpreting the world. It must also be remembered that it is not a question of understanding the world better in order to adapt to it, but, at a much deeper level, through this contact with the changing realities of the world (scientific, social, political, and economic), it is a question of re-reading the scriptural sources themselves with a new eye. In doing this, it is essential to remember that the corpus of the *Sharia* is a human construction and some aspects of it may evolve just as human thought evolves and just as some aspects of the Qur'an and the Sunna were revealed over time. This is precisely the meaning of the Prophetic tradition that "God sends to this community, every hundred years, someone to renew its religion." This renewal is not a modification of the sources, but a transformation of the mind and eyes that read them, which are indeed naturally influenced by the new social, political and scientific environment in which they live. A new context changes the horizon of the text, renews it and sometimes gives it an original purport, providing responses never before imagined.

The three notions in the heading act exactly in this way. Beginning from the state of society, they invite the mind to re-read the sources and give it the means either to find a response that has already been given (for example, in another similar case), or to think of a new legal development (when the texts say nothing that applies to the case in question), or to state a specific legal opinion allowing some adaptation (more or less restricted to circumstance and time). This is an essential process for Muslims living in the West, even if, these tools must be used with a certain number of necessary conditions if one is to avoid falling into the trap of racing into adaptation, which is either timid or risky, and never wholly reliable.

Al-Maslaha: The Common Good

The notion of *maslaha*, as a legal term, has given rise to numerous debates since it was first used, principally by the ulama of the Maliki school, against the fierce opposition by the *Zahiri* school, and in particular by Ibn Hazm. These quarrels were very often ill-founded, and, more than anything, they were often a question of defining relations to the sources and to the corpus of the *Sharia*.

In more recent times, this notion has been used to justify all sorts of new decrees, *fatawa* (plural of *fatwa*), even some that were manifestly in contradiction with obvious proofs from the Qur'an and the Sunna, as in the case of rules concerning interest [*riba*] and inheritance.

It is therefore important to recall briefly the early research and studies carried out in this area, not only in order to understand the scope of *maslaha* but also to evaluate the advantages to be derived from applying it in the light of developments over time and from the diversity of contexts. In his legal research, Imam Malik referred to the notion of *istislah*,[1] which meant "to seek the good" and cited the example of the Companions—who formulated numerous legal decisions in accordance with the common good while respecting the corpus of the sources—to point out the fact that "to seek the good" (*istislah*) is one of the fundamentals of the *Sharia*, and so is part of it. After the work of codification carried out by al-Shafii, the ulama began to set out distinctions between what were actually the sources, and their areas of legal application, the hierarchy of values of the regulations, and so on.

Numerous ulama, such as al-Juwayni in his *Al-burhan* and the Mutazilite Abu al-Husayn al-Basri, in *Al-mutamad fi usul al-fiqh* (both ulama lived in the eleventh century) refer to this notion in one way or another. At that time, the polemic—concerning the definition and the exact meaning of this notion and its status within the Islamic legal apparatus—had already begun. It was Abu Hamid al-Ghazali who, with his strict codification, provided the clearest framework for tackling this question from that time to the present. In his *Al-mustasafa min ilm al-usul*,[2] he states very precisely:

> "In its essential meaning, *al-maslaha* is a term which means to seek something beneficial [*manfaa*] or avoid something harmful [*madarra*]. But this is not what we mean, because to seek the beneficial and avoid what is bad are the objectives [*maqasid*] intended by creation, and good [*salaah*] in the creation of humanity consists in the attaining of these objectives [*maqasid*]. What we mean by *maslaha* is the preservation of the objective [*maqsud*] of the Law [*shar'*] which consists in five things: the protection of religion, life, intellect, lineage, and property. Whatever ensures the protection of these five principles [*usul*] is *maslaha*; whatever goes against their protection is *mafsada*, and to avoid it is *maslaha*."[3]

This general definition outlines a structure on which almost all later ulama were to agree,[4] for it refers implicitly to the sources without making a distinction between the objective of the good, which is found in the Qur'an and the Sunna, and how it is humanly stipulated when nothing is clearly stated in the sources. In fact, with this definition al-Ghazali placed himself above the disputes of the ulama, and when this light was shed on the subject, a more detailed codification in the nature of things opened the way for a precise understanding of *maslaha* and what was at stake in the legal argument; his contribution was therefore immense and central.

Al-Ghazali, still referring to the broad meaning of *maslaha*, mentions three different types: *al-daruriyyat* (the imperative), a category which has to do with the five elements of *maqasid al-sharia* (here in the sense of the objectives of the Law) listed earlier, that is, the protection of religion, life, intellect, lineage, and property[5]; *al-hajiyyat* (the necessary, or complementary), which has to do with the prevention of anything that could be a source of difficulty in the life of the community, without leading to death or destruction[6]; and finally *al-tahsiniyyat* and *al-kamaliyyat* (the enhancing and the perfecting), which concern anything that may bring about an improvement in religious practice.[7] These three levels cover all that can be considered as the *masalih* (common good) of the human being considered as a person and as a worshipper of God, and this categorization was hardly ever questioned in any debate and polemic.

What did give rise to disagreements and conflicts in the legal field was the question of determining whether there was a real need for this notion within the Islamic legal framework[8] or whether *al-maslaha* should be considered an independent source, though supplementary, of *Sharia* (and thus a part of the latter and whose scope should be limited),[9] or, finally, whether it should simply be seen as part of another source, such as *qiyas* (analogy).[10] These various positions taken by the ulama on these issues also depended on another qualification that distinguishes three types of *masalih* (this time differentiated according to their classification, not according to their hierarchical importance), by which the ulama established a typology based on the degree of proximity of *al-maslaha* to the sources. If *al-maslaha* is based on textual evidence (i.e. a quotation from the Qur'an or the Sunna), it is called *maslaha mutabara* (accredited), and it must necessarily be taken into account. If, on the other hand, the *maslaha* invoked is contradictory to an undisputed and explicit text (*nass qati*) it is called *mulgha* (discredited) and cannot be taken into account. The third type occurs when there is no text: the Qur'an and the Sunna do not confirm nor do they reject a *maslaha* that became apparent after the age of Revelation. A *maslaha* of this type is call *mursala* (undetermined),[11] for it allows the ulama to use their own analysis and personal reasoning in order to formulate a legal decision in the light of the historical and geographical context, using their best efforts to remain faithful to the commandments and to the "spirit" of the Islamic legal corpus where no text, no "letter" of the Law, is declared.

It is this last type that has given rise to much debate and polemic, the analysis of which is beyond the scope of this study. Suffice it to say here that the main cause of disagreement was the fear, on the part of those opposed to the very concept of *al-maslaha al-mursala* that such a notion, with such broad scope, might allow the ulama to formulate regulations without reference to the Qur'an and the Sunna on the basis of exclusively rational and completely free reasoning, all in the name of a remote hardship or "an anticipated difficulty." These were the main arguments of the Zahirite school, as well as numerous Shafii and even Maliki ulama who did not recognize *al-maslaha al-mursala*— not referring back to the sources—as a legal proof; they saw in it a spurious (*wahmiyya*) proof, not valid for legislation. This was the same instinctive fear of an approach that was purely rational and not connected with the Law that pushed al-Ghazali to restrict work on *al-maslaha* to the area of the application of *qiyas* (analogy), which, of its nature, requires a close link with the text for the deduction of the cause (*'illa*) on which analogical reasoning rests.

Some ulama in the course of history have formulated judgements in the name of *al-maslaha* and sometimes completely changed and disturbed the manner and conditions of the use of legal instruments within the Islamic framework. The particularly interesting example of the famous fourteenth-century Hanbali jurist, Najm al-Din al-Tufi seems to have partly given them just reason to be fearful: al-Tufi ended up giving *al-maslaha* priority over texts from the Qur'an and the Sunna, which, according to him, should be applied, according to Mahmasani, only "to the extent that the common good does not require anything else."[12] Moreover, in our own times we see very strange "modern Islamic legal decisions" based on "modern *masalih*" that are clearly contradictory to the sources. The notion of *al-maslaha al-mursala* thus sometimes seems to justify the strangest behaviour, as well as the most obscure commercial dealings, financial commitments and banking investments, under the pretext that they protect, or could or should protect, "the common good."

But this kind of excess was not typical among those who supported taking *al-maslaha al-mursala* into account as an authentic and legitimate source of legislation. They believed that the formulation of Islamic legal decisions should take place in the light of the Qur'an and the Sunna and in agreement with them and, moreover, upon certain demanding conditions (even if *al-maslaha al-mursala* should be considered as an independent source in the absence of any text). A careful study of the various opinions (for and against *al-maslaha al-mursala*) shows that the ulama are in agreement on numerous important points, even considering the conditions stipulated by supporters of the concept, among the first of whom was the *alim* of Grenada, al-Shatibi (fourteenth century). We find in his works a series of conditions and precise definitions regarding recognition of the "common good" as a reliable juridical source, which restrict its application and prevent the ulama from having recourse to *al-maslaha* without justification. Without going into too much detail, we may summarize the three generally recognised main conditions for situations when it is certain that no text has been enunciated:

1. The analysis and identification must be made with serious attention so that we may be sure that we have before us an authentic (*Haqiqiyya*) and not an apparent or spurious (*wahmiyya*) *maslaha*. The scholar must reach a high degree of certainty that the formulation of an injunction will avoid a difficulty and not do the opposite and increase problems in the context of the Islamic legal structure.

2. The *maslaha* must be general (*kulliyya*) and be beneficial to the population and to society as a whole, and not only to one group or class or individual.

3. The *maslaha* must not be in contradiction to or in conflict with an authentic text from the Qur'an or the Sunna. If it were, it would no longer be a *maslaha mursala*, but a *maslaha mulgha*.[13]

These three conditions[14] give us broad guidelines by which we can understand the concept of *maslaha*, the common good, in the Islamic frame of reference. What is clear above all is the supremacy of the Qur'an and the Sunna over all other references and legal instruments. Yusuf al-Qaradawi[15] rightly recalls, taking up the ideas of al-Ghazali, Ibn al-Qayyim and al-Shatibi, that everything found in the Qur'an and the Sunna is, in itself, in harmony with "the good of humankind" in general, for the Creator knows and wants what is best for human beings and He shows them what they must do to achieve it. We find in the Qur'an, referring to the revealed message: "[the Prophet] who will enjoin upon them the doing of what is right and forbid them the doing of what is wrong, and make lawful to them the good things of life and forbid them the bad things, and lift from them their burdens and the shackles that were upon them [aforetime]";[16] "O human beings! An exhortation has come to you from your Lord, a healing for what is in your hearts, a guidance and a mercy for the believers."[17] We find the preference for the good of humanity in the first of the three revelations that eventually led to the prohibition of intoxicants: "They ask you about intoxicating drinks and games of chance. Say: 'These two things contain great harm for men as well as benefits; but the harm found in them is greater than the benefit.'"[18] Ibn al-Qayyim al-Jawziyya summarised the position as follows:

> The principles and fundamentals of the *Sharia* concerning the injunctions and the good of humankind in this life and the next are all based on justice, mercy, the good of man and wisdom. Every situation in which justice succumbs to tyranny, mercy to cruelty, goodness to corruption, wisdom to foolishness, has nothing in common with the *Sharia*, even if it is the result of an allegorical interpretation [*tawill*]. For the *Sharia* is the justice of God among His servants, the mercy of God among His creatures, His shadow upon His earth, and His wisdom, which is both the proof of His own existence and the best witness to the authenticity of His Prophet.[19]

To seek the good (*maslaha*) of man, in this life and the next, is the very essence of Islamic commandments and prohibitions. If the latter are clearly proclaimed (*qatii al-thubut wa-qatii al-dalala*[20]) in the Qur'an and/or the Sunna, they must be respected and applied in the light of an understanding of the whole body of the objectives of Islamic teaching, *maqasid al-Sharia*:[21] they are, and represent, the revealed good *maslaha*, granted by the Creator to His creature to guide him towards the good.

Nevertheless, the sources are sometimes silent. Facing new situations and problems, the ulama may not be able to find specific responses in the Qur'an and the Sunna. In such cases, and guided by the light of Revelation and the example of the Prophet, they have to formulate judgments that will protect the best interests of people without betraying the frame of reference. These interests are called *masalih mursala* and require the total and constant commitment of the ulama if they are to make it possible for individuals to live as Muslims in all times and places and prevent them from carrying too heavy a burden, for God said: "God wants things to be easy for you, He does not want them to be difficult for you."

This is the framework within which we must consider the notion of *maslaha*, which has been a controversial concept, often because there has been a lack of clarity in the way it is defined and because of the strict and demanding conditions required for its application. It has sometimes suffered from excessive use by some ulama and scholars when they have tried to justify some "modern judgement" or "progress" in the name of *al-maslaha*. We have seen that it is a very specific concept—in its scope, its levels, its types and its conditions—and requires that the ulama constantly refer back to the sources so that they will be able to formulate judgments in conformity with the revealed Message, even when there is no specifically relevant text. They must try—by carrying out a deep, thorough and detailed study—to provide the Muslim community with new rational judgments guided by Revelation. This is the meaning of *ijtihad* which is both the source and the legal instrument that allows a dynamism to be set in motion at the heart of Islamic law and jurisprudence.

Al-Ijtihad: Definition and Classification

When the Prophet sent Muadh, a companion, to Yemen he asked him about the sources on which he would base his judgments and approved of his intention of "putting all his energy into formulating his own judgment" in cases where he could find no guidance in the Qur'an and the Sunna. This personal effort undertaken by the jurist in order to understand the source and deduce the rules or, in the absence of a clear textual guidance, formulate independent judgments, is what is called *ijtihad* in the field of Islamic jurisprudence. Hashim Kamali proposes the following definition:

> *Ijtihad* is defined as the total of the effort expended by the jurist in order to deduce, with a good degree of probability, the rules of the *Sharia* on the basis of the detailed guidance found in the sources. Some ulama have defined *ijtihad* as the jurist's use of all his faculties either to deduce the rules of *sharia* from their sources, or to put them into practice and apply them to specific questions. *Ijtihad* essentially consists in a deduction [*istinbat*] which represents a probability [*zann*], and so does not include the extraction of a rule from an explicit text.[22]

Like *al-maslaha*, the legal instrument of *ijtihad* has been used to justify all kinds of new judgments. So Hashim Kamali quite rightly recalls the general principle (about which the ulama are unanimous), according to which there can be no *ijtihad* when an explicit text exists in the sources [*la ijtihada maa al-nass*]. This means that if there is an explicit Qur'anic verse whose meaning is obvious and leaves no room for any hypothesis or interpretation [*qatii al-dalala*], no *ijtihad* is possible. Similarly, if the jurist finds an authenticated *Hadith* [*mutawatir, qatii al-thubu*] whose content is also completely explicit and unambiguous [*qatii al-dalala*], he must use that as his reference and there is no room for the exercise of *ijtihad*.

Indeed, clear texts that are both authenticated and explicit, even though they are not very numerous, constitute the unalterable foundation, the fixed principles, on which the *Sharia* is based—principles to which the jurist must refer, from which he must analyze, comment on, and explain texts that contain some conjecture [*zanni*], and on the basis of which he should also formulate new judgments through a dynamic process when his community faces new situations. The laws and judgments provided by these clear texts together constitute a specific corpus which the *ulama al-usul* call *al-malum min al-din bil-darura*, which means that they bring out the fundamental essence of Islamic law and that to reject them leads to the negation of Islam [*kufr*].

But the great majority of the verses in the Qur'an and the traditions of the Prophet are not of both a strict and compelling nature. The Qur'an is authenticated in itself [*qatii al-thubut*, of indisputable origin], but most of the verses containing legal judgments [*ayat al-ahkam*] are open to analysis, commentary, and interpretation [*zanni al-dalala*], and this is also the case with the *ahadith*, most of which leave some scope for speculation as much concerning their authenticity [*thubut*] as concerning their meaning [*dalala*]. This means that the *fuqaha* [jurists] had, and still have, an important and essential function in the formulation of laws that may be called Islamic. They fulfill this function particularly through their *ijtihad*, applied at various levels: to understand a specific text (in the light of the whole Islamic legal corpus); to classify texts on the basis of their clarity or their nature (e.g., *qati* [indisputable], or *zanni* [conjectural]; *zahir* [obvious], or *nass* [explicit]; *khass* [specific], or *aamm* [general]); or to formulate judgments where no text exists. *Ijtihad* taken as a whole (as both source and legal instrument) has in fact been considered by numerous ulama as the third principal source of *Sharia*, encompassing *al-ijma* (*ijtihad jamai*), *al-istislah* and *al-istihsan*, as well as other subdivisions recognised among what are called the supplementary sources of the *Sharia*. Muhammad Hashim Kamali has emphasised: "The various sources of Islamic law that feature next to the Qur'an and the Sunna are all manifestations of *ijtihad*, albeit with differences that are largely procedural in character. In this way, consensus of opinion, analogy, juristic preference, considerations of public interest [*maslaha*], etc., are all interrelated not only under the main heading of *ijtihad*, but via the Qur'an and the Sunna."[23]

Al-Ghazali, al-Shatibi, Ibn al-Qayyim al-Jawziyya, and, more recently, al-Khallaf and Abu Zahra have referred to this type of classification, underscoring the importance of *ijtihad* as the third source of Islamic jurisprudence, for *ijtihad* includes all the instruments used to form judgments through human reasoning and personal effort. *Ijtihad* is, in fact, the rational elaboration of laws either on the basis of sources or formulated in the light of them. Thus, even *ijma* [consensus] is the product of a collective human rational discussion, and so one can conceive—even if it would be very unlikely and rare—that a legal decision made by *ijma* might eventually become unsuitable and be referred again for debate. As Professor Hamidullah has said in connection with the Hanafite school of law:

> The opinion of a jurist can, however, be rejected by another jurist who can offer his own opinion instead. This applies not only to individual opinions or an inference but also covers collective opinion. At least the Hanafite school of law accepts that a new consensus can cancel an old consensus. Suppose there is consensus on a certain issue. We accept its authority, but this does not mean that no one can oppose it till eternity. If someone has the courage to oppose it with due respect and reasons, and if he can persuade the jurists to accept his point of view, a new consensus comes into being. The new consensus, then, abrogates the old one. This principle has been propounded by the famous Hanafite jurist Abu al-Yusr al-Bazdawi in his work *Usul al-Fiqh* [Principles of Jurisprudence]. Al-Bazdawi lived in the fourth and fifth centuries of the Hijrah. This work is a great contribution to Islamic jurisprudence. It is an account of his statement that we can say that consensus cannot become a source of difficulty for us. If consensus is reached on some issue and it is found subsequently to be unsuitable, the possibility remains that we may change it through reasoning and create a new one cancelling the old consensus.[24]

This analysis recalls an important principle from the realm of *usul al-fiqh*, which is that the Qur'an and the Sunna are the only two indisputable sources;

sources at whose core the prescriptive verses and *ahadith* (*ayat wa- ahadith al-ahkam*)[25] are divided into two main levels: the *qati* [indisputable] which is clear in itself, and the *zanni* [conjectural, open to hypotheses and interpretations] which requires on the part of the ulama an attentive study of the texts in question before they can deduce appropriate judgments on passages taken from the sources. The aim of this type of *ijtihad* (applied to *zanni* texts)—sometimes called *bayani* (explanatory *ijtihad*)—is to analyse the text [*nass*] in order to draw from it a ruling and its *illa* (the effective cause of this specific ruling); this allows both an adequate understanding of the text and consequent analogical reasoning [*qiyas*] in the light of the historical context. This type of *ijtihad* has given rise to numerous and diverse subdivisions following the various opinions of the ulama.

There is another type of *ijtihad* that is applied when there is no scriptural reference. Here, too, we find numerous subdivisions because of the diversity of opinion among the ulama and the collections of writings and commentaries that have been made in the course of history. At least three types appear:

1. *Ijtihad qiyasi* works by analogical reasoning, taking into consideration the effective cause [*illa*] of a regulation drawn from the sources.
2. *Ijtihad zanni* comes in when it is impossible to refer to an effective cause; this type is often linked with *ijtihad istislahi*.
3. *Ijtihad istislahi* is based on *al-maslaha* and seeks to deduce rulings in the light of the general objective of the *Sharia*.

But the ulama are not unanimous about the specific classification of *ijtihad*, because they do not even agree on its definition and methods of application.

Another distinction has to do with the degree of *ijtihad*, which may be absolute [*mutlaq*] or limited [*muqayyad*]. The first type, also called *ijtihad fi al-shar'*, is based on the ability of the *mujtahid* (a scholar qualified to practise *ijtihad*) to extrapolate and formulate his own judgments on the basis of a direct study of the sources. The second, also called *ijtihad madhhabi* (pertaining to a school), is, by contrast, limited to a particular school of law and the *mujtahid* must formulate his judgments according to the rules of a given juridical school.

The Conditions [*Shurut*] of *Ijtihad*[26]

The framework we have just presented, with the definition and classification of *ijtihad*, has been taken into account by the ulama when determining the conditions for *ijtihad*. In order to analyze and classify, they have focused on the qualities a scholar must possess in order to practice an authentic and reliable *ijtihad*, in order to become a *mujtahid*. As with other classifications, the conditions formulated by the ulama have been numerous and divergent because of their various opinions about legal instruments, the applicability of laws, or, simply, the priority allotted to their implementation.

Before going further in setting out the requirements for being a *mujtahid*, it may be useful to refer here to the concise opinion of al-Shatibi, who differentiated between the very nature of *ijtihad* and its instruments. His overall view, in this sense, is simple and edifying, for he brings together all the conditions under two main rubrics. Thus, according to him, "the level of *ijtihad* is attained when two qualities are present:

1. A deep understanding of the objectives [*maqasid*] of the *Sharia*
2. A real mastery of the various methods of deduction and extrapolation (*istinbat*) based on knowledge and understanding."[27]

The "five essential principles" [*al-daruriyyat al-khamsa*] which we have already mentioned (religion, life, intellect, lineage and property) as well as the necessary distinctions between the indispensable [*daruri*], the necessary or complementary [*haji*] and the embellishments or improvements [*tahsini*] constitute the framework provided by the Lawgiver to guide the research of the *mujtahid*, and so represent the fundamental terms of reference. The *mujtahid* must also know which instruments[28] he may resort to among the general maxims of *fiqh*, *qiyas*, *istihsan* and so on.

From Abu al-Husayn al-Basri and his work *Mutamad fi usul al-fiqh* (eleventh century) to Ibn al-Qayyim al-Jawziyya with his *Ilam al-muwaqqiin an rabb al-alamin* (fourteenth century), numerous ulama have proposed various classifications of the qualities required and conditions to be met in order for a scholar to be considered a *mujtahid*. Some believed that the first condition was knowledge of the Arabic language[29]; others thought that what mattered above all was knowledge of the verses and *ahadith* that had legal significance. In spite of these divergences, which are in fact essentially procedural since their respective conditions overlap, we may summarize the efforts of the ulama in this area in the following seven points: The *mujtahid* must possess:

1. A knowledge of Arabic which enables him to understand the Qur'an and the Sunna correctly and particularly the verses and *ahadith* that contain rulings [*ayat wa-ahadith al-ahkam*]
2. A knowledge of the sciences of the Qur'an and hadith which enables him to understand and identify the evidence [*adilla*] contained in the texts and, furthermore, to deduce and extrapolate judgments from them

3. A thorough knowledge of the objectives [*maqasid*] of the *Sharia*, their classification and the priorities they imply
4. Knowledge of questions on which there was consensus [*ijma*]: this requires knowledge of the works on secondary issues [*furu*]
5. Knowledge of the principle of analogical reasoning [*qiyas*] and its methodology, the causes [*illa*], and circumstances [*asbab*] of a specific judgment, as well as conditions [*shurut*]
6. Knowledge of his historical, social and political context: that is to say, the situation of the people living around him [*ahwal al-nas*], the state of their affairs, traditions and customs, and so on
7. Recognition of his own competence, honesty, reliability and uprightness.[30]

As we have already mentioned, numerous other conditions in different orders, have been proposed, but these seven points more or less cover the most important qualities needed by a *mujtahid*.[31] Some ulama believe that these conditions and qualifications are so advanced and demanding that it has not been possible to reach this standard since the time of the great ulama in about the ninth century. This is how they justify the pronouncement that forever closed the "doors of *ijtihad*" after this very rich period. Other ulama, the great majority, are of the opinion that the practice of *ijtihad* has been partly abandoned for historical reasons that have pressed either the political leaders or the ulama to declare that it was no longer necessary to practice *ijtihad*.[32] Consequently, the doors of *ijtihad* have never been closed; for no scholar would have had the right to make such a decision in the name of Islam because a declaration such as this, by its very nature, is against Islam. In fact, *ijtihad*, as the third source of Islamic law and jurisprudence, is *fard kifaya*, a collective responsibility.

Everyone recognizes that these conditions are demanding and that they are required for a qualified *ijtihad*, but they also point out that these qualifications have never been beyond the reach of the ulama, neither in the past nor the present. Moreover, the progress that has been made in authenticating *ahadith*, easier access to reference works, and computer-aided classification make the work of the *mujtahid* easier and more effective. Consequently, the Muslim community should, through its ulama, still be fulfilling this fundamental duty today, even though it will be necessary to find a way to apply it appropriately in our contemporary context—because of the new complexity of many sciences, such as medicine, technology, economics, the social sciences, etc.[33] *Ijtihad* remains the most important instrument the ulama have at their disposal to fulfill the universal vocation of Islam, through a constant dynamic of adaptation in response to the time and the context.

Fatwa: Definition and Conditions

To understand what a *fatwa* is, we should keep in mind the whole substance of the preceding analysis, for a *fatwa* is a part, an element and, more precisely, a legal instrument, which must be understood in the light of the corpus of Islamic law and jurisprudence. *Fatwa* (plural *fatawa*) means, literally, "legal decision," "verdict," or, following the definition of al-Shatibi: "A reply to a legal question given by an expert (*mufti*) in the form of words, action or approval."[34] A *fatwa* has two essential aspects: it must, first and above all, be founded on the sources and on the juridical deductions and extrapolations arrived at by the *mujtahidin*[35] who practice *ijtihad* when the sources are not clear or explicit (that is, when they are *zanni*) or when there is no relevant text. It must also be formulated in the light of the context of life, the environment, and the specific situation that justifies its being made—and which is in fact its cause.

The place of the *mujtahid* and the *mufti* is of prime importance. As al-Shatibi said:

> The *mufti*,[36] within the community, plays the part of the prophet. Much evidence supports this assertion. First there is the proof of *hadith*: "Truly the scholars are the heirs of the prophets, and what one inherits from prophets is not money [*la dinaran wa-la dirham*], but knowledge [*ilm*]." Second, he [the *mufti*] is the source of transmitting rulings [*ahkam*] in conformity with the words of the Prophet: "Let the one among you who is witness transmit [that to which he is witness] to those who are absent" and "Transmit from me, even if it is only one verse." If this is the case, it means that he [the *mufti*] stands in for the prophet.
>
> In fact, the *mufti* is a kind of legislator, for the *Sharia* that he conveys is either taken [insofar as it has already been stipulated] from the Lawgiver [by way of the Revelation and the Sunna], or deduced or extrapolated from the sources. In the first case, he is simply a transmitter, while in the second he stands in for the prophet in that he stipulates rulings. To formulate judgments is the function of the legislator. So, if the function of the *mujtahid* is to formulate judgments on the basis of his opinion and efforts, it is possible to say that he is therefore a legislator who should be respected and followed: we should act according to the rulings he formulates and this is vicegerency [Khilafa] in its genuine implementation.[37]

Al-Shatibi underlines the importance of the *mujtahid* who stands in for the prophet in the Muslim community after the death of Muhammad. In this way, the *mujtahid* or the *mufti* represents the continuity of knowledge [*ilm*] guided by the two sources, so that it may be rightly applied throughout history. Al-Shatibi made a distinction between clear and explicit evidence (that stipulated in the sources) and that which required the exercise of deduction and inference and put the *mujtahid* in the position of legislator (even though he must seek the guidance of God, the supreme Legislator, and follow the example of the Prophet). This distinction is useful in setting out the two different levels of *fatwa*: when questioned on legal issues, the *mujtahid* will sometimes find a clear answer in the Qur'an and the Sunna because there is an explicit text. In such a case, the *fatwa* consists of a quotation, and a re-statement of the authoritative proof. If, on the other hand, there is a text that is open to interpretation, or if there is no relevant text, the *mufti* must give a specific response in light of both the objectives of the *Sharia* and the situation of the questioner. Al-Shatibi underscores that the *mufti* really does play the role of vicegerent who must come up with a legal judgment for the one who calls on him. The more the issue is related to an individual or a particular case, the more precise, clear and specific it must be. Consequently, a *fatwa* is rarely transferable, because it is a legal judgment pronounced (in the light of the sources, of the *maslaha*, and the context) in response to a clear question arising from a precise context. In the field of law, this is in fact the exact meaning of "jurisprudence."

Many questions have been raised in the course of history about the diversity of *fatawa*. If Islam is one, how could there be differing legal judgments on the same legal question? The ulama have unanimously affirmed that if geographical or historical contexts differ, it is no longer the same question, for it must be considered in the light of a new environment. Thus, properly considered responses should naturally differ, as is shown by the example of al-Shafii who modified some of his legal judgments after travelling from Baghdad to Cairo. So, even though Islam is one, the *fatawa*, with all their diversity, and sometimes contradiction, still remain Islamic and authoritative.

This kind of diversity was understood, accepted and respected, while the problem of disagreement between ulama faced with an identical legal question has given rise to endless debates. Is this possible in the area of religious affairs, and if so, how can Islam be a unifying force for Muslims? Two essential points have been emphasised by the vast majority of ulama:

1) There is no divergence of opinion on the principles, the fundamentals [*usul*] of Islamic law. There is a consensus among the jurists on the fact that these principles constitute the essence, the frame of reference and the benchmark of the juridical corpus of Islamic law and jurisprudence [*fiqh*]. However, it is impossible to avoid differences of opinion on points related to secondary issues [*furu*], for a legal judgment on these points is dependent on and influenced by many factors, such as the knowledge and understanding of the ulama and their ability to deduce and extrapolate judgments. The natural diversity in their levels of competence inevitably gives rise to divergent interpretations and opinions. This even happened among the Companions at the time of the Prophet, and, according to the ulama, such divergences should be

recognised and respected, within their limits, as based upon the fundamentals of Islam.

2) A question naturally arises from this consensus: even if there are various "acceptable" legal opinions on one and the same problem (even a secondary problem [far']), does this mean that all the fatawa have the same value, or, in other words, are they all correct? If that were the case, it would lead to the conclusion that two divergent opinions could both be true at the same time, in the same place and in respect of the same person, which is rationally unacceptable. The majority of ulama, including the four principal imams of the Sunni schools of law, are of the opinion that only one of the divergent opinions pronounced on a precise question can be considered correct. This is indicated in the passage in the Qur'an that relates the story of David and Solomon, where it is clear that, although they had made judgments on the same case and although both of them had received the gift of wisdom and knowledge, only Solomon's opinion was correct: "We made it understood to Solomon."[38] This position is also confirmed by the hadith already cited about the mujtahid's reward: he will receive two rewards if he is right but only one if he is wrong, because his effort and sincere research will be taken into account by God.

So to accept that there may be a diversity of legal opinions on precise questions (formulated in the same context, at the same time and for the same community or individual) does not in the least lead to the assumption that there are several "truths" and that all these opinions have the same value and correctness. There is only "one truth," which all the ulama should try to discover, and they will be rewarded for the effort they make towards this. As long as there is no indisputable proof applicable to the problem in question, each Muslim should, after serious consideration and analysis, follow the opinion whose evidence and worth seem to him the clearest and most convincing.

Guided by the Qur'an and the example of the Prophet—the sources of truth for Muslims—the ulama should do their best to discover the truth when the texts are not explicit or simply do not exist. In fact the meaning and content of the delegation granted by God to humankind reaches its peak and is fulfilled when the ulama struggle constantly and tirelessly to arrive at the correct judgment, or that which is closest to what is correct and true. Therefore, these ulama, both mujtahids and muftis, must be determined, demanding and confident in their own judgments, while remaining humble and calm to face and accept the fact that there will necessarily and inevitably be a plurality of opinions. The imam al-Shafii aptly said, concerning the state of mind that should characterise the attitude of the ulama: "[As we see it] our opinion is right though it may turn out to be wrong, while we consider the opinion of our opponents to be wrong though it may turn out to be right."[39]

Notes

1. *Istislah* is the tenth form of the root *sa-lu-ha*, which is also the root of *maslaha*.

2. Abu Hamid al-Ghazali, *Al-mustasfa min ilm al-usul*, Baghdad, Muthanna, 1970.

3. Cf. *Al-mustasfa min ilm al-usul*, vol. 1, 286–7. See also Muhammad Khalid Masud's interesting book, *Shatibi's Philosophy of Islamic Law*, Islamabad, Islamic Research Institute, 1995, 139–40.

4. Apart from the ulama of the Zahirite school, who did not even recognise the concept of *maqasid*.

5. *Al-masalih al-daruriyya* are requirements upon which people's lives depend, as well as the protection of the meaning of their worship of God. Later some ulama added *al-ird* (honour).

6. *Al-masalih al-hajiyya* are requirements related to difficult situations. We find in this category rules concerning, for example, the sick and the old, dispensations (*rukhas*) related to prayer and fasting, etc.

7. *Al-masalih al-tahsiniyya* may deal with, for example, cleanliness and moral virtues which may lead to an improvement in religious practice and be a means of attaining what is desirable.

8. Thus considered that there was no room for speaking of *istislah* since the *shariaa* itself and all its injunctions were founded on *al-masalih*, which represent both the content and the objective of the revealed laws.

9. Al-Shatibi explains, in his analysis in *Al-I'tisam*, that the two sources of Islam and the Qur'an and the Sunna, whose injunctions are based on *al-maslaha* (he agrees on this point with Ibn Hazm); but he is clear that we have to refer to our reason when the texts contain no indication (according to al-Shatibi, this was once done by means of *ijmaa* or *qiyas*). So, when the texts are silent, *al-maslaha* is the point of reference and acts as an independent source in the light of the Qur'an and the Sunna.

10. This was the view of al-Ghazali, who, by subordinating the method of reasoning based on *al-maslaha* to *qiyas*, linked the sources in order to avoid a purely rational formulation which might be remote from any reference to the sources.

11. The meaning of *mursala* has been discussed by numerous scholars and it would be pedantic and unprofitable to discuss it here. The classification "undetermined" means that the proposition is generally admissible and legally appropriate.

12. Subhi Rajab al-Mahmasani, *Falsafat at-tashri fil-islam*, Leiden, Brill, 1961, 117. Cited by Mohammad Hashim Kamali, *op. cit.*, 276.

13. Such was the case when some ulama wanted to justify usury and bank interest (*riba*) in the name of the common good. There can be no *maslaha mursala* here because this matter is the subject of clear and indisputable directions in the Qur'an (*qatii al-thubut wa-qatii al-dalala*—indisputable with regard to both transmission and meaning) and Sunna (*Zanni al-thabut wa-qatii al-dalala*—conjectural with regard to transmission and indisputable with regard to meaning).

14. There are numerous other secondary conditions—for example, the *maslaha* must be reasonable (*ma'qula*) according to Malik, and indispensable (*daruriyya*)

according to al-Ghazali. For more details and deeper analyses, see the specialised works already referred to by al-Shatibi (*Al-I'tsam*), Khallaf, Hassab Allah and Kamali.

15. Yusuf al-Qaradawi, *Al-ijtihad al-muasir, bayna al-indibat wa-al-infiat,* Cairo, Dar al-tawzi wa-al-nashr al-islamiyya, 1993, 66–7.

16. Qur'an 7:157.

17. Qur'an 10:57.

18. Qur'an 2:219.

19. Ibn al-Qayyim al-Jawziyya, *I'lam al-muwaqqiin an rabb al-alamin,* Cairo, n.d., vol. 3, 1.

20. We shall deal with various levels of "clarity" when we study the notion of *ijtihad.*

21. The vast majority of the ulama agree in saying that there can be no *ijtihad* (and hence no *maslaha,* no *qiyas,* no *istihsan,* and no need for *ijma*) as far as religious practice (*al-ibadat*) is concerned, for its judgments and modalities are known to us through Revelation and must be applied as they were revealed to the Prophet and taught and explained by him. Similarly, when there are clear and detailed injunctions (only a few judgments in fact meet these criteria), they must be applied (though of course without neglecting a vision of the whole body of objectives of Islamic law and the social situation, as we have explained).

22. Muhammad Hashim Kamali, *Principles of Islamic Jurisprudence, op. cit.,* 366.

23. Muhammad Hashim Kamali, *Principles of Islamic Jurisprudence, op. cit.,* 366.

24. Muhammad Hamidullah, *The Emergence of Islam,* ed. & trans. Afzal Iqbal, Islamabad, Islamic Research Institute, 1993, 97.

25. There are various opinions among the ulama as to the number of these verses and *ahadith.* For example, al-Ghazali and Ibn al-Arabi counted five hundred verses, while Abd al-Wahhab Khallaf has listed about two hundred and twenty-eight. Al-Shawkani, however, believed that such calculations were not reliable and definitive since some verses can be variously interpreted according to the scholar and the context. One could say the same about the *ahadith al-ahkam,* even if Ibn Hanbal is supposed to have said that there are about one thousand two hundred *ahaīīth* in this category. Cf. al-Shawkani, *Al-qawl al-mufīd fī al-ijtihad wa-al-taqlid,* Cairo, 1975, ch. 2; and Abd al-Wahhab Khallaf, *Ilm usul al-fiqh, op. cit.,* French trans., *Les Fondements du droit musulman, op. cit.,* 46–7.

26. There are many other detailed classifications in the area of *ijtihad,* which is beyond the scope of this work. They are known by specialists in *usul al-fiqh* and are the subject of discussions and controversies among the ulama. An example is the 'divisibility of *ijtihad*' (*al-tajzi'a*), about which pages and pages of argument have been written. It is a very theoretical, and in fact secondary, issue. We shall tackle the question of *ijtihad fardi* (individual) and *jama'ī* (collective) later.

27. Al-Shatibi, *al-muwafaqat fī usul al-sharia,* Lebanon, Dar al-marifa, new edn, 1996, vol. 4, ch. 'The conditions for *ijtihad*', 477ff., *passim.*

28. This is what al-Shatibi himself calls the second quality: having said the first is the objective, he adds that 'the second is the instrument' (*ibid.,* vol. 4, 478).

29. Al-Shatibi, for example, was very demanding in this particular; he thought that no one could attain the true level of *ijtihad* without a deep knowledge of Arabic (*ibid.,* vol. 4, 590ff.).

30. This recognition must also come from other scholars and from the Muslim community.

31. The ulama have set down various conditions for the *mujtahid mutlaq* (absolute) and the *mujtahid muqayyad* (limited) who is content to deduce judgments within the framework of a specific juridical school. The conditions required for the latter are certainly less demanding, and added to them are knowledge of the rules of deduction related to the juridical school in question.

32. For a detailed analysis of these historical reasons, see Muhammad Iqbal, *The Reconstruction of Islamic Thought*, Lahore, Ashraf, 1951, 149–52.

33. This is discussed further in my book *Western Muslims and the Future of Islam* published by OUP fall 2003.

34. Al-Shatibi, *Al-muwafaqat fi usul al-sharia, op. cit.*, vol. 4, 595–602.

35. The ulama have often used the words *mujtahid* and *mufti* synonymously. However, the two functions are not exactly the same either in nature or in degree, even if the areas they cover do overlap. The *mujtahid* works on the sources and tries to deduce legal judgments from them, while the *mufti* must give specific answers to his questioner (whether this is an individual or a community) and so depends on the *mujtahid*. He must have most of the qualities referred to above, unless his *fatawa* are restricted to a specific subject area (*juzi*). We shall deal with the various levels of *fatwa* shortly.

36. In this explanation, al-Shatibi identifies the *mufti* with the *mujtahid*.

37. Al-Shatibi, *Al-muwafaqat fī usul al-sharia, op. cit.*, vol. 4, 595–6.

38. Qur'an 21:79.

39. Al-Shafii, *Al-risala, op. cit.*, 128.

2

Elements of Government in Classical Islam

Tamara Sonn

Since the dawn of colonialism, people outside Islam have tried to classify it as distinctly anti-democratic and inherently authoritarian. These efforts have occasioned refutations and responses from the likes of Jamal al-Din al-Afghani (1883) and Syed Ameer (1992) to Rachid Ghannouchi (1990) and Mohammed Khatami (1998).[1] There is general agreement that the Orientalists are wrong about Islam, but differences of opinion remain in the Muslim community on the question of just what are acceptable forms of government in Islam. What qualifies as an Islamic form of government has been debated within the Muslim community since the demise of the Ottoman caliphate. While some have maintained the ideal of a single Muslim polity transcending regional and cultural differences, the majority have accepted the distinction between religious and political unity. But even accepting the need for localized governments within a spiritually or morally unified Muslim community, the question of the proper Islamic form of government remains open. Is it one that is simply headed by a Muslim, regardless of its form? Is it one in which only Muslims participate? Is it one that is based on models derived from a particular era of Islamic history? Is it, indeed, one? Is there a singly Islamic form of government?

A good example of the kind of debate still going on in the Muslim community occurred in the recent elections in South Africa. A few years ago, when South Africans were about to hold their second ever democratic elections (2 June 1999), a group calling itself the Islamic Unity Convention called on Muslims in South Africa not to vote and thereby participate in un-Islamic politics. In response, another group of Muslim scholars, religious and civic leaders, individuals and organizations launched a petition calling on "all Muslims

— 21 —

to exercise their social responsibility by participating in the forthcoming elections." They explained their position as follows:

> These elections have not come cheaply; they are the results of many years of struggle wherein many of our fellow citizens, including Muslims gave their lives. We have been in this country for more than three hundred and fifty years and are an integral and critical part of its present and its future. We are proud of the role that Muslim individuals and organizations have played in the liberation of our country from the injustices of the past. In the various tiers of government, state organs and in civil society, our brothers and sisters are making a positive contribution to the reconstruction of our nation after years of discrimination and exploitation under apartheid. We uphold the right of all citizens to their own opinions regarding the forthcoming elections and we reject with contempt the notion that most Muslims support the call to boycott these elections.[2]

Which is the correct position? How can a government be judged Islamic or not? Some efforts to answer these questions have focused on historic precedent. For example, in the 1920s the Khilifat Movement of India advocated the restoration of the pre–World War I boundaries of the Ottoman Empire and the maintenance of the Ottoman sultan as the leader of the Muslim faithful worldwide. The current principalities (emirates) and kingdoms in the Muslim world also can be seen as remnants of the political structures that characterized the Islamic middle ages. But these historic models actually coexisted with theoretical models from which they often deviated. Those classical theories are the topic of this paper.[3] An examination of the essential elements of Islamic government in the views of classical theorists will demonstrate that while there is no single official Islamic form of government in the classical sources, there are elements which are deemed critical to the Islamic identity of any form of government. I will conclude with observations about the implications of classical Islamic theory for the current debates about Islamic forms of government.

Background

The fact that Islamic political theory developed relatively late in Islam is the first clue to understanding Islamic views on political structures. Unlike Judaism and Christianity, Islam developed from the very beginning in the context of political power. But Prophet Muhammad left no detailed political theory, no institutions empowered to develop one. Classical Islamic theory, therefore, developed only gradually and in dialogue with actual political developments.

The characteristic political institution of Islamic history is the caliphate. From the death of Prophet Muhammad in 632 until 1924, there was—at least theoretically—a successor (in Arabic, *khalifah*) to the Prophet's political lead-ership. But Muhammad's prophetic mantle was not inherited by his successors. Nor did the Prophet devise a specific political system or designate a successor (according to Sunni belief). The Prophet was himself considered a source of divine revelation and a just arbiter. In a document believed to have been dic-tated by him when he established the community at Medina (622 CE), the "Constitution of Medina," he defined his political role as that of arbitrator of disputes. After designing the rights and responsibilities of the community members toward one another, he said, "Wherever there is anything about which you differ, it is to be referred to God and to Muhammad for a decision." Elsewhere, "Whenever among the people of this document there occurs any disturbance or quarrel from which disaster is to be feared, it is to be referred to God and to Muhammad the Messenger of God."[4] Clearly, it was assumed that Muhammad's behavior was divinely guided and that his judgment was sound. But his prophetic and practical roles were not fused; the Prophet received rev-elation which was inerrant, and his decisions concerning the application of divine revelation in daily life were considered normative as a result of his prophetic role. But his judgment in practical matters was human and therefore fallible. In fact, he is reported to have told his community that they are the best judges in practical matters, except where the Qur'an directs otherwise. "I am a human being. If I command you with a matter of your religion, carry it out, but if I command you with something according to my opinion, I am merely a human being."[5] He was even commanded by the Qur'an to make decisions on practical issues in consultation (*shura*) with members of the community. In addition, the Prophet periodically elicited from the community an oath of allegiance to his leadership (*bay'a*). But beyond establishing these norma-tive precedents, and of course delivering the Qur'an for ultimate guidance, the Prophet apparently left it to the community to devise its own ways of governance.

Prophet Muhammad's successors were generally expected to behave accord-ing to the guidance left by the Prophet and to be personally pious as well, but there was no formal theory upon which to either determine who were to be leaders of the community or to judge the legitimacy of anyone's leadership. The first successor, Abu Bakr (r. 632–634 CE), was chosen by consensus of the elders of the community in Medina. Abu Bakr appears to have suggested his successor to a council of community leaders who approved the choice ('Umar). The next two successors ('Uthman and 'Ali) are also reported to have been chosen by such a council, the choice again presumably ratified by the oath of allegiance of the community. Yet it is unclear even what titles these leaders used. Abu Bakr was called "successor to the messenger of God" (*khali-fat* [caliph] *rasul Allah*), while 'Umar seems to have preferred "leader of the faithful" (*amir al-mu'minin*). However, as W. Montgomery Watt points out, there is no evidence of clearly defined significance of either designation.[6] The Qur'an had simply commanded, "Obey God and the Messenger and those among you in authority." (4:62) We have no record that the early Muslim community believed it was doing anything more or less than that.

The caliphate only came to be institutionalized gradually and on an *ad hoc* basis, specifically as Muslim sovereignty began to spread and the office of caliphate came to be a coveted prize. In 661 CE, following violent competition, the descendants of a leading Meccan family, the Umayyads, took control of the caliphate and established their headquarters in Damascus. If the distinction between Muhammad's prophetic and practical pronouncements implied varying levels of authority in Islam, with the Umayyads we begin to see an explicit distinction between specifically religious and coercive/executive levels of political authority. Damascus became effectively the political or administrative capital of the empire while Mecca remained the religious center. But still there was no theory upon which the government was based. Umayyad policy concerning their administration (particularly regarding matters of taxation) was generally to leave in place the system that had prevailed before Muslim conquest. That varied from region to region depending upon whether the area had previously been under Roman (Byzantine) or Persian administration, the means of acquisition (whether by conquest or treaty), etc.[7] Thus, significant segments of policy were incorporated into the Islamic administrative system with virtually no input from religious sources. Furthermore, the Umayyads introduced into their administration the office of judges (qadis). These were political appointees with varied administrative responsibilities, including police and treasury work, but generally charged with settling disputes in accordance with local custom. They were accorded a great deal of latitude, exercising their own discretion with regard to what was permissible in view of Islamic principles and administrative necessities.

However, it soon became apparent to some at least that Umayyad leadership no longer was the model of wisdom and piety that Islamic leadership ideally symbolized. This recognition fostered the growth of opposition groups. Among them were scholars whose objections to Umayyad policies were based on what they perceived to be Islamic principles. It was only in this context that the Islamic community began to develop the foundations upon which to build political theory: the scholars' articulation of the components of legal reasoning, which gave rise to the four schools of Sunni Islamic law.[8]

By the mid-eighth century, there was a body of scholars who were popularly regarded as having the authority to identify and interpret the sources of normative Islamic practice (Islamic law). They fell into schools of thought which generally developed according to regional practice. In Medina, for example, a school of Islamic law developed based on local practice and in view of the interpretations of scripture and hadith reports known locally. It was expressed in the work of Malik ibn Anas (d. 796), around which developed what is referred to as the Maliki school of law. Another center, with different local customs and different hadith reports, grew up in Kufa: the school of Abu Hanifa (d. 767), largely developed by Abu Yusuf (d. 798) and al-Shaybani (d. 804), and known as the Hanafi school. The development of these schools was essentially democratic; determination of what was normative in the Qur'an and Sunna was based on local consensus, *ijma'*. In cases where there were no apparently applicable precedents in the Qur'an or Sunna, legal scholars were to use their discretion to determine the implications of what they did find in the Qur'an and Sunna with regard to the novel situation. They were to practice *ijtihad*, the name given to this interpretive work.

The Umayyads maintained control over the caliphate until they were overthrown in another revolution by the 'Abbasid family in 750 CE. As members of the opposition to the Umayyads, the legal scholars (*fuqaha'*) were naturally favored by the 'Abbasids (750–1258 CE) and came to play an important role in their administration. But their incorporation into the imperial administration made apparent the need for greater rigor in legal thought, in the hopes of greater uniformity of practice throughout the empire. Thus a third school of Islamic law developed, attributed to al-Shafi'i (d. 820 CE), who held that only the consensus of the entire Islamic community (not just the various regions) was considered authoritative. But that was virtually impossible to attain given the extent of the Islamic community by the time he was working. Therefore, it was preferable to follow precedent as much as possible. For al-Shafi'i, then, the third source of Islamic law—after the Qur'an and the oral reports (hadith) of the Prophet's normative precedent (Sunna)—was the already established consensus regarding the meaning and application of the Qur'an as interpreted in light of hadith reports. Ijtihad could be practiced only as a final resort, but it too was circumscribed: the intellectual effort to determine the implications of the Qur'an and Sunna was to be according to syllogistic reasoning, or reasoning by analogy (*qiyas*). A fourth school of Islamic law eventually developed which placed even greater emphasis on precedent as expressed in the Sunna.[9] That was called the Hanbali school, after al-Shafi'i's student Ahmad ibn Hanbal (d. 855).

The articulation of the components and processes of Islamic law would become the basis for a comprehensive theory of political sovereignty. As legal historian N. J. Coulson put it, "The legal scholars were publicly recognized as the architects of an Islamic scheme of state and society which the 'Abbasids had pledged themselves to build, and under this political sponsorship the schools of law developed rapidly."[10]

The Centrality of Law in Islamic Governance

Coulson's observation points to the key element of Islamic governance: the centrality of law. There has been agreement from the earliest days of Islam that the essential element in Islamic life is Islamic law. This is indicated first of all by the fact that the major effort of intellectuals was devoted to establishing the Islamic legal system. The contrast to Christianity is instructive. When Christianity became politically institutionalized in Rome in the fourth century, it devised a way to determine who was in fact a Christian by developing a creed, a list of beliefs. Whoever claimed to agree with the creed was a Christian and therefore a full citizen; those who rejected the creed were non-Christian and considered therefore a threat to the Christian community. In Islam, on the other hand, those who followed Islamic law were considered Muslim, while Jews and Christians were not only allowed but expected to follow their own law (provided it did not contravene Islamic law). Al-Shafi'i, often described as the "architect of Islamic law," articulated as much when he discussed agreement within the community on legal rulings (*ijma'*). He said that whoever agrees on this body of law is considered a Muslim and whoever does not will be considered an opponent of the community.[11]

This idea—that to be a Muslim is to accept Islamic law—became the standard description of a Muslim, so that even if one lived outside the jurisdiction of Islamic law, one was expected to remain guided by it.[12] This was the essence of what became standard terms used to identify various communities: *dar al-Islam, dar al-'ahd* or *sulh*, and *dar al-harb. Dar al-Islam* refers to those territories in which the law of Islam prevails. *Dar al-ahd* (the abode of covenant) and *dar al-sulh* (the abode of truce) are both regions whose leaders have agreed to pay the Muslim leaders a certain tax and to protect the rights of any Muslim and/or their allies who dwell there, but who otherwise maintain their autonomy, including their own legal systems. *Dar al-harb* is a region whose leaders have made no such agreement and where, therefore, Muslims and their allies are neither guaranteed the right to live by Islamic law nor are they protected by it.

It is the centrality of law to Islam, in fact, that has allowed the Muslim community to remain coherent despite the political upheavals that have marked virtually its entire history. Regardless of what was going on with the ruling families, the really critical work continued: developing the guidance and examples into practical law so that people could be guided in their daily lives. Highly motivated scholars took upon themselves the responsibility to draw out the implications of revelation for cases not directly covered in the sources, and to articulate the reasoning involved. Throughout the turmoil of the dynastic revolutions, it was the legal scholars who maintained continuity within the Muslim community.

Developing Political Theory

The centrality of law to Islamic life also explains the secondary status of political theory. The need for a comprehensive political theory apparently did not present itself until the early eleventh century, by which time the 'Abbasid caliphs were facing strong competition from regional usurpers, particularly in Egypt and even in Baghdad, the 'Abbasids' capital. It was this challenge that finally gave rise to a theory of government, that of Shafi'i jurist al-Mawardi (d. 1058).[13]

Al-Mawardi's *Al-Ahkam al-Sultaniyya* was the first comprehensive work on the topic. It is essential to remember that al-Mawardi was working under the 'Abbasids, and in the context of serious challenges to their rule. It is not surprising in this milieu that he substantiated the legitimacy of the caliphate. (Had he not done so, it is unlikely his work would have been promulgated or even survived.) Thus, according to him, the office of the caliphate was established in order to continue the work of the Prophet both in his capacity as defender of religion and in "worldly governance."[14] Al-Mawardi says it is necessary that someone hold this position. Reason tells us that without political leaders, people would fall into chaos and savagery. Therefore, rational people agree to submit to some kind of authority. But revelation also confirms the need for political authority. Al-Mawardi quotes the Qur'an's command to "obey God, the Messenger, and those in authority among you" (4:59). For those who wondered about the legitimacy of the particular group in control at the time, al-Mawardi relates a hadith according to which the Prophet said, "Other rulers after me will rule over you, the pious according to his piety, the wicked according to his wickedness. Hear them and obey in all that accords with the truth. If they do good, it will count for you and for them. If they do evil, it will count for you and against them."

Because of this legitimation, some critics now call al-Mawardi a tool of the 'Abbasids. But a closer look at al-Mawardi's description of the leader's duties shows that his responsibilities are carefully circumscribed. According to al-Mawardi, the duties of the caliph fall into three categories: defense, treasury, and executive. He is to defend the community from attack (article 3), maintain frontier defenses (article 5), and wage war against those who refuse to either become Muslims or enter into treaty with Muslims (article 6). Regarding fiduciary responsibility, he is to collect both the alms payments required of all Muslims to be spent on the needs of the community at large, and the legitimate spoils of wars (article 7). He is to fairly determine and pay salaries from the treasury (article 8), and make sure those he appoints handle treasury moneys honestly (article 9). Most importantly, he is to make sure that the established principles of religion are safeguarded (article 1), and that legal judgements and penalties are enforced (articles 2 and 4). Nowhere in al-Mawardi's description is the caliph accorded legislative or judicial authority. His authority is strictly executive/coercive.

How is the executive to be chosen? Al-Mawardi says that in his day most rulers are designated by their predecessors. But in case there were no designated leader, he said the community should come up with a group of candidates eligible for the position, and a group of electors to choose from among the candidates. And what are the ideal qualifications of this leader? He had to be sound of mind and body, of course, and ideally a descendant of the Prophet's family. (Again, this provision must be seen in context. Since the 'Abbasids claim to legitimacy rested on this lineage, al-Mawardi could hardly discount its importance.) He also says the caliph should be able to exercise ijtihad (independent legal judgement). But he also says that the caliph can delegate certain tasks, and those associated with law are among them (undoubtedly another concession to existing reality). Another Shafi'i scholar, al-Juwayni (d. 1085), put it the other way around. The legal scholars do not get their authority from the caliph, al-Juwayni says; the real authority in the community belongs to the legal scholars in the first place. So the caliph could be a *muqallid* (follower of precedents, rather than an independent thinker) so long as he consulted the scholars.[15] Either way, the first element of Islamic government in the classical theories is that executive authority is distinguished from legal authority, and may even ultimately derive from it.

Three centuries further into Islamic history, Hanbali jurist Ibn Taymiyya (d. 1328) is even more explicit about the requirements for Islamic government and the distinction between legal/judicial authority and executive authority. He is the first to maintain that there is no single official Islamic form of government in the classical sources. "The general and particular features of the various positions of authority . . . are not defined in the Shari'ah," he says. They depend . . . "on various opinions (*alfaz*), circumstances (*ahwal*), and custom (*urf*)."[16] Nevertheless, he continues, there are certain requirements that must be met in order for a government to be considered Islamic. He sets these out in his magnum opus, *Al-Siyasah al-Shar'iyyah*, where he generally follows the outline established by al-Mawardi. He agrees that there must be political leadership because "the children of Adam" can only achieve their (common) interest together, "because every one of them is in need of every other one."[17] Besides, he said, the Qur'an commands obedience to those in authority among us. However, he says, those who hold command are two classes, the scholars ('*ulama*') and the executives (*umara*'). Again, the separation of powers in Islamic governance is affirmed.

Ibn Taymiyya says that in his day, in Syria and Egypt the military act as executive authority. They carry out legal punishments and certain limited litigation in cases where there is no evidence, leaving the legal authorities to deal with cases where there is documentary evidence. In the Maghreb, on the other hand, he says that the military has no juridical authority and acts solely as executive to the judiciary. But Ibn Taymiyya makes his position concerning how things should be very clear. He says the legal scholars are the only authoritative interpreters of the law. Their authority is delegated by the political leader, he says. He says that the executive should be a model of good behavior, as the first four caliphs were, but in any case, the political leader's job is to make sure legal decisions are carried out. So again we see legal authority distinguished from executive authority in Islamic governance. Furthermore, the nature of executive authority may vary from place to place, depending upon circumstances. But legal authority—articulating and adjudicating the law—remains not only distinct from the vagaries of executive administration, but logically primary.

The next question, then, concerns the identity of these scholars or legal authorities who are so important in Islamic governments. Who are they? Where do they come from? How do they get to be in positions of such authority? And what is the extent of their authority? According to the classical sources, they are, effectively, volunteers. Theoretically, anyone can enter the ranks of the *fuqaha'*, provided one is willing and capable of undertaking the study of language, logic, and tradition required to qualify among one's peers. Al-Shafi'i says the well-informed scholar is one fully acquainted with the Qur'an, the Prophet's example as reported by authoritative sources, and decisions made by earlier generations through consensus.[18] These qualifications can be achieved by anyone with sound judgement (*dhu'l-ray*) and good character, he says. Furthermore, al-Shafi'i says achieving this kind of knowledge as religious duty of the whole community (*fard kifaya*). Not everyone has to do it, but enough people have to do it in every community that the job gets done.[19] Ibn Taymiyya will hold the same opinion, using the language of advising the government, the responsibility to enjoin good and proscribe evil required of all Muslims by the Qur'an. As he puts it, it is the responsibility of everyone to offer their advice (from the hadith: *al-din nasiha*: "Religion is advice").

Wael Hallaq argues that the very science of jurisprudence was developed precisely to set out the procedures whereby anyone with proper training could participate in this branch of the government:

> The primary objective of legal theory . . . was to lay down a coherent system of principles through which a qualified jurist could extract rulings for novel cases. From the third/ninth century onwards this was universally recognized by jurists to be the sacred purpose of *usul al-fiqh* [the roots of Islamic legislation].[20]

In this sense—that legal scholars are essential to Islamic government and that theoretically anyone could become a scholar—Islamic government could even be considered populist. Others have called it elitist, due to the degree of training required to become a qualified scholar. Either way—populist or elitist, legal scholars are the core of Islamic government in the classical sources. But even though they are essential to an Islamic government, Ibn Taymiyya wants to caution against the idea that the interpreters of Islamic law are infallible. He says people have to realize there is a difference between *shari'a and fiqh*. Shari'a is God's eternal will for human beings. That means that it is infallible, of course. Fiqh is the human effort to articulate the divine will, and people should not confuse the two. Ibn Taymiyya says:

> People who [confuse Shari'a and fiqh] do not understand clearly the distinction in the meanings of the word Shari'a as employed in the Speech of God and His Apostle (on the one hand) and by common people on the other.... Indeed, some of them think that Shari'a is the name given to the judge's decisions; many of them even do not make a distinction between a learned judge, an ignorant judge and an unjust judge. Worse still, people tend to regard any decrees of a ruler as Shari'a, while sometimes undoubtedly the truth (*haqiqa*) is actually contrary to the decree of the ruler. [21]

Legal judgements, therefore—being human—are fallible. Furthermore, even a valid judgement is subject to amendment in light of new evidence, so Islamic legislation must remain flexible. For that reason, Ibn Taymiyya is opposed to the practice of *taqlid*, imitation of legal precedents. He does not deny authoritative judgements, determined on the basis of consensus, by the founders of the four schools of Sunni law.[22] But he says their decisions were authoritative only because the scholars based their opinions on the authoritative sources—the Qur'an and the Sunna, not because of the authority of the scholars themselves. For him there is no validity in ijma'/consensus separate from the authority of the sources on which it is based. And like al-Shafi'i, Ibn Taymiyya says that given the vast extent of the Islamic community, consensus among the legal scholars is no longer feasible. But even if it were, that would not relieve jurists of the responsibility to examine all evidence in every case and all pertinent arguments in their own school and in others, and then determine on the basis of the Qur'an and the Sunna the most suitable judgement. If the jurist determines that there exists a precedent resonant with the spirit of revealed truth, that precedent should be applied regardless of the school of law in which it is found. If he does not find an appropriate precedent, he shouldn't hesitate to judge independently—to exercise ijtihad in accordance with the principles he has determined most conducive to justice. [23]

Therefore, for Ibn Taymiyya, careful scrutiny of the cumulative tradition of Islamic law was essential to the life of the Muslim community. But the fact that an opinion may have been suitable at a given time and place was no guarantee that it would be suitable in another time and place. That is why he rejected taqlid, and with it the infallibility of the scholars. He said: "[T]he imams themselves have demonstrably admonished the people against their imitation and commanded that if they found stronger evidence in the Qur'an or in the Sunnah, they should prefer it to their own." [24] He quotes Abu Bakr, the first caliph: "Follow me where I obey God; but if I disobey Him, you owe me no obedience." The founder of his own school, Ibn Hanbal, is quoted: "Do not imitate me or Malik or Shafi'i etc., but investigates as we have investigated." [25] Accordingly, every community and generation is required to refer to the sources in their efforts at legislation rather than assume that the decisions of previous generations are necessarily correct. And because human opinion is fallible, disagreement among the scholars is inevitable. Like the judgements of fuqaha', different communities' practices can diverge to a certain extent, as long as the core of moral unity remains. As long as sincere effort is being made by properly trained scholars using the revealed sources to determine what is best for individuals and for the community, given that the goal of Islamic law is to establish justice—to enjoin good and proscribe evil—the community is doing its duty. [26]

Conclusion

The classical Sunni sources agree that there is a distinction between the legal and executive branches of government, that the legal branch is logically prior, it is technically open to anyone willing to undertake the training to qualify, and it is a moral responsibility that enough people do so that the government remains properly guided. Does that solve the dilemma of the South African Muslims, for example? Not at all. The classical sources do not deal with Muslim minority communities except as part of *dar al-sulh*. And it would be anachronistic to ask of the classical sources an answer about Muslims' participation in a pluralistic, democratic government, although a good case can be made for participation, based on the responsibility to enjoin good and forbid evil.

But the South African example does raise another interesting point about Islamic government having to do with the independence of the legal authorities from the executive branch in the contemporary world. In many Muslim countries today religious authorities can be denied a voice if their positions do not support those of the executive authorities, those with coercive power. The phenomenon of religious authorities who find a way to legitimate whatever the government does is also a familiar one. But religious scholars in a minority community like South Africa, perhaps because they are a minority, are not essential to national political stability and are therefore left to their own devices. As a result, the community is free to engage in genuine debate and to air honest differences of opinion based on sincere efforts to understand the sources. The positions being debated in the

South African example, although sometimes diametrically opposed, are formed by trained scholars, giving the community at large the opportunity to exercise its own judgement in choosing between the positions.

The important element of this example is not the fact that South African Muslims are a minority, however. It is the fact that the South African Muslim community voluntarily supports scholarship at all levels, generally through the age-old institution of *awqaf*. Awqaf (singular: *waqf*) are charitable endowments made in perpetuity for the support of the common good. That can include mosques and schools, the mosques and schools in which the scholars train, and scholarships to send students wherever they need to go to get adequate training to deal with today's world.

Throughout Islamic history scholarship was supported through autonomous waqf foundations. There were notorious exceptions and unfortunate examples of corruption in the administration of awqaf. And one of the legacies of colonialism was that awqaf were confiscated by the state, with the ultimate effect of making schools beholden to the state for support, and professional legal scholars employees of the state. This clearly compromised their ability to act independently. Nevertheless, the ideal and principle of the independence of legal authorities from the executive branch remains a vital part of Islamic heritage.

Do these principles have any relevance for today's discussions of the nature of government in Islam? They do allow some comparison between the dominant Western forms of government and Islamic principles of government. What Westerners think of as the three branches of the government are split in classical Islamic theory between those who wield coercive power (the executive branch) and the legislative-judicial branch. The former has authority over matters of defense and is charged with managing the treasury according to the law as well as executing the laws and judgements of the legal scholars. But by far the greatest emphasis is given to the latter branch, particularly in its legislative capacity.

The Sunni sources also reveal that there is a paradigm clash between classical Islamic and Western notions of governance. Whereas the West describes its government in terms of the source of legislation (the people: "democracy"), Islamic governance is identified by the law itself. The most common term for an Islamic system of governance is *al-siyasat al-shari'iyyah*, government according to Islamic law. That law is based on divine revelation but is humanly interpreted. So there is clearly a certain commensurability between the two systems. But it is the insistence that the ultimate source of legislation is divine and that any human effort at interpretation be limited by the absolute norms of revelation that makes Islamic governance unique.

Beyond allowing comparison with Western norms of governance, recognition of the Islamic emphasis on its unique legislation explains the existence of multiple interpretations of Islamic governance. It makes it clear that lack of agreement on a single correct form of Islamic government is neither a defect nor a weakness in Islamic theory. Rather, it results from the fact that political theory is secondary to legal theory in Islam. It also demonstrates that unity in the Islamic community is not based on political structures but on law. Just as political theory is secondary to legal theory, political unity is secondary to legal conformity. Muslims in various circumstances are bound to have different opinions on the most effective forms of administration, because administration is a practical matter and must therefore be suited to the conditions in which it is meant to be effective. Therefore, differences in political forms/structures are virtually inevitable in the Muslim community. And even that conformity is not necessarily based on uniformity of actual legal codes. These may differ as well, depending on the circumstances. Islamic unity is based on consensus regarding the sources of legislation and solidarity in the effort to implement them in the overall effort to carry out the Qur'an's command to "establish justice" and thereby submit to the will of God. In other words, multiple political units and diversity of political systems are not only acceptable, but to be expected, within context of spiritual or moral unity, according to classical Sunni sources.

Notes

1. See Jamal al-Din al-Afghani, "Answer of Jamal al-Din to Renan" in Nikki R. Keddie, *An Islamic Response to Imperialism* (Berkeley: University of California Press, 1983), 181–87; Syed Ameer Ali, *The Spirit of Islam: A History of the Evolution and Ideals of Islam* (London: Christophers, 1922); Rashid al-Ghannushi, *Fi'l-Mabadi' al-Asasiyyah li'l-Dimuqratiyyah wa Usul al-Hukm al-Islami* (The Principles of Democracy and the Fundamentals of Islamic Government) (n.p.: 1990); Mohammed Khatami, *Islam, Liberty and Development* (Binghamton, NY: Institute of Global Cultural Studies, Binghamton University, 1998).

2. Petition circulated by Professor Abdul Kader Tayob, University of Cape Town; Mr. Farouk Cassiem, MP; Dr. Farid Esack, Commission on Gender Equality; Imam Rashid Omar, Claremont Main Rd. Mosque; Dr. Rafiq Khan; Shaikh Sirah Hendricks; and Na'eem Jeenah, President, Muslim Youth Movement of South Africa.

3. I will confine the discussion to Sunni sources, especially the works of al-Maward and Ibn Taymiyya, because they provided comprehensive treatments of the topic and are therefore representative of classical thought.

4. Articles 23 and 42 of the Constitution of Medina, from Ibn Hisham's *Al-Sirah*, translated by W. Montgomery Watt, *Islamic Political Thought* (Edinburgh: University Press, 1968), 132–33.

5. Reported by Muslim and al-Nisa'i.

6. Watt (*Islamic Political Thought* [Edinburgh: The University Press, 1968], 32ff.) discusses the meanings of the term *khalifa* at the time Abu Bakr seems to have used it.

His conclusion that the term had no more specific meaning than "one who comes after" is generally accepted among scholars, although the term is used in the Qur'an in several places with the connotation of "deputy," "vicegerent," or "steward." See, e.g., 2:30, 6:165, 7:69, 7:74, 10:14, 10:73, 27:62, 35:39, 38:26.

7. The general pattern was for the Muslim conquerors to exact some sort of tribute to reflect their sovereignty while leaving it to the local authorities to collect the taxes according to their established customs. The degree of autonomy of the local officials was often affected by the nature of the conquest. When the lands were acquired by means of military conquest, the administrative system established generally reflected more the conqueror's discretion than those acquired by a treaty of capitulation. At times, however, a system of taxation was simply imposed regardless of means of conquest, or the amount of tribute expected may have been fixed in advance of the conquest and only means of collection left to local officials. Iraq, for example, was conquered by military victory over the drained Sasanid forces and with the help of the Shayban Bedouin. The native Arab subordinates were left in control of taxation and followed the Sasanid tradition. The Sasanid system included both a land tax and a poll tax which varied according to the degree of wealth among the populace, except for the aristocracy, who were exempt from the poll tax. In order to maintain this exemption, the aristocracy generally converted to Islam. In Syria, on the other hand, where Islamic dominance was achieved largely by treaty, the tax collection and tribute was left to the discretion of the native administrators. They followed in general outline the fiscal system of the previous Roman overlords. More complex than the Persian system, the Roman model included a personal tax only on colonists and non-Christians and a property tax which varied with the size of the estate. A small parcel was apparently taxed according to the measure of its cultivation while larger estates were taxed according to the number of people working the land. In Iran and the Caucasus/Central Asia, the Sasanid system of land tax and poll tax, regardless of conversion, seems to have remained intact. A Tribute was simply fixed by the conquerors and the local chieftains were left to administer taxes as they saw fit. See al-Baladhuri, *Futuh al-Buldan*, ed. DeGoeje (Leyden: E. J. Brill, 1866 and translated by Phillip K. Hitti as *The Origins of the Islamic State*, New York: Columbia University Press, 1916), 110–12; Ahmad G. Abi Ya'qub al-Ya'qubi, *Ta'rikh*, ed. Th. Houtsma (Leyden: E. J. Brill, 1883), 2:150–51; al-Tabari, *Tarikh al-Rusul wa'l-Muluk*, ed. M. DeGoeje, et al. (Leyden: E. J. Brill, 1879–1901), 1:2111–13, 2121–24; Ibn 'Asakir, *al-Ta'rikh al-Kabir*, ed. 'Abd al-Qadir Badran and Ahmad 'Ubayd (Damascus, 1329–51), 1:130; Ibn al-Athir, *al-Kamil fi'l-Ta'rikh*, ed. C.J. Thornberg (Leyden; E. J. Brill, 1867), 2:312–13. See also Daniel C. Dennet, Jr. *Conversion and the Poll Tax* (Cambridge, MA: Harvard University Press, 1950), 12ff.; C. Cahen, "Djizya," *Encyclopedia of Islam*, 2nd ed., 2559; H. Lammens, *Etudes sur le regne du Calife Omaiyade Mo'awia Ier* (Beyrouth: Imprimeire Catholique, 1930), 226.

8. See N.J. Coulson, *A History of Islamic Law* (Edinburgh: The University Press, 1964), chapters 2–3, upon which this account is based.

9. See Ibid., 70–71, and Wael B. Hallaw, "Was al-Shafi'i the Master Architect of Islamic Jurisprudence?" in *International Journal of Middle East Studies*, 25/4 (November 1993): 587–605.

10. Coulson, op. cit., 37.

11. "He who holds what the Muslim community holds shall be regarded as following the community, and he who holds differently shall be regarded as opposing the community he was ordered to follow." Tr. Majid Khadduri, *Islamic Jurisprudence: Shafi'i's Risala* (Baltimore: The Johns Hopkins Press, 1961), 287.

12. It must be borne in mind that law in Islam is not simply a list of rules and regulations enforced by the state. As Fazlur Rahman put it, Islamic law "is not strictly speaking law [in the Western sense], since much of it embodies moral and quasi-moral precepts not enforceable in any court." "[O]n closer examination," he said, it is "a body of legal opinions or," as Santillana put it, "an endless discussion of the duties of a Muslim, rather than a neatly formulated code or codes."

13. In Marshall G. S. Hodgson's analysis, the dynastic families had seized control of the central political power of the Muslim empire (the army and the treasury that supported it) before there was any theory of political legitimacy in Islam. But by the tenth century, regional principalities had emerged and while they were generally content to pay nominal allegiance to the Baghdad caliphate, they posed a challenge the central caliphate's real power. Hodgson says, "The caliphate itself was in question, in a world ruled by arbitrary amirs [princes], and the caliphate had proved willing to turn to Shar'i principles in its crisis. Hence the scholars set about developing the theory of a *silyasah shar'iyyah*, Shar'i political order." See *The Venture of Islam*, Vol. II: *The Expansion of Islam in the Middle Periods* (Chicago and London: The University of Chicago Press, 1974), 55. It should be noted, however, that even in al-Mawardi's formulation, the term "imamate" is used, rather than "caliphate." Scholars agree, however, that the terms are interchangeable in this context.

14. The following account is taken from 3–6, 14–15, and 19–20 of al-Mawardi's *Al-Ahkam al-Sultaniyya*, translated by Bernard Lewis in *Islam*, Vol. I: *Politics and War* (New York, Hagerstown, San Francisco, London: Harper Torchbooks, 1974), 171–79.

15. This is Wael Hallq's interpretation of the following passage from Muhammad al-Juwayni, *Ghiyath al-Umama*. ([Iskandariyya, 1979]: 274–75): "If the sultan does not reach the degree of ijtihad, then the jurists are to be followed and the sultan will provide them with help, power, and protection." See Wael Hallaq, "Was the Gate of Ijtihad Closed?" in *International Journal of Middle East Studies* 16 (1984):13.

16. Al-Hisbah fi'l-Islam, Damascus 1967, 8.

17. Ibn Taymiyya quotes Prophet Muhammad in this regard: "If three of them were on a journey, they should choose one of them as a leader [*qa'id*]." Ibn Taymiyya, *al-Siyasah al-Shar'iyyah fi Islah al-Ra'i wa'l- Ra'iyyah* (ed. Muhammad al-Mubarak. Beirut: Dar al-Kutub al-'Arabiyyah, 1966. Except where noted, English quotes are taken from translation by '*Umar Farrukh, On Public and Private Law in Islam* (Beirut: Khayats, 1966), 187–9.

18. *Islamic Jurisprudence: Al-Shafi'i's Risala*, Khadduri's translation, 306.

19. Ibid., 87.

20. Wael B. Hallaq, "Was the Gate of Ijtihad Closed?" in *International Journal of Middle Eastern Studies* 16 (1984): 5.

21. The quote continues:

The Prophet himself said, 'You people bring disputes to me; but it may be that some of you are able to put their case better than others. But I have to decide on evidence that is before me. If I happen to expropriate the right of anyone in favor of his brother let the latter not take in, for in that case I have given him a piece of hell-fire.' Thus, the judge decided on the strength of depositions and evidence that are before him while the party decided against may well have proofs that have not been put forward. In such cases the Shari'a in reality is just the opposite of the external law, although the decision of the judge has to be enforced. Fazlur Rahman, *Islam*, 112, quoted from Ibn Taymiyya, *Al-Ihtijaj bi'l-Qadar* in his *Rasa'il*, Cairo, 1323, II:96–97.

22. See his *Raf' al-Muam 'an al-Aimmah al-A'lam* (In defense of the Learned Imams) (Beirut: Al-Maktab al-Islami, 3rd, 1970).

23. See his *Fatwa fi'l-Ijtihad* in the appendix of *Raf' al-Malam 'an al-A'immah al-A'lam*.

24. Translated by Victor E. Makari in *Ibn Taymiyyah's Ethic: The Social Factor* (Chico, CA: Scholars Press, 1983), 98 from Ibn Taymiyya's *Al-Fatawa al-Kubra* (Cairo: Dar al-Kutub al-Haditha, 1966), Vol. I, 484.

25. See Makari, op. cit., 106–7.

26. See Henri Laoust's classic discussion in *Essai sur les Doctrines Sociales et Politique de Taki-d-Din b. Taimiya* (Le Caire: Institute Francais D'Archaeologie Orientale, 1939), 253ff. discussing Ibn Taymiyya's treatise on the topic of difference of opinion among the *'ulama: Ikhtilaf al-Ummah fi'l-'Ibadat*.

3

Obedience to Political Authority:
An Evolutionary Concept

Asma Afsaruddin

The construction of religious and political authority in Islamic thought hinges to a considerable degree on the understanding of the critical Qur'anic verse (4:59), which states, "O those who believe, obey God and the Messenger and those in possession of authority among you" (Ar. "*Ya ayyuha alladhina amanu, ati'u Allah wa-ati'u al-rasul wa-'uli 'l-'amr minkum*). The phrase *uli 'l-amr* in this verse has given rise to various interpretations in different historical contexts. This paper will discuss some of the earliest significations of this verse available to us and compare them with later, including modern, interpretations and dwell on the implications of the evolutionary transformations that emerge. Works of exegesis (*tafsir*), *hadith* works, and political treatises have been consulted in this project of retrieval and comparison.[1]

Medieval Exegetical Works

The earliest published work of exegesis we have at our disposal is the one by the late seventh century/early eighth century exegete Mujahid b. Jabr (d. 720). In his *Tafsir*, Mujahid states that this verse was revealed in reference to "those possessing critical insight into religion and reason" (*ya'ni uli 'l-fiqh fi 'l-din wa'l-'aql*). A second variant report recorded by Mujahid relates that the phrase refers to "those possessing critical insight, knowledge, [sound] opinion and virtue" (*ya'ni uli 'l-fiqh wa'l-'ilm wa-'l-ra'y wa-'l-fadl*). Both of these reports, which are not prophetic in origin, are attributed to the Companion 'Abd al-Rahman [b. Awf].[2] Particularly noteworthy in these glosses is the emphasis on knowledge, independent reasoning, and critical discernment as the distinctive characteristics of the *uli 'l-amr*, who are not identified with any particular group of people or occupational category.

Another early exegete, Muqatil b. Sulayman al-Balkhi (d. 767), records in his Qur'an commentary that the key phrase *uli 'l-amr minkum* was revealed specifically in reference to the military commander Khalid b. al-Walid in a particular historical context, and more broadly refers to the commanders of military contingents (*saraya*).[3] Muqatil refers to an unnamed military campaign during which the two Companions Khalid b. al-Walid and 'Ammar b. Yasir had a disgreement regarding the status of a prisoner of war, to whom 'Ammar had granted protection (*aman*) since the man had publicly uttered the *shahada* (sc. become a Muslim). Khalid refused to recognize 'Ammar's conferral of protection and rebuked the latter for insubordination; this led to an acrimonious exchange between them. Upon their return to Madina, they presented their case to the Prophet. The Prophet recognized the validity of 'Ammar's action; at the same time, he forbade 'Ammar from disobeying a commander (*amir*) a second time. At that, 'Ammar left in an aggrieved state and the Prophet adjured Khalid to catch up with him and apologize to him. Khalid did as he was told but 'Ammar rebuffed him; consequently this verse was revealed in reference to this specific circumstance.

Muqatil considers Qur'an 24:51–52 as an analog (*nazir*) of 4:59, which helps to further elucidate the meaning of the latter. Qur'an 24:51–52 state, "When the believers are invited to God and His messenger so that He may judge between them, they say, 'we hear and we obey'; these are the successful. For those who obey God and His messenger and fear God and heed Him, they are the ones who are victorious."[4] Thus, in comparison with these verses, Muqatil understands 4:59 to be prescribing obedience to God and His messenger only, with the *uli 'l-amr* excluded.

These two interpretations find reflection in another early *tafsir* work *Tanwir al-miqbas fi tafsir Ibn 'Abbas* attributed to the Companion Ibn 'Abbas. In this work, the phrase *uli 'l-amr* is glossed as referring to both "the leaders of military contingents" (*umara' al-saraya*) and "the learned people" (*al-'ulama'*) in the opinion of some. 'Abd al-Razzaq al-San'ani (d. 827) in his early *tafsir* work reports on the authority of the famous Successor (from the generation following the Companions) al-Hasan al-Basri (d. 728) that *ulu 'l-amr minkum* refers to "the learned people" (*al-'ulama'*) and on the authority of Mujahid that the phrase refers to "people of insightful understanding and knowledge" (*ahl al-fiqh wa-'l-'ilm*). He further records a *hadith* from Abu Hurayra in which the Prophet declares in exegesis of Qur'an 4:59, "Whoever obeys me obeys God; whoever disobeys me disobeys God, and whoever obeys my commander (*amiri*) obeys me, and whoever disobeys my commander disobeys me."[5] It should be noted that this *hadith* reflects the early understanding of *amir* as referring specifically to a military commander. In his exegesis, 'Abd al-Razzaq thus also subscribes to the view prevalent in the first two centuries of Islam that *uli 'l-amr* refers to a) the learned and insightful people in general and b) the Prophet's designated military commanders in specific circumstances.

In the *tafsir* section of his famous collection of statements attributed to the Prophet Muhammad entitled *al-Sahih*, the *hadith* scholar al-Bukhari (d. 870) relates a report from Ibn 'Abbas in which he states that verse 4:59 was revealed in reference to the Companion 'Abd Allah b. Hudhafa when the Prophet dispatched him on a military campaign.[6]

The celebrated ninth/tenth century Qur'an commentator al-Tabari (d. 923) gives an account of the various meanings attributed to this phrase and gives us a sense of the evolution in its interpretation. In his commentary on Qur'an 4:59, al-Tabari cites several Companion reports (sc. reports that end with an attribution to one of the associates of the Prophet and not to the Prophet himself) which show that this verse was understood by them to refer to diverse groups of people. He records two reports from Ibn 'Abbas: in the first report, Ibn 'Abbas relates that the verse refers to an unnamed man who was dispatched by the Prophet on a military campaign, while in the second, he identifies him as 'Abd Allah b. Hudhafa.[7] Another report from Maymun b. Mahran affirms that the verse refers to all the Companions who took part in the military expeditions (*al-saraya*) dispatched by the Prophet.[8] Al-Tabari refers to the eighth century exegete al-Suddi (d. 744), who, in confirmation of Muqatil, understands this verse to refer to the specific campaign led by Khalid b. al-Walid and his altercation with 'Ammar b. Yasir.

In another report recorded by al-Tabari, Ibn Zayd, from the second generation of Muslims, quotes the Companion Ubayy b. Ka'b as saying that the verse was a reference to the political rulers (*al-salatin*),[9] an interesting anachronistic usage of this word here since sultans did not rise in the Islamic world until about the ninth century, well after the time of the Companions.[10] Al-Tabari then goes on to refer to a number of authorities who understood this verse as referring to "the people of knowledge and insightful understanding" (*ahl al-'ilm wa-'l-fiqh*). Among these authorities are Jabir b. 'Abd Allah and Mujahid. Other variants of this report which identify the *uli 'l-amr* as "the possessors of insightful understanding in religion and of reason" (*uli 'l-fiqh fi 'l-din wa-'l-'aql*); "people of insightful understanding and religion"; "people of knowledge"; and "the possessors of knowledge and insightful understanding," are recorded on the authority of various sources.[11] Another cluster of reports identifies the *uli 'l-amr* as "the perspicacious and learned people"—this is how the Arabic terms *al-fuqaha' wa-'l-'ulama'* employed in these instances should be translated for the early period. Understanding these terms to refer to the later occupational categories of jurists and scholars (from the ninth century on) would be anachronistic here. These terms together should rather be understood as analogs of the early phrase ahl al-fiqh wa-'l-'ilm, understood more broadly as referring in general to people who possess unusual discernment and knowledge. Other early commentators like Mujahid, according to al-Tabari, were inclined to understand this verse as referring to all the companions of Muhammad (ashab Muhammad).[12]

Al-Tabari next lists a report that has a noticeable partisan flavoring. This Companion report, emanating from 'Ikrima, states that the verse refers to Abu Bakr and 'Umar, clearly a report that shows the influence of the debates over legitimate leadership of the Muslim polity between the Sunnis and the Shi'a.[13]

The twelfth century exegete Fakhr al-Din al-Razi (d. 1209) offers a detailed exposition of this verse and its various interpretations. We see further interesting reflections in his tafsir work of certain theological and juridical developments that had become part of mainstream thought after the ninth century. He states, for example, that Qur'an 4:59 indicates that anything beyond the purview of the four usuls or fundamentals of jurisprudence—the Qur'an, sunna, ijma' (consensus), and qiyas (analogy)—is invalid and to be rejected (mardud, batil). For, he says, these fundamentals encompass all situations regarding which specific prescriptions based on texts may be found; in such cases, absolute obedience is required. In other situations, where no such specific prescriptions based on texts may be found, they may be adduced by resorting to independent reasoning (ijtihad).[14]

Such a discussion consequently entails the discussion of who specifically are the ulu 'l-amr, since they are the ones capable of engaging in ijtihad and are to be resorted to after the Qur'an and the sunna have been consulted with regard to legal and theological matters. Al-Razi thus proceeds to elucidate the meaning of this term. He begins by listing the various interpretations already current by his time, which are now familiar to us. He notes that various exegetes have been of the opinion that uli 'l-amr indicates the Rightly-Guided Caliphs; others regarded the phrase as referring to the various military commanders, among whom were 'Abd Allah b. Hudhafa, and Khalid b. al-Walid during the Prophet's time. In the case of Khalid b. al-Walid, al-Razi recapitulates the disagreement between him and 'Ammar b. Yasir. Finally, he records the interpretation of the Qur'an commentator al-Tha'labi (d. 1035) who had related from the Companion Ibn 'Abbas and the Successors (al-tabi'un) al-Hasan [al-Basri], Mujahid, and al-Dahhak, that the phrase refers to the scholars "who make legal pronouncements regarding the religious law and instruct the people in their religion."[15]

Al-Razi then indicates his preferred interpretation of the phrase and he opts for what the eleventh century exegete al-Tha'labi had reported from Ibn 'Abbas, among others. He asserts that the phrase *wa-uli 'l-amr minkum* establishes that *ijmaʿ* is a categorical proof (*hujja*), since *ijmaʿ* cannot be created except through the pronouncements of the scholars (*bi-qawl al-ʿulama*'), who are able to extrapolate the commandments of God from the texts of the Qur'an and the *sunna*. And these scholars are the *ahl al-hall wa-'l-ʿaqd* (lit., "the people who loosen and bind"), as they are so termed in the juridical literature; they are thus identical to the *uli 'l-amr*. Al-Razi points to the jurists alone as being intended in this phrase, for he says, only this type of scholar (*hadha al-sinf min al-ʿulama*') has the ability to command and prohibit on the basis of the religious law. Interestingly, he maintains that the theologian (*al-mutakallim*), the exegete, and the *hadith* scholar who cannot deduce legal principles from the foundational texts are not to be included in the *ahl al-hall wa-'l-ʿaqd*, and, therefore, not to be counted among the *uli 'l-amr*. Al-Razi's exposition is a clear indicator of the primacy of *fiqh* (jurisprudence) and of the pre-eminent position of the jurists in the religio-intellectual circles of his own time.

Another late medieval exegete, Ibn Kathir (d. 1373) records the variant and variegated interpretations of this verse in his influential exegetical work, documenting both its earliest interpretation as referring to "people of discernment and religiosity" (*ahl al-fiqh wa-'l-din*) and/or to specific military commanders during the Prophet's lifetime.[16] However, it is clear, that Ibn Kathir himself is inclined to the view predominant in his time (the Mamluk period) that the Qur'anic term *uli 'l-amr* refers primarily (if not exclusively) to those who have political authority. He enlists as proof-texts a disproportionate number of *hadiths* which enjoin obedience to the political ruler in general and counsel the faithful to maintain stoic forbearance during the reign of an unjust ruler, since the latter is bound to be punished for his excesses in the next world. The text of the *hadiths*, however, betray no connection to Qur'an 4:59; that is to say there is no indication within the reports themselves that the Prophet had uttered them in direct explication of this verse. We have previously mentioned that al-Bukhari in the ninth century, in his commentary on 4:59, had not invoked such *hadiths* as proof-texts to indicate that the verse mandated obedience to political rulers. Consonant with one of the two earliest views, al-Bukhari had maintained rather that the verse refers to the specific case of the Companion ʿAbd Allah b. Hudhafa and did not understand it to have a broader application.

It seems clear, however, that once the word *amr* came to be understood as primarily referring to political authority by sometime after the ninth century, prophetic reports (of varying degrees of reliability according to the criteria developed by the medieval *hadith* scholars) advising against causing social upheaval (*fitna*) by engaging in political rebellion would be associated with Qur'an 4:59 and thus marshaled as religious warrants for promoting political quietism and authoritarianism. One such *hadith* annexed for this purpose is

derived from the Prophet's sermon delivered at the conclusion of the last pilgrimage of his life in 632 CE. In this sermon, the Prophet addresses the crowd
of pilgrims and advises them to "Obey and listen, even if an Abyssinian slave
with a head like a raisin were to rule over you (*amara 'alaykum*)." It is noteworthy that this *hadith* has generally been understood to underscore the egalitarian
nature of the Islamic polity and to point to the primacy of requirements such as
personal piety and moral excellence in selecting a leader for the polity. According to this prophetic utterance, race, ethnic background, and social class were to
exert no influence, so that even a lowly slave, on account of his greater moral
excellence, could be regarded as being more worthy of the leadership of the
polity than a high-born, free Arab who was less morally excellent. Ibn Kathir
appropriates this *hadith* in this context, however, to more firmly anchor the
notion of practically unqualified obedience to the ruler, regardless of whether
he was deemed agreeable or not, it would seem, by the general populace.

In this section of his exegesis, Ibn Kathir, however, further includes the customary caveats against obeying the ruler who is guilty of violating God's commandments (*ma'siyat Allah*).[17]

Modern/ist Exegetical Works

We will now skip ahead several generations in view of length constraints and
consult the early twentieth-century exegete Rashid Rida's important Qur'an
commentary *Tafsir al-Manar* and his treatment of this critical verse. Rida con-
curs with al-Razi that the phrase *uli 'l-amr* refers to "the people who loosen and
bind" among Muslims and they are the *umara'* (whom he understands to be the
political rulers), the judges (*al-hukkam*), the religious scholars (*al-'ulama'*), the
chiefs of the army (*ru'asa' al-jund*), and the rest of the rulers and leaders (*sa'ir
al-ru'asa' wa-'l-zu'ama'*) to whom, he says, people resort to in their need and for
their general welfare.[18] In this work, the term *amir* or *umara'* is explicated as
referring exclusively to political leaders and rulers, since Rida clearly distinguishes the *umara'* from military leaders whom he terms *ru'asa al-jund*. In this
he departs from the classical and medieval understanding of *umara'* as referring
primarily to military commanders, at least in exegetical works.

Rida also warns, however, that Qur'an 4:59 does not call for obedience to the
uli 'l-amr but only to God and His Messenger, the reason being that the verse
continues with "And if you should differ with regard to a matter, then refer it to
God and His Messenger." If the *uli 'l-amr* rule according to the precepts of God
and the *sunna*, then obedience is due to them; if they do not and in fact resort
to tyranny and oppression (*zulm*), then obedience is no longer an obligatory
duty (*wajiba qat'an*), but is rather forbidden (*muharrama*).[19] He continues by

saying that the actions of the temporal, political rulers (*al-umara' wa-'l-salatin*) are bound by the legal opinions (*fatawa*) of the scholars (*al-'ulama'*), for the '*ulama*' are in fact "the leaders of the leaders" (*umara' al-umara'*).

In this interpretation, Rida is echoing in part the exegesis of the eighth-ninth century commentator Muqatil b. Sulayman, who similarly understood the verse as enjoining obedience to God and His messenger only, and not to the *uli 'l-amr* as well, as we mentioned previously. The *uli 'l-amr* have primarily a consultative role; their counsel is to be solicited when the Qur'an and the *sunna* do not provide categorical answers in certain matters. Acting upon the *uli 'l-amr*'s recommendations is consequently a discretionary option, rather than binding. These conclusions are implicit in Muqatil's exegesis but more explicitly formulated in Rida's.

Further on, Rida, who equates the *uli 'l-amr* with the "people who loosen and bind," broadens the description of this group of people in a modernist vein. The "people who loosen and bind" include all those in whom the Muslim community, the *umma*, has faith: they would include the scholars, the leaders of the army, and the leaders of various sectors of society who promote the general interests of the people (*al-masalih al-'amma*). Among these sectors are trade, industry, and agriculture. Therefore, labor union leaders, political party leaders, members of the editorial boards of respectable newspapers and their chief editors are all included in the category of the people "who loosen and bind." Rida asserts that obedience to them constitutes obedience to the *uli 'l-amr*.[20] We must not forget that Rida was the editor of the highly regarded periodical *al-Manar* and his mentor Muhammad 'Abduh was one of the key figures associated with the influential journal *al-'Urwa al-Wuthqa*; no doubt he was including himself and 'Abduh among the *uli 'l-amr*.

Al-Rida's exegesis echoes the interpretations of the early exegetes. The late seventh-early eighth century exegete Mujahid, like al-Rida, had defined the *uli 'l-amr* broadly. Mujahid had described them as people endowed in general with critical insight into religious matters and reasoning (as previously mentioned), not restricting them to specific occupational categories, as would later commentators, like al-Razi. The latter, as we saw, was of the opinion that among all categories of scholars, only the jurists, because of their ability to engage in legal reasoning, could be regarded as constituting the *uli 'l-amr*. Rida's understanding of this locution is as broad as Mujahid's but he also identifies specific occupational groups peculiar to the modern world, who, in addition to the traditional groups of scholars, jurists, and theologians, contribute to the general welfare and guidance of society as well.

The more recent Islamist thinker and Qur'an commentator Abul A'la Mawdudi (d. 1979) in his exegetical work *Tafhim al-Qur'an* ("Comprehension of the Qur'an") echoes Rashid Rida's broad understanding of *uli 'l-amr* as referring to "intellectual and political leaders of the community, as well as to administrative officials, judges of the courts, tribal chiefs and regional representatives."[21] Mawdudi counsels obedience to them in general, with the caveat that this obedience is contingent on the *uli 'l-amr* being believers themselves and on their being obedient to God and the Prophet. In the event that a Muslim is commanded to carry out a deed that would be in contravention of God's laws, he or she must not obey such a command.

In this context, Mawdudi goes to some length to explain a sound *hadith* recorded by al-Bukhari in which the Prophet describes the situation after his death to his Companions during which time there would be rulers, both just and unjust. Some of the Companions asked if they should fight against the unjust rulers and the Prophet counseled them to desist "as long as they [sc. the rulers] continue to pray." Mawdudi refers to another *hadith*, recorded not by al-Bukhari but, among others, by Muslim (d. 875) and al-Tirmidhi (d. 892) (two more compilers of authoritative *hadith* works), in which the Prophet advises his Companions in response to a similar question not to rise up against oppressive rulers, "as long as they establish Prayer (sic) among you."[22] Mawdudi considers the second report as providing further clarification of the purport of the first report cited: that the rulers are to be obeyed not on account of their personal observance of the duty of prayer but on account of "the establishment of the system of congregational Prayers in the collective life of Muslims." He states further that "[t]his concern with Prayer is a definite indication that a government is essentially an Islamic one."[23]

Mawdudi's argument, it should be noted, is a rather disingenuous one. His argument hinges particularly on the Arabic verb *aqama*, which in specific contexts may refer "to establish" something. The usual meaning of this verb in connection with prayer is simply "to perform" and "to carry out." The Qur'an frequently uses this word in relation to prayer, and often in reference to the individual believer and his or her personal obligation to pray (for example, 2:177). Even if one were to understand the verb as "to establish," it still would not a priori convey the meaning of "to establish something publicly." One may infer this meaning if one is so inclined but this meaning is not explicit in the verb itself. Consistent with his politicized understanding of a number of Qur'an verses, however, Mawdudi finds this particular signification to be conveniently appropriate.

And, finally, on to Sayyid Qutb (d. 1966), whose religio-political thought on so-called "Islamic government" and "divine sovereignty" (Ar. *al-hakimiyya*) has and continues to have considerable influence on those whom we call Islamists today. In his exegetical work *Fi Zilal al-Qur'an* ("In the Shade of the Qur'an"), Sayyid Qutb, interestingly, does not dwell as much on the phrase *uli 'l-amr* itself as one might have expected him to, but regards the "people possessing authority" as being practically subsumed under the commandment to obey God and His messenger. At two points, he glosses the term *uli 'l-amr*. In the first instance, he says "as for the phrase *uli 'l-amr* the text [i.e. the Qur'an] distinguishes who they are"; that is, they are those believers (*al-mu'minin*) in whom the condition of faith and the precepts of Islam (*hadd al-Islam*) . . . are realized." He continues by stating that these precepts have to do with obedience to God and to the Messenger, and with divine sovereignty—*al-hakimiyya*—and the right to legislate for the people from the very outset on the basis of the Qur'an and the *sunna* alone. Slightly earlier in his *tafsir*, Sayyid Qutb makes clear that sovereignty belongs to God alone and governs every aspect of human life, for God had prescribed His law as contained in the Qur'an.[24]

In the second instance, he says that the phrase *uli 'l-amr* refers to "believers who stand upon the law of God (*shari'at Allah*) and the *sunna* of the Messenger,[25] which is a more succinct rephrasing of his first gloss.

In effect, Sayyid Qutb's highly politicized understanding of verse 4:59 with its linkage to the novel term *al-hakimiyyah* represents the culmination of Mawdudi's vision of a hegemonic political Islam. In his exegesis of 4:59, Qutb does not include the customary caveat, common in exegetical works composed by the earliest authors down to Mawdudi, against obeying the ruler if his actions or dictates are deemed to be in violation of the religious law (although, it should be noted, some of his political tracts make clear that the duty of obedience to such a ruler lapses under such conditions). His brief explication of this critical verse also leaves little room for consultation with the people at large and solicitation of their advice (*munasaha*), a procedure Ibn Taymiyya had insisted upon.[26] A dangerous determinism appears to undergird Qutb's schema for an Islamic government. The *uli 'l-amr*, that is, those who have political authority, are clearly to be obeyed along with God and His messenger, since they are tautologically understood to be the best equipped to interpret and apply Qur'anic injunctions and the *sunna* on account of their status as *uli 'l-amr*. Clearly, such an assumed providential arrangement brooks little or no opposition from those who might see things differently.

And yet, as we know from his other works, Sayyid Qutb also advocated the application of the Qur'anic principle of *shura* (consultation), and his utopian Islamic community is comprised of Muslims who infer (practically infallibly) the will of God from the Qur'an and *sunna* and implement it in active and respectful consultation with one another. The disjunction between these two positions may be resolved by bringing in Qutb's concept of *al-tali'a* ("the vanguard") which, since it perfectly comprehends God's will, is in charge of spearheading the worldwide Islamicizing movement.[27] Before the final establishment of the Islamic utopia, this vanguard is a minority of rightly-guided individuals adrift in a sea of misguided people, imbued with the reckless and godless notions of the pre-Islamic era (*al-jahiliyya*). Under such circumstances, the vanguard is not required to consult with the larger community, in fact, it is forbidden to do so, but must instead close ranks and strive to bring everyone into line with their manner of thinking. Although Qutb does not make this connection explicitly in the works I have looked at, the *uli 'l-amr* of his conception are none other than the vanguard of his coming revolution.

Political Treatises

Pre-Modern Works

Now to turn to political treatises. The earliest monograph-length political treatise under consideration in this study is the *Risalat al-'Uthmaniyya* of the celebrated medieval belle-lettrist and polymath 'Amr b. Bahr al-Jahiz (d. 869). This treatise, considerably older than the one penned by the famous political theorist al-Mawardi (d. 1058) but less well-known, preserves the full gamut of the meanings ascribed to this phrase in the early works of *tafsir* and also provides new insights into the early trajectory of this term. In this work, al-Jahiz indicates the range of possible interpretations of this verse: some Qur'an exegetes, he says, have understood the phrase *ulu 'l-amr* to have a restricted application and to apply only to specific agents (*'ummal*) of the Prophet, to his specific delegates or representatives (*wulat*) and/or to specific commanders of his armies, such as Abu Musa al-Ash'ari. Others have understood it to refer to political rulers (*salatin; umara'*). Yet others have interpreted this phrase to refer more broadly to the Companions of the Prophet as a group, and/or to Muslims in general.[28] In the early ninth century, al-Jahiz' political treatise still does not show a preference for the meaning of *amr* as "political authority"; rather his work continues to document the broad range of meanings that were ascribed to the word over time. The last exegetical gloss recorded by al-Jahiz would invest the entire Muslim community (or, at the very least, its righteous members) with moral and political authority. Interestingly, this range of meanings given by al-Jahiz is more in accordance with recent, modernist interpretations of this verse (as we have seen in the case of Rashid Rida and his expansive view of "the people who bind and loosen") than with the interpretations of most late medieval exegetes who seem not to have favored such semantic and exegetical inclusiveness.

The standard and better known political treatises of the later period do, in fact, increasingly begin to restrict the term *uli 'l-amr* to the political rulers of the various Muslim communities. Al-Mawardi in his classic *al-Ahkam al-Sultaniyya wa 'l-Wilaya al-Diniyya* ("Governmental Ordinances and Religious

Administration") refers to Qur'an 4:59 and explicates it as ordaining virtually unquestioning obedience on the part of Muslims to their appointed leaders (*al-a'imma al-muta'ammarun*).[29] He cites in this case a *hadith* narrated by Abu Hurayra in which the Prophet states: "After me there will be rulers/governors (*wulat*), the righteous (*al-barr*) with his righteousness and the corrupt (*al-fajir*) with his corruptness; listen to them and obey them in what is in accordance with the truth (*al-haqq*). If they should rule wisely or justly (*ahsanu*) then it counts in your and their favor. And if they should act unjustly (*asa'u*), then it counts in your favor and against them."[30] It is pertinent to note that this *hadith* counseling political quietism is attributed to Abu Hurayra, whose reputation as a *hadith* transmitter is mixed at best, and which reputation should impel us to regard the reliability of this report (and others like it attributed to him) as less than completely assured.[31]

In the fourteenth century, the well-known jurist and theologian Ibn Taymiyya (d. 1328) in his collection of sermons entitled *Fatawa*, refers to Qur'an 4:58–59 and interprets these verses as enjoining obedience to God and His Messenger, without mention of the *uli 'l-amr*. He goes on to paraphrase *uli 'l-amr* as *wulat al-'amr*, thus clearly understanding the Qur'anic phrase as referring to political leaders and administrators.[32] These *wulat al-'amr*, he maintains, are also due obedience tempered by solicitation on their part of good advice (*munasaha*) from those he rules over.[33] In his political treatise *al-Siyasa al-Shar'iyya*, Ibn Taymiyya is even more insistent that the ruler confer with the learned scholars (*'ulama'*), political and military leaders, and other prominent representatives of the people.[34] This description is reminiscent of the ninth century scholar al-Jahiz' definition of those who constitute the *uli 'l-amr*, although it should be pointed out that Ibn Taymiyya does not use this Qur'anic locution to refer to those whom the ruler consults. It should be pointed out that he further asserts in the *Siyasa* that Muslims must discharge their duties to the ruler (*al-sultan*) to the fullest, "even though he may be corrupt (*fajir*)."[35] He does not, however, invoke Qur'an 4:59 at this point in the *Siyasa* to underscore an assumed religiously mandated duty of practically unconditional obedience to the ruler. Ibn Taymiyya, therefore, appears to be of two minds on the issue of political authority. In the alarming world he lived in besieged by ferocious invaders, unconditional loyalty to the ruler (or, as we would say today, "rallying around the flag") was a given. At the same time, he could not, in good conscience, let lapse the Qur'anically prescribed duty of consultation among the faithful (3:159; 42:38), which on implementation serves as a check on arbitrary, strongman rule (*istibdad*). In these two works, we thus observe Ibn Taymiyya's attempt to effect a rapprochement between a religious responsibility and realpolitik.

Modern Political Tracts

In his writings on political Islam, the Islamist activist Mawlana Abul A'la Mawdudi has maintained in regard to the "Islamic state" that "the basic conception underlying all its [sc. the "Islamic state"] outward manifestations is the idea of divine sovereignty."[36] In his *The Process of Islamic Revolution*, for example, he does not refer to the *uli 'l-amr* as such, but he describes those ideal leaders and servants of the state who "will all work with a sense of individual and collective responsibility to God, not to the electorate, neither to the king nor the dictator"[37]; ideas he repeats in his *al-Hukumah al-Islamiyya* ("Islamic Government").[38] When Mawdudi's political treatises are read in conjunction with his exegetical work, it is clear that these ideal leaders and cadres are the *uli 'l-amr* he describes in his *Tafhim al-Qur'an* in interpretation of 4:59, who hold themselves accountable only to God and answer to no human being since they have comprehended the divine will perfectly.

These ideas greatly influenced his ideological disciple, Sayyid Qutb, who links them more directly to Qur'an 4:59. In his political manifesto *Ma'alim fi 'l-Tariq* ("Signposts on the Path"), Sayyid Qutb does not refer to the first part of 4:59, with which we are primarily concerned, but only refers to the second part which states, "If you should differ in regard to anything, then refer it to God and the Messenger."[39] As is the general understanding, Qutb stresses that this verse adjures the faithful to follow the book of God and the example of the Prophet. The verse, according to Qutb, further places a limitation on the authority of human beings and establishes that no one may arbitrarily promulgate a piece of legislation without acknowledging "the supreme sovereignty" (*al-hakimiyya al-'ulya*) of God. This entails recognition that the only source of political authority (*al-sulutat*) is "God, the Almighty, not the people, not the [political] party, not any individual."[40]

He makes similar statements in his *al-'Adala al-Ijtima'iyya fi 'l-Islam* ("Social Justice in Islam") about the authority of the ruler and links them to Qur'an 4:59. He further adds that the ruler derives his legitimacy from the consent and freedom of the Muslims.[41] Although this sounds quite democratic on the surface, it should be remembered that Qutb had very specific and exclusivist notions of exactly who qualifies as a "true" Muslim.[42]

The verse also makes clear, Qutb asserts, that no human being can claim to speak/have spoken in the name of God except the Prophet; thus there is no resemblance here to European notions of theocracy and of divine kingship. In this, of course, Qutb is absolutely right. The Muslim polity in its basic conception is no more a theocracy than the modern United States which understands itself to constitute "one nation under God." It is more accurate to describe the Muslim polity as a nomocracy, as has been argued before, referring to the primacy of law, in this case the Shari'a in the abstract and *fiqh* in practice, in governing the polity. Sunni Islam also does not conceive of a class of clerics to rule the polity, which is another characteristic of a theocracy. In fact, historically speaking, religious scholars, more often than not, have assumed oppositional roles vis-à-vis governments in the Islamic world; a reversal of this situation in recent history has occurred in some traditionally Muslim countries.

Qutb's incomplete exegesis of 4:59 in the *Ma'alim* must be supplemented by his commentary in the *Zilal* (as already outlined above) for us to determine whom he intends by the *uli 'l-amr* and what role they play in his political schema. These two works taken together tell us that Qutb, like Mawdudi, envisaged the *uli 'l-amr* as those who acknowledged the sovereignty of God in the Muslim polity, and as a consequence, were best qualified to implement the divine laws conveyed to mankind by the Prophet Muhammad and elaborated upon comprehensively in his *sunna* as became codified in the *hadith* literature. Unlike classical Islamic jurisprudence which added analogical reasoning and consensus of the community as supplemental sources of jurisprudence in the absence of explicit texts, Qutb recognizes no other possible source for legislative activity. In his ahistorical apotheosis of the religious law, there is no room for accommodation of customary and cultural practices (*'urf*) nor for multiple readings of scripture and ancillary texts, or for invocation of public commonweal as grounds for legal ratiocination, as actually occurred in the praxis of Muslim communities throughout time. The *uli 'l-amr*, among whom Qutb undoubtedly places himself and his cohorts, and who, therefore, constitute the vanguard of the "Islamic revolution" in the making as discussed earlier, appear to be above the need for such human endeavors. Instead, in this conceptualization, they have flawlessly discerned God's will through a literal, monovalent reading of sacred texts, which in themselves provide all the unambiguous answers to life's every exigency, making superfluous, and ultimately subversive, recourse to human reasoning and the resulting possible ambiguity.

The Diachronic View

Based on our diachronic survey of relevant literature, it is safe to say that we can plot a clear trajectory of transformation and evolution in the primary meanings assigned to the critical Qur'anic phrase *uli 'l-amr*. Through the first two centuries of Islam, this phrase was understood to refer only to "people of knowledge and discernment" and "military commanders" during the time of the Prophet, according to the exegetical literature. In other words; it referred in the broadest possible sense to people possessing moral authority based on a sound knowledge of religious and legal principles and more narrowly to specific individuals who were appointed to positions of military leadership by the Prophet himself. In either case, this locution was not understood by the first two generations of Muslims in particular to have overt political implications. By the ninth century, the semantic scope of this phrase expanded to include political leaders, signified by the introduction of the terms *salatin* and *umara'* into the exegetical discourse on this issue, and the assignment of a secondary meaning of political authority to the term *amr*, as we saw in al-Jahiz' explication and al-Tabari's discussion. We also saw the influence of sectarian debates regarding legitimate leadership of the polity so that some Sunni exegetes were of the opinion that the phrase referred to the *Khulafa' al-Rashidun* (the Rightly-Guided Caliphs), particularly the first two caliphs.

A further semantic expansion occurs in late medieval and modernist works in which *uli 'l-amr* is understood to be the equivalent of *ahl al-hall wa-'l-'aqd*. The latter collocation allows different kinds of authority, particularly religious, moral and political, to be encapsulated within it. A significant shift occurs in Rashid Rida's modernist exegetical work, in which he interprets *uli 'l-amr* qua *ahl al-hall wa-'l-'aqd* as including, in addition to scholars, jurists, and political figures, other public figures who contribute to the overall commonweal of the polity—labor leaders and prominent journalists, for example. We may say here that Rida secularizes the concept of *uli 'l-amr* to a certain extent.

Contrasted to this progressive expansion in the signification of the concept *uli 'l-amr*, we have a dramatic narrowing of the same in the case of late medieval political theorists and modern Islamist ideologues. In the case of the two Islamists we have discussed, our survey reveals that both Mawdudi and Qutb are influenced to a mild extent by the later medieval political treatises and not at all by the classical and early medieval exegetical works. Eschewing the rich semantic repertoire of this critical phrase in early *tafsir* works—from those attributed to Ibn 'Abbas and Muqatil b. Sulayman, for example, which later find reflection in modernist exegeses—and early political treatises like that of al-Jahiz, medieval political theorists like al-Mawardi and Ibn Taymiyya and contemporary Islamists are compelled by the historical and political exigencies of their time to focus narrowly on political authority alone. Moreover, they include the *uli 'l-amr*, understood primarily as political leaders, as deserving of obedience along with God and His messenger, in contradistinction to earlier exegetes like Muqatil, who expressly excluded the *uli 'l-amr*, understood more broadly as people in general endowed with critical understanding and intellect, from being the recipients of such obedience.

In their introduction and usage of the term *al-hakimiyya*, Mawdudi's and Qutb's exegeses and political treatises in the modern period resort to an unprecedented sacralization of religio-political authority. Qutb, in particular, yokes the concept of divine sovereignty to Qur'an 4:59, representing a sharp rupture from the well-established, mainstream understandings of this critical verse in the pre-modern period.[43] The term *(al-)hakimiyya* and its signification derive rather from the deviant and marginalized tradition of the Kharijiyya, who in the seventh century would argue before 'Ali b. Abi Talib that "judgment/ dominion belonged to God alone" (*la hukm illa li-llah*). The term *al-hakimiyya* itself was not known to the Kharijiyya but the authoritarian religio-political charter adumbrated by Qutb in his exegesis of 4:59, however, may be regarded as a lineal descendant of this stance of the Kharijites. This is demonstrated in his exegesis which, as we have seen, completely bypasses the more widespread and fluid interpretations of the phrase *uli 'l-amr* and the broad conceptualizations of different kinds of authority which prevailed in the early medieval period. Thus even though al-Mawardi, as an apologist for the Abbasid government in the eleventh century, focused primarily on *amr* as political authority, he did not conceive of it as solely or largely divinely mandated. His work on "Governmental Ordinances" appeals not only to Qur'anic and *hadith* warrants for a specific concept of legitimate political authority but also to pre-Islamic and non-Islamic, such as Persian, sources and precedents, to point to the necessity and structure of temporal political leadership. For example, in his section on the contract of the imamate, al-Mawardi appeals to verses of pre-Islamic poetry as proof-texts rather than to religious texts to establish the incumbence upon the polity to appoint leaders in order to contain social and political disorder (*fawda*).[44] His conception of *amr* as political authority is a pragmatic, worldly, and eclectic one, whose necessity is motivated by both religious and secular concerns. The first part of the title of his seminal work—*al-Ahkam al-Sultaniyya*—points to mundane political, not theocratic, authority; since the lexeme *sultaniyya* and other derivatives from the same root, point to the rule of the sultan, the temporal and non-religious ruler of Muslim realms. The second part of the title *al-Wilaya al-Diniyya* ("Religious Stewardship/Administration") acknowledges the necessity of deriving administrative principles from religious precepts but does not concede primacy to them as a source.

By the beginning of the fourteenth century in the Mamluk period, we begin to observe the rise of political absolutism in some quarters, as evident in Ibn Taymiyya's writings. His conception of *al-siyasa al-shar'iyya*—political administration mandated, as he understood it, by the revealed law—which is the title of his famous work, counsels obedience to the ruler of the Muslim polity. Such a ruler, however, could, and should be deflected from unrighteous actions through good advice (*munasaha*) imparted by his associates and subjects and through his frequent consultation with them. It is interesting to note that Ibn Taymiyya takes a non-Qur'anic, essentially secular, term for statecraft—*al-siyasa*—and sacralizes it by conjoining it to the adjectival form of Shari'a, the religious law.[45]

The notion of divinely mandated political administration as the only type was by no means universal, however, in the fourteenth century. The famous Andalusi social historian Ibn Khaldun's views on political authority and legitimacy in the fourteenth century are far more nuanced and far less dogmatic than Ibn Taymiyya's. In his magisterial *al-Muqaddima* ("the Prolegomena"), Ibn Khaldun admits the possibility of both "religious administration" (*al-siyasa al-diniyya*) and "rational administration," (*al-siyasa al-'aqliyya*) but maintains the superiority of the former over the latter, since only religious administration, guided by the Shari'a, fosters both the temporal and spiritual welfare of the ruled.[46] In comparison, Ibn Taymiyya's view of legitimate religio-political authority is more rigid and monochromatic. His autocratic view very likely stems to a considerable extent from the particulars of his personal situation. The insecure historical circumstances of his time—with the marauding Crusaders and Mongols practically outside his door in Syria, which forced him to flee to Baghdad—undoubtedly contributed to his position that the ruler of the polity was deserving of the utmost loyalty and obedience, especially during such critical times, and that the law of the land, believed to be identical to the religious law, must be unquestioningly upheld. Absolutism, after all, is very appealing in times of socio-political upheaval and impending or actual foreign aggression. This stance is replicated to a large extent in much of today's Islamist literature, written under similarly politically fraught conditions.

The term *siyasa* which became increasingly prevalent in the Mamluk period, as we see in both Ibn Taymiyya's and Ibn Khaldun's usage, referred to an overarching system of administrative and penal laws mostly of non-religious provenance, which in some areas was often in contention with *fiqh*, the religiously derived legislation. To the occasional dismay of the *'ulama*, *siyasa* sometimes gained the upper hand over *fiqh*, and provoked the fourteenth century Egyptian historian al-Maqrizi's suspicion that the word *siyasa* was actually a corruption of *yasak* or *yasa*, the Mongol code of dynastic law and customs.[47] Ibn Taymiyya's concept of an expanded purview of the Shari'a encompassing what hitherto had been regarded as mainly worldly, administrative concerns, signaled by the title of his major political treatise *Al-Siyasa al-Shar'iyya*, allowed the religious law to coopt *siyasa* and bring it under its domain. Such a development allows for the speculation that Ibn Taymiyya consciously wished to posit an all-pervasive religio-legal-administrative code to compete with and undermine the Mongol *yasak/yasa*, adopted by several Mongol states, a trend he (and some of the other *'ulama* of the time) found terribly threatening from all accounts.

Our diachronic survey categorically establishes that political thought in the later period described above represents a dramatic departure from early Muslim conceptualizations of legitimate political and religious authority. Modernist-Salafis like Rashid Rida, in truth, are far closer in their thinking and understanding of the term *uli 'l-amr* to the first and second generation of Muslims than are Islamists who claim to be reviving the thought and practices of the earliest Muslim community. In an interesting inversion of conventional usage, the term "fundamentalist" in the most literal sense—signifying a return to the fundamentals of something, especially a religious tradition—should be applied in this case to Muslim modernists rather than to Islamist radicals, whose so-called "fundamentalist" enterprise of reviving the earliest Muslim practices and thought appears not to extend back in time much beyond the thirteenth-fourteenth centuries. It is, in fact, distinguished by a convenient amnesia of the first and second centuries of Islam. When the memory of these first two centuries is invoked by them, it is usually filtered through the sensibilities of late medieval exegetes and scholars that are sometimes more in accordance with theirs (or made to appear to be).[48]

Conclusion

To a large extent, modern scholarship on political and religious authority in Islam has focused primarily on later political treatises which posit a conception of the Muslim polity along authoritarian lines. This has allowed a number of Western commentators, particularly from a generation ago, to talk about Islamic conceptions of socio-political organization as relentlessly conducive to a peculiar brand of "Oriental despotism," as, for example, does Max Weber.[49] Some Orientalist scholars have pointed to Qur'an 4:59 as *prima facie* evidence of a politically authoritarian impulse intrinsic to Islam, being completely unaware of the diverse and primarily non-political understandings of this verse through at least the first three centuries of Islam. Bernard Lewis, for example, has brashly asserted that Qur'an 4:59 teaches that "the primary and essential duty owed by the subjects to the ruler is obedience." He further comments, "The duty of obedience to legitimate authority is not merely one of political expediency. It is a religious obligation, defined and imposed by Holy Law and grounded in revelation."[50] As we can see from our exposition, this position is clearly not tenable and that it was indeed on account of political expediency that the notion of practically unqualified obedience to the ruler, legitimate or otherwise, progressively gained ground (but not without opposition) in certain quarters. Lewis' misunderstanding stems in part from his erroneous translation of the Qur'anic phrase *uli 'l-amr minkum*, which should be rendered as "those possessing authority *among* you," and not "those in authority *over* you," as he has it. The Arabic preposition *min* does not translate as "over," but, in this context, as "among."[51] His misreading suggests individuals vested with authority and placed in positions of command *over* others, while the Arabic refers in a non-committal way to people who have (particularly moral) authority on account of personal qualities and aptitudes *among* their peers, and not on account of any kind of formal, especially political, appointment.

The problem of retrieving the earliest conceptualizations of moral and political authority in the Islamic milieu is compounded by the fact that the Islamist activists Mawlana Mawdudi and Sayyid Qutb in the modern period have promulgated the politicized concept of *al-hakimiyya* as a feature of the "Islamic state" that is supposed to have existed from the earliest period, which tends to be accepted at face value in some circles. Qutb further weds this new-fangled concept to Qur'an 4:59, which in his understanding, legitimizes it. A full-length treatment of the Qur'anic lexeme *hukm* from which *al-hakimiyya* is derived (although this derivative does not occur in the Qur'an) is not possible at the present (although necessary). But, once again, even a cursory survey of early and late medieval exegetical works reveals that, like the Qur'anic term *amr*, *hukm* too lacks an early political genealogy.[52] The commentary of the late eighth century exegete Muqatil b. Sulayman glosses *hukm* as referring only to God's [moral] judgment (*al-qada'*) of human beings [sc. of their deeds], both in this world and the next,[53] as does al-Tabari in the tenth century.[54]

It is thus worth emphasizing that the antecedent for the modern Islamist concept of *al-hakimiyya* (but not the term itself) may be found rather in the doctrine of the seventh century extremist group, the Kharijiyya, who went on to fight against 'Ali b. Abi Talib (d. 661) for having submitted to human arbitration in the dispute between himself and Mu'awiya, later the first Umayyad ruler. The Kharijiyya stridently maintained in this context that "judgment or arbitration (*al-hukm*) belongs only to God," refusing to accept the validity of human intercession in this conflict. They were consequently anathematized on account of their extremism and proneness to violence. Paradoxically, then, in spite of their vaunted adherence to the custom of the pious *salaf* ("Muslim predecessors from particularly the first generation"), the Islamists are on record as *not* adopting the precedent of 'Ali, a celebrated Companion of the Prophet, who resorted to human reasoning and interpretation at a politically critical moment, but rather of his rank enemies who did not do so and who were subsequently labeled as deviant by the consensus of the community.

The concept of the caliph ruling, for all practical purposes, invincibly as God's deputy on earth (*khalifat Allah*) is exogenous to Islam. Recent, careful scholarship has shown that such notions seeped into the Islamic milieu through the infiltration of ancient Persian and Hellenistic ideas of divine or sacred kingship by the ninth century.[55] The early egalitarian Islamic community largely recognized differences among the faithful on the basis of personal piety and moral excellence alone, tending to devalue kinship and social status in conscious contradistinction to the pre-Islamic period, as I have discussed elsewhere in detail.[56] Such a moral attitude found broad reflection in the socio-political organization of the early polity as well. Leadership positions mostly (but not always) tended to devolve upon those who had already distinguished themselves for their exceptional piety and meritorious service to the Islamic community. A case in point was Salman al-Farisi, a non-Arab convert to Islam without a distinctive lineage, appointed to the governorship of Persia by 'Umar, the second caliph. In the Sunni conception of the caliphate, the caliph, *primus inter pares*, was, certainly in theory, liable to be deposed for wrongdoing and could be chided (and often was) for straying from good governing practices or for failing to confer with those he governed. Muslim jurists, in fact, recognized the right of the people to rebel against unjust rulers as a matter of conscience and set up specific criteria to distinguish justified political rebellion from treason and brigandage, for example.[57]

The first caliph Abu Bakr's inaugural address, recorded in a number of sources, remains a model of humility and accountability to the people. In this key address, he is quoted in an early source as counseling the people gathered before him,

> You must be Godfearing, for piety is the most intelligent practice and immorality is the most foolish. Indeed I am a follower, not an innovator: if I perform well, then help me, and if I should deviate, correct me.... O gathering of the Ansar [sc. Madinan Muslims], if the caliphate [lit. "this matter"] is deserved on account of inherited merit and attained on account of kinship, then the Quraysh is more noble than you on account of inherited merit and more closely related than you [to the Prophet]. However, since it is deserved on account of moral excellence in religion, then those who are foremost in precedence from among the Muhajirun [sc. the Makkan emigrants to Madina] are placed ahead of you in the entire Qur'an[58] as being more worthy of it compared to you.[59]

The assembly of people is reported to have been convinced by the cogency of Abu Bakr's arguments and proceeded to offer their allegiance to him.[60] The conception of legitimate leadership adumbrated in this key address is referenced by the Qur'anic view that the most morally excellent are the most qualified for political stewardship on earth (for example, 7:128–129; 24:55). Abu Bakr accordingly argues his case before the public establishing his credentials for the office based on this Qur'anic view, and asserts his accountability before those he will govern. Conspicuously lacking in this speech and in the early accounts that follow of Abu Bakr's investiture is any notion that unreflective obedience would consequently be due to him from the people he governed.

This early emphasis on personal piety as the primary criterion for assessing an individual's moral and social, and consequently political, standing never fully eradicated the pre-Islamic (*jahili*) valorization of noble descent and tribal affiliation; this valorization remained in uneasy tension with Islam's radical egalitarianism for most of the formative period. With ideas of political absolutism and social customs of particularly Persian provenance gaining ascendancy under the Abbasids from the eighth century on, Jahili notions of showing deference to the high-born and the politically prominent began to make a diffident comeback as well. The pious were aghast at such developments; we have their dissenting voices recorded in primarily the ethical and humanistic literatures of the period, which often scoff at and lament the self-aggrandizing pretensions of their rulers.[61]

The idea of the caliph as God's religio-political representative on earth (reflected in such titles as "God's shadow on earth")[62] entitled to virtually unquestioning obedience from his subjects is quite antithetical to indigenous Islamic notions of legitimate leadership. For example, it is well-known that Abu Bakr would only use the title *Khalifat Rasul Allah* ("successor of the messenger of God") and recoiled from using *Khalifat Allah* ("God's deputy") because of the undue presumptuousness implicit in its adoption.[63] 'Umar who followed him was at first simply called *Khalifat Abi Bakr* ("Abu Bakr's successor") and then later more commonly *Amir al-Mu'minin* ("leader/commander of the faithful").[64] Under the Abbasids, imported ancient foreign formulations of absolutist political rule, however, began to cloak the caliph from the eighth century on with an undeniable mystique (reflected in the adoption of the title of "God's deputy"), progressively placing him beyond the reach of his humble populace. Over time, certain political theorists would lend an Islamic patina to such notions, allowing for a comfortable accommodation with political reality. Islamist ideologues (and others with authoritarian proclivities) who aver an early Islamic genealogy for the concept of a divinely-mandated government on earth, headed by God's representative(s) who must be obeyed, would be hard put to point to any Qur'anic verse that could legitimize such a concept, and that was so understood from the earliest period, least of all Qur'an 4:59 as we have established.

Notes

Earlier drafts of this paper were presented at the annual conference of the Center for the Study of Islam & Democracy, Washington, D.C., May 17, 2003, and at the second symposium on Qur'an: Text and Interpretation, held at the Centre for Islamic Studies, School of Oriental and African Studies, University of

London, October 16, 2003. I am grateful to the members of both audiences for their thoughtful remarks and penetrating questions.

1. Since only Sunni thought is being discussed here, only Sunni works have been consulted in this study. Shi'i views on legitimate leadership progressively diverged markedly from Sunni thought over time and would require a separate study.

2. *Tafsir Mujahid* (Islamabad, n.d.), 1:162–63.

3. *Tafsir Muqatil* (Cairo, 1969?), 1:246.

4. Ibid., and f.n. 2.

5. *Tafsir 'Abd al-Razzaq* (Beirut, 1999), 1:464–65.

6. *Sahih Bukhari* (Beirut, n.d.), 6:376.

7. *Tafsir al-Tabari* (Beirut, 1997), 4:150.

8. Ibid., 4:151.

9. Ibid.

10. See the article "Sultan," in the *Encyclopedia of Islam*, new edition, ed. G. E. Bosworth et al. (Leiden, 1997); henceforth abbreviated as *EI*²), 9:849–51.

11. *Tafsir al-Tabari*, 4:152.

12. Ibid.

13. Ibid.

14. Al-Razi, *al-Tafsir al-Kabir* (Beirut, 1992), 4:116.

15. Ibid., 4:113.

16. Ibn Kathir, *Tafsir al-Qur'an al-'Azim* (Beirut, 1990), 1:490–91.

17. Ibid.

18. *Tafsir al-Manar* (Beirut, 1999), 5:147.

19. Ibid., 5:150.

20. Ibid., 5:152.

21. Abul A'la Mawdudi, *Towards Understanding the Qur'an*, tr. and ed. Zafar Ishaq Ansari (Leicester, 1988), 51.

22. Ibid.

23. Ibid., 52.

24. *Fi Zilal al-Qur'an* (Cairo, 2001), 2:691.

25. Ibid., 2:692.

26. See below.

27. See Qutb's *Ma'alim fi 'l-Tariq* (Beirut, 1982), 11–12. This work is further discussed below.

28. 'Uthmaniyya (Cairo, 1955), 115 ff.

29. *Al-Ahkam al-Sultaniyya* (Beirut, 1996), 13.

30. Ibid., 13–14.

31. See, for example, Ibn Qutayba, *Kitab Ta'wil Mukhtalif al-Hadith* (Cairo, 1982), 39, 61, where it is reported that 'Umar (the second Caliph), 'Uthman (the third Caliph), and 'A'isha (the Prophet's wife) tended to reject Abu Hurayra's reports.

It is worthy of note that the *hadith* attributed to Abu Hurayra by the late seventh-century exegete Mujahid, mentioned above, counsels obedience to the Prophet and his appointed military commander only, consonant with the early usage of the word *amir*. The text of this *hadith* is thus more credible.

32. The Arabic root *wly*, among other meanings, connotes "to rule, administer." The participle form *wali* (sing.); *wulat* (pl.), refers in a political context to administrators of various kinds, usually provincial governors.

33. *Majmu'at al-Fatawa* (Riyadh, 1998), 18:7.

34. *Al-Siyasa al-Shar'iyya* (Cairo, 1951), 161–64.

35. Ibid., 28.

36. See his *The Process of Islamic Revolution* (Lahore, 1979), 13.

37. Ibid., 13–14.

38. Idem, *al-Hukuma al-Islamiyya* (Cairo, 1980), 15–20.

39. *Ma'alim fi 'l-tariq*, 105.

40. Ibid.

41. *Al-'Adala al-Ijtima'iyya fi 'l-Islam* (Cairo, 1949), 107–8.

42. For further discussion of Qutb's thought as developed in this particular work, see William Shepard, "The Development of the Thought of Sayyid Qutb as Reflected in Earlier and Later Editions of 'Social Justice in Islam,'" *Die Welt des Islams* 32 (1992): esp. 217 ff.

43. Some contemporary commentators have tended to exaggerate the significance of Ibn Taymiyya's political thought (and of medieval political thought in general) in the formation of radical Islamism today. For example, Emmanuel Sivan in his *Radical Islam, Medieval Theology, and Modern Politics* (New Haven, 1985), 94 ff., strains himself trying to prove Ibn Taymiyya's seminal influence on particularly Mawdudi's and Qutb's Islamist schemas. There is no doubt a measure of influence as their own writings suggest, especially in their invocation of the term *jahiliyya*, but these Islamists also took stances contrary to Ibn Taymiyya's on significant issues. For example, Qutb disagreed with Ibn Taymiyya on the requirement that the caliph had to be from the tribe of Quraysh because it violated the principle of egalitarianism (as the Kharijiyya had maintained) and that the caliph, once duly selected, had to be obeyed even if he proved to be unjust to avoid chaos, as Ibn Taymiyya maintains in his *al-Siyasa al-Shar'iyya* (see above, n. 35). Mawdudi and Qutb also had a pretty dim view of medieval jurists (Ibn Taymiyya not being exempt) and of jurisprudence in general, viewing them as often having contributed to the distortion of pristine Islamic principles as they conceived them. For a fuller treatment of Qutb's thought in particular, see Ahmad S. Moussalli, *Radical Islamic Fundamentalism: The Ideological and Political Discourse of Sayyid Qutb* (Beirut, 1992), 147 ff.; and Yvonne Haddad, "Sayyid Qutb: Ideologue of Islamic Revival," in *Voices of Resurgent Islam*, ed. John L. Esposito (New York, 1983). The most important fact remains that the concept of *hakimiyya*—which is the principal building block of Mawdudi's and Qutb's "Islamic state"—was their invention and neologism alone (Mawdudi's to be precise and adopted by Qutb) that has no precedent in the pre-modern period. Radical Islamism of this ilk, predicated on *hakimiyya*, has no genealogy before the twentieth century (prefigured, however, in the extremist stance of the Kharijiyya in the seventh century) and thus before the constellation of specific historical circumstances that abetted its rise—particularly the abolition of the caliphate in 1924 and the disarray in much of the Islamic world under Western colonial occupation. A heightened sense of Islamic identity conceived in primarily political

and statist terms at a time of great political vulnerability was *a* response to the perceived political and ideological hegemony of the West. On account of their deviant lexicon and haphazardly concocted theology of intolerance severed from the rich diversity of Islamic thought that developed over time, "Sunni respectability" continues to elude these radicals, despite Sivan's glib assertions to the contrary.

44. *Al-Ahkam al-Sultaniyya wa'l-Wilaya al-Diniyya* (Cairo, 1983), 5.

45. See the article "Siyasa" in *EI²*, 9:693–94.

46. See Muhsin Mahdi, *Ibn Khaldun's Philosophy of History* (London, 1957), 236 ff.

47. See al-Maqrizi, *Khitat* (Cairo, 1934), 2:220. See further the article on "Siyasa Shar'iyya," *EI²*, 9:694–96.

48. See my article, "Reconstituting Women's Lives: Gender and the Poetics of Narrative in Medieval Biographical Works," *The Muslim World* 92 (2002): 461–80, which discusses how the early biographies of the women *salaf* ("predecessors") from the first and second generations record the assertive, public roles played by many of them, which depictions were then doctored by some fourteenth and fifteenth century biographers to make their image conform more to Mamluk sensibilities, since by that time a more restrictive role had been imagined for women in the public sphere.

49. For an extended discussion of his views, see Bryan Turner, *Weber and Islam: A Critical Study* (London, 1974), specially 7–21; also 107–21.

50. See Bernard Lewis, *The Political Language of Islam* (Chicago, 1988), 91.

51. Ibid; similar sentiments are expressed by Elie Kedourie, *Democracy and Arab Political Culture* (London, 1994), 7. Recently, Bernard Lewis has parlayed this kind of narrative about an intrinsically authoritarian political culture engendered by Islam itself into a highly commercially successful venture. He has repeated these misguided notions in his best-selling *What Went Wrong? Western Impact and Middle Eastern Response* (Oxford University Press, 2002) to great effect. See further note 62 below.

52. For an opposite viewpoint, see Sayed Khatab, "*Hakimiyyah* and *Jahiliyyah* in the Thought of Sayyid Qutb," *Middle Eastern Studies* 38 (2002): 145–70. In spite of his assertion that the notion of *hakimiyyah* is early, Khatab, however, could not come up with a single early commentator who refers to this obviously late, non-Qur'anic term. He wisely leaves out any reference to the Kharijiyya and their understanding of *hukm*, since that would not have exactly bolstered his position.

53. See *Tafsir Muqatil*, 1:564 for verse 6:57; 1:565 for verse 6:62; 2:343 for verse 12:40, etc. Similarly in *Tanwir al-Miqbas*, 145 for verse 6:62; 251 for verse 12:40, etc.

54. *Tafsir al-Tabari*, 5:216 for verse 6:62; 10:97 for verse 28:70, for example.

55. Louise Marlowe, *Hierarchy and Egalitarianism in Islamic Thought* (Cambridge, Eng., 1997), 114ff.

56. Asma Afsaruddin, *Excellence and Precedence: Medieval Islamic Discourse on Legitimate Leadership* (Leiden, 2002), esp. Chapter One.

57. For a detailed, monograph length study of this topic, see Khaled Abou El Fadl's *Rebellion and Violence in Islamic Law* (Cambridge, Eng., 2002).

58. The Qur'anic collocation *al-Muhajirun wa-'l-Ansar* has been understood to indicate the Muhajirun's precedence in Islam in general since they were placed before the Ansar in order.

59. *'Uthmaniyya,* 202.

60. Ibid.

61. For example, see Ibn Qutayba, *'Uyun al-Akhbar* (Cairo, 1963), 2:115, where a certain Sudayf laments that under the 'Abbasids, political leadership was no longer consultative and had become despotic.

62. Contra Lewis, *What Went Wrong,* 97, where he states without any qualification that for the Muslims, "the caliph was his [sc. God's] vice-gerent, 'his shadow on earth.'" He thus presents this notion as always having existed within Islamic thought, without any allusion to specific historical developments and external influences which progressively led to the articulation of such views in certain official texts. For someone who claims to be a historian, Lewis is thus remarkably "essentialist and ahistorical" in the views which he propounds in this work, as Adam Sabra has commented recently in his review entitled "What Is Wrong with *What Went Wrong?*"in the *Middle East Report,* August 2003. As we have seen, Lewis' ahistorical approach is particularly evident in his assumption of a reified political tradition in the Islamic world which, in his portrayal, appears not to have been susceptible to change, growth, and distortion in diverse historical circumstances.

63. Ibn 'Abd al-Barr, *Kitab al-Isti'ab fi Ma'rifat al-Ashab* (Hyderabad, 1908), 3:972; Ibn Sa'd, *al-Tabaqat al-Kubra* (Beirut, 1957), 3:183–84.

64. Ibn 'Abd al-Barr, *Isti'ab,* 3:971; Ibn Sa'd, *Tabaqat,* 3:281.

Regional Debates
on Islam and Democracy

4

Islam, Ethnicity, Pluralism and Democracy: Malaysia's Unique Experience

Osman Bakar

Introduction

Religion, ethnicity, democracy and pluralism are four civilizational[1] forces that have shaped the Malaysian nation since its birth in 1963.[2] The first two of these forces, namely religion and ethnicity, with few exceptions always intertwined throughout human history are centuries-old traditional forces whose beginning can be traced to the first Malay collective consciousness of being a distinctive people among the world's numerous racial groups, with a homeland, a nation, and a culture or civilization that they can proudly call their own.[3] The other two forces, that is democracy and pluralism, are mostly modern phenomena associated with the British colonial rule. The British introduced Westminster-style parliamentary democracy in Malaysia in 1955, two years before its independence. However, democratic values and practices, albeit in an Islamic context, have not been entirely absent from Malay-Islamic political culture,[4] which is the dominant culture in Malaysia's multi-ethnic society. Again, religious and ethnic pluralism that is so characteristic of modern Malaysia was a fateful product of the British colonial rule. The needs of economy in the nineteenth and the first half of twentieth centuries had brought waves of ethnic Chinese and Indian migrants from China and India respectively to the Malayan Peninsula. Not only had the British re-imported Chinese and Indian religions,[5] they also facilitated the growth and expansion of Christianity of all denominations. A major cultural transformation in the land was thus under way. The place and role of Islam in this transformation has been duly recognized and it has not ceased to be debated until now.

The main aim of this chapter is to provide an overview of the place and role of Islam in the transformation of independent Malaysia into a democratic and plural nation. In particular, it seeks to offer a new interpretative account of how the Islamic transformation of Malaysia during the last two decades has created new tensions in its national politics, thereby forcing a rethinking among many Malaysians on a number of vital issues related to religion, ethnicity, pluralism, and democracy. Heated debates are now raging in the country on such issues as whether Malaysia is a secular or an Islamic state, the compatibility between Islamic state and pluralism, and the future of Malay political dominance and ethnic-based Islam in the light of the growing appeal of Islamic universalism among Malay Muslims. We will also look briefly at the possibility of the emergence of a democratic two-party system that is based on Muslim political dominance and leadership. If such a system is to emerge, then Malaysia will be entering a new historic phase in its democratic experiences that may be described as an Islamic democracy.

Brief History of Ethnic and Religious Pluralism in Malaysia

In order to appreciate better Malay Islam's position on ethnicity and pluralism, a brief history of ethnic and religious pluralism in the country is called for. In the long history of the Malays that spanned thousands of years, they have undergone several phases and patterns of relationships between religion and ethnicity corresponding to changes in their religious affiliations. From the point of view of their religious history, there have been five such major phases. In the beginning, the Malays had their "native religion" prior to the coming of Hinduism. Then they became Hindus, and in the third phase came Buddhism. Many became Buddhists, but many others remained Hindus.

The fourth phase saw the coming of Islam. The spread of the new religion had been evolutionary and peaceful. From the time of its first arrival around the eleventh century, five or six centuries had to elapse before Islam finally became the religion of the overwhelming majority of the Malays throughout the archipelago.[6] In the fifth phase, beginning in the sixteenth century, the Malay world witnessed the coming of Christianity brought about by Western colonial powers, namely the Portuguese, the Spaniards, the Dutch and the British. This phase has been exceptionally violent with numerous military conflicts and "civilizational wars" between these colonial powers and the natives as militant Christianity sought to conquer Malay Islam.[7] While Christianity has made enormous gains in converts over the years, especially in the Philippines which eventually became Catholic except Muslim Moro provinces in the south and such Indonesian islands as Maluku, Islam remains to this day the dominant religion of the Malay world. In the light of its rich religious experience and heritage, we may assert that the Malay world has been well exposed to the phenomena of religious pluralism and diversity much earlier and to a greater extent than many other regions of the world.

Despite these several major religious experiences and transformations that the Malays have gone through, certain traits of the Malay ethnic character have remained unchanged, constituting as it were the permanent elements of the Malay soul, which may be described as the "traditional Malayness" of the Malays. In the words of Burhanuddin al-Helmi (1911–1969), a prominent twentieth-century Malay intellectual activist, "the Malays adopted their religion voluntarily as a matter of free choice and not under compulsion or through force, just as they now embrace the religion of Islam voluntarily and freely. But in their Malayness, they remain Malays."[8] The complex relations of religion and ethnicity manifest themselves in various forms, which vary from religion to religion. Transformed by the power of Islam, the interrelations of religion and ethnicity in Malay life and thought have assumed new dimensions and new intensity and complexity. One of the major domains of Malay civilization to have undergone this new Islamic transformation is political life. In this domain, primarily as a response to Western colonialism, a new idea was born, namely the idea of Malay-Islamic nationalism, a unique blending of religious and ethnic ideals.

The essence of Malay-Islamic nationalism is the triple love of religion (*agama*), race and ethnic identity (*bangsa*), and homeland (*watan; Negara*). This trinity of the Malay nationalist political creed, presented by its believers as being sanctioned and legitimized by Islam, is of utmost importance to our understanding of the nature and substance of the Malay liberation struggle against colonial rule and the struggle for a postcolonial nation-state that is predominantly Malay-Islamic in its religious-ethnic character. As we shall see later, the Malays of Malaysia succeeded in establishing such a state with all the consequences and challenges for its religious and ethnic pluralism with which it has to grapple until today. Malay-Islamic nationalism manifested itself centuries before the appearance of secular nationalism of the modern Western type. Its first globally significant manifestation was in 1511 when Malacca in the Malay Peninsula, founded as a Malay-Islamic sultanate only a century earlier, was conquered and ruled by the Portuguese for 130 years. Portuguese colonial rule was followed by Dutch (1641–1824) and British rule (1824–1957) until Malayan independence. Faced with more than four centuries of colonial rule that is for the most part repressive and threatening the very survival of Malay religion-ethnic identity, religion and ethnicity in Malay life and thought became ever more intertwined. In the realm of ideas, the challenge of colonial rule over such a long period has given generations of Malay thinkers ample opportunities to reflect on the meanings of ethnic identity and salvation within Islam and to articulate a philosophy of nationalism that would harmonize the immediate political goal of Malay survival with Islam's more permanent goal of social justice and ethnic equality.[9]

As stated earlier, pluralism is for the most part a modern societal phenomenon in the Malay-speaking world. However, a certain amount of religious pluralism has prevailed in the region prior to the coming of western colonial powers and Christianity and their sponsored migrations of workers of various ethnic backgrounds from outside the region. The coming of Portuguese Catholicism to Malacca in 1511 and with it the establishment of the first church had created the first Christian community in the Malay world.[10] Mixed marriages between Portuguese merchants, soldiers and administrators with native women had not only enlarged the new faith and community but also produced a new breed of Portuguese descendents[11] with a distinct ethnic identity that has survived to this day. By the last quarter of the century, the Portuguese had made Malacca a Catholic city.[12] Thus with Portuguese colonialism, a new element and a new dimension of pluralism in the religious landscape of the Malay world was introduced.

The change in colonial power from the Portuguese to the Dutch had resulted in changes not only in administrative but also in religious policy. The Dutch brought with them their Protestantism, which forcibly conflicted with the Roman Catholicism in place.[13] Through this development, that is the presence of Christian intra-faith pluralism in Malacca with its Catholic-Protestant feuds, the Malays were to encounter a new phenomenon in religious pluralism that has hitherto escaped their religious history. Religiously speaking, the Malay-Muslims have always been a homogeneous lot, belonging to only one theological school, the Sunni Ash'arite, and only one legal school of thought, namely the Shafi'ite. Colonial rule has not altered the religious homogeneity of Malay society. Consequently, the Malays have been spared sectarian intra-faith conflicts that have plagued a number of Muslim lands. Christian pluralism, however, continued to increase in complexity. With the arrival of the British in the late eighteenth century, who had generally been disposed toward supporting Christian missionary works of all denominations, Malaysian Christianity grew significantly both in its denominational pluralism and overall adherents. The first Anglican Church was established in Penang following the British takeover of the island from the Sultan of Kedah in 1786. The Methodist Church began its missionary work in Singapore in 1885 before spreading to Penang and other parts of Malaysia. Churches of other denominations were latecomers that did not make their entries into the country until the twentieth century.[14]

Seen from the point of view of Malaysia's history of religious and ethnic pluralism the British era may be regarded as the most significant and the most far-reaching especially in its religious and political consequences for the country.

Not only have the British expanded the horizon of Christian denominational pluralism almost to the point of making the religion a microcosm of world Christianity, they have transformed Malaysia into an entirely new and unique multi-ethnic and multi-religious society. Ethnic and religious pluralisms in Malaysia in their present forms and structure have their roots in British colonial economic policy. In early nineteenth century, the indigenous Malays were to witness the emergence of the first immigrant communities from outside Southeast Asia, such as the Straits Settlements Chinese communities in Penang, Singapore, and Malacca. However, the main impetus for the mass migration of workers and traders to the Malay Peninsula was the rapid growth of the tin industry in the second half of the nineteenth century and of rubber industry in the first three decades of the twentieth century. To cater to the needs of this fast expanding colonial economy, new waves of multi-ethnic immigrants invaded the shores of the Peninsula, consisting mainly of ethnic Chinese from China to work in tin mines and Tamils from South India to work in rubber plantations and railway services. So rapid and en masse was the migration influx, that by the 1930s the native Malays have been reduced to a minority.[15]

With the Chinese came their culture and religions like Taoism, Confucianism, and Buddhism. With the Tamils came Hinduism. Hinduism and Buddhism had been pre-Islamic indigenous religions, but through the new immigrants the two religions have found modern vehicles for their re-importation into the region. With all these new developments in the pre–World War II Malayan population, identification of religion with ethnicity had become more pronounced. The emerging racial arithmetic that revealed a delicate balance between the major ethnic groups gave rise to an ethnic-based pre-independence politics that was to endure to the present period. The Malays launched a massive nationwide political movement to reassert their dominance and with success. The overriding concern of the non-Malays was to secure citizenship rights in a land they have chosen to be their own. As for the British, postwar circumstances had made them responsible for both Malay rights and the unity and inclusivity of Malayan national identity.[16] Out of the British-engineered multi-ethnic compromises that paved the way for independence, a kind of "social contract" permeated Malaysia and a Malay-Islamic character was born.

The Character of the Malaysian State: Religious or Secular?

In Malaysia today, Muslims form only slightly more than half of its total population of 22 million. With the presence of numerous religious and ethnic groups, Malaysia has often been praised as a progressive and relatively successful Muslim nation in dealing with religious and ethnic pluralism. The country has known very few religious or ethnic conflicts and strife. The worst racial riots that had left a dark spot in the country's otherwise clean record of inter-religious and inter-ethnic cooperation occurred more than three decades ago, on May 13, 1969 following the general elections that year that saw the ruling Alliance Party, the present National Front's predecessor, losing a lot of seats to the Opposition. Understandably, there was much nervousness and apprehension in the country when in the 1999 General Election, UMNO, the backbone of the multi-ethnic ruling coalition, gave a repeat performance of the 1969 debacle, even worse, losing control of two states to the Opposition Islamic Party and performing badly in Mahathir's own state of Kedah. But amidst Opposition charges that certain UMNO leaders had fomented the 1969 racial riots, the general mood in the country was one that exerted a great pressure on Mahathir to prevent its repetition. When Malaysia successfully avoided the much-feared post-election racial clashes, many Malaysians congratulated themselves on what they perceived to be their newfound political and national maturity in inter-ethnic relations.

But has Malaysia really come of age in respect of inter-ethnic cooperation? It is certainly true that, generally speaking, the country has enjoyed inter-ethnic harmony, peace and stability during the last four decades. But many of those in Malaysia concerned with national unity and who are keeping track of the nation's progress in inter-ethnic relations are not yet confident that the racial and ethnic and religious fabrics of the nation can withstand severe tests of political turmoil and economic crisis of a major proportion. In the last three years, those national fabrics had been tested in the wake of new political and economic challenges. Asia's 1997 financial crisis has brought about major economic and political consequences for Malaysia that could lead to ethnic tensions and conflicts. That crisis was a major factor in leading to a better political feud between Mahathir Mohammad and his deputy and heir-apparent, Anwar Ibrahim, resulting in the latter's sacking in September 1998 from both the Government and UMNO. The series of events and developments in the country that followed Anwar's sacking, by Malaysian standard, can only be described as a political upheaval of a major proportion unmatched in post-independent era. Anwar's exit from power and his controversial and intensely disputed trial on corruption and sodomy charges of which he has been convicted with a 15-year prison sentence have angered and alienated many Malays from UMNO to the point of undermining its traditional position as the most dominant Malay political party in the country. Many observers and analysts of the Malaysian political scene have made claims that UMNO has lost the support of the majority of Malays.

With UMNO's popularity at its lowest ebb in decades, Malaysia is set to enter a period of political uncertainty that could herald the beginning of a new political era for the country. Undoubtedly, what lies at the heart of all these uncertainties is the future of Malay politics and the place and role of Islam in that politics and by extension national politics. The raging political battles are essentially an intra-Malay affair between UMNO and PAS with the other ethnic groups and their representative political parties largely remaining spectators but with the awareness that their own future is going to be affected in one way or another by the outcome of the battles. To recover its lost political ground to PAS, UMNO seeks to impress upon the Malays that what is at stake is nothing less than Malay unity, and the preservation of Malay political dominance and Malaysia's Malay-Islamic character. Mahathir goes even further to decalare that Malaysia is already an Islamic state. In so doing, he tries to convince the Malays that Malaysia under UMNO rule has already been transformed into an Islamic state that they can see with their own eyes unlike that advocated by PAS, which is yet to be created and which they even do not know how to describe.[17] PAS countered by saying that Malay unity is a non-issue since the Malays as a community have never been disunited in the first place. It is UMNO that is fractured and disunited as a result of the Anwar political saga. PAS also emphasized that Malaysia is not an Islamic state as claimed by Mahathir. However, on this particular issue of the Islamic state, the debate is no longer confined to the two Malay political parties and the Malay community. Fearing their future could adversely be affected by the outcome of the Islamic state debate, many non-Muslims have begun to participate in that debate. This is indeed something novel in the history of Malaysian politics. The consequences for the nation could also be far-reaching.

In the light of this ongoing debate on the Islamic state, it may be pertinent to touch briefly on the character of the Malaysian state that was founded four decades ago and its evolving character, especially when partisans in the debate often invoke the Constitution in support of their respective positions. Now, in speaking of Malaysia's national character, one may venture to claim that, as a Muslim nation, it is quite unique in a number of respects. One important dimension of Malaysia's uniqueness pertains to the religious character of the state. It is our view that Malaysia is not an Islamic state in the technical sense understood in the traditional science of the Divine Law of Islam (Shari'a), which is regarded as the decisive criterion of Islamicity that really matters. From the traditional point of view, Malaysia was not an Islamic state at the time of its birth nor it is one now, notwithstanding Mahathir's claim, or at any point of time in its independent history. But it is equally true that Malaysia has never been a secular state in the strict sense of the word. If the essence of secularism as a political ideology is the separation of religion and state, and if it is this characteristic that defines a secular state, then clearly Malaysia does not fit into the category of secular states whether Muslim or otherwise. We will argue that Malaysia is a religious state of some kind that conforms to many of Islam's requirements.

Malaysia was founded with Islam as a highly significant integral component of the state and with a national character that is dominated by Malay-Islamic political values and institutions. The Malay-Islamic character of the Malaysian state may be argued on the following basis. First, Islam is enshrined in the Federal Constitution as the sole official religion of the country, but other religions may be practiced in peace and harmony. Second, the state is a constitutional monarchy, which is essentially a Malay-Islamic political institution. The Supreme Head of the Federation called Yang DiPertuan Agong (King), and Rulers in their capacities as Heads of Islam in their respective states are conferred with constitutional powers pertaining to the practice, observance or ceremonies of Islam. The monarchy therefore provides some kind of a permanent authority for the institutionalization of the place and role of Islam in the state. Third, Islam is further imprinted on the state character by virtue of the fact that Malays are constitutionally defined as Muslims, and their dominant position as the backbone of the nation is reinforced by various state institutions and mechanisms.

There are other arguments pinpointing to the Malay-Islamic character of the Malaysian state. But just the three factors cited above are more than sufficient to prove our point. Why is Malaysia then described, especially in the West, as a secular Muslim state? This description appears to have been countered more often in recent years as attempts are made in various quarters to distinguish in clear terms between what Malaysia is actually now and what Malaysia will be under "Islamic fundamentalism." Even before the September 11 event and recent revelations by a number of Southeast Asian governments of a regional Muslim terrorist network in pursuit of the Islamic state, there has been the expressed concern that Southeast Asia's secular traditions are being threatened by the rise of radical Islam. It has been pointed out in particular, that Malaysia's traditional secularism is in increasing danger of being replaced by radical Islam. Conservative and radical Muslim political activists are claimed to be attempting to transform largely secular Malaysia into an Islamic state.[18]

How fitting is the use of the term "secular state," especially when applied to contemporary Malaysia? The claim of a "secular Malaysia" needs a serious examination, at least for two good reasons. One reason is that Malaysia has undergone quite a significant "Islamic transformation" since its birth. If at the time of its birth, as previously argued, the state had already acquired certain notable Islamic characteristics, then the more so now can we identify as Islamic its dominant national character. From the times of its first Prime Minister, Tunku Abdul Rahman, until the present Mahathir administration, the state has been involved to various degrees in promoting Islam and the religious welfare of the Muslims. Consequently, especially under the Mahathir-Anwar Administration, with its Islamization of policies, the space of "Malaysian secularism" has been steadily shrinking to make way for the Islamic domination of national policies.[19]

Another reason is that the claim is apparently based on a loose understanding of the word "secular" as well as misunderstanding of the concept of Islamic states and the various possible types of state that can emerge in between. Moreover, it seems that many people outside Malaysia have unquestioningly accepted the characterization "secular Malaysia" just because within the country itself, various groups have been claiming that Malaysia is indeed a secular state. Interestingly however, the same claim has been asserted by people coming from the opposite ends of the Malaysian political spectrum, and obviously with different political reasons. On one end of the spectrum are the secularists, who have maintained that Malaysia was founded as a secular state, and it should remain so for the sake of its future wellness as a multi-racial and multi-religious country. On the opposite end are Muslim political ideologues and activities who are working toward the establishment of an Islamic state. This group too, mainly associated with PAS, sees a secular Malaysia. Consistent with that position, they have rejected Mahathir's declaration that Malaysia is an Islamic state. It is precisely because the country is deemed secular that they are determined to transform it into an Islamic state of their interpretation.

The most vocal defender of the secular state position is perhaps Lim Kit Siang, a former Parliamentary Leader of the Opposition, and his dominantly Chinese Democratic Action Party. A non-Muslim religious coalition, the Malaysian Consultative Congress of Buddhism, Christianity, Hinduism and Sikhism (MCCBCHS), has also come out strongly in asserting the secular character of Malaysia. The main argument advanced in support of the secular position is an interpretation of "Islam the religion of the Federation" that the Alliance Party had submitted in its memorandum to the Reid Constitutional Commission that was entrusted with the task of drafting the Constitution for the newly independent nation. The memorandum makes the following constitutional proposal: "the religion of Malaysia shall be Islam. The observance of this principle shall not impose any disability on non-Muslim natives professing and practicing their religions and shall not imply that the State is not a secular State." It thus seemed to be the view of the Alliance that 'having Islam the state religion' and 'being a secular nation at the same time' were not contradictory prepositions. The Party did not express at the time any serious concern, if at all it was aware, that in due course the two propositions would come into conflict.

However, in the actual Constitution that came to be adopted, the reference to the "secular State" in the Alliance proposal was not included. Not once is there a mention in the Constitution of a secular State. The phrase "secular State" appeared only in the Reid Commission Report when it reproduced the Alliance proposal in question, and in the Government's 1957 White Paper, which was really a constitutional document on reviews of the Reid Report.[20] The fact thus remains that the Constitution is devoid of an explicit recognition of Malaysia as a secular state. The famous clause (1) of Article 3 merely says: Islam is the religion of the Federation; but other religions may be practiced in peace and harmony in any part of the Federation. So neither is there an explicit constitutional recognition of Malaysia as an Islamic state. What we have are supporting documents of the original interpretation of this clause, that is, "Malaysia is a secular state." Tunku Abdul Rahman as Leader of the Alliance, "father of independence," and Prime Minister subscribed to this interpretation. He had also made assertions that the country is not truly an Islamic state.[21] It is mainly on this original interpretation of the Constitution favored by the Alliance that the secularists' claim of a secular Malaysia rests its arguments. Political and religious secularists staking out this claim are also insisting that Malaysia should stay secular, since such a national character was what was agreed upon in the 1957 social contract that founded the nation. They further argue that any attempt to alter Malaysia's secular character by turning it into an Islamic state is deemed unconstitutional. Their charges of unconstitutionality are directed at both Mahathir's UMNO for having declared Malaysia as an Islamic state and PAS for passionately pursuing their Islamic state dream.

What about proponents of an Islamic state claiming Malaysia is secular? What are their arguments in support of the claim? Their main and persistent argument is that Islamic law (Shari'a) is not being implemented in its entirety in the country. To be an Islamic state, Malaysia needs to accept and implement the Shari'a as a complete legal system and as the supreme law in the land to which all other laws are subservient. For this religious group then, what decisively distinguishes a secular state from an Islamic one is the place and role accorded to Islamic law. Public space is defined essentially as the domain that is determined and regulated by Islamic law. Moreover, it is their unshakeable belief that with the implementation of the Shari'a all societal ills can be cured. For this reason, PAS and other like-minded groups have taken a somewhat legalistic approach to societal problems.

It appears to us, on the basis of their respective arguments, those claiming Malaysia is a secular state have taken the common standpoint that in its national character Malaysia can only be one of two things. Either it is an Islamic state or a secular one. There could not possibly be another kind of state that is neither secular in the Western sense nor Islamic as envisioned by PAS or as actualized in Saudi Arabia and Afghanistan under the Taliban. It is also quite clear that these claimants have ignored the Islamic transformation of Malaysia to which we have earlier alluded. The crux of the matter is that present-day Malaysia in its religious features is no longer the same as Malaysia under Tunku's leadership. The question that arises then is whether or not such an Islamically transformed

Malaysia can still be described as a secular state, even if it is not yet an Islamic state. In the light of this transformation, if a special characterization of the contemporary Malaysian state has to be made, many Muslims would be inclined to think of it as "an Islamic state in the making" or "a largely Muslim state that is in its advanced stage of transformation into an Islamic state." In other words, Malaysia is already largely Islamic, not largely secular.

But Mahathir in facing the biggest challenge in his political career has responded with a surprising answer: "Malaysia is already an Islamic state." Of course, he knows fully well Malaysia's significant Islamic transformation. After all, he was its chief architect. Prematurely or otherwise, he decided that Malaysia has reached the point of acquiring enough qualifications to be called an "Islamic state." But that decision may well turn out to be historic, marking a major turning point in the history of the relations of Islam and the State in Malaysia.

The Significance of Mahathir's Islamic State

Mahathir's "Islamic state" declaration has puzzled and infuriated many people, but it has also received wide support. No one can accuse him of not knowing the 1957 interpretation of Malaysia as a secular state. So he must have pondered on the implications of his "Islamic state declaration" for his politics, UMNO and the nation he lead. It is still too early for anyone to assess its impact on Malaysian politics and its implications for the development of Islam. Likewise, it is too early to detect whether his political fortunes are turning for the better as a result of that declaration. Whatever indications there are up to now, it looks as if Mahathir's declaration has enlivened even more and at once broadened and complicated the nation's "Islamic state debate" that hitherto has been dominated by PAS and the DAP.

Interesting though the nation's "Islamic versus secular state" debate has been, it has been dominated by politicians with their sectarian politics. Polemics and rhetoric abound, but intellectual discourses are still lacking. Even among academics, there has been a glaring lack of objective and scholarly analyses of the major issues brought up in the debate that can help minimize ethnic and religious tensions. Until now, the debate has taken place more or less along ethnic and religious lines, with Malays who are Muslims supporting some form of Islamic state and non-Malays who are mainly non-Muslims defending the secular state. The stand taken by the non-Muslim religious coalition to defend Malaysia's secular character has reinforced those religious divisions. Muslims whose religion abhors secularism find it hard to understand why Hindu, Buddhist, and Christian religious leaders seek to defend the secular state, if not because of their hostility to the Islamic state.

They find it even harder to understand why these religious leaders are even opposed to Mahathir's liberal "Islamic state" which is not something yet to appear but something that is "here and now," the present Malaysia in which they are all living. If present Malaysia is secular to non-Muslims and Islamic to Muslims, then isn't the furor over the "Islamic state" just a quarrel over "forms" rather than "substance"? On their part, the non-Muslims are deeply concerned about their religious and civil rights in an Islamic state. They fear they will become second-class citizens in their own country, and they do not want to become second-class citizens. The debate has the potential of developing into a highly emotive polemic and degenerating into sectarian conflicts. However, in a way, Mahathir's "Islamic state" declaration may help to transform the debate into one that transcends ethnic and religious affiliations. For a start, non-Malay and non-Muslim political leaders in Mahathir's multiethnic ruling coalition find themselves having to defend UMNO's version of Islamic state. Now that UMNO has its own Islamic state to defend, it has to take a more aggressive stance against PAS' Islamic state. All these developments will help to blur the religious lines along which the debate has been pursued until now.

Apart from helping to intensify the traditional debate on the character of the Malaysian state, Mahathir's Islamic state has also helped to break new grounds for public and intellectual discourses on the meaning of secularism and Islamicity in the Malaysian context. Very likely, Mahathir's declaration will have major consequences on the nation's politics and inter-religious discourse. But for the moment we will limit ourselves to pointing out the immediate significance of that declaration. We will argue for three major areas of significance. Firstly, the declaration will force the major actors in the Islamic state debate to address in a more serious manner the issue of whether the state constitution is secular or Islamic. For a start, the DAP has challenged the constitutionality of Mahathir's declaration. Interestingly, even before that declaration, several PAS leaders had made known their stand that the constitution is basically Islamic. Tuan Guru Haji Hadi Awang, the Deputy Leader of the Party and Chief Minister of the state of Terengganu maintains that if PAS were to come into power, its version of Islamic state will only require a minor amendment to the existing state constitution. Secondly, the declaration helps to bring home the message to Malaysians that there is not just one model of the Islamic state. They have the freedom to choose either the UMNO model or the PAS model, or to reject both of them. In fact, Kit Siang and his DAP have rejected all versions of Islamic state as long as they carry the name "Islamic." But there are non-Muslims who feel that to the extent an Islamic state in Malaysia is inevitable given Islam's dominance in the State and in society, and to the extent Malaysia is a democracy, they have to exercise their freedom of choice, either in favor of UMNO's Islamic state or that of PAS.

Thirdly, related to the earlier issue of possible models of Islamic state, Mahathir's declaration is likely in the long run to generate a more substantive discourse on the meaning of Islamicity. If present Malaysia is already an Islamic state in the eyes of UMNO, something that PAS rejects, the contention between these two political rivals on what constitutes an Islamic state boils down to their different interpretations and criteria of Islamicity. To demonstrate he is serious in his version of the Islamic state, Mahathir assembled the ulama' (religious scholars) of UMNO to come up with a theological justification of the declaration. That justification has been documented. In a follow-up, he has challenged PAS to come up in writing as well with its own version of the Islamic state so that Malaysians can see for themselves and make the appropriate judgment. But UMNO is being challenged on another front. The DAP is insisting Malaysia is secular, and UMNO has to articulate accordingly why the country is not secular but Islamic. In attempting to strengthen the Islamic arguments for his Islamic state, Mahathir could not find a better ally than Anwar, his current political foe and former ally. Not that had he still been Mahathir's deputy, Anwar would agree with him declaring Malaysia an Islamic state at this stage of development of Islam in the country, most probably settling for a lesser claim for Malaysia's "Islamic" status, but his alternative approach to Islam, Islamic state, and Islamic law would be of tremendous help to Mahathir in articulating on his Islamic state. It was observed that both during his ABIM (Malaysian Muslim Youths Movement) and UMNO years, Anwar had been cultivating an alternative approach to Islam, emphasizing different areas and criteria of Islamicity from those pursued by PAS. He is in disagreement with several major aspects of the Islamic state concept espoused by PAS. Emphasizing more on substance than on forms, he speaks of a struggle for a nation and a socio-political order founded on moral principles and the fundamental Islamic values of justice and tolerance. In his general response to PAS' insistence on the immediate implementation of *hudud* laws, Anwar pleads for a sense of priorities in the implementation of Islamic Law, tolerance and understanding of Malaysia's religious and cultural pluralism, and the rationality of the country's evolutionary path to an Islamic nationhood. In thus believing in another interpretation of "Islamic state" and in an evolutionary path to its realization, he represents another school of Malaysian political Islam of which he is perhaps the most vocal member.

The most significant thing about the Islamic state debate in Malaysia is that it has been carried out all these years in a political democracy and in a multi-ethnic and a multi-religious society in which non-Muslims account for nearly half the population. In a democracy like Malaysia, the fate of the Islamic state, whether that of UMNO or of PAS, will be as much decided by the ulama' and intelligentsia as by ordinary citizens at the ballot box.

The Role of Political Democracy in the Development
of Malaysian Islam

Malaysia was born a democratic nation. Its Westminster-style parliamentary democracy is a British legacy. The first democratic multi-party election was held in 1955, two years before independence, to choose the party that would lead the country to self-rule. The Alliance, a coalition of ethnic-based political parties representing the three major racial groups in the country—Malays, Chinese, and Indians—headed by Tunku won 51 out of a total of 52 parliamentary seats. The Islamic Party won the remaining one seat. From then until now, Malaysian politics has been dominated by ethnic-based politics.

What about the place and role of Islam in Malaysia's political democracy? Has that democracy been secular or otherwise? It may be asserted that Islam and democracy in the country have been closely intertwined right from the beginning. We will present here a brief account of their interactive growths and development. To begin with, Malaysian democracy has never been strictly secular. The country's dominant Malay-Islamic character could not but shape the contours and the formal characteristics of its democratic system. Political parties using religious names and campaigning on Islamic platforms are legalized. As we have seen the Islamic Party participated in the first general elections and won a parliamentary seat. Islam is a perennial issue in Malaysian politics. It is true that at various times in the nation's post-independent history, especially during Tunku's rule, there have been UMNO leaders who have called for the separation of religion and politics, thus providing PAS with political bullets to fire charges of ideological secularism against UMNO. In practice, however, no one really observes a separation of the two. Islam is too powerful and influential a force in Malay society, thus by extension Malaysian life, to be ignored by politicians. It may be asserted without exaggeration that Islam has played a central role in the foundation of the nation's democratic system and in the evolution of its democratic institutions and practices.

In what sense may Islam be regarded as the foundation and source of institutional and political frameworks of the country's democratic system? There are three relevant points to be noted. These are (1) the special position of Islam as the sole official religion, (2) the special position of the Malays as the destined political guardians and vanguard of Islam, thus necessitating their political dominance and special rights in various domains, and (3) the unique blending of traditional Islamic and modern western political institutions in the creation of new democratic institutions. Pertaining to the first point, Islam's position as the state religion gives the government in power the right and freedom to develop the religion as it wishes and as it sees fit. With or without democracy, by virtue of that constitutional provision on Islam, the government of the day has a moral and political obligation to develop and implement policies on the religion. But over the years Islam has benefited not only from its constitutional status but also from the practice of political democracy with its multi-party system. Indeed, one of the major factors for the steady expansion of Islamic space in Malaysian life in the last few decades is the ever-increasing need to develop Islam to appease the Muslim electorate. Appeasement of the Muslim community has become a kind of societal need that is growing in importance especially in the wake of Islamic resurgence.[37] Political parties and politicians, Muslims and non-Muslims alike, have to give prominence to the appeasement issue due to Malay-Muslim political dominance. Moreover, Islam is traditionally the main source of political legitimacy. Conversely, political democracy has benefited from the positive socio-cultural impacts of the practice of Islam by the majority population such as the widely acknowledged tradition of openness and tolerance that has characterized the Malay-Indonesian Muslims, the role of Islam as a stabilizing force, and Islam's distinctive commitment to social justice. It is a measure, a significant one, of the positive reception and commitment of Malay-Muslims to democracy that save for a brief period when it was suspended following the May 1969 riots, Malaysian democracy has functioned for more than four decades.

The second point, the special position of the Malays, constitutionally guaranteed, is a major shaper of the country's political democracy. Islam, Malay political power, and democracy as the legitimate means to power, which are closely interrelated, are of major concern to Malay politics. Islam can only maintain its present position as the state religion with all its privileges and responsibilities if the continued dominance of Muslim political power is guaranteed. Since the great majority of the nation's Muslims are Malays and all Malays are Muslims by constitutional definition, the national duty to protect and advance the cause of Islam has to fall on the Malays. It is the issue of Malay-Muslim political power that is at the heart of Malaysian politics. To the question how Malay-Muslim political dominance can be preserved, the Constitution provides part of the answer. A constitutional provision is made, that gives a definition of "Malay" in terms of his Islamic identity. This definition establishes and ensures an inextricable link between Islam and the country's largest ethnic group. Consequently, Islam and the Malays emerge as each other's protector. This close identification of religion with race has been both a source of strength and a source of weakness of Malaysian Islam. In recent years there has been an increasing criticism of this constitutional definition, from among both Malays and non-Muslims. Critics have argued the definition violates the freedom of belief since it bars Malays from converting to other religions without losing their Malay identity and privileges. Christian missionaries have often cited the definition as a major obstacle to their making an inroad into the Malay community.

Another way the Constitution seeks to empower the Malays is to give recognition to their special privileges as the indigenous people. This provision enables the government to help the Malays to elevate their socio-economic status on par with non-Malays. Although in principle all accept the special privileges policy, the government's implementation of the policy has often come under severe fire from both Malays and non-Malays. Another part of the answer to the question how Malay-Muslim political dominance can be ensured is provided by the country's democratic system. Greater political weight is given to rural areas where the great majority of the Malays live. Accordingly, parliamentary and state constituencies have been drawn up to reflect that political bias.

Malay-Muslim national leaders who have ruled Malaysia consider it their greatest challenge to reconcile the imperative of maintaining Malay and bumiputera political dominance and advancing their socio-economic status with the need to give justice and equality to the non-Malays within the constitutional framework. As a matter of fact, the entire Malay community sees the challenge in terms of a trust that is morally binding on them. This moral picture partly explains why UMNO and PAS are competing hard to convince the nation that they are the better party to overcome the challenge. Until now, UMNO has won the competition, but in recent years it has faced a more formidable challenge from PAS. The path Malaysia has chosen in realizing its political democracy is the sharing of political power among its numerous ethnic groups. A national power-sharing formula was worked out purportedly to the general satisfaction of all ethnic groups, particularly the Malays, the ethnic Chinese, and the ethnic Indians. This formula gave birth to Malaysia's tradition of democratic pluralism that has survived to this day. It is also in the light of this seemingly workable power-sharing formula that ever since independence, Malaysia has been ruled by a coalition government that is at once Malay-dominated and representative in the broadest sense possible of the country's ethnic groups. This unique relationship in power sharing may be viewed at the same time as a power sharing between Muslims and non-Muslims, that has benefited Islam and Muslims as well as non-Muslims.

The third point, the unique blending of traditional Islamic and modern Western political institutions brings into picture the role of constitutional monarchy in Malaysia's democratic system. The country's unique constitutional monarchy is what survives of the traditional Malay royalty that had been stripped of many of its powers by the British colonial rulers, and to which novel modern features are added. In its compromised modern form, the reigning Sultans of the nine states with Rulers have to elect a King once in every five years, making Malaysia the only country in the world to have an elected King. The Constitution has called upon this monarchy to play a special role in relation to both Islam and democracy. In relation to Islam, the Sultans and Rulers are heads of the religion in their respective states, and the King is the Head of the religion in his own state and in the states without Sultans or Rulers. Although religion is a state matter, The Conference of Rulers may delegate authority to the King to make Islamic pronouncements on behalf of the entire nation. With its constitutional provision, the monarchy is generally regarded as yet another national institution created to protect and advance both Islam and Malay interests.

Over the years Malay-Muslim reception of the monarchy has been mixed. On the positive side, they see the monarchy as having a role to minimize, if not entirely prevent exploitation of Islam by political authorities. They also feel that the monarchy could have contributed more to the progress of Islam if only they have been well advised to play their roles by the relevant religious and political authorities. On the negative side, there has been widespread criticism that the development of Islamic law in the country and the administration of Islam generally is slow moving, because of a lack of concerted efforts and wisdom in streamlining religious policies in the light of decades-old "problematic" relationship between Federal and State religious authorities. The monarchy as heads of Islam, the ulama' as religious advisors and administrators, and the Federal and State governments who hold the political power, all have got their portion of the blame for this "religious mess."

In relation to political democracy, as in relation to Islam, the country has hopes and disappointments with the monarchy. The monarchy is expected to play a role in ensuring the smooth functioning of the nation's political democracy at both Federal and State levels. There have been instances when the monarchy or Sultans and Rulers were either directly involved in controversial political matters or unilaterally engaged themselves in resolving political crises that call into question their faithfulness to their constitutional roles. In the main, however, since the nation has only known the same political party in power in its history, the constitutional monarchy has never been really tested in its role performance. Many Malaysians hope to see the day when the monarchy will be judged well by the people in that role performance, especially in ensuring a healthier growth of democracy. In recent years, much interest has been shown toward the idea of an emerging Islamic democracy in Malaysia. Since the monarchy stands above partisan politics, it is seen as well suited to play an effective role in helping to turn the idea of Islamic democracy into a reality. In particular, Sultans of state which already have the experience of overseeing change of governments from UMNO-dominated to PAS or vice-versa, as in the case of Kelantan and Terengganu, are considered to have the extra "credentials" to promote the idea of Islamic democracy among the Malay-Muslim community.

Several political facts pertaining to the Malay community, some of which are old and others new, would be conducive to the realization of an Islamic democracy that can serve as a stable and permanent foundation for the nation's democratic system as a whole. The most important fact is that the Malay-Muslim community seems to be comfortable with its two-party system, UMNO and PAS to compete for legitimacy as their and the nation's leaders. Notwithstanding the existence of small Malay political parties, UMNO and PAS have been the two parties that really matter to the Malay-Muslim ever since the introduction of political democracy. If the nation feels that these two can work in a coalition system at the national level, then prospects for an Islamic democracy in Malaysia will be good enough indeed.

Interestingly today, in a political democracy dominated by Malay-Muslims, in the wake of PAS victory in Kelantan and Trengganu in the 1999 General Elections and UMNO's shrinking support among the Malays, many non-Muslims have started comparing which of the two parties is giving a better treatment of their religions. In the past, UMNO's traditional strategy to monopolize the political support of non-Muslims has been to impress upon them that they would become second-class citizens and their religious rights badly treated under PAS Islamic rule. But now that non-Muslims, at least in Kelantan and Trengganu, have experienced both UMNO's and PAS's kinds of government, they are better placed to pass a more objective judgment on the "virtues and vices" of the two parties. Many non-Muslims are now also examining closely the "Islamic states" of the two Malay parties to start comparing which is better for their future. How the non-Muslims are going to compare and contrast and to evaluate them in the coming years is going to have a profound impact on the future of Islam and democracy in Malaysia. For now, UMNO and PAS are engaged in a bitter and divisive psychological and political war to convince the Muslims that each is better qualified than the other to establish and run an Islamic state in a multi-ethnic and multi-religious nation. At the same time, the two parties are competing to convince the non-Muslims that each is better than the other in its treatment of their religious interests. This is indeed another interesting development that is conducive to the birth of an Islamic democracy in Malaysia from which both Muslims and non-Muslims stand to benefit.

Conclusion

From the foregoing discussion, it is clear that the four civilizational forces of religion, ethnicity, democracy and pluralism have singularly and collectively played significant roles in the history of modern Malaysia. These forces have interacted in a unique way to shape the country under the pervasive influence of Islam. Standing at the center of these four forces, Islam has made important contributions to inter-ethnic and inter-religious harmony and to the development of the democratic pluralism in the country. But Islam is also on the receiving end in a positive way. Interestingly, it has grown and developed in a political democracy and a multi-ethnic and multi-religious society. Malaysia's unique experience offers lessons to countries that are striving hard to create a democracy out of their multi-ethnic and multi-religious societies.

Notes

1. By "civilizational forces," I mean human ideas and values that through their societal manifestations give shape and character to the culture and civilization of a particular people or nation. Islam views positively the place and role of each of these four forces, especially religion, in the development of human society. On Islam's appreciation of religious and ethnic pluralism as major constructive forces in human civilization, see Osman Bakar, "Inter-Civilizational Dialogue: Theory and Practice in Islam," in Mitsuo Nakamura, Sharon Siddique and Omar Farouk Bajunid, eds., *Islam and Civil Society in Southeast Asia* (Singapore: Institute of Southeast Asian Studies, 2001), 164–176. On Islam's positive views of democracy, see Yusuf al-Qaradawi, *State in Islam* (Cairo: El-Falah for Translation, Publishing and Distribution, 1998); Muhammad Asad, *The Principles of State and Government in Islam* (Berkeley: University of California Press, 1961; Gibraltar: Dar al-Andalus, 1980; Petaling Jaya, Malaysia: Islamic Book Trust); and Niaz Faizi Kanbuli, *Democracy According to Islam* (Pittsburgh: Dorrance Publishing Co., Inc., 1994).

2. Malaysia came into existence on September 16, 1963 when Malaya, itself a federation of eleven states and which gained independence from the British on August 31, 1957 formed a larger federation with Sabah and Sarawak in Borneo and Singapore, all formerly British colonies that were given independence through the Federation. In 1965, Tunku Abdul Rahman, Malayia's first Prime Minister, expelled Singapore from the Federation following his "irreconcilable difference" with the island state's leader, Lee Kuan Yew over race-related issues. The expulsion of Singapore may be cited as the first major casualty of ethnic tensions in the newly born Federation. Since Malaysia adopts Malaya's independence day as its own, the word Malaysia is often used throughout this essay, depending on the context, to mean the independent Malaya.

3. For a classic account of the origins and development of Malay civilizational consciousness and identity, see W. G. Shellabear, ed., *Sejarah Melayu*, or the *Malay Annals* (Singapore: The Malaya Publishing House, 1950); also T. Situmorang and A. Teeuw, ed., *Sejarah Melayu* (Jakarta, 1958). For a modern treatment of the subject, see, for example, Burhanuddin Al-Helmi, *Falsafah Kebangsaan Melayu* (The Philosophy of Malay Nationalism) (Bukit Mertajam: Pustaka Semenanjung, 1954). This popular writing of Burhanuddin, a noted Malay intellectual-activist and a former leader of the Malaysian Islamic Party (PAS), is reprinted in Kamarudin Jaffar, *Dr. Burhanuddin Al-Helmi: Pemikiran dan Perjuangan* (Dr. Burhanuddin Al-Helmi: His Thought and Struggle) (Kuala Lumpur: IKDAS Sdn. Bhd., 2000).

4. On the spread of Islam in the Malay world, see Alijah Gordon, edited and annotated, *The Propagation of Islam in the Indonesian-Malay Archipelago* (Kuala Lumpur:
Malaysian Sociological Research Institute, 2001).

5. On the role of Christianity in the military conquest of Malay-Muslim territories,
see Charles Ralph Boxer, "Portuguese and Spanish Projects for the Conquest of Southeast Asia, 1580–1600," in Gordon, 159–179.

6. See Kamarudin Jaffar, 73.

7. Quite a number of Malay thinkers of the colonial part of the twentieth century
have dealt with the theme of Malay salvation within Islam and the compatibility of
Malay nationalism with Islam. See for example, the writings of Za'ba (Zainal Abidin
Ahmad) (1895–1973) such as "The Salvation of the Malays" in *The Malay Mail* (Parts
I and II, 21 & 22 November 1923) and Burhanuddin al-Helmi such as the previously
cited *The Philosophy of Malay Nationalism*.

8. According to historical records, accompanying the conquering Portuguese fleet
were eight priests, including six Franciscans. One or more of these Franciscan Friars
remained in Malacca to minister to the faithful. See K. M. Williams, *The Church in West
Malaysia and Singapore: Regarding Her Situation as an Indigenous Church*, PhD Disser-
tation, Faculty of Theology, Katholieke Universitat Te Leuven, 1976; see also Ghazali
Basri, *Christian Mission and Islamic Da'wah in Malaysia* (Kuala Lumpur: Nurin Enterprise, 1992).

9. See Vidhu Verma, *Malay, State and Civil Society in Transition* (Boulder, CO: Lynne
Rienner, 2002).

10. Boxer, "Portuguese and Spanish Projects," 159–179.

11. Boxer, "Portuguese and Spanish Projects," 159–179.

12. Boxer, "Portuguese and Spanish Projects," 159–179.

13. For the role of the Dutch in Malay history see John J. Valentine, *"Imperial
Democracy": Dutch Colonizers in Malaysia, Annexation of the Philippines* (San Fran-
cisco: Press of Hicks-Judd Company, 1899). See also Nicholas Tarling, *Anglo-Dutch
Rivalry in the Malay World, 1780–1824* (New York: Cambridge University Press, 1962).

14. For a history of Christianity in Malaysia see Robert Hunt, Lee Kam Hing and
John Roxborough, *Christianity in Malaysia: A Denominational History* (Petaling Jaya:
Pelanduk Publications, 1992).

15. See Ramdas Menon, *Migration Patterns and Migrant Adjustment in Peninsular
Malaysia* (Ottawa: National Library of Canada, 1989). See also Siu-Lun Wong, ed.,
Chinese and Indian Diasporas: Comparative Perspectives (Hong Kong: Center of Asian
Studies, 2004).

16. See Kamariah bte Musa, *Islam, Malays and the Malaysian National Identity*
(Malaysia, 1977).

17. Patricia A. Martinez, *The Islamic State or the State of Islam in Malaysia* (Singapore: Institute of Southeast Asian Studies, 2001).

18. See R. Mageswary, "Talk of 'Islamic State' Causes Malaysian Jitters," *Asian Times,*
November 17, 1999, <www.atimes.com/se-asia/AK17Ae01.html>.

19. See Patricia A. Martinez, *The Islamic State or the State of Islam in Malaysia* (Singapore: Institute of Southeast Asian Studies, 2001).

20. For a brief review of Malaysia's constitutional history and the Reid Commission see Abdul Aziz Bari, "The Evolution of Malaysian Constitutional Tradition," paper presented at the Asian Law Institute Conference, Singapore, May 27–28, 2004, <www.law.chula.ac.th/asli/paper/f13.pdf>.

21. See Min Choon Lee, *Freedom of Religion in Malaysia* (Selangor, Malaysia: Kairos Research Centre, 1999).

5

An Islamic Quest for a Pluralistic Political Model: A Turkish Perspective

Özlem Denli

Introduction

The *coup d'etat* of 1980 brought about major transformations in the Turkish political scene. One significant dimension of the transformations was regarding the direction of official policies toward religion. Alarmed by the heightened political polarization of the 1970s, the high command of the—historically laicist—Armed Forces employed a language that made references to Islamic identity. State investment in the promotion and control of religion increased substantially.[1] The election in 1983 brought into power a civilian government that perpetuated this tendency. In this atmosphere, ideologies and political tendencies inspired by Islam gained substantial leverage and entered into political equations in an unprecedented way.

The increased political importance of Islam was accompanied by a process of differentiation among its ranks. Diverging interpretations laid claim to the sphere opened for Islam in the political realm; the diversity of Islamic interpretation and practice was voiced in a vibrant and proliferating Islamic public sphere of discussion and deliberation. Concepts like pluralism, cultural heterogeneity, civil society, and human rights started to make entry into the Islamic discourse, as they became an intrinsic part of the political vocabulary and public debate at large. Alternative societal projects regarding the relation between the state, society and religion were widely discussed in a rapidly transforming political landscape.

The topic of this article is one such proposal for a new political organization put forward by a prominent Muslim intellectual, Ali Bulac. Bulac advocated plural legal systems as a political model inspired by the Medina Constitution, which was practiced by Prophet Muhammad during the early years of Islam. Bulac presented his proposal in a series of articles published in journals such as *Birikim, Bilgi ve Hikmet, Kitap Dergisi* and in some daily newspapers. The idea was widely discussed and elaborated in the 1990s by members of Muslim groups and organizations as well as intellectuals representing a broad section of the political spectrum.[2]

Bulac's proposal is of crucial significance for instigating new terms for Islamic political critique in present-day Turkey. First of all, Bulac voices concerns of those Muslims who see their faith as a set of norms with a claim to evaluate shared public political institutions and practices. Bulac develops an Islamic framework for reflecting upon the question of modern societal plurality and its fair accommodation. He puts forward an alternative to existing political institutions and procedures while maintaining a commitment to values such as pluralism, tolerance and human rights. Despite his critique, Bulac's interpretation of Islam offers Muslims a way of entry into the values associated with liberal democracy and human rights by making them acceptable on internal Islamic premises. Secondly, the politics of difference Bulac advocates offers an understanding of the priorities arising from an Islamic cultural context, and related variations in human rights approaches.

Modernity, Plurality and the Public Relevance of Islam

The starting point of Bulac's proposal is his evaluation of parliamentary democracy as a comprehensive way of thinking and a way of life, according to which the claim of neutrality in the name of its fundamental principles and procedures is rendered problematic. Bulac sees the nation-state as the principle element whose centrality to modern political institutions is also the main reason for their inability in accommodating genuine plurality and difference. According to Bulac, modern political institutions have a unifying rather than a pluralist gist. In particular, modern nation state is inherently totalitarian. In contrast with the limited intervention capacity of the premodern state, which leaves many areas of life out of its control, modern nation-state has religion, law, education, scientific knowledge, official ideology, dress code and even cuisine within its range of intervention (1994: 8). This "centralized" character endows the nation-state with "the ability to regulate all aspects of life in a totalitarian fashion including the inner life of the individual" (1994: 5). Bulac claims that democracy in this sense is merely a mechanism that deepens the penetration of the nation state in all spheres of life in modern societies.

Furthermore, Bulac claims that modern democracy can only accommodate diversity within a relatively narrow spectrum. What Bulac sees as genuine difference, namely diversity of *sharia* cannot be accommodated in this framework. The way Bulac understands *sharia* is not linked to Islam or belief in a revealed religion. Neither does it mean legal system in a narrow sense. *Sharia* literally means path in Arabic and Bulac follows this definition to argue that it broadly corresponds to path or way of life regardless of their origin; more specifically, to the totality of the principles founding a life lived in accordance with one's conception of the good life (1994: 13).

Although Bulac does not reduce *sharia* to a set of legal norms, he insists that the concept does not exclude the dimension of legal system. According to the view put forward here, every religion, belief system, culture and tradition has its own concept of wisdom, virtue and justice (1992: 109). Law is the jurisdictional dimension of this broad set of norms. As a concrete technique and method, law directs members of a community towards a life lived according to general principles (1994: 13). Bulac insists that for groups and communities being what they really are is inseparable from being able to express themselves in self-defined legal standards (1992: 109). This is the reason why Bulac considers the modern nation-state incapable of accommodating the essence of religious freedom understood in Islamic terms:

> The modern nation-state deprived Muslims of their right to live according to Islamic law while nominally granting the freedom of religion. In this way the very essence of this liberty for Muslims was distorted. (Bulac 1994: 11)

Taking what he perceives as legitimate Islamic demands as his starting point, Bulac presents an alternative proposal that places modern forms of political organization under scrutiny with the intent to improve upon them in terms of safeguarding plurality and difference. In order to give foundation to his proposal, Bulac refers to the historical practices of the Muslim community during the early period of Islam. More specifically he ventures to revitalize the basic principles and procedures associated with the Medina Constitution, which was signed in 622 between Muslims, Jews and pagan Arabs (1992: 110).[3]

Bulac's claim that the current conditions in Turkey render the Medina Constitution as a plausible model to draw upon requires an understanding of the social and political circumstances within which the Constitution emerged.

A Brief Historical Review

Muhammad began to communicate the messages of the new religion in 610 AD but he had very limited success in the beginning. As the number of his fol-

lowers increased Muhammad met considerable resistance, including assassi-
nation attempts. He stayed in Mecca for twelve years in spite of opposition, but
eventually accepted the appeal from the Medinan Muslims to move to Medina
(*hijrah*) in 622 A.D. Medina, unlike other Arab towns such as Mecca and Taif,
provided Muhammad with a suitable environment to proclaim the new religion. In both Mecca and Taif there existed relative peace and security among
tribes. Medina, on the other hand, was being plagued by animosity and conflict.
There were eleven main groups, here to be referred to as "clans," as well as a
number of smaller ones. Three of the main groups professed Jewish faith (Watt
1961: 84). In the century before Muhammad's arrival, there had been a steady
increase in violence and fighting between clans. In the war of 618, there was a
heavy slaughter. Hostilities ceased when the two sides were exhausted, but peace
was not made. After this Medina lived in a state of tension (Watt 1961: 87).

Immediately after his arrival at Medina, Muhammad established a social
and economical system of solidarity between Meccan and Medinan Muslims.
Muhammad Hamidullah argues that the solidarity arrangement in question
developed a somewhat communal life that even entitled parties to inheritance
in the absence of kinship ties (Hamidullah 1994: 84, 85). Bulac states that the
arrangement introduced by Muhammad crystallized three main "social blocs"
in Medina: Muslims, Jews and Pagan Arabs. Subsequently, Muhammad sought
a political arrangement to join these blocs (Bulac 1992: 105). According to
Bulac this social arrangement was completely different from traditional structure in the Arabian Peninsula.

> While traditional tribal social organization was based on blood ties and kinship,
> for the first time in Medina people with different geographical, ethnic and cul-
> tural origin joined to define themselves as a distinct social bloc (community).
> (Bulac 1992: 105)

The Medina Constitution is the document codifying the political agreement
between these three groups in Medina who agreed upon constituting a political unit of a new type (Watt 1961: 94). As Watt states:

> There follows nine articles that mention nine clans and state that each is to be
> responsible for blood money incurred by a member of the group and for ran-
> soming a member of the group who is captured. . . . Of the remaining articles
> about twenty deal with various aspects of the relations of the believers to one
> another and to the unbelievers, while about fifteen treat of the rights and duties
> of the Jews. (Watt 1961: 94).

According to Muhammad Hamidullah the document was not unitary, but
consisted of two juxtaposed parts. Articles 1–23 regulated matters concerning

Muslims and articles 24–47 delineated principles organising the relation between communities. In this way the constitution of the body politic, that was called a "city state," was demarcated (Hamidullah 1993: 190).

The Basic Principles of the Medina Constitution

The essential principles of the Medina Constitution can be summarized as the following:

1. Article 1 defines communities party to the agreement. Accordingly, the people of the Medina "city state" consisted of Muslim emigrants of Quraysh, Medinan Muslims and non-Muslims (Jews and pagans). Together they formed a single *ummah* distinct from other people.
2. Drawing on the verse reading "To you your religion to us our religion" (Al-Kafirun/109, 5),[4] the Medina Constitution declares: "To the Jews their religion and to the Muslims their religion" (Watt 1956: 223). Each and every community was to retain and practice their belief and to solve their problems by referring freely to their own law and religion.
3. The Medina Constitution established a system of financial and military cooperation. Communities agreed to show solidarity on the issues of security and defence. People of the document would not go into agreements with third parties against each other and would protect Medina against whoever warred against them.
4. Muhammad was chosen as a litigator between communities. The constitution states: "whenever there is anything about which you differ, it is to be referred to God and to Muhammad" (Watt 1961: 95). When dealing with cases involving non-Muslims Muhammad was asked to judge according to whichever law the parties wished to be tried.

Reflecting on this last point Hamidullah contends that it was reasonable for the Muslims of Medina to respect and trust Muhammad. His central question is what made the Jewish and pagan clans accept such an agreement, considering that Muslims were only a relatively powerless minority[5] prior to the war of 624 (Hamidullah 1994: 89).[6] This is precisely the question that motivates re-appropriation of the Medina Constitution in present-day Turkey. According to Bulac, considering the balance of power, Muhammad could not have coerced non-Muslims into the arrangement. The arrangement was valid and binding because it was established by a contract among representatives of Muslim, Jewish and pagan communities on the basis of equal participation (1992: 109). In other words the arrangement derived legitimacy from mutual consent of the parties involved who reached agreement as equals.[7]

The political logic of Bulac's argument is based on the way *ummah* was defined in the Medina Constitution. Article 1 of the Medina Constitution reads:

> In the name of God, the Merciful, the Compassionate!
> This is a writing of Muhammad the prophet between the believers and Muslims of Quraysh and Yathrib (Medina) and those who follow[8] them and are attached to them and who crusade along with them. They are a single community (*ummah*) distinct from other people. (Watt 1961: 94)

On this definition, *ummah* is not understood as religious community but as a political unit established by contract between the people of Medina (Muslims, Jews and pagans).[9] For Bulac, for the first time in Medina people with different geographical and ethnic origin, and with different religious convictions joined freely to identify themselves as a political unit. What was achieved was not uniformity at the level of *sharia* but a mutually binding mode of conduct among autonomous legal communities (1992: 105). According to the Medina Constitution, the tribes party to the contract agreed that conflicts they could not resolve among themselves were referred to Muhammed. In this arrangement Muhammed was not a sovereign but a litigator, judging according to whichever law the parties wished to be tried. Under modern circumstances the litigation function will be taken over by special courts dealing with relations between communities and with legal issues between individuals belonging to different blocs (1992: 109).

Bulac sees the practice of Medina as an implementation of the verse revealed in Mecca reading "To you your religion, to me mine" (Kafirun, 6). The Medina Constitution was an unfolding of the vision revealed in Mecca as concrete social, legal and institutional arrangements" (1992: 105–106). On this model, political authority can not hold any official religious doctrine due to the normative plurality constitutive of the *ummah*. According to Islamic Public Law government is established by a contract on the basis of mutual consent. The state is not legitimized on divine or metaphysical grounds. It is merely a functional instrument established in order to perform common and indivisible services.

Constitutive Principles for a Modern Polity

Bulac does not propose to replicate the substantive content of the Medina Constitution under radically different modern circumstances. The argument focuses on fundamental concepts and procedures that depict unforced consent of contracting parties as the basis of legitimate political organization. By using these constitutive principles Bulac aims to extrapolate ground rules that can serve as references for today's society (1992: 110). Bulac argues that the Medina Constitution has a historical character, yet this fact is not relevant in terms of extrapolating from its constitutive principles, and identifies the basic features of the agreement reached in Medina as follows:

1. Constitutive principles of the Medina Constitution are twofold. First, a just and fair social arrangement aiming genuine peace and stability has to emerge out of a contract between different (religiously, legally, philosophically, politically etc. based) groups. Second, this social arrangement has to be founded upon participation, not domination.
2. By virtue of these principles, the agreement affirmed the fact of plurality and established a legally guaranteed framework for respecting diverging forms of life (1992: 108).
3. Bulac delineates parties to the general contract as natural or elected representatives of autonomous communities who will stipulate principles at the inter-community level. At the level of the general contract all communities will be represented on the basis of equality. The principles of the contract will be situated above individual legal systems of the communities and will be mutually binding. Issues upon which agreement cannot be reached will be left to internal legislation (1994: 14). In this way demands that are endemic to the legal system of one community will not be imposed on others.

Parties to the contact will be religiously, culturally, ethnically, politically or philosophically based legal communities. Each legal community will have religious, cultural and legal autonomy. That is, in religious life, legislation, juridical system, education, trade, culture, art, science and in daily affairs, communities will be what they are and will express themselves in self-defined cultural and legal standards. (1992: 109)

Autonomous legal communities are equal parties to the polity-founding contract and cannot demand that the state function according to principles derived from a particular religion or belief.

The Medina Constitution, with its objective rules, is above all religious and social blocs. That is, Muslims, Jews and Pagans cannot move out of its general framework. In this sense the Constitution that emerged out of mutual agreement is above the Quran, Tevrat, and established tradition. (1992: 109)

The suggested model has obvious similarities with the *millet* system of the Ottoman period. Yet it is significantly different as it is based on rejection of the *dhimmi* status which is at the foundation of the *millet* system. The traditional millet system was based on religious communities that were governed according to their internal legislation while political authority was legitimized with reference to Islam. The system was premised upon a hierarchical stratification in which Muslims (*millet-i hakime*) had higher status than non-Muslims (*millet-i mahkume*). In Bulac's proposal, Islamic reference for political organization is dismissed, and replaced by mutual agreement on the basis of equality. The general framework is not Islamic in the traditional hierarchical sense, but contractual with Islamic legitimacy on the Medina model.

The pluralistic vision of the social realm underlying the Medina Project is based on a gap Bulac posits between the divine will,[10] which is absolute, and the acquired knowledge of it, which is relative. Bulac's argument is as follows: the divine will reveals itself in the world of phenomena in a plurality of ways and there is a disparity between the divine essence of the revelation and the human acquisition of it:

> the realm of beings is not reflection of Allah but Allah's will and attributes (names). Its existence is derived, dependent, limited and with an end; it is relative. (1993c: 50)

The divine will is always the co-presence of all its elements. Therefore, the essence behind the complex appearance cannot be inferred from the knowledge of its worldly expressions, which is bound to be relative and partial (1993b: 41). Bulac calls for epistemological modesty due to the limited nature of human understanding:

> Ultimate knowledge belongs to Allah. Human knowledge is limited. Part cannot fully express the whole, neither can the imperfect represent the perfect! (1993c: 50)
> What is divine cannot be reduced to products of human effort. (1993b: 42)

Affirmation of the aforementioned epistemological constraint leads Bulac to welcome plurality of other paths and ways of life as well as the Quranic injunction to accept the freedom of others to follow the dictates of their conscience. Judgment of the religious paths individuals choose to take are left to the hereafter (1993b: 41).

Rather similar grounds are the reason why Bulac avows Islam's internal plurality both in terms of scriptural contentions and the diversity endemic to its lived tradition: Interpretations of the divine will are always plural and embedded in historical circumstances and collective ways of life. Any human understanding of the divine word depends on the society and cultural environment people inhabit, and, therefore, the "meaning" of the revelation will always exceed the human comprehension of it (1993b: 42). Just as the plural expressions of the divine will cannot be reified, the interpretations of the Quran and *sunnah* cannot be frozen either. For Bulac *ijtihad* is a reference to the divine knowledge but is not identical with the revelation itself. Ultimately, it is informed yet subjective opinion of the interpreter. There may exist as many different interpretations as the number of competent interpreters and all *ijtihad* is the outcome of exercising a legitimate right.

Ijtihad interprets the divine message. Yet being merely a human acquisition, every interpretation is the product of human cognitive effort that is bound by time, place and circumstances:

> There can be no single interpretation of the divine word. Islamic ideas and projects are interpretations of the first words and they reflect the trajectory of the historical experience of the *ummah*. (1993b: 42)

Bulac's proposal accommodates internal pluralism of Islam through enabling establishment of multiple Muslim communities. Muslims will have the opportunity to choose between living under secular laws or in communities implementing different versions of Islamic Law. Bulac acknowledges the diversity of belief and practice within Islam and basically supports the utilization of the inter-group model for intra-group relations. Thus, people adhering to different interpretations of Islam will be able to organize as separate blocs based on whichever foundation they choose (1993: 41).

Islam as a Religion of Community

The defining feature of Bulac's proposal, as a political project, appears to be abandoning of the political aim of an Islamic state, and disengaging the concern with salvation from the issue of statehood. According to Bulac there exist two kinds of duties Muslims have to fulfill regardless of the society they live in. First, leading a life according to the norms and obligations of Islam, including abiding by the rules of the Islamic Sharia. Second, communicating Islam to others (*teblig*). According to this reasoning, full realization of freedom of religion for Muslims does not necessitate an Islamic state. Instead, any social organization within which the two fundamental religious duties could be performed would be sufficient for Muslims to consider themselves "in power" in that particular society (1994: 11).

This argument is built on the proposition that Islam does not confer divine legitimacy upon political authority. There are no readily available models of Islamic political organization and institutional arrangements cannot be given closure based on revelation. The fundamental sources of Islam do not provide doctrinal material for a total socio-political project or a fixed model of political organization. Quranic references to *imamat, khalifat, hakimiya,* etc., neither provide substantive ideas nor amount to a model. Furthermore, there is almost a total silence in the Quran about rules of succession and specific institutional arrangements. Bulac maintains that political authority according to Islam is "not a sacralized instance but a mode of organizing the coexistence of Muslims with each other and with non-Muslims in a way congenial to Islamic principles" (1994: 15). Bulac maintains that Islam provides no legal and institutional closure, and its basic tenets can be implemented in a variety of institutional settings. Indeed, the normative spirit of Islam can only be sustained by different arrangements under different circumstances (1994: 15). In this respect Bulac prefers to talk about the state of a Muslim society instead of an Islamic state.

Bulac portrays the dimension of historicity and change with reference to a process of "semantic intervention," through which diverging civilizational elements, modes of thinking and ways of life are appropriated and reconstructed according to constitutive principles of Islam. Accordingly, the substantial content of these forms are created by means of a process where normative principles interact with concrete reality through activities of Muslims:

> Many examples of such process were observed in the Muslim history. Indeed the great civilizations of Umayyads, Abbasids and Ottomans were created as outcome of such interaction. Although these structures were not pure embodiments of the divine revelation, they were not completely independent of the ethos of the Quran. This legacy is not the divine will itself, but what the *ummah* made of it according to the extent of its *taqwa*[11] and ability. (1992: 108)

It is in this sense that Bulac declares Islam a religion of community and insists that continuity of genuine Muslim belief and practice resides in the *ummah*, which embodies diverging interpretations and practices. Quest for a single and conclusive reading would easily be hostage to political authority aiming to promote a particular Islamic interpretation in its own name. There cannot be a single methodology, which would legitimately bring out unity of interpretation. Human acquisitions of the divine will cannot be monopolized by an elite or be placed at the disposal of political authority: Although there exists an "absolute truth" it is located out of the reach of any worldly authority (1993b: 42). Bulac maintains that this fact of "transcendence" enables the Muslim community to "resist against worldly authorities, including Islamic states, which attempt to instrumentalize Islam as official ideology in order to legitimize political power" (1993b: 42).

According to Bulac, the Medina project is a plausible reading under conditions of modern plurality. Yet the contemporary relevance of the Constitution is not taken to imply that arrangements belonging to premodern times were erroneous interpretations. Bulac depicts the Medina model and the *dhimmi* arrangement as plausible readings under different historical circumstances. The Medina model, too, is not accepted as *the* correct interpretation or a trans-historically applicable model giving closure to Islamic political thought.

In this context, Bulac introduces a distinction between two traditions he alleges to have run parallel throughout Islamic history. The first lineage is the Islam of the state, which sacralized political authority. The second trajectory is that the Islamic scholarship and the lived tradition of the Muslim community which remained beyond the boundaries of the administratively incorporated religious establishment. Bulac defines these traditions as the "official" and "civilian" strains of Islam, respectively. On this classification, what is commonly named "political Islamism" falls into the first category. Bulac claims that official Islam is basically locked in the framework of modernity, and aims Islamization of modern political institutions.

The point raised by Bulac represents a recent development in the way Muslims reflect upon the status of political authority in Islam. The majority of Islamist movements emerging in the 1980s took over, even intensified, the state-centered legacy of Turkish political culture. The primary target of mobilizational Islam came to be the state. This dominant position entailed a critique of the direction of state intervention in society and religion, without problematizing the intervention itself. Their political vision can be summarized as gaining political power in order to employ the state apparatus for the pursuit of an Islamic social project.

In contrast, Bulac underlines the potential of "civilian" Islam for transcending this framework and for generating an alternative political organization. The essence of this potential is defined as the diversity of belief and practice characterizing *ummah*. Bulac adopts a critical attitude against state domination of religion as well as the hold of an official interpretation over the dynamics and plurality endemic to the lived tradition. In this sense, Medina project is also a counter proposal to monopolization of Islam in the form of a state creed by an Islamic nation-state. On this particular point, Bulac seems to be in keeping with the traditional skepticism of the Sunni *ulama* towards political authority—in a fashion aggravated by cognizance of the unprecedented intervention capacity at the disposal of the modern state apparatus.

Social Contract and Forms of Life

According to the constitutive principles of the Medina Project, political authority cannot adopt any comprehensive religious doctrine. The state will be organized around a commitment to provide indivisible public services and to uphold the principles of the polity-founding contract. Yet the outlined

Islamic conception of justice is not purely procedural. It defines what is permissible and what is not through a commitment to the substantive values of basic rights. Bulac re-appropriates a classical Islamic scheme with widespread contemporary adaptation and categorizes rights as:

1. Rights of Allah, *hukukullah:* Claims of Allah on the individual, which are belief, worship and submission.
2. Rights of the self, *hukukunnefs:* Claims of individuals on themselves as the expression of the respect we owe to ourselves.
3. Rights of human beings, *hukukunnas* or *hukuku'l ibad:* Claims of fellow human beings on the individual (1993: 154).

This scheme, although presented in response to human rights questions, is indeed a classification of rights and duties in a broader sense, including categories with no equivalents in the internationally accepted usage. The category of *hukukullah* (rights of Allah) belongs to the realm of religious commitment and constitutes obligations towards Allah. I believe it is possible to consider *hukukunnefs* (rights of the self) in conjunction with this first category since it does not establish relationships between individuals or collective actors. Rights of the self simply suggest a pious mode of behaviour and avert the individual from conduct such as suicide and masochism. As indicated by the respective addressees of each category, *hukukunnas* (human rights) is the only set of rights that creates a mutual relationship between human beings. *Hukukunnas* establish the specific duties of the individual towards others whose observance, in turn, safeguards the rights and freedoms of the individual herself. In this fashion the individual indirectly becomes the recipient of rights as the beneficiary of the duties of others.

Bulac takes the category of *hukukunnas* as a point of reference when dealing with human rights questions. Accordingly, *hukukunnas,* in the narrower sense of the term, correspond to "birth-given natural rights that are divine in origin." These rights do not emerge as a result of contract between human beings but are products of God's divine benevolence. It is due to their divine origin that birth-given rights are accepted as universal, inviolable and inalienable. These are the rights every individual is born with (*fitri haklar*) and which are held solely by virtue of being human (1993: 154). They can neither be relativized with regard to membership in a certain religious community or citizenship, nor can they be denied or abrogated due to these criteria.

Bulac presents the essence of *hukukunnas* as the five entitlements for whose protection the Islamic body of law is generated and refers to the exegetic work of the classical Muslim thinker Ghazali (d. 1111) to give a basic definition (1993: 154). Ghazali lists these fundamental rights as the protection of life, religion, soul and intellect, progeny, and property. The polity-founding social contract, and political authority legitimate on Islamic terms in general, will have to remain within boundaries set by basic rights. Muslims will be committed to uphold the rights put forward in this scheme as a religious duty (1993: 154). These rights, therefore, will be safeguarded at the level of the broader scheme by mandatory institutions created by agreement among communities. In this sense protection of birth-given rights constitutes the minimum foundation for the legitimacy of basic political contracts entered not only by Muslims but also by non-Muslims. Consequently, not all forms of life can be seen as equally deserving of respect. The polity-founding contract cannot destroy or abolish birth-given rights and consequently, some conceptions of the good will not be admissible in the framework defined as such.

The political morality advocated is not based on uniformity at the level *sharia* but on a mutually binding mode of conduct among autonomous legal communities. Bulac refers to the verse reading "Had Allah pleased, He would have made you one nation but [He wanted] to test you concerning what He gave to you."[12] Relations between human beings are to be organised around the dictates of "being forward in doing good deeds," which lies beyond the specifics of any religion or belief:

> According to the Islamic doctrine, every religion, tradition and culture has its own concept of wisdom, virtue and justice. Islam does not invite humanity to unite under a common religion—in the sense of sharia and law—but to a common moral tradition. It is certainly desirable that everyone finds salvation through Islam. Yet both history and the experience of our times show that this is not a realistic expectation (Yusuf, 106). In either case this is not a goal to be reached by compulsion since compulsion is contrary to the will of Allah and the wisdom of creation (Morde, 48). (1993: 154)

In this manner Bulac hints affirmation of a political morality that brackets issues of religion or faith.

It seems possible to categorize the rights that have, so far, become apparent within the proposed social arrangement as follows:

1. Birth-given rights every individual is entitled to regardless of the community she or he belongs
2. Contract-based rights:
   a) Rights that are established by negotiation and mutual consensus between communities.
   b) Rights provided within individual legal systems of communities that are declared in advance and agreed upon entry into the community—and that can, presumably, be extended and improved upon from that point onwards.

We can assume that individuals will choose to live in a community that would best cater for their conception of the good. In this framework it is likely that some communities will be organized according to liberal democratic principles. But some will choose to found their public lives on dictates of various comprehensive doctrines. Choosing to live in one of the latter communities will also mean subscribing to a series of obligations emanating from a particular comprehensive outlook. To put it in a different way, through her voluntary agreement the individual will be living in a community, which, though respecting basic freedoms, will offer a different set of rights and duties in certain respects.

The Medina project allows for establishment of blocs guaranteeing rights and freedoms akin to liberal democracies. Communities organized around more communitarian visions too are catered for. The way the model Muslim community[13] is dealt with constitutes a good case for the latter, though we are presented with the most general contours alone.

The model Muslim community is envisioned in terms of a harmony of complementary interests and mutual correspondence of expectations. Bulac posits complete concurrence between the community and the individual, and rests assured that the individual will freely submit to her religious duties or otherwise she would not have chosen to be there in the first place, and because at all times she retains the right to leave. The model Muslim community is not designed to accommodate internal conflict and differences. To the contrary it tends to purify itself through constant projection of difference as its exterior by encouraging divergent interpretations of Islam to organize as separate communities. Individuals' conception of rights and freedoms cannot be completely divorced from the meanings and practices within their community. Once the internal plurality of a group is reduced, lifting principles organizing public life above the conflicting contents of comprehensive doctrines will no longer be required. In a morally homogenous community, it will, in principle, be reasonable to take a particular conception of the good as the organizing principle of compulsory institutions.

Bulac's argument minimizes the distance between regime types that can be implemented within the limits of the nation-state and extends towards a generic critique of the framework itself. His position is premised on the idea that liberal democracy is a regime based on a comprehensive doctrine pretending to be in neutral distance towards diverging religions and worldviews.[14] Bulac's vision of a fair political arrangement is one where the state has much less intervention capacity—with minimum shared institutions and procedures—and is based on a thinner yet truly neutral normative ground. The state would be required to withdraw from as many areas of life as possible, and the greater part of its current functions would be taken over by individual communities.

Conceived along these lines, the ground rules of the Medina project inadvertently confer critical significance upon two fundamental possibilities that should be kept open for everyone, thus, guaranteed at the level of the general contract. First, the right to change communities and second, when it takes the form of abandoning a religiously based community in favor of another one or a secular group, the freedom of apostasy. Bulac aims to strengthen "civil society" against the state and, by the same token, empower communities vis-a-vis the individual. The Medina project has the potential to culminate in a conception of community that is morally homogeneous. Communities are granted further power through a partial takeover of the functions that are traditionally in the jurisdiction of the modern state. The right to leave one's community constitutes a certain amount of leeway for protecting fundamental rights in the face of strengthened communities under the circumstances of the ideal model. It is also of vital importance in case of any authoritarian deterioration away from the declared principles.

However, it is important to note that even when these freedoms are provided for, the principle of free choice and free exit of legal communities is likely to create certain illusions. Surely, already existing ascriptive communities will not overnight give way to voluntary associations. The fallacy of underestimating the weight of tradition, communal values and attachments will not go without consequences in terms of safeguarding liberties. The general reasoning of the Medina Project must therefore bracket the questions of personal costs of free affirmation and change of communities, and whether it will appear as a realistic option to the individual. Bulac offers a communitarian theory according to which the individual is firmly located in her social group and community within which she acquires her identity. Paradoxically enough, he ends up with a rather demanding concept of individual autonomy. The argument assumes an autonomous agency that can lift herself up her social identities, and, at will, moves among legal communities.

The Medina Project opens up the possibility that communities organize around their deeply held convictions without modifying the broader framework[15] according to their specific demands. Under the delineated scheme, any failure to safeguard all the aspects substantiating basic rights and freedoms by the inter-community contract would delegate it to internal legislation of individual communities. At this level the principle of legal autonomy, in all likelihood, will generate problems akin to those associated with sovereignty and non-intervention in a nation-state based world order.

Bulac conceives social contract in an actual historical sense and not as a hypothetical notion or an "exploratory devise."[16] In a historical contract, deliberations will take place in full knowledge of the position and strength of the parties represented. In this fashion, effects of political bargaining and taking advantage of superior power will re-emerge since stipulations will not be abstracted from contingencies of the deliberating parties. Another related problem is the fact that the ground rules of the Medina project enable establishment of groups that are relatively small in terms of membership. A large number of deliberating parties representing numerous small communities may render unanimous agreement at the level of the general contract a practical impossibility. Therefore, Bulac's persistent opposition to the majority principle may have to lead to a pragmatic bowing to the logic of what is practically achievable.

At this point it should be mentioned that principles of representation as well as other details relevant to implementation (such as parameters of representation, for instance with respect to population) are not specified. Ultimately any suggestions on procedures remain vague. On Bulac's part not elaborating the final contours of a total design is a considered position. Bulac states his purpose as proposing the basics of the alternative project in order to guarantee that the outcome is the joint product of all participants. The idea is starting from a few initial premises and constructing along the way through agreement of the parties involved. What is proposed at this level is not meant to be a fully developed model or an institutional blueprint.

Concluding Remarks

According to Bulac a genuinely pluralist society is one that accommodates more than one legal system. On this basis he proposed an alternative organizational principle which is considered to be an improvement upon the nation-state model, provided that it is adequately elaborated and properly institutionalized.

The Medina project relies upon the moral significance of equality of all human beings in terms of their capacity to have a conception of what is valuable in life. Bulac's most fundamental reference is the Quranic declaration "There is no compulsion in religion; true guidance has become distinct from error."[17] This pronouncement is regarded as the canonical statement prohibiting coercion in matters of religion and faith, upholding Islam as a religion of *teblig* (1993c: 53). The logic of the argument is based on an appreciation of the moral significance of equality. More specifically, equality is endorsed in two senses. First, in terms of the equal worth and moral capability of every individual for affirming or rejecting faith and related ways of life. In the second step, the idea of equality is transferred from the level of the human individual to the level of individual communities. Admissible ways of life embedded in legal communities are granted equal recognition and their representatives are situated with equal standing.

Bulac displays an overarching concern with maintaining the plurality and the richness of the lived tradition of Islam as well as more scriptural aspects of it. This sensitivity towards diversity of Islamic doctrines is, in turn, translated into the language of acknowledging normative plurality in a broader sense. In the case of the model Muslim bloc, Bulac envisions a correspondence of religious community and the body politic. This community is, in turn, placed in the larger political framework of the state, which will be reduced to mainly executive and administrative functions.

By and large, the Medina Project stands for limiting state intervention into the religious life of communities and supporting an institutional framework for diverging ways of life to flourish by producing principled normative arguments that though rooted in Islamic sources can be shared across religious, political, and other normative divides.

Notes

1. In 1982 with an initiative from the military, religious instruction was made part of the required curriculum in all primary and secondary schools—except schools of religious minorities. Obligatory religious instruction took a confessional attitude, and was synonymous with teaching Sunni Islam and instructing religious practice.

The number of schools to train prayer leaders and preachers (the *Imam Hatip* schools) increased sharply from 258 to 350 during the three-year tenure of the armed forces. The number of students attending those schools rose dramatically to 270,000. Along with the *Imam-Hatip* schools there has also been an expansion in the lower grade Quranic schools. Before the coup of 1980 there were 2,610 such schools; by 1989 the number had grown to 4,715 (Ahmad, 1994: 21–221).

2. A similar yet not identical vision of plural legal systems was included in the program of the *Refah* (Welfare) Party and was defended by the party leader Erbakan in his public speeches. *Refah*'s programmatic commitment to plural legal systems constituted a factor for dissolution of the party by the Constitutional Court (16 January 1998) and was mentioned among reasons offered for the affirming judgement of the European Court of Human Rights (31 July 2001).

3. Bulac gives a brief account of how the Medina Constitution came to the attention of students of Islam. Wellhausen was the first Western scholar who drew attention to the Medina Constitution. After the publication of his book "Skizzen und Vorarbeiten" 1899 several researchers including Grimme, Caetani, Buhl, Wensinck, Korehl, Ranke, Müller and Guillaume showed interest in the topic and there followed a substantial amount of publicity about the Constitution. It was Muhammed Hamidullah who revived the discussions on the Medina Constitution in the Muslim world, providing detailed information about the document itself as well as the historical and social circumstances surrounding its coming into existence (Bulac 1992: 103).

4. Translation of the verse is provided by Watt.

5. Hamidullah gives the numbers as 1,000 Muslims and 10,000 non-Muslims (Hamidullah 1994: 89).

6. Of course it also seems understandable that the Arab tribes having yearned for peace for such a long time agreed to sign an agreement under the leadership of Muhammad. But Hamidullah does not consider this answer as satisfactory.

7. This historical claim provoked controversies within Islamist circles in Turkey. Without going into these critiques I would like to give a summary of the matter of historical validation as I perceive it:

While there seems to be a general consensus on the authenticity of the document, there is uncertainty about its date. The present form of the Constitution consists of two documents. Watt claims that the Constitution might have taken its present form at a much later date, more precisely after 627 when three main Jewish clans were liquidated (Watt 1961: 93–94). If this is the case, it would mean that Jews were not accepted as equals, neither did they freely consent to be a part of the contract. Instead, they were coerced to participate since they have already lost their autonomy after the war of Badr.

Bulac seems to totally disregard the conclusions of Hamidullah (whom he declares as the primary reference for his work) regarding the matter, which happens to fall in line with aforementioned statement of Watt. Bulac basically follows the arguments of Wensinck that supports the version of contract between equals (Ege 1993: 27).

Although the historical support is significant in terms of the internal consistency of the initiative, lack of agreement on historical data does not prevent the discussion of the implications this particular interpretation brings. For the purposes of this study, the significance of the Medina Constitution does not derive from validation of the historical argument but from the fact that it is interpreted in a specific way in order to set foundations for a novel Islamic project. I will concentrate my discussion on the possible conclusions that may be drawn from this contemporary re-appropriation.

8. Followers understood as Jews and pagan Arabs.

9. See note 7 above.

10. Expressing itself in the realm of beings as well as through revelation.

11. *Taqwa*: keen spiritual and moral consciousness and motivation.

12. (Al-Maida/5, 48).

13. The model Muslim community does not refer to the exemplary character of their particular design but simply indicates that I am dealing with a particular Islamic community conceived by Bulac.

14. Bulac argues that democracy should be regarded as a religion and *sharia'* (s. 40, 59).

15. The broader framework of the state and other mandatory institutions and practices at the level of the general contract.

16. Kymlicka defines social contract as "a device for testing out the implications of certain moral premises concerning people's moral equality" (Kymlicka 1990: 60).

17. Al-Baqara/2, 258.

References

Ahmad, F. (1994) The *Making of Modern Turkey,* London: Routledge

Bulac, A. (1992) "Medine Vesikasi Uzerine Genel Bilgiler," *Birikim,* no:38/39, 102–112

———. (1992b) *Din ve Modernizm,* Istanbul: Beyan Yayinlari

(1)*Islam ve Fanatizm,* Istanbul: Beyan Yayinlari

———. (1993b) "Medine Vesikasi Uzerine Tartismalar I," *Birikim,* no:47, 40–46

———. (1993c) "Medine Vesikasi Uzerine Tartismalar II," *Birikim,* no:48, 48–58

(2)"Birarada Yasamanin Mumkun Projesi: Medine Vesikasi," *Bilgi ve Hikmet,* no:5, 3–15

Ege, R. (1993) "Medine Vesikasi mi, Hukuk Devleti mi?," *Birikim,* no:47, 21–39

Hamidullah, M. (1993) *Islam Peygamberi,* Istanbul: Irfan Yayin

Hamidullah, M. (1994) *Islam Tarihine Giris,* Istanbul: Beyan Yayinlari

The Qur'an, translation Fakhry, M. (1997), Lebanon: Garnet Publishing

Watt, W. M. (1956) *Muhammad at Medina,* London: Oxford at the Clarendon Press

Watt, W. M. (1961) *Muhammad: Prophet and Statesman,* London: Oxford University Press

6

Islamic Thought between Formal Conservatism and Indigenous Liberalism: Lessons from the Sudanese Heritage

Mahgoub El-Tigani Mahmoud and Carolyn Fluehr-Lobban

Unlike the cultural and religious setting of the western industrialized societies, Muslim societies are strongly influenced by *Shari'a* law as a crystallized form of Islamic jurisprudence, as well as Sufi sects as a prominent component of popular Islam. In this study, our interest is centered on the impact of religious thought on a few issues of modernity and development in the Sudan. To clarify these aspects, a brief background sheds light on the popular Sudanese Sufi tradition as a historical constituent of the Muslim community of Sudan. Another section discusses the doctrine of Al-Mawardi as a classical Arab Muslim jurist whose political doctrine continues to influence conservative Muslim thought. The concluding sections analyze the ideas of Hassan Al-Turabi, Sadiq Al-Mahdi, and Mahmoud Mohamed Taha that played a significant role in the contemporary public life of Sudan.

By analyzing the ideas of these thinkers, we aim to clarify the agreement or disagreement between their thought as Muslim leaders. To what extent have their ideas developed the classical schools of *Shari'a* law? What solutions did they offer to modernize the country? In what way did the classical Arab Islamic thought influence their thought versus the Sufi popular tradition? These and other critical questions will be adequately discussed in the subsequent sections.

Al-Mawardi: A Classical Arab Islamic Model

Al-Shaikh Al-Iman Abu Al-Hassan Al-Mawardi (born 974 D.C.) is an orthodox Muslim jurist who authored a significant book on Al-Ahkam Al-Sultaniya wa Al-Willayat Al-Deeniya [State Rules and Religious Governorates]. Many conservative Muslim groups consider Al-Ahkam as a legitimizing text for the Muslim striving to rule Muslim societies by Islamic jurisprudence. Al-Mawardi believed that "the Caliphate is founded on succession of the Prophet for the tasks of safeguarding religion and running the worldly affairs." The actual performance of Muslim Caliphs, however, suggests that the *Shari'a* teaching on governance that dictate the commitment of Muslim rulers to God-fearing justice have not been implemented for the most part. Instead, the centralized authority of the Caliphs did not allow the occurrence of any viable system of check and balance between the ruling group and the vast majority of the population who were often compelled to change their rulers by force (Al-Marqrizi).

Mawardi spoke of several conditions for a Muslim to be eligible for the Caliphate's prominent position. As he put it "There are seven conditions, chief of which is justice with all its general terms. Another condition is the knowledge that is pertinent to the *Ijtihad* [scholary work] of making judgments. The other conditions include good health, sound opinion to maintain the interests of people, bravery to protect religion from enemies, and affiliation with Quraish the tribe of the Prophet."

It was extremely difficult to find a successor for the succeeding Caliphs since the death of the Prophet, whether by a direct selection of the *Ahl Al-Aqd wa Al-Hal* [the learned ones entrusted with the task of leading and guiding society] or by the *Shura* [consultation] principle. Thereafter, the conditions of Muslim societies have consistently changed over time due to the forces of urbanization, migration, and colonialism. The Muslim population experienced significant transformations in the social structure, political economy, and State bureaucracy. The discrepancy between modern forms of development administration, individual lifestyles, women's rights, and religious freedom on one hand and the classical interpretation of Islamic *Shari'a* Law further increased for a number of reasons. The reasons include education and the entry of women in the modern labor force, the failure of Muslim conservative groups to insure individual freedoms and human rights, and the increasing awareness in modern societies of the need to enjoy equal citizenship rights, regardless of sex and gender relations or the ethnic, religious, or politic-economic status.

The Sufi Tradition of Sudanese Popular Islam

The cultural heritage of the Sudanese Muslim communities was largely reflective of the multi-ethnic and cultural diversity of the country more than any strict adherence to the Arab-Islamic models of which Al-Mawardi clearly adopts a Quraish-descent Caliph to rule Muslim societies—which is virtually impossible in contemporary societies. Up to the establishment of the Abdallab and the Funj Muslim dynasties that succeeded the Christian kingdoms of Sudan the spreading of Islam was rather nominal under the direct influence of Bedouins and traders who were not highly knowledgeable of Islamic jurisprudence. The Sufi leaders like Qulam-Allah ben 'Ayid and Hama Abu Dannana later on increased the dissemination of *Shari'a* law in the country (Hassan, 1974: 3–5).

When the Funj consolidated their rule, they encouraged many jurists to teach Islam as a different faith from the Sudanese indigenous habits or Christian customs. The absence of *Ijtihad* [scholarly work] from the Muslim world at that time, however, helped the Sufi spiritual groups, rather than the formal *Shari'a* judges or jurists, to prevail as a major feature of the Sudanese Muslim culture, affirms Hassan (Ibid: 10).

The pioneering Sufi leaders taught the principles of Islam in a simple way by committing their disciples to a special moral and worshipping practice with a specific recitation. The Sufi leaders observed a life of austerity, piety, and spiritual influence. The disciples and other supporters believed in the miraculous actions and the blessing nature of the Sufi as a *Walli* [saint] who must be strictly obeyed.

These Muslim Shaikhs became a great spiritual force protecting the poor and other powerless groups from the injustice of ruling families. Most of the Sufi leaders, however, were not strictly committed to the formal rules of Islamic jurisprudence with respect to marriage relations, women's status or rights in inheritance, etc. These situations helped to mix simple Sufi teachings, rather than *Shari'a* jurisprudence, with many cultural elements of mythology and folklore, as well as superstition and lethargy.

There is not yet adequate research on this area. And yet, many anthropological studies indicate the continuity of African cultures in the country as they creatively accommodated the new Islamic faith (see for example, Adams, 1978; Fluehr-Lobban, 1984; Fruzzetti and Ostor, 1990).

In the Sudan today, the increasing consciousness of the Sudanese non-Arab non-Muslim population about the African heritage in the issues of national identification will motivate the need for anthropological and sociological research on the unique role that the Sudanese African cultures played in shaping the Muslim tradition of the country and the vital recognition of the diversity of Sudan in all spheres of the political, social, and religious life.

It is timely to affirm the fact that the Funj of the Muslim medieval kingdoms of Sudan might well have been the Shulluk of southern Sudan, the Ingessana and Nuba of central Sudan might well have been the norther Nubians who ruled both Egypt and Sudan in ancient times, and the other Nilotic groups of the Dinka, Nuer, and Anwak might well have been the same "Ethiopian" or

"Nubian" Cushite of Axom and Nubia, as well as the west African groups whose cultures still influence large regions of the contemporary Sudan.

The Arabs and the Arab Muslim jurisprudence and culture have undoubtedly impacted the social and political life of Sudan for long centuries. But the African cultures and indigenous creativity have equally, if not more, adapted the Arab culture and jurisprudence to the Sudanese African society and state. It is therefore expedient to refer to Sudan Muslims as a variety of Muslim communities and ideologies of which the African version of the Sufi tradition that has been widely spreading across the Sahara since the Mali and Berber empires is most influential. Hassan (Ibid: 12) finds that the kings and Sultans equally believed in the *awliya* [saints]. They would not initiate any important task without their advice, as in the case of Idris wad Al-Arbab with the Abdalab leader Ageeb and King Badi of the Funj. With this prestigious status, the Sufi leaders collaborated closely with the ruling groups at the same time they maintained stable social and religious relations with the people that largely believed in their spiritual powers. This medieval portrayal of Sudanese political life contradicts the Mawardi configuration of *Shari'a* political structures at length.

In his famous book *Al-Tabaqat*, Mohamed Al-Nour ibn Daif-Allah documented with rich information the biographies of medieval Sudan Sufi leaders. These included Khugali ben Abdel-Rahman ben Ibrahim, the *Walli* of the Tuti Island who was taught by Aisha the jurist, daughter of Al-Gaddal Mohamed ben Ibrahim Al-Farddi, as well as the renowned Sufi, Al-Shaikh Idris wad Al-Arbab. Khugali was a most dignified leader that stayed away from the ruling class, not even corresponding with them, but asking them to respect the rights of the poor.

These accounts of the Sudanese early Islam indicate the unique liberalism of the Sudanese community under flexible teachings of the Sufi tradition, rather than a dogmatic version of formal jurisprudence as was the case in many other Muslim societies. Throughout the medieval times, the Sufi tradition helped to separate between the spiritual leadership of society and the authority of State managers.

Except the Mahdiya *Shari'a*-oriented rule of the Sudan (1885–1898), the succeeding rulers of the country, including the earlier Turkish-Egyptian rule (1821–1885), did not reduce the Sufi influence. It was possible for the Muslim Sudanese in the medieval times up to the Turkish-Egyptian rule and the aftermath to incorporate many elements of African cultures and the Christian faith into the Muslim Sufi tradition.

The *Walli* would continue to assume the privileges, high-esteem, and miraculous ability of the Nubian Christian saints to protect the poor from injustices of the ruling elite, facilitate the difficulties of life, and develop special economic relations with the Bedouins and peasants within the subsistence economy of the time.

The British administration encouraged the Sufi influence once again for political reason: to avoid the engagement of Islamic Jihad groups in politics of the State. The British acknowledged the religious and social influence of the Khatmiya Sufi sect led by Al-Merghani family and the Ansar religious group of the Al-Mahdi family, in addition to the other smaller sects all over the country.

In recent times, however, the emergence and the growth of modern Sudanese groups, namely the Umma Party, the Democratic Unionist Party, Muslim Brotherhood, and the Republican Brothers brought to life a conflict between the Sufi popular Islam and the formal tradition of Islamic jurisprudence, as well as the issue of separating State management from the political control of religious groups.

To analyze the complexities ensuing in these conflicting domains, the thought of Hassan Al-Turabi, leader of the Muslim Brotherhood, Sadiq Al-Mahdi, leader of the Umma Party, and Mahmoud Mohamed Taha, founder and leader of the Republican Brothers, will be discussed in some detail.

Hassan Al-Turabi: Religious Revival or Shari'a Survival

Hassan Al-Turabi (Tagdeed, 1980: 7) emphasizes the need to connect jurisprudence consistently with the reality of contemporary life "to provide for practical methods to rule society, administer the economy, and organize the public life to guide the behavior of the individual Muslim in modern society." The start of Islamic *Da'wa* [mission] was initiated by "theoretical generalizations" to stabilize the origins and fundamental premises of religion. This task has not been adequately apprehended by the perception of society at that time. The Movement of Islam was subsequently advanced to employ "branches" of the emerging jurisprudence in order to find practical solutions for the changing realities of life.

A complete rehabilitation of Islamic jurisprudence is at the top of the agenda for the Movement of revitalizing *Shari'a* law. The reason is that, "the kind of jurisprudence that the Movement possessed is not substantial for the needs of the *Da'wa* or those beholding it whatsoever induction or deduction they might creatively reach on its basis" (Tagdid, 1980: 7–8). As Turabi explains, "Some postulates of the rules that once represented the concept of righteousness in accordance with the criteria of religion a thousand years ago are no more fulfilling to the domain of religion today. They would not accomplish the objectives in demand because the means have also changed and the prerequisites of life have been largely developed. Hence, the results that ensue in the applications of a certain rule in its earlier form [in modern time] are completely out of context" (Tagdid, Ibid.).

Hassan Al-Turabi mentions that the alternative is "to make a new discipline that shall amalgamate the spiritual knowledge received in written or literal forms [i.e., the *Qur'an*, the holy book of Islam, and the revealed *Sunna*, the deeds and sayings of the Prophet with the human sciences that are daily innovated and integrated by both experimentation and vision. With this united science, we would be renewing our knowledge on religion and the requirements it conferred upon our recent life, stage by stage" (Tagdid, Ibid.).

Despite this open invitation to amalgamate scriptural knowledge with the sciences and experiences of the human mind, it is not clear what proportions or forms the proposed amalgam would take. It is not apparent that Turabi is calling for a superimposition of any of the two components of the holy knowledge and the human science over one another. Actually Turabi assumes the existence of an Islamic society without defining its features or conditions. "[The Islamic society]," as Turabi says, "is held together by fixations of unity and collective methods of decision making. These unifying methods are attributed to the Principle of *Shura* [consultation] that gathers together the partners in conflict as well as the Principle of *Ijma'* [consensus] that represents the authority of the Muslim public" (Tagdid, Ibid. 10). He does not, however, explain how the *Shura* [consultation] would be managed on a national level. Nor does he specify the proceedings envisaged in the process of *Shura* or that of Ijma'. He doesn't show whether these principles conform or not to the modern parliamentary systems of representation. The proposed "amalgamated science" requires a qualified caliber to derive from all these sources of knowledge the points of agreement between the classical jurisprudence, the scriptural knowledge, and the human sciences that is most concerned with the requisites of the contemporary life. The idea is that, "Life is not a stagnant reality. Nor is the religiosity or the kind of problems dealt with by the early jurists the only form of Islam," affirms Turabi. "The Muslims must change their [present] forms of life to handle these challenges with the origins of Muslim beliefs and the *Shari'a* Law as the sole Muslim law," Turabi further asserts (Tagdid, Ibid. 10–11). A major problem remains unsolved: the "most appropriate form of Islamic life" and "the form of religiosity" as adhered to by the early Muslims, as Turabi seems to suggest. Most important, the needs of contemporary Muslims are not easily satisfied by many rules of the classical *Shari'a* law.

Turabi asserts that, "When Islam was embracing the whole life [in early Muslim communities], the public economic and political practices were committed to religion. This [public commitment] activated the fundamental rules that were suitable to that peculiar life. The jurists were not tackling, for the most part, problems of the public life. Thus the public life evolved away from them . . . the fundamentals of jurisprudence moved to a concern with rituals, marriage, and divorce" (Tagdid, 1980: 15).

"The questions of *Al-Siyasa Al-Shari'ya Al-Kuliya* [i.e., the comprehensive legal policy, how a society's life would be run as a whole] were issues the *Awliya Al-Umur* [responsible leaders] were not interested in. These included the processes of production, distribution, importation, exportation, and the treatment of a high cost of living or depressing it. Likewise, the questions of the public economy and political conditions were equally ignored" (Tagdid, 1980: 14–15).

The dispute is precisely centered on the historical stage at which "Islam was overwhelmingly influential." Is this stage relevant to the State of Medina, that of the Prophet with the light of revelations overshadowing the Muslim community for generations, or does the period in question contain other succeeding times, irrespective of the State of Medina? What then are the characteristics of such a period?

If these contradictory statements are not tautological as well, where is the determining variable, which alone, or in interaction with other influential factors, ensures a whole embracing of an Islamic life—one activated by "suitable" fundamental rules yet consonant with modernity? Where and how would Muslims set the limits to sort out the kind of jurisprudence Turabi theorizes for their private and public life? Who are the jurists entrusted with scholastic authority to decide upon these assertions when Turabi claims that the most authenticated version of Islamic jurisprudence is "redundant" in some ways and "inadequate" for the present time? The alternative suggested by Turabi to classical jurisprudence is tautological since it has adopted the same major elements of that jurisprudence, albeit an ambiguous reference is made to "a life commitment that wholly embraces Islam." However, he has not explained the nature of that commitment or the legal, social, and political obligations it bears on Muslims today. The biggest problem of Turabi's thought should be linked to his contempt of the Sufi indigenous tradition and his tendency to impose individual configuration of Islamic jurisprudence on the collective life of people regardless of their heritage and cultures.

This critique does not mean that the idea of establishing a new Islamic thought is not important. On the contrary, it is an idea that echoes many of the preceding claims of many Islamic revivalists such as Jamaluddin Al-Afghani and the Imam Mohamed Abdu. Turabi fails to present a detailed program for the social and religious change anticipated in Sudan by his theological model.

His thesis suffers a serious lack of definitions, clarity of concepts, and coherency. This failure might partially explain Turabi's active involvement in the coup of June 30, 1989, to exercise de facto governance, in the words of Ali Abd-Allah Abbas, President of Sudanese state and society, via an authoritarian model of a religious state.

Sadiq Al-Mahdi: The Modernity of a Traditional Majority

It may be true that Sadiq Al-Mahdi, as a Sudanese Islamic thinker, made a practical contribution in his works to elaborate on the possibility of applying the broad theoretical assumptions of the Turabi model. Sadiq's intention seems to hinge on the establishment of "a new amalgamated science" to undertake a modern and scientific rehabilitation for the Muslim world today. In *Al-'Uqobat Al-Shar'iya wa Mawqi'a min Al-Nizam Al-Ijtimai Al-Islami* [Shari'a Punishments and Their Position in the Islamic Social System], Al-Mahdi writes explicitly that, "The most enlightened picture of Islamic thought is the earliest one, the oldest stage of Islamic thought that was most lively and offering, a state at which Muslims exemplified a society of mercy, justice, and forgiveness. Islamic thought was most persuasive to the whole universe in terms of reform, success, freedom, vividness, and creativity" ('Uqobat, Undated: 123).

This is the viewpoint that is completely contrary to the Turabi assessment of the earliest era of Islam as one that was restrictive to the pioneer Muslims by limitations of jurist rules. Sadiq's evaluation is quite consonant with a number of Islamic revivalists, such as Ibn Taymiyah and Mohamed Ahmed ben Abd-Allah, the Grand Mahdi, his own great grandfather, both of whom developed a revivalist thought upon that of the earliest Muslims.

On the need for a "revision of the classical jurisprudence," Sadiq phrases "the Islamic vigilance," since the early 1980s to serve as an emblem for his religious scheme (see *Al-Sahwa Al-Islamiya wa Mustaqbal Al-Da'wa* [Islamic Vigilance and the Future of Islamic Call], issued by the Ansar Students' Movement, 1981).

Sadiq Al-Mahdi rejects the extremism of right-wing groups and the secularism of left-wing parties. He is equally resentful of the rashness of persons who are enthusiastic [about Islamic revivalism] without planning, or the opportunists who have no real faith in their attempt to apply Islam [in society and the state]. Contemporary Islamic application is challenged with problems that cannot be simply resolved by wishful thinking or enthusiasm. To straighten out Islamic applications, the problem of the [existing] rules of jurisprudence must be readily resolved" (Ibid. 24).

Al-Mahdi is satisfied with the fact that, "The references consulted by all those who desire to apply *Shari'a* are books of the *Madhahib* [schools of jurisprudence]. Although the rules have been established according to texts and sources of the *Shari'a*, they were expressive of a reality that has greatly changed over time. Therefore, it is not right to establish a contemporary Islamic application with these rules" (Ibid. 124).

The conclusion reached by Sadiq was earlier shown in the criticisms of Turabi. The difference between the two writers is that Turabi only promises to create "a new amalgamated science" as an alternative to the "nullified" version of Islamic jurisprudence [which is not specified in his writings]. Turabi antic-ipates such contribution only "if granted a wider opportunity to deal with the jurisprudence of religious sources and their systems, by using more accurate methodology and deeper analysis" (Tagdid, 1980: 46).

Sadiq, for his part, is determined "to transfer the area of general research to a field of specific know-how of Islamic application" ('Uqobat, Undated: 22). This is done by a series of discussions in some of his works on the needs, themes, and limits of a new *Ijtihad* to form a modern version of Islamic jurisprudence.

Al-Mahdi begins with a polite appreciation of the efforts of the ancestors, the older generations: "The consensus of the Muslims in the issues [of jurisprudence] was a function of time as [that jurisprudence] had been the most just in the circumstances. But after twelve centuries passed away, a revi-sion is necessarily manifesting itself [for that jurisprudence]" (Ibid. 124).

Sadiq then discusses the need to repeal specific *Shari'a* rules of concern to the non-Muslims since they "degrade their status below that of the Muslims. This motivates the non-Muslim minorities in Islamic countries to reject the application of Islamic *Shari'a*" (Ibid. 125). The remaining issues are pertinent to the imposition of *hudud* [punishment prescribed by Allah] on specific violations (for example wine drinking); women's rights; slavery; exercising authority of the state; transgression; apostasy; and the implementation of rules on citizens of other states.

Based on the intensive citations of authentic jurisprudence, Al-Mahdi high-lights a fundamental fact of Islamic thought, namely that diversity of opinions has always existed among the *'ulama* [scholars] and jurists. A learned and enlightening dispute has consistently underlined that diversity because the scholars and jurists were originating their viewpoints in the fundamental ori-gins and branches or religion, rather than any personal feelings.

Sadiq Al-Mahdi criticized "all ill practices made in the name of Islamic Vig-ilance. The strongest allies of secularist thought and action are founded on a misunderstanding of the Islamic Vigilance and a wrongful application of Islamic *Shari'a*." In this statement, Al-Mahdi differentiates secularism from Islam in a way that posits secularism as an antithesis of Islam. Al-Mahdi believes that "For an Islamic system of succession to arise on the basis of pop-ular representation, the political movement of society must liberalize society of all coercive regimes, and to render the political will of society determined via free and fair election of people. The ensuing parliamentary order shall oversee and decide by majority vote the system of rule desirable for a majority of people by their majority representatives" ('Uqobat, Undated: 196).

The experience of Sudan under Sadiq's democratically elected governments does not substantiate fully his contention. The 1986 elections, for example, did not allow the Southerners to participate in the national suffrage because the north-dominated central government failed to establish a workable political settlement with the South. The majority will, vote, and the system of rule did not bring the stability Sadiq is talking about. After every national elections, war still continues and a deeper conflict splits the Sudanese society between secular forces (especially those of the National Democratic Alliance opposition groups) and the ruling pro-*Shari'a* supporters. Again, Al-Mawardi's thought finds no real support in Sudanese politics and religious affairs.

Both Al-Mahdi and Turabi stress the significance of economic factors in societal affairs. Turabi speaks to the International Conference of Islamic Call at Khartoum (1981) as follows: "the common factor in the cultures of mankind is the initiation of religiosity that springs from the human nature. This is a state clarified by experiences of mankind and validated by civilization. One aspect in mind if the oneness of God and the meaningfulness attributed to it for the liberalization of mankind, emphasizing the unity and dignity of man, and the equity of all people without racism or discrimination" (Khitab, 1981: 12–113).

"Other aspects include a reluctance from pagan lethargy and a commitment to freedoms of man within the economic and political relations based on equality, freedom, justice, and solidarity. In this is an illumination of the ethos of religion as an accomplishment of the economic interests, which have been a top concern for the believers. Economy may thus have been the [most influential domain] to preserve religion in contemporary times" (Khitab, 1981: 122–23).

The aforesaid text calls openly for the use of economy "to preserve religion." It is a clear-cut acceptance of the power of the economic factor and its influential effect on this era. The class context of this direction, which Turabi never mentions, suggests the possibilities of strengthening certain strata of the population while weakening the others, unless this particular result is nationally rectified by political agreement.

Because Islam strongly calls for the venerations of modesty and simplicity of life, a question still lingers. How would the "just Islamic principles" be implemented in the era with all its overwhelming material and economic concerns? How could we avoid class division and class conflict if the economy is so used as an instrument to divide societies into rich minorities and an impoverished majority? If class stratification is an indispensable fact in relation to economic growth within "the required ethnic and religious hegemony" Turabi perceives?

For Al-Mahdi, "the teachings of Islam allow the incorporation of the beneficial and the righteous [aspects of life] according to certain jurisprudence techniques. These teachings include standards and principles to correct any deviance from the right path of Islam, thus they provide solutions to correct the miserable conditions of the Third World" (Ibid. 55).

Pointing at the strong impact of the capitalist market in the present time, Sadiq criticized "its negative effect on the attitude of the middle classes of the Third World as it converts them to mere agencies and fronts in the service of international companies. The policies imposed by systems of rule over middle classes exert a strong impact negatively upon them. They are unstable systems because they exchange political allegiance for privileges and loans to their favorites. They deprive the qualified [persons or groups] by that bias while parasitic elements excessively abuse financial resources" (Ibid. 33).

Sadiq states, "The rich classes in the Islamic world are frightened of the hazard that nationalization present to their ownership. Also, they smuggled the largest portion of their money abroad. These classes will not be able to invest in the 3rd World or in the Islamic World compared to economic development of the European and American middle classes [in the preceding times]" (Ibid.).

"The left-wing governments resorted to the establishment of a coalition of many classes. They organized political parties to lead that coalition. The alliance was superimposed from the top and, in its name, totalitarian regimes rule these societies while still promising in the name of "progressive" alliances the achievement of a speedy and just socialist development" (Ibid.). "But all these systems and claims did not bear any fruit," claims Al-Mahdi. "Instead, they were abused by elite regimes so isolated from the people. They persecuted people in the name of socialism, and wasted the national wealth. In addition to political spending to buy off supporters and to enable the favorites to live a soft life, for which they never made the least effort, [these elite groups] ruined the national wealth with spending on security apparatuses and false propaganda" (Ibid. 33–35).

Sadiq's analysis touches upon social classes and their roles in development administration. He elaborates on liberalism with a form belief in "freedom and popular participation by fair elections." Turabi admits that economy is vital to "the need for and the growth of wealth." Obviously, he has reserved a lion's share for the Muslim Brotherhood to transform Muslim societies both politically and economically. But he does not elaborate on the issue beyond assertion. Nor does he use analytical methods in his work.

The thought of Al-Mahdi and Turabi exemplified the shortcomings of classical jurisprudence as they try to apply it to handle the complex issues of modernity and national unity. If Mawardi's doctrine simply fails to cope with contemporary life, as Mahdi indirectly mentions concerning the condition of affiliation to the Quarish tribe of the Prophet, the resort to state politics to impose *Shari'a* rule in the diverse society is non-realistic, let alone a political ideology or party programs. *Shari'a*, however, would continue to influence the Sudanese Muslim society as a significant component of the social life for which *Shari'a* and Sufi traditions should be developed by community activity apart from any State intervention.

The Intriguing Thought of Mahmoud Mohamed Taha

Mahmoud Mohamed Taha is a unique Islamic thinker who envisioned a progressive way to revive Islam versus the Muslim Brotherhood and the other conservative groups. The latter group sought to revive *Shari'a* Law in contemporary societies by necessary changes on *Shari'a* Law without a real change of the tenets of the classical jurisprudence. Taha struggled all his life to establish a new mission of Islam that would selectively interpret the Meccan verses of the Qur'an, as possibly applicable in the present time.

Taha, however, shares with the Islamic conservative thinker Sayed Qutb some of his condemnations of the contemporary civilization of mankind, the one relevant to the sciences and life styles of the twentieth century. As Mahmoud puts it, "Nowadays, in the 2nd half of the twentieth century, mankind lives in a Second *Jahiliya* [ignorance], at a level much higher than ignorance of the seventh century" (Tariq Muhammad, Undated: 16).

In the early 1960s, Sayed Qutb sorts out in his book Ma'alim fi Al-Tariq [Features or Milestones on the Way] the *Jahiliya* of the century and condemns its contradictions with classical *Shari'a* Law. But the adaptations of each thinker [i.e., Taha and Qutb] of a way to salvage mankind, in general, and Muslims, in particular, from *Jahiliya* are different.

One difference between the two trends is that Qutb and the Muslim Brotherhood groups developed a political doctrine based on the use of *Jihad* [holy striving including the use of force] to change the political structure of Muslim societies. Taha and the Republican Brothers called for a peaceful transformation of society by a new system of thought, as will be shortly discussed. Another difference at hand is that Mahmoud confines the task of salvaging humanity "with God's will, from the darkness of the Second *Jahiliya* into the light of Islam" (Ibid: 27) to Ahmedism. This is the Second Message of Islam, exactly as Muhammadism, the First Message of Islam, formerly saved humanity from the darkness of the First *Jahiliya*. Mahmoud Mohamed Taha to some extent admires the remarkable achievements of the century's "rational sciences," "materialist evolution," "progression," etc. Like Turabi and Mahdi, he insists on calling upon society to take advantages of the fruition of science and technology, although they disagree with each other about many ideological concerns regarding modernity of the age.

The conclusions of Taha throughout his writings are not harmoniously interrelated as expected with a comprehensive theoretical approach. The critique of this writer of the Turabi scheme of modernizing classical jurispru-dence by means of a "new amalgamated science" holds true in the case of Mah-moud. Both of them advocate a number of presumptions to project the rise of a "new" Islamic entity. But they do not present the details required to delineate the prerequisites, relations, and interrelations of the "new" Islamic society or nation of Islam with respect to the existing global doctrines and world powers.

Unlike Turabi who never clearly condemned the use of force to install an Islamic society in the Sudan, Taha abhors the acts of violence as a means of religious revivalism. "Violence is forbidden in Islam; but the *Shari'a* of Islam is not the whole Islam. *Shari'a* is an approach to Islam. The original sources of Islam dictate: "Call for the path of thy Lord with wisdom and good preaching, and discuss with them in the best manner." When the real legislature of Islam comes about in its most flourishing time, it will not rest on anything other than a rejection of violence" (Rasaiyl, 1973: 33).

Taha assures the rise and growth of Islam on the basis of individual volun-tarism and peaceful argumentation. Blaming the groups that strive for an Islamic Call without perceiving the ethos of Islam, in essence, he criticizes, "Those who speak about 'Islamic Call and the sword': misunderstand the ethos of Islam and the rule of the time, simultaneously. They would do good to themselves, as well as Islam, if they abandon this inhibiting call" (Al-Thawra Al-Thaqafiya, 1972: 33).

He attacks, on the other side, the religious and political forces that struggle for a *Shari'a* constitution: "The Islamic Constitution the existing propagan-dists (i.e., the Front of Islamic Charter, sectarianism, Ansar Al-Sunna, and *Shari'a* jurists) are calling for is not an Islamic one. It is ignorance hiding behind the sacredness of Islam. They pursue an Islamic Constitution in the Islamic *Shari'a*; but the constitution is interwoven in the *Qur'an* (the actual Islamic Constitution) not in the Islamic *Shari'a*, which has nothing to give in political affairs but guardianship. The *Shari'a* does not have any [place for] socialism in wealth. Women have no equality with men in *Shari'a*."

Finally, Taha holds that, "The fundamental rights, which are the spirit of constitution, are based on these three domains: democracy, socialism, and the equality between men and women. The *Qur'an* embodied the constitution. And the *Qur'an* needs a new interpretation to give rise to the origins abrogated in the past by its branches" (Ibid. 28).

Mahmoud presents a philosophical perspective, rather than a program of action, towards a new Islamic Constitution in terms of a new Message of Islam. It is irreversible, however, that Mahmoud shares with the other thinkers a concern for the general challenges of the Sudanese society. Taha asserts, for example, that social development hinges upon "the geographical, political, and national unity of the Sudan. The first step is to bring the remote areas of the country into a close connection with each other, using a modern technology of communications and transportation." For him, this national unity is so critical that it deserves a special handling. "Political unity," thinks Mahmoud, "takes place in a number of levels that must start with peaceful coexistence among all ethnic sections of the population, including their different and hostile tribes. A stoppage of the armed conflict between North and South is the best start to make. National unity means that the multitude of tribal groups, nationalities and ethnic groups of the Sudan be molded in a melting pot to make of themselves a united population with a common destiny, similar characteristics, and a shared perception."

"National unity requires [the collaboration of] all scientific, cultural, and intellectual efforts. It does not become true, as a rule, unless all activities are sufficiently utilized. We maintain in principle that the Cultural Revolution and the Intellectual Revolution will not arise until all activities are energetically pursued. They are firmly founded on a religious revivalism" (Al-Deen wa Al-Tanmiya, 1974: 20–22).

This important citation figures out as an educational strategy for an idealist group that believes in religious revivalism as a life outlook much more than political and social struggles. In actual fact, the solutions sought for the bitter realities of Sudanese diversity and civil striving require detailed policies and practices within a well-defined plan of action. Mahmoud Mohamed Taha has not offered such details but rather confines his intellectuality to the Second Message of Islam as a focal point of his philosophy.

"'A new thought and a new science' should be processed to lead Muslims to 'a new horizon,'" says Taha. He draws heavily upon a new realm of ideas to prepare the ground for the Second Message of Islam. "The rule of time stipulated that Muhammadism had to depart from Ahmedism a great deal to be able to guide people, according to the level of their rationality, applying rules addressed to their simple needs. That departure occurred by a shift from the verses of origins in the *Qur'an* to the verses of branches of the *Qur'an*. The latter became the rule of the time, abrogating in legislative terms the verses of origins" (Tariq Muhammad, Undated: 70).

This ideal construct is further elucidated as follows: "It is better to decide firmly that there are two forms of *Shari'a*, the classical *Shari'a* which is the *Shari'a* of the First Message of Islam [Muhammadism] and the new *Shari'a*, that of the Second Message of Islam [Ahmedism]. The difference between them is a matter of degree. The *Shari'a* of the First Message is a base that of the Second Message is a step forward towards the top of a pyramid whose basis in a *Shari'a* and its top is morality. This pyramid picture generates a clear impression that the *Shari'a* of the First Message is not locked up; it is opened onto the *Shari'a* of the Second Message."

"There is also an inter-relationship between [the two forms of *Shari'a*] that renders some postulates of the First Message's *Shari'a* valid alongside the Second Message, for example, the *Shari'a* of *'Ibadat* [worshipping], *hudud* [God's penalties], and retribution. The continuity of these valid aspects of the First *Shari'a* is explained in our book Al-Risalah Al-Thaniya min Al-Islam [The Second Message of Islam]. The remaining trasactions' *Shari'a* in political, monetary, and social affairs has inundated much of its functions to the extent of exhaustion. Its development thus became a necessity" (Tatweer, 1971: 71).

Taha ascertains that, "It would be a shortcoming of the minds to transmit Shari'a from its [appropriate] environment to another one, that is not located for it, in the pretext that the Islamic *Shari'a* is fit for every place and every time. All verses stipulating guardianship over women are abrogated, starting from this day, by the verse, 'And women shall have rights similar to the rights against them, according to what is equitable; but men have a degree of advantage over them' [II: 228]. All verses of guardianship upon men, and upon women, are abrogated from this day by the verses "Remind, you are only a reminder. You are not mastering them'" (Ibid. 69–70).

The same views are said about capitalist economy: "All verses on capitalism in the *Qur'an* are abrogated by the verse: 'they ask you about what to spend. Say: forgiveness.' Forgiveness has a top and a bottom. Its top will be reserved for the area of morality. What concerns us here is its base because it is the lowest degree of socialism, i.e., the prevention of ownership of the means of production by a single person, or by a few individuals. With that, the path would be opened to develop a legislation on which the Second Message of Islam relies" (Ibid).

Mahmoud Mohamed Taha is a creator of a new "Islamic" thought. Although he spoke highly about the Sufi leaders who did not act hypocritically with rulers or pursue worldly affairs, the known Sudanese Sufi groups did not approve of his Second Message of Islam. The classical jurists, in general, rebuffed his ideas and have thence resisted them. Among many layers of the Muslim population several scholars thoughtfully discussed his doctrine in academia, at the halls of philosophical studies and research. Still, his main doctrine to apply a new approach of Islamic thought instead of the classical *Shari'a* law seems to find increasing support in the light of the drastic failures of Muslim Brotherhood rule of Sudan, years after his death.

Sudanese Muslims: Which Way to Go?

What possibilities does Sudan's cultural and religious diversity offer to help achieve national integration, instead of authoritarian rule? This study reveals that the Sudanese Muslim society experienced multicultural interpretations and practices of Islam since the seventh century. The Sufi tradition, as Daif-Allah clearly documented, adapted the cultural heritage of the formerly Christian population of the country and the other African religious groups that adopted Islam to a flexible version of Muslim traditions.

In the post-independence era (1956 onwards), both civilian and military regimes seized the secularly oriented government of Sudan. Strong support by Turabi and the Muslim Brotherhood, the military governments of Nimeiri (1969–1985) and Omer Al-Bashir (1989 to the present) made serious attempts to eradicate the influence of the popular Sufi Islam of Sudan. They tried to expand upon serious falsification of Sudan applying the Arab Islamic Ideology as a sole ethnic and religious national identification. All these attempts failed to reduce the persistent African cultures of the country that merged with the Sufi tradition to create a unique Sudanese Muslim social esteem, spiritual philosophy, national ideology, and a political reality in its own right.

A drastic attempt was the application of a strict version of *Shari'a* law by the tyrant Nimeiri in 1983 using the so-called September laws. The Ansar group and the Umma Party led by Sadiq Al-Mahdi were opposed to the September laws. When Al-Mahdi was elected Prime Minister of Sudan after the overthrow of Nimeiri by the April Popular Uprising in 1985, however, he failed to abolish the September Laws. He engaged in political rivalry with the Khatmiya-based Democratic Unionist Party and finally gave way to a new military dictatorship led by the national Islamic Front (NIF). Hassan Turabi, the NIF leader, spent the early 1990s in full control over the military rule as speaker of the national Council and top security leader. He was again imprisoned, however, by the Bashir-led NIF military faction for political reasons. Most recently, Sadiq Al-Mahdi withdrew from the National Democratic Alliance after he signed an agreement with the NIF-controlled government. Mohamed osman El-Merghani, the Khatmiyya leader NDA President, maintains strong alliance with the southern groups, the SPLM and USAP, and all the other secular groups (communist party, trades unions, professional groups, and the regional groups of the Beja, the Federals of DarFur, and the Legitimate Command of the Sudanese Armed Forces).

Taha died, a martyr of his thought, after he challenged the authority of Nimeiri's "Islamic" state by a strong rebuke of the regime's *Shari'a* application to make war with the South and to terrorize the opposition. In January 1985, led by Ja'far Nimeiri, the Authority executed Mahmoud Mohamed Taha extrajudicially.

As the Sudanese nationals and the whole world continue to realize the significance of the cultural, social, and religious diversity of Sudan, the NIF-Bashir regime resort to the use of violence to impose their will in the populace. It is therefore important to allow a greater freedom of thought and expression for the Sudanese than is available thus far to voice the national sentiments and aspirations of the People of Sudan on the basis of their cultural, religious, and social diversity. The intellectuals themselves must always show tolerance and appreciation with respect to their different views and schools of thought.

Sudan is a country composed of a pluralist culture that defies all forms of Authority to enforce the will power of people in national decision-making. The maintenance and advancement of the people of Sudan depends on the observance of human rights and civil freedoms, without any restrictions or hesitation on the part of the Authority.

All political parties, military groups, and trades unions must appreciate the freedoms of thought and expression to ensure civil and political rights, as a prerequisite of social stability and progression. This is a deep contention of the Sudanese masses, which has always guided their struggles for civil rights and democratic freedoms. It will continue to prevail in the next transition rule of Sudan.

References

Adams, William (1978): *Africa, the Corridor to Africa*, Allen Lane, London.

Al-Fadil, Mohamed Daif-Allah Ibn Mohamed Al-Ja'ali (Undated): *Kitab Al-Tabaqat fi Khosos Al-Awliya wa Al-Saliheen wa Al-'Ulama fi Al-Sudan*, Beirut.

Fluehr-Lobban, Carolyn (1987): *Islamic Law and Society in The Sudan*, Frank Cass, London.

Fruzzetti, Lina, and Akos Ostor (1990): *Culture and Change along the Blue Nile*, Westview Press, Boulder.

Hassan, Yusif Fadl (1974): *Tabaqat Daif Allah*, 2nd edition, University of Khartoum, Khartoum.

Al-Mahdi, Sadiq (1981): *Al-Sahwa Al-Islamiya wa Mustaqbal Al-Da'wa.*

———. (Undated): *Al-'Uqobat Al-Shar'iya wa Mawqi'a min Al-Nizam Al-Ijtimai Al-Islami*, Umma Publications.

Al-Maqrizi, Al-Inam Tariq Al-Deen Ahmed (845H): *Al-Khitat Al-Maqriziya: Al-Mawaiz wa Al-I'tibar bi Zikr Al-Khitat wa Al-Athar*, Maktabat Al-Adab, Cairo, 1996.

Al-Mawardi, Al-Imam Abu Al-Hassan (Undated): *Al-Ahkam Al-Sultaniya wa Al-Wllayat Al-Deeniya*, Cairo.

Taha, Mahoud Mohamed (1974): *Al-Deen wa Al-Tanmiya Al-Ijtima'iya.* 1st edition.

———. (1973): *Rasayil wa Maqalat.* 1st edition, May.

———. (1972): *Al-Thawra Al-Thaqafiya.*

———. (1971): *Tatweer Shari'at Al-Ahwal Al-Shakhsiya.*

———. (Undated): *Tariq Muhammad*, Omdurman, 1st edition.

Al-Turabi, Hassan (1984): *Al-slam wa Nizam Al-Hukm fi Al-Sudan.* Papers of the 1st International Conference, op. cit.

———. (1984): *Khitab Al-Umma Al-Sudaniya li Qul Al-Milal Al-Ukhra*, Khartoum University Press.

———. (1980): *Tajdid Usul Al-Fiqh Al-Islami*, Matboat Al-Fikr, Khartoum, 1st edition.

Chapter 7

Recent Developments in Shi'i Thought: A Brief Introduction to the Views of Three Contemporary Shi'ite Thinkers

Ali Paya

Introduction

Since the advent of the Islamic Revolution in Iran in 1978–1979, radical changes have taken place in the views of many of the Iranian Shi'ite scholars concerning the major issue of the nature of religious belief in general and their own understanding of the main tenets of the Shi'i Islam in particular. These changes seem to have far-reaching consequences not only for the future of the Islamic State in Iran, but also for almost all other Muslim communities around the globe. In this paper, following a short historical introduction to the development of Shi'i thought in the past centuries, I shall concentrate on some of the theories and arguments presented by three contemporary Iranian Shi'ite scholars, who are representing a new wave of religious thought in present-day Iran.

The three scholars whose ideas will be selectively and briefly introduced are: Abdulkarim Soroush, a pharmacologist by training turned philosopher of science and more recently turned philosopher of religion; Mohammad Mojtahid Shabestari, a clergy and a professor of theology at the Faculty of Divinity, University of Tehran; and Sa'id Hajjarian, a political theorist with a background in mechanical engineering.

It will be shown that these scholars, despite their different backgrounds, have developed views and ideas which are remarkably similar in tone and content, and at the same time substantially different from the views held by the previous generations of the Shi'ite scholars. The ideas developed by this new breed of Shi'ite thinkers contain the seeds of a rational interpretation of religious thought which heralds a truly revolutionary approach to Islam in the twenty-first century. Amongst the fruits of the "paradigm-shift" due to this conceptual revolution, one which is of great practical importance, will be a better understanding and greater readiness for forging closer relations between the Sunni and the Shi'ite Muslims.

A Brief History of Shi'ism[1]

The Shi'ites or the Shi'ats (a name derived from the Arabic Shi'at Ali, "the party of Ali") constitute one of the two major branches of Islam, the other, larger branch being the Sunnites or the Sunnis (the followers of *Sunnah* = tradition). The emergence of these two main branches was, partly though not entirely, due to political disagreements: following the death of the Prophet Mohammad (632 CE), disagreement arose at the *Saqifah* assembly as to the necessary qualifications and exact functions of his successors as leaders of the Muslim community.

The Shi'ites emphasized the spiritual function of the Prophet's successor, the Imam, in whom the Prophetic Light is ever present in this world. According to the Shi'ites, Imams are divinely protected against sin and error (in passing judgements on religious issues) and have an infallible understanding of the Quran.

The Shi'ites insisted that only members of the Prophet's family, specifically, the descendants of Mohammad's daughter Fatima and her husband Ali ibn Abi Talib (the Prophet's cousin), could qualify as Imams. They further stressed that, the Prophet during his lifetime on numerous occasions had pointed out that Ali and some of Ali's male offspring should be regarded as his righteous successors.

One such occasion, reported in all authentic and authoritative Shi'i and Sunni sources alike, has been interpreted by the Shi'ite as the formal endorsement of Ali's right to succession and his designation to the position of community's leader by the Prophet. On the eighteenth day of the month of *Dhu'l-hijjah*, in the eleventh year of his *Hjjrah* (632 CE), at a place called the *Ghadir* (pool) of *Khumm*, the Prophet who was returning to Medina from his last pilgrimage to Mecca, made a fateful proclamation which has been reported in different versions, the most popular being: "He for whom I was the master, should hence have Ali as his master فهذا علي مولاه من كنت مولاه."[2]

The Sunni Muslims, while accepting the authenticity of the *Ghadir* story, put a different gloss over it: in their view the term *master* (*mawla* مولا from the root term *wali* ولي) in the Prophet's proclamation should be interpreted as friend and patron rather than leader. They advocated the view that the Prophet had deliberately left the question of succession open, leaving it to the Muslim community (*ummah* ﺍﻣﺔ) to decide who would be the most competent person to assume leadership.

Whatever the true intention of the Prophet, it was the Sunni view that prevailed at the *Saqifah* assembly. Abu Bakr, a distinguished member of the community and the Prophet's father-in-law was chosen as the first Caliph of God's messenger. He was succeeded by Umar ibn Khattab, another close companion to the Prophet and also his father-in-law, and Uthman ibn Affan, a member of the important and wealthy Umayyad clan at Mecca and a son-in-law of Mohammad. His murder in 656 was followed by a strong display of popular support for Ali to assume the mantle of the Prophet.[3]

However, by the time Ali, who came to be known as the last of the four Rightly-Guided Caliphs of the Prophet, took charge, great changes had taken place in the rapidly growing Islamic community. Changes that had made the community a very different entity from the one the Prophet himself had created and used to guide. The wealth accumulated from the successful expansion of the territories of Islam had transformed some of the families and clans into new power-contenders. They had little sympathy with Ali's insistence on transparency and accountability in managing the affairs of the community and had no intention of going back to the strict regime of the Prophet's days to which Ali was inviting them.

Ali was murdered in 661, and Mo'awiyah, a close relative of Uthman who used to be Syria's governor during Uthman's rule and who had fought with Ali over the caliphate, declared himself as caliph in Damascus and founded the Umayyad dynasty. The Shi'ites, however, supported Ali's sons as the legitimate successors of the Prophet and rightful Caliphs of the Islamic community. Ali's eldest son, Hasan, was forced to sign a peace treaty with Mo'awiyah. Although, notwithstanding his weaker position, he managed to include a clause in the treaty according to which the Caliphate would return to him after Mo'awiyah's death. Hasan however died mysteriously c. 669, and Hossein, his younger brother, who challenged the appointment of Yazid, Mo'awiyah's son as the next Caliph, was killed by Umayyad troops at Karbala (in Iraq) in 680.[4]

From then on, despite many uprisings and even occasional creation of short-lived small independent territories and political bodies, the Shi'ites were pushed out of political power and their Imams, who were descendants of Hossein ibn Ali, were barred from political activities and effectively remained under constant surveillance, or kept under house arrest, or imprisoned or killed by the Caliphs of the two powerful dynasties of Umayyad and Abbasid.[5]

In view of the continuous threat to their lives and the security of their followers, the fifth Imam, Mohammad ibn Ali (Baqir) and his son and successor Ja'far ibn Mohammad (Sadiq) initiated a new trend of cultural and educational activities in place of direct political confrontation. Through this strategy, the

Shi'ite Imams, despite all imposed restrictions, succeeded in promoting the Shi'ite creed through training a large number of competent disciples.

It was only with the establishment of the Safavid Dynasty in Iran in the sixteenth century that Shi'ites found a place to live under the rule of fellow Shi'ite rulers.[6] However, the doctrine of *Imamat* or *Imamah* (the Leadership of the infallible Shi'ite Imams) which was one of the main ingredients of the Shi'i belief system, would mean that in the eyes of the Shi'ites even these rulers did not enjoy political legitimacy during the occultation period of the twelfth Imam, Mahdi (Messiah) who disappeared in the ninth century (837). According to the Shi'ites, he will return near the end of time to inaugurate a reign of truth and justice. Until he returns, all laws and doctrines should be interpreted by *Fuqha* (the jurists) and *Mujtahids* (religious doctors, those who exercise their independent legal judgment).

This doctrine meant, among other things, that for the rulers of the Shi'ite communities to achieve political legitimacy, they needed to coordinate their deeds with the Shi'ite *Fuqha* and attain their approval. However, a radical interpretation of this very doctrine by Ayatollah Ruhallah Khomeini in the mid-twentieth century gave birth to the theory of the Absolute Guardianship of the *Faqih* (the jurist). According to this interpretation, the task of *Fuqha*, who (according to Ayatollah Khomeini) are the deputies of the Prophet and the Imams, is not just to interpret the Islamic laws and doctrines, but to manage the affairs of the state on behalf of the occult Imam.

The principle of the Absolute Guardianship of the *Faqih* is now part of the revised constitution of the Islamic Republic of Iran, though it is not universally accepted amongst the Shi'ite scholars (*Ulama*). The significance of such a principle becomes more evident if one bears in mind that the central political institution of the Sunni Islam which governs both temporal and religious affairs in the Muslim community, was and still is the Caliphate. The Sunni Muslims from very early on in the history of Islam, in order to deal with the task of conducting the vexed affairs of the state in the absence of the Prophet or his righteous successors, had made recourse to a number of juristic notions, including, *maslaha* مصلحة, the public interest, and *siyasah* سياسة, the public policy. These were notions which are very useful and indeed necessary for the governance of complex and sophisticated societies in dealing with issues where the *Shari'a* شريعة (religious) law can offer no guidance, or where emergency or political necessity requires the ruler to act his discretion outside the bounds of the *Shari'a* law.

Moreover, the Sunni Muslims, in line with their view concerning the issue of succession, developed a political system whose key political concepts were different from the one developed by the Shi'ite *Ulama*. For the Sunnis, concepts such as *ijma'* (the consensus of the elite), the "people who loose and bind"

(العقد و الحل اهل *ahl al-hall wal-'aqd*), *Khalifah* (the caliph), and *bay'ah* بيعه (taking the oath of allegiance to the caliph by his electors) gained prominence. These concepts and their corresponding mechanisms, which were thoroughly pragmatic in nature, guaranteed that the personality of the ruler, i.e., his piety or otherwise, does not unduly intervene in the intricate problem of the leadership of the community.

The Shi'ites, who distinguished themselves from early on by their more rationalistic rather than pragmatist approach, however, followed a different path. For them concepts like *imamat, wilayah,* and *ismah* (infallibility of Imam) became important. Since they were in minority and were not in charge of running the affairs of the state, they could afford holding a more theoretical (abstract) position. They were arguing that given God's justice (*adl*) and benevolence (*lutf*) towards human beings it was inconceivable that He should have left the issue of the leadership (*imamat*) undecided. It cannot be the case that such an important office could be occupied by impious individuals. The same rational considerations which necessitate the sending of the Prophets also require that in their absence faultless and infallible leaders should be appointed for guardianship (*wilayah*) of their followers.

The Shi'ites concentration on the attributes of the *Imams* as the leaders of the Islamic community gave a more elitist flavour to their political philosophy in comparison to the Sunni's more pragmatist outlook. The difference between the two groups, however, did not confine to political matters. In doctrinal issues, while the Shi'ites shared with the Sunnis the Principles of Religion, namely, *Tawhid* توحيد (Monotheism), *Nubuwwat* نبوت (Messengership of Mohammad), and *Ma'aad* معاد (Judgment day), they promoted two other principles of *Adl* عدل (Divine Justice), and *Imamat* to the rank of doctrinal principles.

The insistence on preserving a distinct identity served the Shi'ites as a strategy for survival. Being a minority group, they could only survive if they had an identity of their own. It is in this sense that one can talk of the distinguishing features of Shi'ism. Such features, as the late Hamid Enayat (1982) has pointed out, should be sought not only in Shi'i fundamental principles, but perhaps more importantly in its ethos, in the tone of historically developed attitudes which have informed and infused the Shi'ites stance on the issues which were raised as significant challenges to Muslims throughout their history. In trying to understand this ethos, one has to deal with "Historical Shi'ism," namely, a Shi'ism which has taken shape as a form of life, in the actual, living experience of specific groups of Muslims, through attitudes which stemmed sometimes clearly from the Shi'i tenets, and sometimes from individual interpretations and a slowly emerging consensus, without necessarily being recognised as fundamental principles in the Shi'i sources.

A quick look at the intellectual output of the Shi'i thinkers in various fields such as *fiqh*, *kalam* (theology), *falsafeh* (philosophy), *'irfan* (mysticism), *akhlaq* (ethics), *tafsir* (interpretation of the Quran), reveals some of the distinguishing features of Shi'ism. The Shi'ites, by and large, have had a tendency for abstract reasoning, metaphysical thinking and philosophical system building; for esotericism, for aloofness from politics and opposition to the worldly powers; for idealism and utopianism; for emotionalism; and for particularism and elitism.

A sense of purpose and global mission can also be discerned among the features characteristic of Shi'ite thought. Thus, for example, in modern times, it was a Shi'ite cleric, Seyyed Jamal al-Din Asad Abadi from Iran, who distinguished himself as the first religious reformer in the nineteenth century to launch a programme of revitalising Islamic thought by introducing the notion of "going back to the sources," promoting radical reforms in the practices of the clergymen modelled on Luther's Protestantism, and advocating the idea of pan-Islamism.

Shi'ism in its long history and in response to diverse political and ideological challenges has evolved in ways which have resulted in the appearance of a number of distinct trends within it. Among these trends those which are more prominent may be provisionally dubbed as the orthodoxy, traditionalism, fundamentalism, modernism, and critical rationalism, for want of a better terminology. Needless to say, within each of these trends, many variations and nuances are discernable. Nevertheless, the broad features of each can be summarised as follows.

The orthodoxy can be best traced in the beliefs and practices of the average clergymen who are in charge of the local mosques in various places and through them they influence and shape the views of the majority of the citizens. According to the orthodox reading of the Shi'ite creed, a good Muslim should follow the instructions of his/her chosen *mujtahid* as they appear in his *resalah* رساله (the book which contains the *mujtahid*'s religious edicts or *fatwas* فتاوا). The follower of the orthodoxy is, for the most part, apolitical and subscribes to the view that, "live and let live." He/she observes a commonsensical code of moral conduct and regards *Mafatih al-Jinan* مفاتیح الجنان (literally: *The Keys to the Heavens*—A collection of the Shi'ite prayers) as his/her most important daily guide.[7]

While the orthodoxy is the belief system of the populace, traditionalism is a more elitist trend. For traditionalists it is not the reason (intellect) but the faculty of intuition (in the classic meaning of the term) that provides the believer with a sure means for extracting the truth of the Book and the Tradition.[8] This faculty could be invoked during the religious practices for purifying the soul. The main objective of religion is to care for the spiritual needs of the faithful and not to create a heaven on earth. Traditionalists welcome religious and political pluralism and maintain that personal salvation can be achieved even for those Shi'ites who live in non-religious societies or under secular regimes. Traditionalists are critical of many aspects of modern, secular civilisation, in that they view it as a misguided adventure by modern man who has neglected and suppressed his divine nature.[9]

Fundamentalists like traditionalists reject the authority of reason in revealing the truth of the Book and the Tradition. However, contrary to traditionalists, they strictly follow the literal reading of these sources. They maintain that the aim of religion is to take care of all aspects of the lives of the believers in this world and the other. This means, among other things, that for fundamentalists establishing a religious state is a necessity. They are not in favour of religious and political pluralism and hold that at any given time there could only exist one official reading of the tenets of the religion which all the believers ought to follow. Fundamentalists are also critical of the modern Western civilisation. However, their position in this respect is much more stronger than traditionalists in that they regard it as not only corrupt and decadent but also deeply hostile to Islam.[10]

Modernists emphasize the role of reason in understanding the mind of God through careful studying of the Book and the Tradition. They believe in the compatibility of religious doctrines and the achievements of the modern reason and try to provide rational interpretations of religious tenets and doctrines. They are interested in the establishment of an Islamic state with a liberal, and not a fundamentalist, outlook. However, they do not pursue such a goal zealously and like traditionalists maintain that personal salvation is not impossible under the rule of secular regimes. They greatly value personal moral conducts of the believers and are at ease with religious and political pluralism.[11]

While in the modernists' view reason, notwithstanding its utmost importance, must be regarded as subservient to the Revealed Message, for critical rationalists reason is autonomous in its deliberations and does not recognize any higher authority. The Book and the Tradition could only be understood through never ending processes of interpretation which is carried out by the autonomous reason that is informed and enriched by particular forms of life. For critical rationalists faith is a personal matter and the faithful by exercising the power of their intellect (reason) and combining it with their spiritual experiences enhances their understanding (in the rich sense of the term) of the realm of the sacred. Critical rationalists are pro pluralism and not in favour of ideological states. Unlike the fundamentalists and some of the modernists, they have almost no interest in such theses as pan-Islamism and are more concerned with the local and global issues which pertain to the national interest. Like the traditionalists they maintain that religion deals with the spiritual needs of the individual. As far as managing the affairs of the state and the society are concerned, they believe that the main problem, contrary to the views of the orthodoxy and the fundamentalists, is not finding the most pious individuals to be appointed as leaders, but putting into place rational and reliable systems and institutions or structures which would facilitate the creation of a fair and just society.

The three thinkers whose views are partially introduced in this paper belong to the last trend among the currents discernable in the contemporary Shi'ite Islam. The fact that their common objectives and shared interests, notwithstanding their different backgrounds and approaches, have resulted in a large set of similar, if not identical, results which are at once original and challenging, is a testimony to the internal coherence and richness of this latest trend in the Shi'i thought.

Abdulkarim Soroush: Shi'ism from the Viewpoint of a Philosopher

Abdulkarim Soroush first came to be known by the general public in Iran during the last few months of the Royal regime, and in the early days after the victory of the Revolution in 1978–1979. In a number of books published in that period, Soroush, drawing on arguments from Karl Popper, dealt a devastating blow to Marxists dogmas which were prevalent amongst the leftist groups in Iran.[12] However, subsequently, in the late 1980s, having taught courses in the philosophy of science at a number of universities and institutes for higher education for a number of years, Soroush turned his attention to issues concerning the philosophy of religion.

Since then, through delivering talks at seminars or publication of papers and books, Soroush has produced a set of doctrines that has challenged, to varying degrees, the better-known trends in the Shi'ite thought. His prime targets however, have been the orthodox and fundamentalist accounts which are being advocated by the (ultra) conservative clergies and their hard-line followers. Soroush's main theses can be summarised as a set of distinctions in the following way[13]:

1. A distinction needs to be made between any religion *per se* and *our understanding* of that religion. While the former is, in the view of its beholders, a set of sacred and unchanging truths, the latter is an ever changing set of personal experiences and publicly accessible ideas and theories which, at any given time, reflects the state of our knowledge of the tenets of that religion. Thus, for example, in the case of a revealed religion such as Islam, only the (uninterpreted content of) the Quran and the Tradition of the Prophet (and the Shi'ite Imams, in the case of the Shi'i Islam) should be regarded as "Islam," the religion.

Our understanding of "Islam" is, by definition, something human and this-worldly and as such is being influenced by, among other things, our background knowledge, our place in history and our geographical location, our social, cultural and political environment, and the like. Changes in each of these external factors and many others, which together shape our particular "form of life" or "life-world," would cause changes in our understanding of "Islam." The more familiar a believer with other fields of knowledge and the richer his/her form of life, the more enhanced his/her understanding of the tenets of the religion.

2. A second distinction pertains to "the essential and the accidental" aspects of "Islam." The true essence of "Islam," and any other genuine Divine religion for that matter, is only to remind the believers that they are not God. That, the whole realm of being, including human societies, is but God's creation and each human being, as God's viceroy on earth, should bear in mind that his/her duty is to live a life in this world which best prepares him/her for the other world. The rest are accidental, that is, temporal, historical, and context-dependent facts or norms which constitute, not "Islam" but the body of the Islamic (interpreted) doctrines. Thus, for example, the Prophet could have been a Chinese who lived in the fourth century (CE); the Quran could have had more (less) chapters and verses; the Tradition could have been partly or totally different; there could have been no rift between Shi'ism and Sunnism; this or that religious ritual could have had a different form; and so on.

3. A third distinction concerns minimal and maximal interpretations of "Islam." Maximalists are those who maintain that "Islam" not only takes care of the believers' lives in the other-world, but also contains the comprehensive guidelines for all individuals and societies in all times and places to conduct their worldly affairs. Minimalists would deny this. In their view the management of this-worldly affairs is the task of the so-called "*collective intellect*." People, by exercising the power of their intellect and through processes of trial and error devise more effective ways for managing their lives. "Islam" is not a set of doctrines which aims at teaching the believers what sort of political, social, and economic systems to adopt, or how to go about making scientific discoveries and technological innovations. As far as management of the mundane affairs is concerned, "Islam" has only provided the faithful with the bare minimum and not detailed guidelines.

4. The next distinction is about the value systems which are internal to religion and those which are external to it. Soroush argues that values such as freedom, justice, rights, truthfulness, respect for the others, and the like are not emerging from within religions but belong to systems which

are external to the main core (essence) of the religious doctrines. These values, or to be more precise, the interpretations given to them, are the products of the collective reason. Religions usually endorse these values and incorporate them into their belief systems.

5. Another distinction sheds light on the differences between religious faith and religious belief. The former is arrived at via existential experiences. It can vary in its intensity and belongs to what Popper would call world-two: the subjective realm of human inner experiences. Religious beliefs, on the other hand, are states of mind which can be expressed in terms of sets of statements/assertions which together form our understanding of "Islam." They belong to the Popperian world-three: the objective realm of human intellectual constructs.[14]

   As such, they can be publicly and critically assessed. The Prophet's existential experiences have a pivotal role in shaping and forming "Islam," the religion. The personal experiences of the faithful who are following in the footsteps of the Prophet in various times and places, when translated into written texts or oral narrations, would enrich the realm of religious beliefs and would add to the corpus of the Islamic (interpreted) doctrines.

6. A sixth distinction focuses on dissimilarities between religion in the sense of a combination of both religious faith and religious belief system on the one hand and religion as an ideology on the other. As an ideology, religious doctrines act like an instrument for effecting changes in the world. They provide the believers with easily comprehensible and rather simplistic views of the world: usually black and white pictures with the believers on one side (the side of the privileged ones) and the rest on the other. Ideologized religious doctrines are typically devoid of meaning ambiguity. They are being presented to the believers under official interpretations. Religious faith and religious belief, in contrast, are the ever-changing outcomes of never-ending spiritual quests on the part of the faithful for finding meaning and answers for the so-called ultimate questions: who am I? Where am I from? Is there life after death? And so forth.

Based on these distinctions, Soroush has offered a model for understanding religion in general and "Islam" in particular which places emphasis on the role of religion as a spiritual quest rather than a social and political ideology. In Soroush's view, "Islam" has been established through the personal experiences of the Prophet during his lifetime. The community of the faithful throughout history look at the Prophet as their role model and try to follow in his footsteps. This pursuit results in accumulation and expansion of the ever-growing body of religious doctrines (religious beliefs) which are accompanied and complemented by religious rituals and activities.

The body of beliefs and doctrines which gradually takes shape around the core which is known as "Islam," of necessity is being categorised under various rubrics and headings. These categories together form what is known as Islamic Sciences (*Ma'aref-e Islami* معارف اسلامی). Among the various branches of the Islamic Sciences two subjects, namely, the Islamic Jurisprudence (*Fiqh*) and the Islamic Ethics (*Akhlagh-e Islami* اخلاق اسلامی), are of practical (and not just theoretical) importance, in that they manage the faithful public and private affairs in accordance with the Islamic norms.

Taking a minimalist approach towards religion, Soroush maintains that *Fiqh*, rather undeservedly, has taken the centre-stage and has passed itself as *the* temporal manifestation of "Islam." Whereas in reality, in its present form, *Fiqh* can only provide limited legal guidelines on a range of issues which are restricted in their scopes. According to Soroush *Fiqh*, as is being exercised in all Islamic countries, is duty-oriented in its outlook: it mainly deals with the duties and obligations of the faithful towards God. In Soroush's view—which is evidently influenced by liberal thinkers such as John Rawls—such an orientation would make traditional *Fiqh* unable to deal with the complex problems of modern world which are rights-based. That is to say, they stem from the recognition of the fact that human beings *qua* human beings, and not as believers or Muslims, have certain fundamental rights. For Muslim jurists to be able to contribute meaningfully to the life of modern Muslim societies, they must undergo a conceptual paradigm-shift which would transfer them, figuratively speaking, from the middle-ages to the present time.

It is Soroush's conviction that adoption of this new paradigm, among other things, would amount to recognition of the fact that "Islam" has not endorsed any particular form of government. This means that all sorts of political systems can be imposed on a religious society. His own preference, however, is a religious (Islamic) democracy. He believes that an Islamic democracy can be established in a society whose majority citizens are Muslims and in favour of democracy. He also emphasises on the value of freedom as a necessary measure for assisting the faithful to realize their potentials and to enrich their religious experience. In this respect, he believes that one can easily find compatibility between certain interpretations of liberalism and religious way of life. However, amongst the most basic values without which a proper religious community cannot flourish, he holds that it is the value of equity that reigns supreme and stands above all other values. Following philosophers like Richard Dworkin, Soroush is of the view that equity not only informs other values but also sheds light on laws and prepares the ground for creating more humane legal systems and fairer societies.

Mohammad Mojtahid Shabestari:
Shi'ism from the Viewpoint of a Shi'ite Theologian

Whereas Soroush has made good use of his familiarity with the works of modern analytic philosophers in producing a fresh approach to understanding "Islam," Mohammad Mojtahid Shabestari, who has spent some years in Germany and Austria, is making use of German hermeneutic tradition in his arguments against the orthodox and the fundamentalist readings of the Shi'i Islam. In three closely related books, which are collections of his essays and papers,[15] Shabestari has advocated views more or less similar to those of Soroush's. His style of argumentation however, notwithstanding his emphasis on the hermeneutic method, is rather like G. E. Moore's method of philosophising with his emphasis on the role of commonsensical understanding of the big philosophical issues.

In his most recent book, *A Critique of the Official Reading of Religion: Crises, Challenges, and Solutions*, Shabestari has argued that the official reading of the Shi'i Islam which is being promoted by the conservative clergies in Iran is suffering from an acute legitimacy crisis the causes of which are both theoretical and practical.

At the theoretical level, insistence on two unjustified claims has undermined the status of "the official reading."[16] These are firstly, that Islam, as a religion, contains powerful political, economic and legal systems—all produced by *fiqh*—which are capable of providing sound solutions for all problems in all times and circumstances. And secondly, that the main objective of an Islamic government is to implement the Islamic rules and laws (*Shari'a*) in the society.

At the practical level, the insistence of the conservative clergies to impose their *bona fide* interpretation against the will of the people has alienated a large number of the citizens and has encouraged them, especially the younger generations amongst them, to turn their back against not only the official reading of Islam, but also against all attempts to preserve Islam as an established and over-arching institution within the Iranian society.

Against this backdrop, Shabestari argues that the conservatives' two unwarranted claims neither conform to the basic tenets of Islam nor are supported by the reality of Muslim societies in the past one and one-half centuries. According to Shabestari, before the advent of the modern era and the eventful encounter between a powerful West and the weak regimes and backward societies in the Islamic lands, all Muslim communities were being managed by a combination of local customs and traditions plus religious edicts issued by *fuqaha* فقها (the jurists). These *fuqaha* would explain to the believers which actions are obligatory (*wajib* واجب), which are prohibited (*haram* حرام),

which are recommended (*mostahab* مستحب), which are better not attempted (*makruh* مکروه) and which belong to the category about which the *Sharia'h* is silent (*mobah* مباح).

However, this simple way of life underwent dramatic changes since the mid-nineteenth century in the aftermath of the encounter between the West and the Muslim communities. The new forms of life which have gradually emerged out of this encounter and have forced themselves upon the Muslim societies have a number of characteristics which are entirely unprecedented in the past history of Islam. In modern societies, traditional concepts such as "*Haakim* حاکم" (the ruler), "*ra'yat* رعیت" (the subject), "*itaa'h* اطاعه" (obedience), "*ahl hall wa'l aqd* اهل حل والعقد" (people who loose and bind: electors, the elite), "*bay'at* بیعت" (oath of allegiance to rulers), "*hisbah* حسبه" (censorship, surveillance of public morals), "*Nasihat-al aeimat-al Muslimin* المسلمین تصیحه ائمه" (advice to the rulers of the Muslims), and the like, have been replaced by modern concepts such as, "citizen," "individual rights," "public partnership," "people's guardianship," "political and social liberties," "rational planning," and the like. These new concepts have been devised in order to cope with a host of new theoretical and practical problems which are highly complex and involved.

In Shabestari's view, *fiqh* which was traditionally responsible for finding appropriate solutions for newly emerged issues in three areas of *ibadat* عبادات (ritual acts of worship or religious duties), *mu'amalat* معاملات (mundane transactions), and *siyasaat* سیاسات (temporal politics), may still be able to function in modern times in the first two areas, albeit in a much limited capacity. However, as far as the third area is concerned, traditional *fiqh*, as it is known today, is structurally and inherently incapable of addressing the complex problems which are constantly emerging in the realm of modern politics. Shabestari argues that the Muslim jurists in the traditional societies had introduced their religious edicts in a paradigm which was completely different from the modern paradigm. The whole system of *fiqh*, at least as far as *siyasaat* is concerned, was geared to answering questions that have nothing to do with the modern issues in this area. Issues such as democratic government, crime prevention, social justice, human rights, and the like do not have a counterpart in the traditional paradigm in which the customary *fiqh* flourished.

Shabestari is of the view that to introduce more acceptable readings and interpretations of Islam which are compatible with the norms of the modern world, Muslims should make use of hermeneutic methods and phenomenological approaches in understanding religious texts. All religious statements must be studied with due regard to their historical contexts. Moreover, those who embark on such studies must be aware that they are carrying with themselves their own excess baggage of presuppositions and assumptions. This means that, *inter alia*, nobody could claim he/she is in possession of the whole truth concerning the Divine message.

Contrary to those who try to pass their own reading of Islam as the only authorised and acceptable interpretation, Shabestari insists on the plurality of understandings and interpretations. In his *Hermeneutic, the Book, and the Tradition* (1996) he writes: "Understanding the word of God is not something which takes place once and for all. Its understanding is tantamount to its continuity. I do not know a sweeter story than this. A story which is identical with the reality of man."

For Shabestari, modern reason, assisted by the hermeneutic methods and enhanced by personal experiences, is the ultimate source for understanding the word of God. He sees no incompatibility between his rationalist approach and his religious faith. In his view the faithful in their religious quest must think freely and act responsibly. Shabestari regards freedom as a value of utmost importance and, somewhat like the Motazilites, maintains that the value of freedom is intrinsic.

His concern for freedom has made him take issue with those who intend to impose arbitrary restrictions on the life of the believers in the Islamic communities. He argues that the notion of "human rights" is a novel construct of the modern age which has had no precedent in the past history of Islam. This notion has arisen in the context of real social and political changes in modern times and as such must be dealt with through invoking appropriate theoretical machinery. In Shabestari's view it is not impossible to show that the notion of "human rights" is entirely compatible with the tenets of Islam. However, to show this one needs to make careful use of sophisticated hermeneutic methods and not try to portray this notion as a purely metaphysical (i.e., abstract and ahistorical) concept.

Shabestari stresses that the Shi'ite *ulama* and *fuqha* as well as their followers must accept the human rights in their totality for all human beings and abandon their customary distinctions which make non-Muslims or even Sunni Muslims and Shi'ite women second-class citizens. In his view, the *mujtahids* must make complete revisions of many of the traditional *fatwas* (religious edicts) in the light of this notion. He refers to the edicts concerning apostasy as a case in point and reiterates his view that no one should be punished or persecuted because of his beliefs.

According to Shabestari, Prophets were not inventors of new legal or moral systems. They, however, lent their spiritual support to such systems and thus gave prominence to morality and human rights in the lives of human beings. Neither had they prescribed any particular system of government. In this respect too, they were following the tradition of their own time. This means that at present, Muslim communities can adopt democratic systems of governance just as they can adopt the notion of the human rights and make use of the developments in modern legal systems.

To have a democratic system, Muslims should make room for political and cultural pluralism in their societies, they should recognise the fundamental rights of "the others," and should learn to play the game of the politics in accordance to a system of morals in which tolerance and respect of the other are paramount values. However, Shabestari emphasises that to name such democratic systems which would be operating in the Muslim societies as "Islamic democracy" is a misnomer since democracy is just a method of governance and as such it is neutral with regard to religious or non-religious value systems. A society is either governed by democratic rule or by a dictatorship, there is no third alternative. Although, no doubt, a democratic system of governance in an Islamic society will be informed and inspired by the values which are held by the majority of the populace, just as a democratic system of governance in a Christian society will be informed by the values prevalent in that society.

Sa'id Hajjarian:
Shi'ism from the Viewpoint of a Political Sociologist

Hajjarian, who after obtaining his BS in mechanical engineering from the University of Tehran, and before completing a PhD in Political Science, spent some years in the city of Qom to study *fiqh*, has developed a radical theory concerning the evolution of the Shi'i *fiqh* in modern times.[17] According to Hajjarian the Shi'i *fiqh* has, in modern times, undergone a process of secularization, i.e., a transformation from the realm of the sacred to the realm of the secular. He distinguishes two different, though not unrelated, meanings of the term "secularization" and maintains that the aforementioned transformation that has accelerated in the Shi'i *fiqh* in Iran since the advent of the Islamic Revolution has, so far, mostly remained confined to the first *sense* of this term.

Secularisation, in the first sense, is known in the Arab world as *almaniyat* علمانيّت and in Iran as *urfi shodan* عرفی شدن. Etymologically speaking, the first term comes from the root word *aalam* عالم (the world),[18] whereas the second term refers to *urf* عرف, that is, what is commonly held and exercised by the people. However, what is meant by these terms as a translation of the term "secularization" in its first sense is a transition from the sacred categories and concepts *Norms,* to the secular ones. The latter are not regarded as anti-religious in tone or content but as either rational concepts or categories (which are stated or asserted in *etc.* terms of factual [true or false] statements) or rationalized concepts or categories (i.e., conventions, normative assertions, socially constructed insitutions, and the like) which are determined/introduced by the reference groups in each society.

In its second sense, secularisation indicates a structural separation between the political and the religious institutions. Hajjarian, however, makes it clear that in his view "secularisation" in the above two senses is different from "secularism." While the latter is an ideology which has its own value system, the former is a historical process. It is the studying of recent developments of this historical process in the context of the Iranian society which constitutes Hajjarian's main research interest as political scientist.

Hajjarian maintains that Shi'ite *fiqh* has inherent capacity and built-in mechanisms for such a transition from the realm of the sacred to the realm of the secular. Traditionally, for the Shi'ite jurists there are four main sources which assist them in making religious rulings. These are the Book (the Quran), the Tradition (of the Prophet and the Imamas), *ijma* اجماع (consensus of the *fuqha*),[19] and *aql* عقل (the intellect, the reason). Now, while the insistence on literal interpretations of the first two main sources has been strong among a large number of the Sunni *moftis* (those jurists who issue religious edicts) as well as the so-called *akhbaris* اخباریون (traditionists: those who give priority to the Tradition over other sources) among the Shi'ite *fuqha*, in Hajjarian's view the mainstream of the Shi'ite *fuqha* throughout the past centuries have developed ways and mechanisms which would enable them to exercise a less literal and more liberal approach in making use of the main sources. These mechanisms, a partial list of which is presented below, has greatly facilitated the process of "secularisation" of the Shi'ite *fiqh* in post-revolutionary Iran.

- The endorsement of many aspects of the pre-Islamic social norms (فقه الجاهلیه *fiqh al-jahiliyyah*) by the Prophet. Some of the *fuqaha* have interpreted this as the permissibility of endorsing modern social norms which are much more humane than the pre-Islamic norms.
- The expansion of the realm of acts and deeds which belong to *Sharia*-free zone (*manteghtul fragh* منطقه الفراغ), i.e., the realm of *mubahat* مباحات. Some of the *fuqha*, by exercising their commonsensical judgements have helped expand this realm in such a way that the realm of compulsory/forbidden deeds (*wajibaat / muharammat* واجبات ~ محرمات) could (eventually) be reduced to the personal relations between man and God.
- To declare that the traditional *fiqh* has nothing to say on some subjects. This is a powerful mechanism which can easily put the whole realm of modern economic, social and political sphere out of the reach of the traditional *fiqh*. A case in point, to show the power of this mechanism, is the controversial issue of *riba* (usury). Some of the *fuqha* would argue that since the ruling concerning the unlawfulness of the usury only applies to those goods which are deemed to have intrinsic value like gold and jew-

elry, it cannot be applied to a socially constructed entity like "paper money" which does not have an intrinsic value. Many other modern concepts that likewise have no precedent in *fiqh* can be declared to be out of the proper realm of its applicability.

- The so-called rule of *ma la nassa fih* ما لا نصّ فيه (what to which there is no reference either in the Quran or in the Tradition of the Prophet and the Shi'ite Imams). Some of the *fuqaha* quite successfully have applied this rule in filtering out many of the textual references as non-relevant authorities for issuing religious edicts and thus have provided a greater role for the approaches customarily held amongst the populace (*urfi* solutions).

- Making use of analogical arguments (*qiyas-e fiqhi* قیاس فقهی) in issuing religious edicts. The significance of this measure can only be appreciated if one notices that traditional Shi'i *fuqha* have always prided themselves for arriving at their religious edicts via deductive patterns of reasoning or syllogism. They have also looked suspiciously at the practice of the Sunni *moftis* and *ulama* who were using analogical reasoning from the early days in the history of Islam. However, in practice, the Shi'ite *fuqha* have resorted to *qiyas* and therefore have given a greater say to the *urfi* reason.

- Resorting to the Prophetic sayings such as "My *ummah* (followers) never, in their entirety, agree upon something which is against the will of God and his Prophet," or "Whatever is endorsed by the Muslims is also endorsed by God." Such sayings were traditionally being used by the Sunni *moftis* as a justification for making use of *ijma'*, however, the use of these same traditions by some of the Shi'ite *fuqaha* has paved the way for more customary (*urfi*) judgments to prevail.

- Endorsement of the view that the deeds of a duty-bound (*mokallaf* مكلف) Muslim should only not conflict with the *basic* tenets of *Sharia*. Such a stratagem provides the secular (*urfi*) reason with a larger room for manoeuvre in dealing with newly emerged issues in relation to the religious edicts.

Hajjarian argues that there are also a range of other mechanisms which can be used, and in fact have been used, by the *Shi'ite fuqhah* in paving the way for more liberal and less restricted approaches in issuing edicts. Some such mechanisms are: *Anavin Sanavieh* عناوین ثانویه (secondary religious judgements which replace the primary judgements in exceptional circumstances); *Ahkam-e Mofawedah* احكام مفوضه (a category of rules which is left to the *faqih*'s discretion); *Ijtihad-e Poya* بویا اجتهاد (dynamic and flexible *ijtihad*); *Qaedeh-e Lotf* قاعده لطف (the principle of "kindness of God to people"—God does not impose difficult tasks on people); and *Izterar* اضطرار (being compelled out of lack of choice or pressing necessity).

However, Hajjarian goes on to argue that all these mechanisms for facilitating the transition of the Shi'ite *fiqh* become pale in comparison to effects of a revolutionary theory proposed by the late Ayatollah Khomeini, namely, the theory of the Absolute Guardianship of the *faqih* ولايت مطلقه فقيه " (*Wilayat-e Motlaqeh Faqih*). This theory, among other things, has given birth to a new *fiqh*, namely, *Fiqh-al Maslaha* فقه المصلحه (expedient jurisprudence) which, according to Hajjarian, will replace the traditional *fiqh*, and plays a significant role in speeding up the process of secularization of the Shi'i *fiqh* in our time.

Hajjarian maintains that according to the theory of the Absolute Guardianship of the *faqih*, the *faqih* acts as a mediator between the two realms of the sacred and the secular. As such, he wears, as it were, two different hats. In his first role, which is called *Yalel-Rab* يلي الرّب (what is related to God), *faqih* is the representative of the Prophet and the Imams and is being appointed by the twelfth (occult) Imam. In his second role, *Yalel-Khalqh* يلي الخلق (what is related to the people), *faqih* acts as the representative of the people and is being elected by them.

In his first capacity, *faqih* has absolute authority over the system of *fiqh* and the *Shari'a*. He can introduce new religious laws and rulings in the same way that the Prophet and the Imams would do. His views, in religious matters, carry the same weight as what can be found in the primary sources such as the Book and the Tradition. This is because in his role as the representative of God *faqih* acquires his legitimacy from God alone.

In his second capacity, *faqih* acquires his power and legitimacy through a "social contract" with the faithful. In this role he is the representative of the people and the symbol of the national sovereignty and is obliged to look after the public good and the national interests.

Hajjarian believes that the combination of these two aspects in the theory of the Absolute Guardianship of the *faqih* paves the way for a rapid process of secularization of the Shi'ite *fiqh*, in both senses of the term "secularization." The reason is rather simple: to do his job as the representative of people, *faqih* has no choice but to resort to pragmatic measures in conducting the affairs of the state. Here the notion of utility takes precedence over all other values. However, since he is also representing the realm of the sacred, his recourse to pragmatic measures drives a wedge between the state, as the manager of the worldly affairs and the more spiritual and personal aspects of the religion. And this, according to Hajjarian, is exactly what is happening in Iran since the early years of the Islamic Revolution.

Ayatollah Khomeini, as the epitome of a *faqih* who is at once representing God and the people, in a groundbreaking edict emphasized that: "The Islamic state, which is a part of the absolute guardianship of the Prophet, is one of the primary principles of *Shari'a* and as such takes priority over all the secondary principles even the Prayer صلوه, the Fast صوم, and the Pilgrimage to Mecca حج.... The state can stop any practice, related to religious rituals or otherwise, whose implementation is against Islam's [i.e., Islamic state's] interest until this remains the case."[20]

Referring to Jean Bodin's theory of modern state, Hajjarian points out that national sovereignty is absolute, unconditional, non-transferable, and undividable. These are incidentally the same characteristics of the absolute guardianship of the *faqih*. In other words, such a system actually represents a modern state and as such it must be equipped to all the means available to modern states.

To establish a modern state whose main concern is the national interest, Hajjarian argues, the *Wali-ye Faqih* (the Guardian Jurist) has no choice but to make use of the notions of utility and expediency. Ayatollah Khomeini, mindful of this delicate issue, explicitly and emphatically stated that, "The preservation of the [Islamic] system is the most important task amongst those religious duties which are compulsory (*oujab-e wanjebat* اوجب واجبات)." This means that to safeguard the interests of an Islamic system (Islamic state) and to preserve it the guardian *faqih* or his representatives can resort to all sorts of expedient measures that are deemed necessary.

It was this concern which prompted Ayatollah Khomeini to order a new council of experts, the expediency council شوراي تشخيص مصلحت, to be established. The members of the first council, though Muslim, were by and large secular (rational) in their outlook. The creation of this council, which was met with objections from the more conservative *fuqaha*, on the one hand assisted those in charge of running the government to do their tasks more effectively, and on the other, pushed the traditional *fiqh* even further towards the issues which only deal with the personal relationship between the believers and God.

Hajjarian believes that the inevitable process of secularisation of the *Shi'i fiqh*, which, ironically, has been greatly facilitated by the creation of an Islamic state under the model of the absolute guardianship of the *faqih* would eventually result in a metamorphism within the very realm of *fiqh* which historically has enjoyed a dominant position *vis-à-vis* other branches of the so-called Islamic Sciences. Traditional *fiqh* would reduce in size and will be limited to what is known as *fiqhul ibadah* فقه العباده (religious rulings concerning customary religious rituals). Other aspects of the traditional *fiqh* will merge with various branches of modern science of law.

The process of secularisation of the Shi'i *fiqh*, in Hajjarian's view, is irreversible and is much more stable than some of the seemingly similar processes which have occurred in a number of Islamic countries. The reason for this difference according to Hajjarian is that while the changes which have taken place in other Islamic countries have been mostly due to the influences of external factors and non-religious elements, in the case of the Shi'i *fiqh* the process of radical and revolutionary change is being fuelled from within and is based on the internal resources of this entity and especially the theoretical structure of the theory of the Absolute Guardianship of the *faqih*.

In the longer term, the Islamic state will be run by what can be dubbed as the "secular reason (intellect)." Those *fuqha* who have joined various departments of the sate will become civil servants in the usual sense of the word. The rest would concentrate on more individualistic (personal as against the public) aspects of the religious doctrines and rituals. In this way, a division of labour will take place within the Shi'ite *fiqh* in which "secularisation" in the second sense of the term will also be realized.

Conclusion

The three representatives of the Shi'i modern thought whose views were selectively and briefly discussed in this paper, despite their different backgrounds have lots in common: they are fluent in Arabic and at least one European language, well acquainted with the Islamic Sciences, well versed in modern social and human sciences, and actively involved in the political and intellectual reform project in contemporary Iran. Their approaches, in their respective fields, are also problem-oriented. They try to tackle newly raised issues by making effective use of the traditional and modern resources available to them. And above all, in their efforts to find sound modern solutions for modern problems of our age, they are making extensive use of the modern reason which is, by definition, autonomous. In doing so, they have, in a sense, revived the deeply rooted idea of *ijtihad* in the Shi'i Islam.

The trend represented and advocated by these modern-day Shi'i *mujtahids*, though only has gained prominence in the past few years is clearly in the ascendant. The number of scholarly articles, in explaining and expanding the positions of this new trend, which consistently appear in the Iranian academic journals, is a good indication of its broad base and the pace of its growth.

Critical rationalism is an elitist trend. This is of course in line with one of the Shi'ite classic features. However, the significance of this new trend in the post-revolutionary Iran is that its appeal goes much further than the members of the educated middle class. Many of those who either belong to more traditional social strata like the bazaaris (traditional entrepreneurs) and the clerics, or to the workers' class, are also being attracted to the views advocated by the critical rationalist who belong to the middle class. In this sense a complete shift in the importance of the social groups have taken place in Iran since the revolution: a shift from populism to elitism. While during the 1960s and 1970s it was the values of the lower class which were being promoted and praised by the intellectuals, the leftists and the Muslim intellectuals alike, in the post revolutionary period it is the values of the middle class, that sets the social norms.

The new discourse which is gradually gaining prominence in Iran under the influence of the new trend seems to be preparing the ground for a fundamental paradigm change in the approaches of the Shi'ites to Islam and to modern life. Thus, for example, the recognition of the fact that in dealing with the intricate problems of managing the affairs of the state recourse to pragmatic measures is inevitable would help the Shi'ite to better appreciate the predicaments of the Sunni *moftis* in the past history of Islam and look upon their practices more sympathetically. On the other hand, the prominent role given to the *urfi* reason by the Shi'ite critical rationalists in dealing with the doctrinal issues is bound to be appealing to the Sunnis who have favoured such a reason from early on. This in turn means the models which are being proposed by the new trend of the Shi'ite thinkers could also have far-reaching effects on the approaches and practices of the Sunni Islam. The significance of such an influence becomes even more apparent, if one, like some of Arab writers, maintains that the Arab/Sunni world is, by and large, not adequately open to modern ideas and ideals.[21]

The end result of all these new developments could be a better mutual understanding on the part of the two main branches of Islam and therefore, greater possibilities for closer cooperation which should prove to be beneficial for the humanity at large.

Notes

1. For a short but authoritative account of history and main doctrines of the Shi'i Islam see, Mohammad Hossein Tabatabai, *Shi'ite Islam*, trans. S. H. Nasr, London, 1975. Hamid Enayat's *Modern Islamic Political Thought*, London, 1982, also offers a brief scholarly explanation of emergence and evolution of Shi'i Islam. S. Hussain Jafari, *The Origin and Early Development of Shi'a Islam*, Beirut, 1977 discusses some of the conceptual and historical issues related to Shi'i Islam at some length. *Shi'ism: Doctrines, Thought, and Spirituality*, edited, annotated, and with an introduction by S. H. Nasr, H. Dabashi, and S. V. R Nasr, 1988, State University of New York Press, introduces main themes in Shi'ite doctrinal system. I have heavily relied on Enayat's book for the historical background of Shi'ism.

2. Enayat, 1982.

3. Enayat, *op. cit.*

4. The violent death of Hossein, is celebrated annually with orations, plays, and processions and is one of the most important occasions in the Shi'ite calendar. These celebrations have had a significant social and political role in the history of Shi'ism. They have also influenced Sunnite believers in some part of the Islamic world, including Afghanistan and India, who participate in similar passion plays.

5. The success of the Abbasids' revolt against the Ummayads was to a great extent due to the support of the Shi'ites who were hoping to restore the leadership of the *Ummah* to their Imams. However, despite their initial promises, the Abbasids did their best to keep the Shi'ite Imams out of political arena.

6. Shi'ite Islam has a number of subdivisions. The majority are called Twelvers (*Ithna Ashariyya* اثنی عشریه), because they recognize twelve Imams, beginning with Ali. Other Shi'ite Imams who are descendants of Ali are, Hasn ibn Ali, Hossein ibn Ali, Ali ibn Hossein, Mohammad ibn Ali, Ja'far ibn Mohammad, Musa ibn Ja'far, Ali ibn Musa, Mohammad ibn Ali, Ali ibn Mohammad, Hasan ibn Ali, and Mohammad ibn Hasan (Mahdi).

Among the other Shi'ite sects, which are much smaller in comparison to the Twelvers, the better known are the Zaydis (Yezidis) of Yemen who recognize five imams, the Ismailis who recognize seven imams and live mostly in Pakistan and India, and the Druzes who live mostly in Lebanon, Israel, Jordan, the West Bank, and Syria. Some of the Shi'ite sects may believe in at least one Imam who is not among the list of Imams believed by the mainstream Shi'ite. For example, while the main body of Shi'ite regard Musa ibn Ja'far as their seventh Imam, the Isma'ili recognize instead his brother Isma'il and since his disappearance, they await his return.

7. The orthodoxy has many representatives. Ja'far Sobhani, a senior cleric in Qom (Iran), is a typical one who has written many books on philosophy and *fiqh*.

8. Tradition, in this context, means the sayings and the deeds of the Prophet, including his endorsement of the states of affairs he has witnessed and about which he has approvingly remained silent. For the Shi'ites, the term also applies to the infallible Imams.

For a comparison between the classic and the modern meanings of the term "intuition," see Ali Paya, "Intuition according to the Analytic Philosophers," in *Analytic Philosophy: Problems and Prospects*, Tehran, Tarh-e Nou, 2003.

9. A well-known proponent of this trend is Seyyed Hossein Nasr, a professor of Islamic Studies at George Washington University. See, for example, his *Traditional Islam in the Modern World*, London and New York, Kegan Paul, 1987.

10. Mohammad Taqi Mesbah Yazdi, a prominent Ayatollah in Qom (Iran) who used to be one of the orthodoxy's more vocal representatives, in recent years has increasingly identified himself with the fundamentalist trend and is now being regarded as one of its main ideologues.

11. The modernist trend has had its heyday mostly in the pre-Revolution and the first few years after the victory of the Islamic revolution in Iran. Some of the most influential figures of this trend are Ali Shari'ati, a Sorbonne educated sociologist; Morteda Motahhari, an eminent Ayatollah who was a member of the Revolutionary council; and Mahdi Bazargan, a French-educated university professor and the prime minister of the provisional government after the Revolution.

12. Soroush [1978] *Cheh Kesi Behtar Mitavanad Mubarezeh Konad* (Who Can Fight Better); Soroush [1979] *Idéologi-ye Shaytani* (The Satanic Ideology).

For an overview concerning the influence of Popper's thought on the Iranian intellectuals, see Ali Paya, "Karl Popper and the Iranian Intellectuals," *American Journal of the Islamic Social Sciences*, Spring 2003.

13. Soroush has expanded his views on religion in general and Islam in particular in a number of publications, including *Ghabz va Bast-e Theoric-e Shri'at* (A Theoretical Account of the [Epistemic] Contraction and Expansion of the Religion), Tehran, Serat Publications, 1992; *Farbeh tar az Ideology* (More Capacious than Ideology), Tehran, Serat, 1994; *Bast-e Tajrobeh-e Nabavi* (The Expansion of Prophetic Experience), Tehran, Serat, 1999; *Akhlagh-e Khodayan* (God's Ethics), Tehran, Tarhe-Nou, 2001.

14. For Popper's view on these concepts see his *Objective Knowledge*, Oxford, Oxford University Press, 1979.

15. Mohammad Mojtahid Shabestari, *Hermeneutic, The Book and the Tradition*, Tehran, Tarhe-Nou, 1986; *Faith and Freedom*, Tehran, Tarhe-Nou, 1987; *A Critique of the Official Reading of Religion: Crises, Challenges, and Solutions*, Tehran, Tarh-e Nou, 2000.

16. By "the official reading" Shabestari means mostly the fundamentalist approach which is being advocated by a group of conservative clerics who wield considerable influence among more radical Shi'ites inside and outside Iran. The views held by these clergies and their supporters have many elements in common with the orthodox reading with the major difference that the fundamentalist approach is much more politicised and socially active.

17. Hajjarian's views can be found in his two most recent books: *Republicanism: Demystification of Power*, Theran, Tarhe-Nou publications, 2000, and *From the Sacred Witness to the Profane Witness*, Tehran Tarhe-Nou, 2001.

18. Some also believe that this term should be pronounced as *elmaniyat* from the root word *elm* (modern or rational science).

19. Although both the Shi'ite *fuqa* and the Sunni *moftis* make use of the concept of *ijma'*, however there is a fine difference in the way the two groups understand and interpret this term/concept. The Sunnis, relying on a saying of the Prophet, that the whole of the Muslim community, in their totality, cannot err, claim a high degree of validity for *ijma'*. The Shi'ites, on the other hand, maintain that *ijma'* can only be valid, if an infallible Imam takes part in the process of decision making or somehow influence its outcome. Difficulties in implementing the required criteria has meant that the Shi'ite *fuqha*, in the past, were not so keen in making use of this source.

20. Ayatollah Khomeini, *Sahifeh Nur* (Book of Light), Tehran.

21. See Foad Ajami, "Iraq and the Future of the Arab World," *Foreign Affairs*, January–February 2003.

Global Discourse
on Islam and Democracy

8

The Politics, Theory, and Philosophy of Islamic Democracy

M. A. Muqtedar Khan

The Grand Narrative on Islam and the West

The grand narrative on Islam and the West has posited several binaries to distinguish between essentialized notions of Western and Islamic civilizations. Both Muslim as well as Western historians and political commentators have meticulously constructed narratives about "the Islamic civilization" and "the Western civilization," and in these endeavors their dominant strategy has been to identify, highlight and even exaggerate real and perceived differences between the two cultural and historical entities. Interestingly secular as well as religious scholars from both sides are involved in maintaining this discourse of difference. The only exceptions are the Islamic modernists, who recognize that the West has gone further than Muslims in extending political freedoms and human rights guarantees to their citizens, and those scholars who are part of the Esposito school of thought.[1] Islamic modernists break away from the grand narrative to register their dissent through appreciation of democracy and arguing that there is more in common between Islam and the West.[2] They insist that what Islam and the West share is vast and profound in comparison to what separates them.

One of the curious elements of this grand narrative is that neither of the two competing epistemic communities—Islamist scholars and Western scholars—is honest. Western scholars either selectively compare Western present with a highly caricatured Muslim present, or they compare Western ideals, such as democracy and religious tolerance, with the worst manifestations of Muslim realities such as the extremism of the Taliban. Islamists too respond in kind.

They compare a glorified Islamic past with selected aspects of Western present. For example, they contrast the explosion of science and philosophy in the heydays of the Islamic civilization with promiscuity, drugs and crime in the West. Needless to say, very few Islamists have anything to say about the explosion of science, InfoTech, space travel and medical sciences in the contemporary West. Similarly while there are many western studies documenting the plight of Muslim women in places like Afghanistan, there are no studies available that compare the family lives of hundreds of thousands of successful Muslim women professionals with those of their counterparts in the West.

The point I seek to make is neither completely original nor complex. How the Western discourse on Islam constructs Islam as the inferior "other" in order to produce and reproduce the idea of a modern, advanced and rational western civilization has been explained with great eloquence by Edward Said, Aziz Al-Azmeh, John Esposito and many others.[3] My only point is that Islamists too have now joined this grand narrative on Islam and the West and are using it for a similar purpose—to produce a theocentric, just, universally valid, divinely mandated and morally superior Islamic society that uses the modern West as its constitutive other.[4] Thus the perpetuation of the Islam and the West discourse as a dominant global narrative is essential to both chauvinistic Westerners and jingoistic Islamists to sustain their utopias through the creation and demonization of a civilizational other. This discourse simultaneously generates the Western as well as the Islamic identity.

The discourse on Islam and democracy and its constituent debates is just one theme of the grand narrative on Islam and the West. Some of the important themes of this discourse include "the threat of Islam," "Islam and secularism," Islam and development," "Islam and modernity," "Islamic terrorism" and "Islamic holy wars." This narrative also includes the themes of "colonization," "imperialism," "Zionist racism" and "globalization." The first set of themes seeks to establish the twin objectives of Western superiority over Islam, and the threat of Islam to the West. These twin goals reproduce the Western identity, and justify military actions against the Muslim World. Notice how since the attacks of September 11 not only have these themes become common but so has pride in being American and belonging to the Western world. Specters of Islamic threat always reinforce the conceptions of the self in the West in general and in the U.S. in particular. It is therefore not coincidental that both Americans and Muslims now see the U.S. as the flag bearer of the Western world.

The second set of themes helps Islamists in carving out a distinct Islamic identity by creating a self whose dominant characteristic is ever increasing distance from the West.[5] These themes, like the first set of themes also provide motivation and justification for violence against the West. A consistent manifestation of this tendency is the linking of all Muslim-U.S. issues to the Arab-

Israeli conflict. By linking the U.S. with the brutality and the land grabbing policies of Israel, Islamists extend the demonizing labels of colonization and imperialism to the U.S. to justify terrorism against it.[6] It is within this textual arena where construction of identity and justification of violence takes place that one can locate the discourse on Islam and democracy. The discourse on Islam and democracy is composed of two distinct debates. One debate is primarily political. The central question that is debated is the reasons for the marked absence of democracies in the Muslim World. The second debate is quasi-theological, or in a sense concerns the political theology of Islam. This debate is about the compatibility of Islam and democracy. Unfortunately both the debates are implicated by the politics that spawns them. My discussion here is more about uncovering the politics behind the political theology of Islam and democracy rather than exploring the substantive issues in the various debates.

The Politics behind the Discourse on Islam and Democracy

In many ways the politics of the discourse on Islam and democracy is as interesting and worthy of examination as the alleged compatibility or lack thereof between Islam and democracy. I have already discussed how the grand narrative on Islam and the West is necessary for the reproduction of the Western as well as Islamic identity. It is noteworthy that the debate on whether Islam and democracy are compatible starts with an unproblematized assumption that there are indeed two unique political systems, one belonging to Islam and one to the West. There is no serious examination as to why democracy is assumed to be Western, and what is uniquely Islamic about the institution of *Khilafa* or the principle of *Shura*.[7] The discourse is in a way tautological because it starts with the assumption that the two civilizations or systems are different and usually ends with the conclusion that they are different yet compatible or different and incompatible.[8]

Western Politics

As far as several Western scholars who write on this subject are concerned they seem to have essentially two demagogic objectives behind their discourse. One, to project Islam as a totalitarian ideology that seeks to undermine personal and political freedoms; Islam as a system, they argue, is opposed to individual rights and is a barrier to the creation of a tolerant, pluralistic and democratic society. The political, and consequently economic underdevelopment of the Muslim World—primarily Middle East and South Asia—is therefore a consequence of its adherence to Islam and not as a result of either European colonization or American neo-colonization. The global system does not privilege or marginalize any of the Third World nations. Muslims are in a bad shape only and only because they are Muslims—believers in Islam. Needless to say this argument not only seeks to exonerate the West of any culpability for the extremely negative consequences of its global domination in the past and in the present but also seeks to establish the utilitarian superiority of the so called Western ideals over Islamic values. Any astute student of political science will immediately recognize that this is the old theory of modernization in a new garb. The West is modern because it is modern and the East is backward because it is traditional (Islamic).

Secondly the argument that Islam and democracy are incompatible is a supplementary argument for the justification of continued U.S. support for Israel in the Middle East after the end of the cold war. This discourse maintains that Israel is the only democracy in the Middle East and therefore merits the uncritical support of its democratic allies—the West. It also implies that because Israel allows its Jewish citizens several democratic privileges, the international community must not look too negatively at its horrendous treatment of the millions of people it subjugates within its borders by designating them as non-citizens. For Israel to maintain any form of legitimacy in the West it is imperative to portray Muslim societies as fundamentally undemocratic, and therefore fundamentally anti-Western.[9]

Thus the unique identity of the West and the security of Israel are the stakes that drive the politics underpinning the discourse on Islam and democracy as far as non-Muslim Western scholars are concerned. Needless to say there are some notable exceptions and most of these exceptions have joined forces with Muslim Democrats in trying to enunciate and elaborate the hitherto un-enumerated democratic foundations of Islam.[10]

Muslim Politics

It is not easy to map Muslim politics for several reasons. The basic reason for this difficulty is that majority of Muslims often remain silent and most of the voices in the cacophony of Muslim politics represent aggressively active minorities. Also there are diverse Muslim positions; the most fundamental division within them is between secular Muslim approaches and the so-called Islamist approaches. Within Islamist voices too there are several positions. It is, however, interesting to note that while in South Asia, Islamists tend to be mostly authoritarian and secular Muslims are more democratic, in the Middle East, Islamists tend to be more democratic and secular Muslims are more authoritarian. Since secular Muslims hold power in most of the Muslim World except in Iran, South Asia is more democratic than the Middle East. The ultimate indication of this is the fact that both Bangladesh and Pakistan have had women heads of states, who were freely elected to office.

While in Pakistan and Bangladesh, Islamists have found it increasingly difficult to come to power through the ballot; they wish to do so through other means. The Pakistani experience with the dictatorship of General Zia in the 1980s may have convinced the Islamists that a friendly general is their best way to impose the *Sharia* (Islamic Law). Under General Parvez Musharraf's reign, a man with clearly secular orientations, the Islamists have done exceedingly well at the ballot box. They presently govern two out of four provinces and are the second largest party in the national assembly.[11]

In the Middle East, Islamists have discovered that democratic institutions such as political parties and parliaments, no matter how weak and subservient to the kings and dictators, still allow them opportunities to partake in the public sphere and bring their voice and ideas to the masses. Without some degree of democratization they would be completely silenced and marginalized. Therefore unlike their South Asian counterparts, Islamic movements in the Middle East are more in favor of democracy. Mind you this is a purely pragmatic issue. It does not mean that Islamists in the Middle East are more inclined towards the argument that Islam and democracy are compatible. Their preference for democracy is perhaps more political than theological.[12]

In the West, particularly in America, the debate within the Muslim community on Islam's compatibility with democracy is inextricably linked with the debate over whether Muslims should participate in American politics or not. Muslims are clearly divided on this issue. I describe those who argue that Islam and democracy are compatible as Muslim Democrats. They insist that Muslims must enter the American political arena to safeguard their rights and advance their social and political interests from within the system. I describe those who claim that democracy is un-Islamic as Muslim Isolationists. They are interested in keeping Muslims isolated from American mainstream.[13]

Some Islamic movements equate being pro-democracy as pro-Western. It is a confessional position. Since by insisting that they are against democracy they essentially claim that they are against the West, especially the U.S. Therefore their resistance to democracy is an extension of their resistance to U.S. global domination. They see democracy in the same way as they see MTV, as a Western cultural artifact that will corrupt and de-Islamize Muslim societies. When they see the marginal role that Christianity (or rather the Christian clergy) plays within western societies, particularly in Europe, their fear of democracy as anti-religion is enforced and makes them more adamantly opposed to democratization. The Wahhabis, the Salafis and the Hizb-ut-Tahreeris, in spite of their internal differences are united in this fear of democracy as antithetical to religion.

From the above discussion it must be evident that the discourse on Islam and democracy often serves as a proxy debate for several contentious issues within the Muslim community. The Muslim World is still recovering from the cultural and psychological devastation caused by colonialism, which basically truncated their history. Colonialism was an external force that disconnected the Muslim world from its past and its traditions. Decolonization then disconnected it from its present. The resulting alienation has created a deep cry and need for authenticity, for relevance, for connection, and has generated a communal search for a "self." The discourse on Islam and democracy while not exactly addressing these existential issues is definitely permeated by its philosophical implications.

The Challenge of Democracy

Both Islam and democracy have become powerful global trends. Islam is today the fastest growing religion in North America, Europe, Australia, Asia and Africa. Islam is not only growing in numbers but in significance. Islamic politics is now easily the most important global concern even overshadowing the effects of globalization and global warming. Islam and its various interpretations are not only shaping politics but also economics. The experiments with Islamic economics are commonplace in much of the Muslim World. Islamic Development Bank is an important institution and now Dow Jones has an Islamic index and Harvard University has Islamic legal and Islamic finance projects that deal with day-to-day aspects of these fields.

Democracy too has seen a phenomenal growth. After the end of the cold war, the democratic way of political organization has become perhaps the only legitimate form of polity. Societies are either democratic or abnormal and therefore absence of democracy, an abnormality, needs explanation. The most malignant case of this political illness is in the Arab World and is therefore scrutinized by polemicists as well as philosophers alike. The logic is simple, much of the Muslim World does not have democracy but has Islam, and the rest of the world apparently does not have Islam but has democracy or is getting there. Thus it is inevitable that Islam and democracy must be antithetical forces. Democracy clearly is desirable and therefore Islam must be undesirable unless of course it ceases to be an obstacle and recasts itself not as a challenge but as compatible with democracy.

Here again the discourse presupposes essentialist notions of Islam and democracy. Societies can be free and democratic without necessarily looking exactly like the U.S. The Islam articulated and advocated by Liberal Muslims is vastly different from the one advocated by the scholars of Saudi Arabia or conservative movements that share the beliefs of the Salafi ideology. Liberal Muslims have consistently argued the compatibility of Islam and democracy and even went as far as to assert that Islam cannot be fully realized in the absence of political freedoms.[14]

But regardless of what Islam's theoretical position is vis-à-vis democracy, the globalization of democracy does pose a serious challenge to the Muslim World: democratize or produce an alternate form of government that realizes the aspirations of all its citizens and ensures that women and minorities are guaranteed, at the minimum, the basic human rights enshrined in international law. So far the alternatives that the Muslim World has offered are woefully inadequate. Some Muslim nations have managed to democratize to admirable degree. Bangladesh, Turkey, Malaysia, and Indonesia have shown that democracy can take root in the Muslim World. But Afghanistan, Saudi Arabia and Sudan have demonstrated that the Islamic alternative to democracy is a rather medieval form of autocracy. Only Iran has managed to some extent to find a middle path that embraces Islam as well as democracy, but the failure of Iran's polity to escape the clutches of the clergy, make Iran's experiment with Islamic governance undesirable.

The current structures of authoritative governance cannot be sustained in the Muslim World. The Muslim World cannot wait until the Islamists define and articulate a conception of the Islamic state that appeals to all. There are no other alternatives at present except democracy and the Islamic state. I believe the Muslim world would do well to democratize first, and then use the open society to debate how to accommodate Islam in its governing structures. So far the debate about the role of Islam in politics is being conducted in an environment of intimidation and tyranny. Where Islamists are in power they disallow demands for freedom as in Iran and Saudi Arabia, and where the secularists are in power they oppress Islamists, as in Egypt and Syria. Democratization will provide the free environment where Muslims can debate and develop their vision of an Islamic society, without the fear of repression by either secularists or Islamists. In fact it is not difficult to imagine Muslim democracies with political parties that advocate secularism, Islamism, and Islamic liberalism, each trying to shape policies based on their particular ideological and theological visions.[15]

But even to move towards democracy as a transitory state is not easy. Democracy must triumph in theory before it can be realized in practice. Muslims must widely and unambiguously accept that Islam and democracy are compatible and that meaningful faith requires freedom. Once we accept these principles we can address the political issues more easily. But before Muslims can accept democracy as an Islamic principle, Islamic political philosophy must accomplish the following tasks:

1. Link political legitimacy not to the application of a legal code that is prior to politics, but to the binding character of Shura (consultation).
2. Reject the idea of a fixed Shari'a in favor of keeping Shari'a open and dependent on negotiated understanding.
3. Explain how talk of divine sovereignty works to free rulers from accountability to the ruled.
4. Acknowledge the limits of the Islamic legal tradition and eschew it in favor of the Compact of Medina as a basis for Islamic democracy.
5. Treat Islam as a fountain of values that guide conduct rather than a system of ready-made solutions to problems.
6. Past legal opinions must not subvert contemporary political reflections. We will be free only when we can freely determine for ourselves what is the Shari'a. There is no mediation in Islam and the Islamic jurists must step aside. As long as the colonial tendencies of Islamic jurisprudence persist there will be no Islamic democracy.

For nearly a century, Islamic political theorists have been trying to argue that not only is Islam compatible with modernity and democracy, but indeed the advent of Islam was the essential beginning of modern enlightenment. Muslim political theorists are rare commodity but nevertheless few of them who did exist and write have tried to demonstrate the antecedents of modern polities within Islamic experience. But much of their contribution has remained out of the mainstream of Islamic discourse and Muslim conceptions of Islamic scholarship. The political concepts that pervade Muslim discourses today have mostly been crafted by Islamists like Maulana Maududi and Syed Qutb, who were Islamic political theorists in some sense, but their approach was too ideological and polemical.[16] Nevertheless while there are rich sources of Islamic thought on democracy, an Islamic democratic theory has yet to emerge.

As the Muslim World became independent from colonial occupation and began searching for authentic models for their newly independent polities, Muslims were faced with the choice of either imitating the contemporary West, often their former colonizer, or try to reproduce the political and legal structures that preceded the colonial era. Muslim secularists, most prominently Attaturk in Turkey, opted to adopt Western models of secular democracy and some Arab states chose to reproduce medieval models of kingships based on tribal loyalties.[17] It was only when Pakistan emerged as an independent nation that Muslims at that time chose to invent a model of Muslim democracy that recognized the compatibility of Islam and democracy. The debates that shaped the writing of Pakistan's constitution brought out interesting issues about how Islam would shape politics and political structures in the modern era.[18]

The promise of the debate about the authenticity of democracy and the challenge of accommodating religion in a multi-religious modern state of Pakistan was unfortunately never realized. Two mutually reinforcing trends within the Muslim World marginalized the importance of this emerging political theory of democracy in Pakistan. The two trends still dominate the Muslim political landscape and they are Political Islam and its highly politicized interpretation of Islam and the call for an "Islamic State"; the other trend is secular authoritarianism which emerged from Arab socialism. Muslim discourses and Muslim politics in the last fifty odd years has been a debilitating assertion of either secular authoritarianism with military repression or radical Islamism with frequent frenzies of terror and civil strife. One of the casualties of this civil war in the Muslim world was the emerging democratic theory of an Islamic polity in modern times.[19]

The juxtaposition of Islamic state or secular democracy, the Iranian model versus the Turkish model, as the only two alternatives for a Muslim polity not only undermined the development of Islamic democratic discourse but also marginalized liberal Muslims and intellectuals.[20] But recent developments in global politics and the most surprising emergence of President George Bush as an advocate of the compatibility of Islam and democracy and his determination to facilitate the establishment of such a polity in Iraq, has once again given vitality and centrality to the incipient theory of Islamic democracy.[21] One is now witnessing a plethora of academic journals publishing special issues on Islam and democracy, think tanks conducting debates and symposia on Islam and democracy and even newspapers are now exploring the nuances of faith and freedom.[22] Recently we have also witnessed a series of books that seek to address the issue from both political as well as theoretical perspective.[23]

Theologians, Jurists and Political Philosophers

The new interest in Islam and democracy will certainly revive old ideas and generate new interpretations; however, the contemporary momentum is driven by theologians, jurists and activists and not by political theorists. The activists are convinced that democratization is the panacea for all Muslim problems and they are happy to run with the slogan that Islam and democracy are compatible and hence we should hasten with the process of democratizing the Muslim world. From a political perspective their zeal and enthusiasm is advantageous but they do not really contribute much to the theoretical content of the claim that there is a strong convergence in Islamic values and democratic principles except for the rhetorical equation of democracy with *Shura*. *Shura* is the Quranic term for consultation and Muslim advocates of democracy find a theological vindication for their quest in this Quranic injunction to consult: *"And their affairs are conducted through mutual consultation"* (Al Quran 42:38). But a democratic theory cannot just emerge by itself from a part of a verse.

The theologians do approach the issue in a comprehensive and systematic way. They go to Islamic roots and identify and exemplify those elements that correspond to liberal democratic principles. An excellent example is the recent work of Abdulaziz Sachedina who shows, relying basically on Quranic sources and eschewing other socially constructed discourses, how Islam strongly advocates pluralism.[24] Sachedina's work is not a treatise in political theory and he does not intend it as such. He himself envisages his work as a preventive diplomacy tool for Muslim and non-Muslim politicians seeking to advance the cause of pluralism.[25] One of the most important limitations of *The Islamic Roots of Democratic Pluralism* is its treatment of pluralism and democracy as stable, uncontested ideas enjoying widespread consensus.

The work also focuses on religious pluralism without actually distinguishing between religious and political pluralism. For example, while one can find in it excellent resources to argue for religious tolerance and equality of all from a purely Islamic standpoint, one cannot however justify the toleration of competing political ideologies such as capitalism and communism. Will an Islamic state allow political parties to exist and compete for power that are ideologically opposed to state ideology? Can communists share power or even come to power in an Islamic democracy? Will people of different faiths enjoy equal rights under Islamic pluralism? Does the system also tolerate political pluralism? As a theologian, Sachedina focuses on theological differences and offers a theological solution to religious differences but he does not offer a theological or a political solution to political differences. Can a political theorist treat Sachedina's work as a resource to build an Islamic theory of political pluralism? Possibly. Sachedina's work is not only path breaking but also points to new paths and underscores the necessity for the full-blown development of Muslim/Islamic democratic theory. In this book too, Sachedina's chapter on the role of Islam in the public square, underscores the importance of political theology and the relationship between theology and political philosophy.

All arguments that advocate Islamic democracies or the compatibility of Islam and democracy take the Quran as a revealed document, whose text is absolute but meanings are open to alternative interpretations. There is even a Quranic basis to claim the absoluteness of text and relativity of meanings (Al Quran 3:7). The Quran acts as the anchor, the absolute point from which Muslim thinkers begin and end their thinking. Therefore when we talk of pluralism and democracy it is important to clarify which democracy—liberal, radical, socialist, deliberative, and which pluralism—religious, epistemological, cultural or political? While arguing the compatibility of Islam with pluralism or modernity or democracy, the merit of these notions cannot be taken for granted. They must be unpacked and their virtues examined from the moral and ethical foundation of the Quran.[26] This is the responsibility of Muslim political theorists.[27] Muhsin Mahdi makes an interesting point to emphasize the compatibility of theology and political philosophy while explaining the political philosophy of Al Farabi. He argues:

> Political philosophy had to pay particular attention to theology for many reasons. To begin with, there was the political impetus that gave rise to theology [Revealed theology in the Islamic community arose in response to differences concerning the legitimate ruler of the community as well as to clarify and defend God's justice and its implications for man's life on earth]. . . . Furthermore theology was the religious science most open to the call of reason. All this required the political philosophers to delimit the respective spheres of theology and political philosophy, distinguish their respective principles and aims, and define the proper relationship between them.[28]

While theologians and their work can become a fundamental resource for Islamic political theorists, the *Fatwa* (religious edict)[29] wielding Islamic jurists, who with one stroke can make democracy *Halal* (permissible in Islam) and political philosophy *Haraam* (forbidden in Islam), remain an important barrier to the development of Islamic political theory. An illustrative example of how even well meaning Islamic legal scholars unable to escape their juristic outlook, can undermine the Islamic roots of democracy while actually advocating Islamic democracy is the recent argument on the subject by Khalid Abou El Fadl. In his essay, El Fadl combines an Islamic ethical and juridical outlook to identify various sources of compassion, tolerance, equality and justice in Islamic sources and unlike Sachedina he does not limit himself to essentially the Quran but explores secondary sources too. But in the conclusion of the article he allows the colonial tendency of Islamic legalism to subvert his quest for an Islamic democracy.[30]

Islamic intellectual tradition, which includes Islamic legal thought (*Usul al-fiqh* and *fiqh*), theology (*Kalam*), mysticism (*Tasawwuf*) and philosophy (*falsafa*), is easily one of the most developed and profound traditions of human knowledge. However, for various historical reasons, this intellectual heritage of Islam remains strikingly underdeveloped in the area of political philosophy. One of the reasons for this lacuna in Islamic thought is the colonial tendency of Islamic legal thought. Many Islamic jurists equate Islam with Islamic law and privilege the study and exploration of the *Sharia* (loosely understood as Islamic Law) over and above all else thereby colonizing Islamic thought and marginalizing other fields of inquiry. This dominance of legal studies has allowed only episodic exploration of the idea of a polity in Islam. Today, all over the Muslim World there are hundreds of Islamic schools and universities that produce hundreds of thousands of Islamic legal scholars but hardly any traditional school produces political theorists or philosophers. Except for rare exceptions, this intellectual poverty has reduced Islamic thought to the status of a medieval legal tradition.[31]

In spite of the intellectual imperialism of the Islamic jurists, Islamic political theory has managed to survive in some form. In the twentieth century we have witnessed the emergence of two distinct approaches to Islamic political theory.[32] The Islamists who advocate the establishment of an Islamic State, an authoritarian and ideological entity whose central concepts are al-Hakimiyyah (the sovereignty of God) and Sharia (the law of God),[33] and the liberal Muslim political theorists who advocate an Islamic democracy whose central themes are Shura (consultation) and Sahifat al Madinah (Constitutionalism a la the Compact of Medina).[34]

Political Islamists do posit the principle of Shura as an important element of their Islamic State but their concept of Shura is limited and essentially does lip service to the idea of consultation. For them consultative governance is not necessary for legitimacy, since legitimacy comes from the enforcement of the Sharia regardless of the will of the people. Thus if Shura contradicts their notion of what constitutes the Sharia their Islamic State will immediately abandon its consultative status and become a totalitarian ideological entity ready to wage Jihad to enforce their view of the law of God even against the will of the people. It is exactly here that political theorists of the Islamist tendency become as authoritative as the jurist, whose understanding of what is God's will is law and always above the will of the people. Needless to say, for the liberal Muslim theorists, Shura is paramount and Sharia too must be arrived at through consultative processes and not taken as given.[35]

The extraordinary influence of the idea of "Islam as Sharia" has made law prior to state/polity. Because law comes first and then the political community, the structure and the form of the polity becomes subservient to the application of law. Polity derives legitimacy from its ability to implement Sharia rather than the very idea of law/Sharia emerging to serve the need of the polity. This philosophical error, which amounts to placing the cart in front of the horse, also underpins El Fadl's otherwise erudite discussion of the compatibility of Islam and democracy. This is particularly striking in his conclusion. I expected his treatise to end with some kind of delineation of an Islamic democracy. On the contrary, he concludes by imposing, a priori, Sharia based limitations on democracy. He clearly states that a case for democracy from within Islam should not substitute popular sovereignty for divine sovereignty and should recognize that democratic lawmaking respects that a priori nature of the *Sharia*. He begins his essay as a political philosopher and ends it as an Ayatollah laying the edict—you can have democracy but only as long as people are not sovereign and *Sharia* is not violated.

Prof. El Fadl's essay is brilliant in its discussion of the moral and ethical principles within Islam that can help make a case for democracy from within Islam, he nevertheless reinforces traditional barriers rather than deconstructing them. One of the most prominent Islamic theologians, Sheikh Ibn Taymiyyah (1263–1328 AD) who in many ways is a source of great inspiration to conservative Muslims who advocate authoritarianism, argued for an Islamic leviathan that would defend the Islamic world from external military threats and Islamic doctrines from internal heresies.[36] He claimed that the object of an Islamic state was to impose the *Sharia*. El Fadl argues similarly that an Islamic democracy should recognize the centrality of *Sharia* in Muslim life. This is scary. It raises several questions. Who gets to articulate what constitutes the *Sharia*? Islamic Jurists? Who determines who is an Islamic jurist? Who determines which schools can provide the education that will produce jurists? Who determines when a specific democratically passed law is in violation of the *Sharia*? Who determines the issues on which people will have freedom of thought and action and the issues on which the so-called *Sharia* will be unquestionable? The answer to all of these questions is the same—the Muslim jurist. A close reading of El Fadl's arguments suggests that his conception of an Islamic democracy is essentially a dictatorship of the Muslim jurists. Sounds too much like contemporary Iranian democracy that is often held hostage by the clerics.

There will be no democracy unless jurists are willing to let go and allow the *democratization of interpretation*. Let every citizen be a jurist and let her interpret Islam and *Sharia* when she votes. In a democracy the vote/opinion/fatwa of every individual must be considered as equal since ontologically all humans are equals. An essentialization of the *Sharia* with a concomitant assertion of its uncontested centrality is a recipe for authoritarianism. Sure, I recognize that El Fadl is interpretively more liberal than his traditional colleagues and his vision of what constitutes the *Sharia* is definitely more inclusive, but until we dismantle the exclusivist and often dictatorial authority of the jurists, and democratize *Ijtihad*, there can be no Islamic democracy. Sure the moral quality of this Islamic democracy will depend on the extent of Islamic knowledge of the citizens and their commitment to Islam; we have to accept that and live with it. Any attempts to guarantee "Islamic outcomes" through any other provisions such as "the essential *Sharia* must be applied" will necessarily entail the subversion of democracy. Also the Prophet of Islam, peace and blessing be upon him, reportedly said that "My Ummah will not unite upon error"[37]; there is no such endorsement available about the infallibility of the opinions of the jurists clearly suggesting that Islam only privileges the overall will of the people.

The point is simple, even what is *Sharia* and what is Islamic Law should be a democratically negotiated conclusion emerging in a democratic society. In the absence of this free and open negotiation, Islamic democracy will be a procedural sham that uses voting mechanism selectively in non-crucial matters. Clearly until political philosophers and theorists have developed a cumulative, substantive discourse on democratic theory in Islam, the less the jurists intervene the better it will be. Indeed the quest for democracy in the Muslim World is a twin project, it seeks to free the human conscience from the political tyranny of the dictators and also free the human soul and intellect from the legalist tyranny of the Islamic jurist. Islamic jurists by monopolizing the right to understand and interpret Islam are depriving all other Muslims of their basic humanity—the right to exercise their reason and be free Muslims.[38]

El Fadl in his response to the above criticism exemplifies the problem of the centrality of jurisprudence within contemporary Islam. He interprets my rejection of the exclusivist authority of the jurists as a rejection of the *Sharia* itself.[39] It is illustrative that he equates rejection of the domination of jurists as rejection of the essence of Islam. The jurists have for too long seen themselves as the sole articulators of what constitutes Islam, often reducing the way of life to a simplistic compendium of do's and don'ts creating a closed corpus of tradition that stands as a barrier to progressive development of Muslim societies. We saw how the desire to "implement the *Sharia*" as the paramount objective of an Islamic state led to the barbarian state of Afghanistan under the Taliban and the medieval state of Saudi Arabia, which according to its own citizens is economically in the twentieth century but intellectually in the fourteenth century.[40]

I am not rejecting the significance or the importance of divine principles (*Sharia*), I am merely articulating a more egalitarian or democratic process for arriving at what we call *Sharia*. El Fadl surely understands that the *Sharia* is socially, politically as well as historically constructed. There is definitely a consensus around rituals and cardinal beliefs but these are very few and hardly contentious. But on most political issues there is hardly any consensus on the interpretation of divine texts and its contextuality. At some point in history (its discussion is beyond the scope of this chapter) the jurists usurped the articulation of *Sharia* heralding the era of intellectual tyranny in Islamic thought.

El Fadl rejects my suggestion that everyone should have the right to do *Ijtihad*.[41] He wishes to reserve the right to opine and have a legal position only to the *fuqaha*! This is an explicit rejection not only of democracy and the principle that all human beings are equal but also the Quranic idea that all human beings, not just the jurists and not just Muslims, are God's vicegerents on earth (Quran 2:30). This is surprising since he himself articulates human vicegerency as an important reason why Islam and democracy are compatible. It is my contention that his juristic training precludes him for drawing such philosophical conclusions. When the Quran claims that all human beings are God's vicegerent's on earth, it essentially is articulating the equality of all human beings and that extends to freedom of thought and conscience. Rejecting the right of all individuals to do Ijtihad is to reject the freedom of thought and conscience of all.

El Fadl's discourse has an interesting quality. It is steeped in an arrogant self-declaration of El Fadl's own competence and familiarity with Islamic juristic tradition. He seems to suggest that his traditional expertise and his rendition of the tradition is uncontested. Statements such as "My point here is that every part of my context—my intellectual upbringing, personal history and theological training—lead me to find Mohammad Fadel's claims about salvation foreign and odd,"[42] are indicative as to how El Fadl assumes that he is Islamic tradition personified. He makes this statement while rejecting Mohammed Fadel's argument that in Islam salvation is more important than justice.[43] Mohammad Fadel made that point while arguing that El Fadl himself was too far from the tradition. El Fadl claims that since Arabic has no equivalent term to salvation, Fadel's idea of salvation as an ultimate Islamic good is foreign. I stopped several ordinary Muslims in my local mosque and asked them whether they understand this point made by Mohammad Fadel. To my great delight everyone I asked agreed and immediately translated salvation as *maghfirah*, restoring my faith in the competence of all humans to understand the purpose of the divine message. El Fadl might be right that Islam may not have a Christian equivalent of salvation, but it should not have been difficult to guess what Mohammad Fadel was referring to. Mohammad Fadel's position is derivative of the Quranic verse that identifies *piety* (the path to *maghfirah*) as a higher virtue than *Adl* (justice) (Quran 5:8).

El Fadl makes similar dismissive statements about all those who disagree with him including Sheikh Yusuf Al Qaradawi, easily the most preeminent Sunni Muslim scholar in the world, and Fahmi Huwaida, a prominent Egyptian reformist thinker. He makes a presumptuous generalization about Huwaida—without ever discussing any of the thinker's works—"his competence and the knowledge of the tradition [Islam] that he attempts to characterize is seriously in question," he adds about Sheikh Yusuf Qaradawi, "he only has the most superficial and casual knowledge of the institutions and theories of democracy," (121).[44] In all fairness to El Fadl, I have met many other jurists who similarly dismiss El Fadl's contributions as unorthodox and even un-Islamic. This is not an attempt at personalizing an intellectual disagreement. I think it is important to illustrate this particular characteristic of intellectual arrogance often manifest in the work of the jurists who feel free to issue "authoritative *fatwas*." This intellectual arrogance is typical of the jurists because unlike the philosophers and the theologians, they alone presume that they are "speaking in God's name."

When this class of arrogant experts exercises exclusive authority over law, how can the Muslim world ever become democratic? It can only remain a tyranny of the jurists. This intellectual arrogance of the jurists prevents them from extending intellectual freedom and freedom of conscience and opinion to all human beings equally undermining the prospects for democracy in the most fundamental of ways. The development of Islamic jurisprudence at the expense of other disciplines to the extent that jurists now hold sway over what is Islam itself is, in my humble opinion, the biggest barrier to democracy in the Muslim world. Muslim political philosophers therefore cannot abdicate their duty to define the Islamic polity in every time period, else the intellectually imperialist jurist will step in and impose her dictatorship even while defining Islamic democracy.

This tension between political philosophy and jurisprudence that I describe was recognized by Al Farabi and explored by his contemporary commentator Muhsin Mahdi. As the Muslim community begins to (re)understand, (re)define and even (re)constitute the normative basis of its polity/polities, we must not allow jurisprudence to subvert political philosophy and theory. Mahdi describes the political philosopher's relation to jurisprudence as follows:

> As a good member of his own religious community, he had to accept the opinions and perform the actions enjoined as legally binding in his own divine law as determined by the jurist. But as a political philosopher he needed to go beyond jurisprudence and to attempt to understand the foundations upon which the Islamic religious community rested. He had to ask questions that the jurist was neither required to ask nor capable of asking: Why does a political community need to be a religious community? Why does the ruler or legislator of the political community need to be a prophet or the representative of a prophet? Why does a political community need to be governed by a divine law?[45]

While the theologians' approach is useful and the jurists' approach is counterproductive, political philosophers produce a rich discourse on democracy and if allowed to flower and develop, this tradition can advance a progressive, ongoing Islamic democratic theory that can help establish and develop Islamic polities facilitating the causes of both faith and freedom. In this discussion I shall explore the work of the Iranian philosopher Soroush, but before that I will review the work of the greatest Islamic political philosopher, Al Farabi who was also the first Muslim to systematically evaluate the merits and limits of democratic polities.

Al Farabi places democracy in the category of ignorant cities. Ignorant cities are those cities that collectively are unaware of God (The First Cause). They also do not have a singular purpose. He recognizes that since democracies are free societies there will be multiple objectives that the citizens of a democracy will seek. He also suggests interestingly that if people who seek security dominate the polity a democracy can become a national security state (Al Farabi talks in terms of cities of war and peace). But he also makes a very interesting observation which is perhaps the most important lesson contemporary Muslim thinkers can take from him. Al Farabi suggests that because democracies are free and non-homogeneous societies, there will be some who will excel in good as well as some who will excel in evil. But since one can find the pursuit of perfection present within a democracy, a democracy has the best chance of all ignorant cities of becoming a virtuous city. This is a cautionary but powerful endorsement of democracy especially at a time when the options available to Muslim societies largely fall in the ignorant category (monarchies, dictatorships etc.).[46]

Soroush's approach to the compatibility of Islam and democracy is very different from Sachedina and El Fadl. He neither treats Islam as a stable unproblematic concept nor does he treat modernity or democracy as settled issues. In true philosophical spirit he considers all concepts and all assertions of values as open to negotiation, reflection and understanding. For El Fadl Islamic law or *Sharia* is the ultimate criterion as is Quran, the indisputable word of God, for Sachedina. For Soroush the only thing that is given is the human capacity to understand what is moral, what is reasonable, what is ethical and what is worthy of upholding as a value. For Soroush the ultimate criterion is his reason and his understanding of even God's will and words are essentially the outcome of the interaction of reason (*aql*) and revelation (*wahi*). Therefore, before there is either Islam or democracy, for Abdulkarim Soroush there is reason.

All Muslim intellectuals start with a stated or unstated assumption that Islamic principles or Islamic laws are absolute truths revealed by God and hence cannot be at fault. If there is any seeming deficiency it must necessarily be in the interpretations and hence we need to reinterpret or revive the tradition of *Ijtihad*—independent interpretive thinking. But Soroush starts his arguments essentially by asserting reason as a defining characteristic of humanity and freedom as a necessary existential condition for that humanity to thrive. For the philosopher what is primary is the human agency as a "thinking being" whereas for the theologian and the jurists human agency is a "submissive being." The theologian asserts: here is the Truth, understand it. The jurist commands: this is the Truth, obey! The philosopher says: you can think and if you are free to think, think and you may know the Truth. Soroush articulates this philosophical position clearly. And thus the fulfillment of humanity depends upon the fruition of reason and reason cannot thrive, grow or be exercised without freedom. If anything, by linking reason and freedom, Soroush makes this very clear, freedom is necessary for reason and reason leads to faith and truth.[47]

Having established the necessity of freedom for reason to thrive, Soroush then argues that it is incorrect to assume or even consider that reason (*aql*) and revelation (*wahi*) are in some way antithetical to each other. He argues and this has been the position for a long time in Islamic philosophical tradition that revelation is essentially accessed through reason. Reason is the instrument that enables the apprehension of revelation. One cannot understand the will of God without possessing the faculty of understanding.[48] Thus he seeks to subvert the widely touted tensions between faith and freedom and reason and religion. If Islam is compatible with freedom and reason—the constitutive elements of democracy—then Islam should be compatible with democracy. Soroush further argues that democracies are basically means to an end and as long as Islam is understood as a reasoned justification of God's rights over humanity, a religious society should have no problems in establishing a democracy as means to good and just governance.

Soroush's ideas are highly provocative given the cultural context from which they are emerging. But nevertheless they remain at a very high level of abstraction and need to be translated in political theoretical concepts that can be operationalized. How do we integrate reason into general understanding of religion? How do we operationalize freedom as prior condition to faith and government? How do we deal with the existing corpus of Islamic law that is not easily amenable to criticism that will circumscribe its scope and the power of those who wield it? Democracy is not just freedom from the tyranny of political power but also the tyranny of traditional authority? How do we deconstruct the stifling effect of "Sharia obsessive Islam" on reason?

In the discussion so far, I have reflected on the prospects of an Islamic democratic theory in the context of three genres of discourse—theological, jurisprudential and philosophical. My conclusions are that while theological understanding is necessary but not sufficient, philosophical illumination is the answer but needs much more development and jurisprudence is a challenge rather than an ally of Islamic democratic theory. In this essay my goal was to underscore the importance of political philosophy and theory. I am afraid that quick fix solutions as being attempted in Afghanistan and Iraq will not give birth to an authentic Islamic democracy. Neither will the mere reinterpretation of Islam, by emphasizing those elements that facilitate and marginalizing those that subvert democracy, will produce the necessary result.

The barriers to democracy in the Muslim world are both ideational and material. While political activism and even revolutionary change may become necessary to establish democracy, Islamic democratic theory must precede political change in order to remove ideational barriers first. If an authentic Islamic democracy is to emerge, then it must first become an aspiration in Muslim minds and must dominate their discourse. Once the idea exists, the form can follow. This is the challenge for Islamic political theory.

Notes

1. The Esposito school of thought is a view of the Islamic world that sees Islamic resurgence as an authentic expression of Muslim desire to give Islam a central role in their lives. It recognizes that Islamism is a challenge and not necessarily a threat to the West.

2. A good starting point for exploring this discourse is Charles Kurzman (Ed.), *Liberal Islam: A Source Book* (New York: Oxford University Press, 1998). Also see John Cooper, Ronald Nettler and Mohamed Mahmoud (Eds.), *Islam and Modernity: Muslim Intellectuals Respond* (London: I. B. Taurus Publishers, 1998) and Abdul Aziz said, Nathan C. Funk and Ayse S. Kadayifci (Eds.), *Peace and Conflict Resolution in Islam: Precept and Practice* (New York: University Press of America, 2001).

3. Edward said, *Orientalism* (New York: Vintage Book, 1978). Edward Said, *Covering Islam: How the Media and the Experts Determine How We See the Rest of the World* (New York: Pantheon Books, 1981). Aziz Al-Azmeh, *Islams and Modernities* (London: Verso, 1993). John L. Esposito, *The Islamic Threat: Myth or Reality* (New York: Oxford University Press, 1995).

4. See for example G. W. Chowdhury, *Islam and the Contemporary World* (Des Plaines, IL; Library of Islam, 1991) and Khalid Bin Sayeed, *Western Dominance and Political Islam: Challenge and Response* (Albany, NY: State University of New York Press, 1995). For concise summaries of how Islamists use the West and designated Western ideas as the other see the works of Mir Zohair Husain, *Global Islamic Politics* (New York: HarperCollins College Publishers, 1995) and Youssef M. Choueiri, *Islamic Fundamentalism* (Boston: Twayne Publishers, 1990) and Abdel Salam Sidahmed and Anoushiravan Ehteshami (Eds.), *Islamic Fundamentalism* (Boulder, CO: Westview Press, 1996). Most importantly the works of Seyyed Hossein Nasr have contributed a great deal towards developing the idea of Islamic essentialism. The theme that things such as science, methodology and historical periods can have an "essentially Islamic character" runs through all of Nasr's works. Seyyed H. Nasr more than anyone else has helped propagate the idea of an Islamic identity based on Islamic exceptionalism of scientific and philosophical traditions. One wonders if he realizes that some of his works mirror those of Western thinkers who also peddle the myth of Western essentialism. Some of the works where this idea is more visible are Seyyed Hossein Nasr, *The Need for a Sacred Science* (Albany, NY: State University of New York Press, 1993) and Seyyed Hossein Nasr, *A Young Muslim's Guide to the Modern World* (Chicago, IL: Kazi Publications, 1994).

5. For a conceptual analysis of the Islamist discourse see M. A. Muqtedar Khan, "The Political Philosophy of Islamic Resurgence," *Cultural Dynamics*, 13, 2 (Summer 2001), 213–231.

6. The mirror image quality of this discourse was also noticed by Bahgat Korany, "Arab Democratization: A Poor Cousin?," *PS: Political Science and Politics*, 27, 3 (September 1993), 511–513.

7. The term *Khilafah* means succession and implies succession to the Prophet of Islam; the derivative term *Khalifah* refers to the title used by early Islamic rulers. It means successor and it implied the successor to the Prophet of Islam. The term also

derives its legitimacy from a Quranic verse that says that God has appointed human beings as his vicegerent (*Khalifah*) on Earth (Quran 2:30). The principle of *Shura* (the term itself means consultation) is another Quranic concept that refers to God's injunction commanding humans to conduct their affairs through consultation (Quran 42:38). Muslim political theorists who advocate authoritarian regimes focus on the concept of *Khilafah* and those who advocate democracy rely on the idea of *Shura*.

8. For a more comprehensive argument about how Islam and the West are shared civilizations see M. A. Muqtedar Khan, "Dialogue of Civilizations?" *The Diplomat*, 2, 5 (June 1997) 45–49.

9. The most prominent voice in this area is that of Bernard Lewis. He has written several articles, or actually several versions of the same argument, claiming that Islam is fundamentally authoritarian and unlike the West does not have the openness necessary for democracy. Needless to say many scholars have disagreed with this position. Mumtaz Ahmad argues that there is actually an emerging consensus on the compatibility between Islam and democracy. While Ahmad may be a little optimistic, there is much merit in his claims. See Mumtaz Ahmad, "Islam and Democracy: The Emerging Consensus," *Middle East Affairs Journal*, 2, 4 (Summer/Fall 1996), 29–38.

10. An institution, The Center for the Study of Islam & Democracy (www.islam-democracy.org), has emerged from this alliance between western academics that consider Islam as democratic and Muslims who share these beliefs and also wish to democratize the Muslim World.

11. See Muqtedar Khan and Kamran Bokhari, "Pakistani Democracy: Between a Rock and a Hard Place," *The Daily Times* (September 17, 2004).

12. To get a sense of this line of thinking please see a very revealing and frank interview with the spokesman of Jordan's Islamic Action Front. See "Assessment of Democracy in Jordan: An Interview with Shaykh Hamza Mansur," in *Middle East Affairs Journal*, 3, 1–2 (Winter/Spring, 1997), 142–150.

13. See "Constructing the American Muslim Community" in Y. Haddad, J. Smith and J. Esposito (eds.), *Religion and Immigration* (New York: Altamira Press, 2003), 175–198. Also see M. A. Muqtedar Khan, "Muslim Democrats Triumph over Muslim Isolationists," *Washington Report on Middle East Affairs*, 20, 2 (March 2001), 82–83.

14. See M. A. Muqtedar Khan "Radical Islam, Liberal Islam," *Current History*, 102, 668 (December 2003), 417–421.

15. See M. A. Muqtedar Khan, "First Islamic Society, then Islamic State, but Democracy Now!" *The Diplomat*, 2 (November 1997), 48–51.

16. M. A. Muqtedar Khan, "The Political Philosophy of Islamic Resurgence," *Cultural Dynamics*, 13, 2 (Summer 2001), 213–231.

17. For a comparative analysis of postcolonial political developments in Turkey and the Arab World see "Part III: The Modern Transformation," in Ira M. Lapidus, *A History of Islamic Societies* (New York: Cambridge University Press, 1988), 549–717.

18. G. W. Choudhury, *Constitutional Development in Pakistan* (Vancouver: Publications Center, University of British Columbia, 1969). Also see Louis D. Hayes, *Politics in Pakistan: The Struggle for Legitimacy* (Boulder, CO: Westview Press, 1984). See also the chapter "Pakistan: The Many Faces of an Islamic Republic," in John L. Esposito and John O. Voll, *Islam and Democracy* (New York: Oxford University Press, 1996).

19. While political theory debates involving the democratic elements of Islam became marginal in the Muslim world as the Islamism-Secularism debate occupied center stage, the debate between radical and moderate Muslims continued over the nature of an Islamic polity. For a quick review see Mansoor Moaddel and Kamran Talattof (Eds.), *Contemporary Debates in Islam: An Anthology of Modernist and Fundamentalist Thought* (New York: St. Martin's Press, 2000). Also see Ahmad S. Moussalli, *Moderate and Radical Islamic Fundamentalism: The Quest for Modernity, Legitimacy and the Islamic State* (Gainesville: The University Press of Florida, 1999).

20. For a long time now the west in general and the U.S. in particular have been advocating the Turkish experience as a desired model for democracy in the Muslim World. Turkey's membership of NATO, its close alliance with Israel and its radical secularism that has often used undemocratic means to marginalize Islam from the public sphere was the preferred alternative to Iranian or Pakistani style of Islamic states. For Islamists the Islamic revolution of Iran was a major inspiration and they hoped that similar revolutions in key Muslim states, such as Saudi Arabia, Pakistan, Egypt, and Algeria would duplicate the Shii miracle in the Sunni world. For discussions of the Turkish model see Omar Taspinar, "An Uneven Fit? The 'Turkish Model' and the Arab World," *Brookings Analysis Paper* (Washington, DC: Brookings Institution, 2003). For a discussion of Iranian model and its impact, see John L. Esposito (Ed.), *The Iranian Revolution and Its Global Impact* (Miami: Florida International University Press, 1990).

21. While there are several instances when President Bush asserted the compatibility of Islam and democracy, the most outstanding occasion was at the National Endowment for Democracy on November 3, 2003. He asserted "A religion that demands individual moral accountability, and encourages the encounter of the individual with God, is fully compatible with the rights and responsibilities of self-government." The full text of the speech can be found on the World Wide Web at http://www.ned.org/events/anniversary/oct1603-Bush.html. Also see M. A. Muqtedar Khan, "Prospects for Democracy in the Muslim World: The Role of U.S. Policy," *Middle East Policy Journal*, 10, 3 (Fall 2003), 79–89.

22. For examples of special issues see "Islam and the Challenge of Democracy," The Boston Review: A Political and Literary Forum (April/May 2003). Nearly every think tank in Washington DC has hosted a forum on the topic, for example, the USIP's forum on Islam and Democracy, June 18, 2002. See also Steven Martinovich, "Islam and Democracy—Not an Impossible Marriage," *The Christian Science Monitor* (May 8, 2003).

23. See Noah Feldman, *After Jihad: America and the Struggle for Islamic Democracy* (New York: Farrar, Straus and Giroux, 2003); M. A. Muqtedar Khan, *American Muslims: Bridging Faith and Freedom* (Beltsville, MD: Amana Publications, 2002); Larry Diamond, Marc F. Plattner, and Daniel Brumberg, eds., *Islam and Democracy in the Middle East* (Baltimore: Johns Hopkins University Press, 2003).

24. See Abdulaziz Sachedina, *The Islamic Roots of Democratic Pluralism* (New York: Oxford University Press, 2001).

25. Ibid., 13.

26. A forceful case for examining the compatibility and desirability of liberal ideas and values from an Islamic perspective is advanced by Saba Mahmood. See Saba Mahmood,

"Questioning Liberalism, Too: A Response to 'Islam and the Challenge of Democracy'" *Boston Review: A Political and Literary Forum* (April/May 2003).

27. Abdul Karim Soroush, a contemporary Iranian philosopher and political theorist attempts to answer some of these questions, see chapter 9: "Tolerance and Governance: A Discourse on Religion and Democracy," in Mahmoud Sadri and Ahmad Sadri (Trans. and Eds.), *Reason, Freedom and Democracy in Islam: Essential Writings of Abdul Karim Soroush* (New York: Oxford University Press, 2000), 131–115.

28. See Muhsin Mahdi, *Al Farabi and the Foundations of Islamic Political Philosophy* (Chicago: University of Chicago Press, 2001), 43.

29. Technically a *Fatwa* is a legal opinion that is binding only on the jurist who asserts it, however today Muslim clerics use it as an edict. It is the most important item in their arsenal. See John L. Esposito (Ed.), *The Oxford Dictionary of Islam* (New York: Oxford University Press, 2003), 85.

30. See Khalid Abou El Fadl, Joshua Cohen and Debra Chasman (eds.), *Islam and the Challenge of Democracy* (Princeton, NJ: Princeton University Press, 2004).

31. I am not alone in making this argument about the dominance of legal thought. Fazlur Rahman anticipates it in his analysis of Islamic Legal thought and the development of the *Sharia* in Fazlur Rahman, *Islam* (Chicago: University of Chicago Press, 1966), 100–116.

32. Ahmad S. Moussalli, *Moderate and Radical Islamic Fundamentalism: The Quest for Modernity, Legitimacy and the Islamic State* (Gainesville: The University Press of Florida, 1999). See also M. A. Muqtedar Khan "The Islamic States" in M. Hawkesworth and M. Kogan (Eds.), *Routledge Encyclopedia of Political Science* (forthcoming 2004).

33. See S. Abul A'la Maududi, *Islamic Law and Constitution* (Lahore: Islamic Publishers Pvt. Ltd., 1955). See also Vanessa Martin, *Creating an Islamic State: Khoemeni and the Making of a New Iran* (London: I. B. Taurus, 2000). Asghar Ali Engineer, *The Islamic State* (New Delhi: Vikas Publishing House, 1996).

34. See M. A. Muqtedar Khan, "The Compact of Medina: A Constitutional Theory of the Islamic State," *Ijtihad.org* (May 30, 2001). http://www.ijtihad.org/compact.htm.

35. For a review of the ideas of Islamic Liberalism as pertaining to democracy see Charles Kurzman (Ed.) *Liberal Islam: A Source Book* (New York: Oxford University Press, 1998). See the special issue of *Journal of Democracy* (April 2003) on the theme of liberal Islam.

36. See Qamaruddin Khan, *The Political Thought of Ibn Taymiyyah* (Delhi: Adam Publishers, 1982), 23–51. Also see M. A. Muqtedar Khan "The Islamic States" in M. Hawkesworth and M. Kogan (Eds.), *Routledge Encyclopedia of Political Science* (forthcoming 2004).

37. An authentic (*sahih*) tradition of Prophet Muhammad reported in *al Tirmidhi* [4/2167]. Also reported in *Hakim* [1/116].

38. My discussion and criticism of Khaled Abou El Fadl's work relies primarily on my response to his article "Islam and the Challenge of Democracy." See M. A. Muqtedar Khan, "The Priority of Politics: A Response to Islam and the Challenge of Democracy," *Boston Review: A Political and Literary Forum* (April/May 2003).

39. See Khaled Abou El Fadl et al., *Islam and the Challenge of Democracy* (Princeton, NJ: Princeton University Press, 2004), 122–125.

40. See Muqtedar Khan, "Urgent Turn," *Al Ahram Weekly*, May 6–12, 2004.

41. See Khaled Abou El Fadl et al., *Islam and the Challenge of Democracy*, 124.

42. See Khaled Abou El Fadl et al., *Islam and the Challenge of Democracy*, 117.

43. See Mohammed Fadel, "Too Far from Tradition," in Khaled Abou El Fadl et al., *Islam and the Challenge of Democracy* (Princeton, NJ: Princeton University Press, 2004), 81–86.

44. Ironically El Fadl's inability to recognize that the Constitution of Medina was indeed a social contract that established a rudimentary form of constitutional democracy in Medina is perhaps indicative of how his own competence in political theory and philosophy is superficial and limited. In an essay that expounds for 14,000 words on Islam's compatibility with democracy he does not feel the necessity to discuss the constitution on the basis of which the first Islamic polity was established. Especially since several Muslim political theorists have made this argument for over one hundred years. Many of them have been identified in the introduction to this volume.

45. See Muhsin Mahdi, *Al Farabi and the Foundations of Islamic Political Philosophy* (Chicago: The University of Chicago Press, 2001), 40.

46. For an excellent discussion of Al Farabi's understanding of democracy see Muhsin Mahdi, "Al Farabi," in Leo Strauss and Joseph Cropsey (Ed.), *History of Political Philosophy* (Chicago, IL: University of Chicago Press, 1987), 224–226. See Al Farabi, *On the Perfect State*, 315. Also see Muhsin S. Mahdi, *Alfarabi and the Foundation of Islamic Political Philosophy* (Chicago, IL: University of Chicago Press, 2001), 144–146. Also see M. a. Muqtedar Khan, "The Islamic States."

47. See the chapter on "Reason and Freedom" in Sadri and Sadri, *Reason, Freedom and Democracy in Islam*, 88–104.

48. See M. A. Muqtedar Khan, "Reason and Personal Reasoning," *American Journal of Islamic Social Sciences*, 16, 3 (Fall 1999), v–xi.

9

The Role of Islam in the Public Square: Guidance or Governance?

Abdulaziz Sachedina

In the recent decades, especially following the Islamic revolution and the establishment of religious authority as the head of government in a modern nation-state of Iran, the public role of religion in general and the role of Islam in particular has been revisited by social scientists. With the American intervention in Afghanistan and Iraq, constitutional debates have as yet to tackle the role of religious convictions and values in the development of democratic institutions to guarantee basic freedoms and rights in those countries. The major stumbling block to democratization appears to be the way the role of religious values is defined in developing an inclusive sense of citizenship without insisting upon doctrinal/theological uniformity. In both these countries religious leaders have insisted to make the religious law of Islam, the Shari'a, as the principle source of defining freedoms and rights in the national constitution. While it is acknowledged that in the personal status of a Muslim man and woman the Shari'a could continue to provide judicial decisions in the area of personal law, there is also a major concern in the way traditional juridical formulations define a woman's social and political rights. More importantly, religiously pluralistic nature of Muslim societies require to take into consideration not only Sunni-Shi'ite but also interfaith relationships. The need to search for inclusive religious values has assumed urgency.

The challenge that faces the community today is this. There is a deeply held belief among religiously oriented Muslims that as a comprehensive guide to human life Islam must not only guide but also govern a modern state with Muslim majority. Is this conceivable? Are there within the classically inherited tradition resources that can be tapped for the creation of a nation-state that is also a member of the international public order? While the latter question is beyond the scope of the present paper, I want to explore the conceivability of a religious-minded demand in light of the changed circumstances under which modern nation-states conduct their affairs. In order to do that I will begin my search in the foundational sources of Islamic political discourse in the context in which this discourse shaped the political underpinnings of the Muslim empire. My reflections on the foundational sources like the Qur'an and the Tradition that continue to be held in high esteem by the community will provide me the opportunity to offer my thesis and its ramifications for the democratic governance based on some sort of functional secularity. I will return to this secularity later. But let me say this from the outset that I am not imposing this concept on Islamic tradition; rather, separate jurisdictions for God-human and human-human transactions (rather than the separation of church and state) are acknowledged in the sacred law of Islam, the Shari'a.

Let us examine the interaction between religion and history in Islam. Considering the historical development of Islamic tradition, and contrary to our modern perceptions of the role of religion, one is struck by a religious tradition that has been a source of a public project founded upon the principle of coexistence, recognizing self-governing communities free to run their internal affairs under a comprehensive religious and social political system. Of all Abrahamic religions based on the biblical ethos of shaping its public culture Islam has been from its inception the most conscious of its earthly agenda. Islam has been a faith in the realm of the public. The Shari'a regulates religious practice with a view to maintaining the individual's well being through his or her social well being. Hence, its comprehensive system deals with the obligations that humans perform as part of their relationship to the Divine Being and duties they perform as part of their interpersonal responsibility. Public order must be maintained in worship, in the marketplace, and all other arenas of human interaction. Social transactions based on an ethical standard of conduct in the Shari'a deal with enforcing the law by taking into account only what appears in the public sphere of human interaction. Muslim courts have no jurisdiction over private acts unless infringement of rights occurs and is brought to judiciary's attention without prying.[1]

In searching for the guiding principles of a civil society, one must ask whether a faith community can accept the idea that other religious communities have autonomous, self-governing existences. This is the most challenging aspect of one's religious commitment that affects a public order. The essential point to consider is whether religious communities are willing to recognize one another as spiritual equals, each entitled to its distinctive path of salvation. The reason is that in a democratic pluralistic public order political consensus in the public square is dependent upon each group's commitment to inclusive religious convictions.

Here I take religious pluralism to mean the acknowledgment of the intrinsic redemptive value of competing religious traditions. It is expected, however, that beliefs and values essential to one community will contravene those of others; herein lurks the potential for conflict and violence, if religious teachings are not articulated with necessary acumen and practical wisdom in the public square.

The fundamental problem, as reflected in the classical formulation of Muslim political identity, is religious authoritarianism founded upon an exclusive salvific claim, which runs contrary to the emerging global spirit of democratization through acknowledgment of religious pluralism. At the very core of emerging democratic pluralism is respect for the human rights of the non-Muslims living in Muslim societies. Since the beginning of this century, Muslim religious and social thinkers have wrestled with the issue of Islam's capacity to create a political society that would transcend the traditional boundaries between believers and non-believers and thus allow for the human dignity to emerge as the sole criterion for social and political entitlements.

From its emergence in the seventh century as a tradition in which a prophet is sent as a lawgiver and an organizer of the community to lead it to its ideal existence, Islam has provided its followers with a vision. This vision has something to do with a possibility—a potential—in the public domain of human existence, the possibility of an ideal polity that would shape a Muslim identity for citizens who actively "submit" to the will of God as members of a human community. It is primarily the possibility of appropriating the earth for creating a God-centered multicultural and multiethnic society that animates the Koranic vision of interpersonal relations.

It is important to underscore the significance of the Koranic universal discourse calling upon humanity to respond to its original nature capable of discerning rightness and wrongness. No human endowed with reason can fail to understand this moral language. More importantly, as a source of unity that transcends religious differences, this language establishes the necessary connection and compatibility between private and particular spiritual, and public and universal moral guidance. Hence, the Koran binds all of humanity to its natural predisposition not only to be aware of the meaning of justice but also to will its realization. In this universal idiom, no human being, then, can claim ignorance of the ingrained moral sense of wrong and right; it follows that none can escape divine judgment of a failure to uphold justice on earth.

The Koran allows the non-believers to be other in the sphere of ethics, where the natural knowledge of good and evil makes injustice in any form inexcusable. No matter how religions might divide people, ethical discourse focuses on human relationships in building an ideal public order. Human relationships at the horizontal level provide us with a framework for defining the religious or cultural other in terms of "we" and "them." Islamic self-identification as a process of self-understanding becomes accessible to the outsider through its conceptual description of the other.

Such a description of the other is situated in the realm of law, the realm of revelation-based religious and moral activity. Islamic law as an expression of the human endeavor to carry out the divine will on earth is actually identical to the belief that faith is an instrument of justice. When law and faith merge in an individual's life, they create a sense of security and integrity about the great responsibility of pursuing justice for its own sake. And when this sense of security and integrity is projected onto the collective life of the community, it conduces to social harmony. Peace, then, is belief translated into action. It is not sufficient merely to believe in justice for peace to come about. Rather, peace is the outcome of justice maintained at each stage of interhuman relations. The separation of law and faith, on the other hand, results in the lack of commitment to justice that leads to chaos, violence, and even war. Hence, the Islamic prescription for avoiding carnage is to respond to God's revelation, which calls for sincere God-human and inter-human relations. In other words, submission to the will of God becomes a kind of conduit for the creation and maintenance of justice and equity on earth. Ultimately, the vision of intercommunal relations in Islam is firmly founded upon the diverse communities' sharing in cross-religious moral concern with egalitarianism, peace, and justice.

But the interaction between this faith and history has not fostered an interreligious vision of spiritual egalitarianism. In fact, part of the Muslim self-understanding has led to intolerance, even to the exclusion of the other from the divine-human relationship. Such an exclusivist theology can envision a global human community only under Islamic hegemony; Islamic tradition, so interpreted, becomes an instrument for the furthering of Muslim political and social power over other nations.

However, in a diverse intercommunal society, insistence on agreement on matters of belief as a precondition for social organization is highly problematic. The solution offered by secular liberal theory is that effective governance arises not from shared belief but from a system of government incorporating the principle of religious pluralism. International relations today are conducted without any reference to the substantive beliefs of the member states because religious beliefs are considered "non-public." Whatever their irreconcilable differences in matters of faith, all communities are legally bound to do their part in maintaining peaceful social relations. The resolution of conflicts does not require people to uphold certain religious beliefs; nor does it mean that they do not or cannot share vision of a future community that is inspired by the belief in transcendence. According to this line of thinking maintained by the political liberalism, judgments based on religious morality are "inaccessible" because "some of the crucial premises that underlie such judgments are not subject to general acceptance or to persuasive demonstration by publicly accessible reasons."[2] As I shall demonstrate in this paper, Abrahamic traditions in general, and Islam in particular, have much to contribute to a discourse about the desirability of including universal religious argument calling for human cooperation in establishing a just public order. As a Muslim educated both in the traditional seminary and the modern secular university, I face the unique opportunity and special responsibility of taking up the challenge of a self-critical assessment of current Muslim thought and practice to demonstrate the "accessibility" of religious reasons for developing a necessary "overlapping consensus" in a democratic society for the purposes of just governance.

To begin with the purpose of revelation is to guide rather than govern humankind. Accordingly, the Koranic valuation of human beings is not limited to honoring humankind as the vicegerent of God. It is about believing in the abilities and potential of humankind, the value of time, the authority of the human mind in pursuing the truth, and the future of humankind. The critical evaluation of inequalities between men and women, the degradation of human resources, and the disregard of human experiences provides the Muslim thinker with an opportunity to restate human values in an Islamic context and to restore the balance with other considerations such as national interest, priorities, and traditions.[3]

By virtue of explicit recognition of a common ground shared between Muslims and the people of the Book, Islam has never harbored a widespread belief that Jews and Christians are to be denied salvation and hence reduced to *persona non grata* status if they do not first convert to Islam.[4] Unlike the early Christians, the early Muslims felt no need to establish their socio-political and religious identity at the expense of another community.[5]

Moreover, Muslims, unlike the Jews, did not regard their own community as uniquely selected to receive divine guidance in a world otherwise bereft of it. Muslims thought of their community as one among many divinely guided communities, all at their beginning equally blessed. Furthermore, as acknowledged in K. 5:48, the Muslims, like various other religious communities, are also an autonomous social organism with their own law for their own members.

Can Religion Become a Source of Democratic Pluralism?

Exclusion of religion as a source of democratic pluralism has been a common tendency in many societies that foster secular values and a clear demarcation between the public and private spheres of human activity. Religion is to be tolerated and even abstractly supported without affording it a clear voice in the public arena because it lacks the ability to communicate with those outside the community.

All world religions, at one time or other, have succumbed to secular pressure and have subordinated their core spiritual-moral message to the political ambitions of their particular communities. Such marriages of convenience between exclusive faith communities and political power has actually led to the disestablishment of the universal ethical and legal foundations of various religious traditions. Abrahamic religions include among their theological doctrines of divine justice and human moral agency concepts of individual and collective responsibility to further a divinely ordained ethical public order.

Thus arises the concentration of comprehensive religious-secular power in the hands of an exclusivist leadership whose views of private morality are divorced from the communalistic vision of society, with the attendant mistreatment of those within and outside the community who reject that community's religious exclusivist claims. Monotheistic communities have from time to time denied their individual members a right to dissent from or to reject the communalistic interpretation of their respective traditions because of the fear that such internal dissension (usually labeled apostasy) is potentially fatal to the collective identity of the faith community and its social cohesiveness.

There is a strong desire among the people of various religions to prevent any form of internal dissension. The conflicting and even incommensurable theological positions on freedom of religion in different world communities has led to the oppressive use of force to ensure adherence to a single comprehensive religious doctrine. The ensuing intolerance has manifested itself in intrafaith relationships as well. Whereas Muslims treated other religious communities with relative tolerance, they often treated their own dissenters with extreme cruelty. Thus, for instance, under various powerful Muslim dynasties the Shi'ite or Sunni minority suffered more oppression than did the Jews and the Christians.[6]

The Iraq-Iran war in the 1980s and the Gulf War in 1990–1991 brought home a realization that even secularly based imported ideologies like nationalism and socialism could not advance the cause of pluralistic, tolerant political culture. The imported ideologies, to be sure, were enforced from above without people's rational consent or political participation. Hence, they flagrantly failed to generate the necessary consensus for change in conservative Muslim societies.

The Koran does not teach that humanity has fallen through the commission of original sin. But it constantly warns human beings about the egocentric corruption that can weaken the determination to carry out divine purposes for humankind. Human pride can infect and corrupt undertakings in politics, scholarship, everyday conduct, and theology. The last is the most sinful aspect of egocentric corruption because it is done in the name of God.

Besides stressing the "noble nature" (*fitra*) that promotes human sociability and positive bonds between people because of the common ethical responsibility towards one another, the Koran emphasizes the mutual expectations and relations fostered by universal parentage. The Koran commands people to honor their parents:

> Thy Lord has decreed you shall not serve any but Him, and to be good to your parents, whether one or both of them attains old age with thee; say not to them 'Fie' neither chide them, but speak unto them words respectful, and lower to them wing of humbleness out of mercy and say, 'My Lord, have mercy upon them, as they raised me up when I was little.' (K. 17:26)

The importance given by the Koran to interpersonal relationships evidently points to the institutions and culture that promote the creation of a spiritual-moral community made up of individuals willing and able to take up the challenge of working for the common good. It is for this reason that the moral performance of an individual in society is to be measured not so much by reference to some ingrained "noble nature" as by the religious-moral institutions through which history has shaped the community's ethical aspirations. The doctrine of the "noble nature" (*fitra*) in the Koran is properly anchored in history of human struggle toward discovering what it is to be properly human.

What of the claim that tolerance leads to a compromise of religious truth? By encouraging tolerance among its members, the community might claim that its transcending quality and its unique relation to truth are sacrificed to pragmatism. Theological differences about any matters in the revelation are difficult, perhaps impossible to resolve. Yet, the spirit of accommodation and tolerance certainly demands that a common ground should be sought for implementing the common good in society. Working for the common good without insisting on imposing the beliefs and desires each holds most dear can result in a legitimate public space for diverse human religious experience.

Can this public space be realized without considering ideas about the highest end of human existence on the earth? Can they be accomplished through communal cooperation for the collective good or widely different and even irreconcilable individual interests? How can a religious community remain neutral and non-interventionist on ethical issues that from the individual's point of view, might run counter to one's sense of the highest end in life?

The secular prescription of Western democracies seems to suggest that religious toleration can be achieved only when the idea of freedom of conscience is institutionalized in the form of a basic individual right to worship freely, to propagate one's religion, to change one's religion, or even to renounce religion altogether. In other words, the principle of toleration is equated with the idea of individual freedom of conscience.[7] Moreover, it restricts the role of conscience to the domain of private faith, which is clearly demarcated from the public realm—hence the separation of church from state. Whereas one has the free-dom to choose between competing doctrines and pursue one's belief in private religious institutions, one is linked in common citizenry in public state insti-tutions. This is the secularist foundation of a public order in which, in pursuit of freedom of conscience, all considerations drawn from belief in God or other sacred authority in one's private life are excluded from the administration of public life.

Abrahamic traditions are characteristically founded upon the scriptures that locate justice in history through community. This ideal of justice in a divinely ordained community is a natural outcome of the belief in an ethical God who insists on justice and equality in interpersonal relations as part of the believer's spiritual perfection. The indispensable connection between the reli-gious and ethical dimensions of personal life inevitably introduces religious precepts into the public arena. In other words, church and state are closely linked, requiring the involvement of the religious community in taking responsibility for law and order.

Freedom of Conscience and Religion in the Koran

Freedom of conscience and religion has been correctly recognized as the cor-nerstone of democratic pluralism.[8] Any pluralistic social order requires the active articulation of rational as well as revelational sources of protection for individual autonomy in matters of personal faith within society as part of the divine-human covenant. The question of individual autonomy and human agency might seem peculiar to the modern vision of a public order in which a group of individuals share core ideas, ideals, and values geared towards main-taining a civil society[9]; yet living together in a society requires mutuality not only in matters of commerce and market relations, but it also presupposes a shared foundation of morality and binding sentiments that unite autonomous individuals who are able to negotiate their own spiritual space—and these cri-teria apply to all societies in all eras.

In general, by virtue of the natural human urge to social interaction, diverse groups fall back on their religious teachings to derive and articulate the rules affecting public life. The recognition and implementation of the religious val-ues of sharing and mutuality creates a civil religion that encourages coexis-tence with those who, even when they did not share the dominant group's particular vision of salvation, can share in a concern for living in peace with justice. Hence, as I shall contend, the concern for human autonomy, especially freedom of worship (or not to worship), is as fundamental to the Koranic vision of human religiosity as it is to that of other civilizations. The Koran requires Muslims to sit in dialogue with their own tradition to uncover a just approach to religious diversity and interfaith coexistence. Moreover, a rigorous analysis of the Koran will demonstrate that, without recognition of freedom of religion, it is impossible to conceive of religious commitment as a freely negotiated human-divine relationship that fosters individual accountability for one's acceptance or rejection of faith in God, commitment to pursue an ethical life, and willingness to be judged accordingly.

The difference between a moral and religious response to God's guidance is critical here. In relation to the divine purposes for humanity, according to the Koran, God provides two forms of guidance: universal moral guidance that touches all humans qua humans, and particular revelatory guidance that is given to a specific faith community. On the basis of universal guidance, it is conceivable to demand uniformity because an objective and universally binding moral standard is assumed to exist that guarantees true human well-being. In enforcing that basic moral standard, resort to compulsion through legitimate enforcement is justifiable. However, on the basis of particular guidance through scripture, it is crucial to allow human beings to exercise their volition in matters of personal faith because any attempt to enforce religious conviction would lead to its negation. And although the comprehensive nature of scriptural guidance provides a detailed description of ideal human life on earth that is consonant with the historical and cultural considerations of community life in Islam, it removes the God-human relationship from human jurisdiction.[10] So construed, the aspect of revelatory guidance that regulates the God-human relationship is concerned with "reminding" and "warning" people to heed the divine call through "submission" to God's will. As the head of the community, the Prophet could not use his political power to enforce a God-human relationship that is founded upon individual autonomy and human agency. In fact, the Koran repeatedly reminds the Prophet that his duty was simply to deliver the message without taking it upon himself to function as God's religious enforcer (K. 17:54; 50:45).

This clarification regarding the two forms of guidance that the Koran speaks about provides us with a scriptural basis for freedom of religion. Not only does it maintain the idea of universal and objective moral values that are cognitively accessible to human nature without any distinction between believer and non-believer; it also upholds the notion of a fallible conscience that might fail to respond to God's call. This notion of the possibility of rejecting religious guidance results in the toleration of human autonomy in matters of religious choices.

Freedom of Religion in the Context of Islamic Public Order

But the tension begins as soon as the Koran speaks about the just order. There are numerous prescriptive propositions that deal not only with individual religious freedom, but also with the creation of a just social order. I have shown elsewhere how under certain conditions the Koran gives the state, as the representative of society, the power to control "discord on earth," a general state of lawlessness created by taking up arms against the established Islamic order.[11] The eradication of corruption on earth, taken in the light of the Koranic principle of instituting good and preventing evil, is a basic moral duty to protect the well being of the community. In the Islamic polity, where religion is not divorced from the public agenda, leaving adherents of competing doctrines free to pursue their beliefs engenders an inherent tension between religious communities that has to be resolved through state regulation.

The "millet system" in the Muslim world provided the pre-modern paradigm of a religiously pluralistic society by granting each religious community an official status and a substantial measure of self-government. The system based on the millet, which means a "religiously defined people"[12] was a "group rights model"[13] that was defined in terms of a communitarian identity and hence did not recognize any principle of individual autonomy in matters of religion. And, this communitarian identity was not restricted to identifying non-Muslim "protected minorities" (*dhimmi*s);[14] the millet's self-governing status allowed it to base its sovereignty on the orthodox creed officially instituted by the millet leadership. Under the Ottoman administration this group status entailed some degree of state control over religious identification, overseen by the administrative officer responsible to the state for the religious community.[15] In addition, the system allowed the enforcement of religious orthodoxy under the state patronage, leaving no scope for individual dissent, political or religious. Every episode of the individual exercise of freedom of conscience was seen as a deviation from the accepted orthodoxy maintained and enforced by the socio-religious order.

Such evaluation of the dissent within the Muslim community was also treated with much intolerance that was thoroughly institutionalized in the laws dealing with apostasy and religious rebellion. Juridical studies have shown with ample evidence that Muslim jurists have not engaged in a conceptual investigation of the ethical-legal presuppositions of certain commandments in the Koran. In particular, the absence of a thorough analysis of the Koranic ethical-legal categories on the one hand, and the ethical-religious on the other, has generated rulings that fail to recognize separate jurisdictions for God-human from human-human relationships. For instance, the Koran assigns Muslim public order the obligation of controlling "discord on earth." This phrase is part of a long verse that prescribes the most severe penalties for rebellion:

> The punishment of those who fight against God and His Messenger, and hasten to do corruption, creating discord on earth: they shall be slaughtered, or crucified, or their hands and feet shall alternately be struck off, or they shall be banished from the land. This is degradation for them in this world; and in the world to come awaits them a mighty chastisement, except for those who repent before you lay your hands on them. (K. 5:33–34)

That the Koran presents comprehensive commandments in which moral, religious and civil are not always easy to distinguish is demonstrated by the equal gravity under civil law accorded to moral and religious transgressions by Muslim jurists.[16] Moreover, Islamic law treats these transgressions as affecting not only humans, but also God. There is a sense in which both humans and God may have claims in the same infringement, even if the event seems to harm only one of them. Although punishment of crimes against religion are beyond human jurisdiction, the juridical body in Islam is empowered to impose sanctions only when it can be demonstrated beyond doubt that the grievous crime included an infringement of a human right (*haqq adami*, or private claim). The supreme duty of the Muslim ruler is to protect the public interest, function for which the law afforded him an overriding personal discretion to determine how the purposes of God might best be achieved in the community.

Since criminal law in Islam was a system of private law that fell under the ratifying and enforcement powers of the established political regime, prosecutions for offenses like false accusation of unlawful intercourse or theft, crimes that offend against both God's will and just human relations, take place only if initiated by the victim, and the plaintiff must be present both at trial and the execution.[17] In the case of unlawful intercourse the witness plays a crucial role. There must be four witnesses to the actual act of intercourse. Moreover, at the time of punishment, if the witnesses are not present (and, if the punishment is stoning, if they do not throw the first stones) the punishment is not carried out. If the thief returns the stolen object before an application for prosecution has been made, the prescribed punishment lapses; repentance for highway robbery before arrest causes the punishment to lapse; and if an offense is treated as a misdemeanor (*jinayat*) and the complainant is willing to pardon, blood money may be paid instead or the punishment remitted altogether. In the cases of offenses against religion that are not sanctioned by specific punishments—apostasy, for example (for which there is no defined punishment in the Koran)—the effects of repentance are even more far-reaching.

Determining the Role for Islam in Iraq

I do not wish to leave my subject at the level of theory without relating it to the concrete situation dealing with defining the role of Islam in the development of democratic constitution in Iraq. Off and on there has been a call for integrating the Shari'a in the new constitution in Iraq. At different times, religious leaders, mainly Shi'ites, but also some Sunnis, like the professor of the Shari'a and the imam of the Friday prayers in Baghdad, Dr. al-Qubaisi, have indicated the Islamic nature of the Iraqi society and the need to make Islamic social and political values part of the overall new political system of Iraq. To assess the seriousness with which this call is made one needs to identify the authority that gives the statement. It is not far-fetched to assert that the religious leadership in Najaf is interested in seeing that the Iraqi constitution reflects the majority view wishing to fulfill the religious dream of situating the Shari'a law at the heart of the political governance.

However, such a call needs to take into consideration fundamental problems that arise in the Iraqi situation as a modern nation-state. First is the fact of ethnic pluralism that exists in developing a sense of national identity. This has also implications for the development of a democratic constitution in which the notion of citizenship becomes the principle for power distribution. Second is the fact of sectarian plurality that informs religious identities within the broad national culture. This latter identity has gained a heightened sense in the context of enforced Ba'athist, secular ideology, during the last three decades. In fact, with favored status of the Sunni community under Saddam, a sectarian identity assumed the source of prime identity in terms of claims and rights that were in many instances denied to the Shi'ites by the Ba'athist government. This entrenched sectarian identity might also become the source of the derailment of any progression towards democratization of political institutions; transcending ethnic and sectarian divide today.

The new democratic constitution will be impossible to draft without addressing some of the issues that were raised above and which arise out of religious convictions. The question of guaranteeing the rights of non-Muslim minorities has come up quite often in the present deliberations. While it is important to make sure that the new constitution guarantees the fundamental human rights of all citizens, the major issue that needs even more immediate attention is the treatment of women as a "minority." There is a strong possibility that both political as well as religious leaders can disregard the Iraqi women's rights. Cultural obstacles are imposed by patriarchal traditionalism that prevails in the religious center like Najaf; whereas discriminatory evaluation of a woman's personal status is enshrined in the inherited juristic law, the Shari'a. Both these elements can result in the irreparable damage to the status of a woman in new Iraq, which can deny giving a clear and legitimate voice to women who constitute over half of the Iraqi population.

Nevertheless, attention must be paid to the cultural sensitivity to anything Islamic in Iraq. Even the atrocious secularism of the Ba'athists could not suffocate this connection of the people with Islamic values. The moderates or reform-minded intellectuals in Iraq, mostly the product of the secular education, tend to ignore the popular voices whose loyalty to their religious leaders is unquestioning. The bridge to this connection with the populace today is to provide authentic information on how Islam or Islamic law can or cannot become the source of governance in modern Iraq. Ignoring this important ingredient in building the necessary consensus on how the political system will evolve can actually lead to the rise of militant responses, flared by some of the politically opportunist religious leaders, intent to fill the power vacuum today.

There is little doubt that a fresh understanding of the Shari'a in the public arena should be in place to further its gradual acceptance by the people. Secularism with its insistence on the separation of "church" and "state" ("seminary" and "state" in Iraqi context) is not responsive to the culture that demands keeping religious values at the core of the emerging national culture. To put it differently, "disestablishment" of Islam will not work. In fact, not responding to such demands will actually backfire and will be seen as intentional marginalization of religious institutions and leaders, who are now actively demanding to be heard after a long period of their suffocation by the state. At the same time, the main problem that haunts any religious system, including the Shari'a, in a multifaith situation is its claim to exclusive loyalty. It is worth keeping in mind that, as discussed above, the Shari'a does not advance a concept of egalitarian citizenship—the core of civil rights and responsibilities in a modern nation-state. It simply divides the people as "Muslim members" with full privileges, and "non-Muslim minorities" with protected status under its divinely ordained system. Furthermore, it ordains laws for both the religious and the social-political aspects of everyday life. Herein lies the main cause for its incompatibility with the modern democratic system that conceives of its nationals as equal citizens, with equal rights and obligations. More importantly, in the area of gender relationships, the traditional system has instituted inequalities between men and women that could derail the democratic system built on equal rights of all its citizens, regardless of their gender or any other differentiations.

Hence, Islamic heritage has no paradigm at this time that can offer realistic solutions to the Iraqi situation that are demanded by its ethnically, culturally and religiously pluralistic population, unless, as demonstrated above, a fresh reading of this heritage is undertaken. Since the majority of the population is Muslim, one can begin to explore the possibilities of retrieving the core values of Islamic system to offer this fresh Islamic paradigm. This paradigm is actually derived from the religious law of Islam, the Shari'a itself. Let us consider this in the context of Iraq's need for a democratic constitution.

To begin with, we need to search for freedom of religion to enforce an individual's right to adhere to any or none of the confessional communities, without the interference from the state. In other words, this is the foundation stone of a democratic Muslim state in which religious freedom to forge one's spiritual destiny is offered to all citizens without any coercion or discrimination. Is it possible to speak about human-God relationship in which the state has absolutely no right to intervene or to impose uniformity?

The Shari'a provides the paradigm of a civil religion by separating the jurisdictions (*nitaq sulta*) in all its laws. I call this a principle of "secularity" (*sifa madaniyya*). This principle allows religion to manage God's relationship with humanity without interference from any human institutions, including the mosque and the seminary. All those laws that regulate God-human relationship are beyond any adjudication by human courts. There are no penalties for missing the obligations that one performs as part of his/her relationship to God. Only God reserves the right to demand an explanation for such a breach between individual believer and God. This area of the law covers the Ibadat—that is all those actions that are done clearly with the intention of pleasing God.

The second major area of the Shari'a deals with interpersonal social transactions. All laws regulating human relationships are covered under this section. This area of the law is known as Mu'amalat—that is, social transactions that must be conducted between individuals and groups, including the state, in keeping with the demands of justice in all areas of human existence. In this area, human courts have jurisdiction to enforce its decisions and to demand obedience. More pertinently, it is in this area of the law that reforms affecting social issues have taken place through the reinterpretation of the religious sources. Hence, the theoretical immutability of the sacred law does not get extended to this area.

This separation of jurisdictions is the closest the Shari'a can come to the secularism adopted in the western constitutions. It allows for functional secularity that can generate civic equality and mutual responsibilities at the human-human level of relationship, while maintaining the particularity and independence of the religious tradition from state administration. In other words, the separation of the jurisdictions in the Islamic law can respond to the needs of the modern nation-state, where the state must adopt non-interventionist policies in the matter of religious convictions of its citizens, but guarantee civic equality on the basis of human-human relationships, as required by the Shari'a. More importantly, this aspect of interpersonal relationships could be advanced for the improvement of women's moral and political equality with men, especially when the law concedes that the women have sufficient capacities to enter contracts as equals. In the traditional formulations there is an inconsistency in the law regarding men-women inequalities, which needs to be addressed in terms of the needs of a nation-state committed to democratic values.

Is it reasonable to expect that the fresh adoption of the classical formulations about separate jurisdictions might help carve for Islam an important place in public arena as the ethical-religious voice of guidance rather then governance? In the Iraqi culture it is ultimately the religious authority trusted by the people that can make such a meaning of the Shari'a acceptable. Without the cooperation of religious scholars at this time, it is hard to sell even democracy to the people who are conditioned to political and religious authoritarianism that prevails in Baghdad and Najaf, respectively. The fear is: Will secular form of authoritarian politics replace prone to authoritarian religious politics? It is certain that without the cooperation of moderate religious leadership, Islam in Iraq, especially the version that is heard at the present time, will retain its classical grip of claiming a total control over all the spheres of human activity ushering the rule of the uncharted sacred realm. Herein lies the danger to the core democratic values of civic equality of all citizens under a modern nation-state. Islamic heritage must guide rather than govern a modern nation-state. Iraq can benefit from its religious heritage provided it treats all its citizens as "equal in creation." Without this foundation no political system can claim to be democratic and pluralistic.

Concluding Remarks

The role of religion in creating the dichotomous relationship between two senses of loyalty—loyalty to one's nation and loyalty to one's religious tradition—is important in Muslim political culture. The divided loyalty is also a source of two identities in Muslim consciousness, the identity generated by one's relation to God, consolidated by observance of the sacred law of the Shari'a, and the identity created by one's experience of living as a member of a corporate body. The tension arises when the two sources of identities, revelation and reason, make incompatible and incommensurable demands upon an individual to hold exclusive and inclusive membership in the community and modern nation-state, respectively. The solution is provided in the recognition of a principle that can serve as the foundation for a civil society. This principle can lead the two identities to converge on a common goal—the overlapping consensus—about what is the common good in society. Regardless of one's religious affiliation, the principle, enunciated in one of the administrative documents of classical Islam, recognizes humans as "equal in creation" and in need of guidance and not governance from religion to inculcate values that will sustain a meaningful life. The document was written by the caliph 'Ali (d. 660) at the time when he appointed his governor for Egypt and its provinces. It is important to bear in mind that Muslim conquerors were in minority in Egypt. Egypt had a large Christian population, to whom a proper status had to be granted for administrative purposes. To reduce the majority to a "non-Muslim" tolerated people was detrimental to the development of a sense of civic responsibilities to the conquering Muslim army. In this context, the idea of civic equality was introduced in the following document written by the caliph himself to underscore the fact that the communitarian membership was not incompatible with the civic equality based on human dignity. As long as the role of faith was to instill moral and spiritual awareness leading to responsible behavior in society, the governance could be founded upon a more universal principle of recognizing other humans as one's equal in creation. In other words, the real concern of religion was to generate respect for all humans as sharing the dignity and honor as God's creation:

> Infuse your heart with mercy, love and kindness for your subjects. Be not in face of them a voracious animal, counting them as easy prey, for they are of two kinds: *either they are your brothers in religion or your equals in creation.* Error catches them unaware, deficiencies overcome them, [evil deeds] are committed by them intentionally and by mistake. So grant them your pardon and your forgiveness to the same extent that you hope God will grant you His pardon and forgiveness. For you are above them, and he who appointed you is above you, and God is above him who appointed you. (emphasis added)[18]

The recognition of non-Muslims as "equals in creation" is certainly a status that can be accorded to a citizen regardless of his/her religious affiliation. The role of religion, then, is to foster norms, attitudes, and values that can enhance peaceful relations among different ethnic and religious communities. The norms like "your brothers in religion or your equals in creation" can and should serve as the founding principle of governance through the creation of a civil society.

The question that needs to be addressed is whether a modern society with its pluralistic and diverse citizenry in terms of religious and cultural affiliations can afford to ignore such valuable guidance in matters of its governance of a paradigmatic city of humans "brother in religion or equals in creation." The response is very clear in the Koran 5:48:

For every one of you [Jews, Christians, Muslims], We have appointed a path and a way. If God had willed He would have made you but one community; but that [He has not done in order that] He may try you in what has come to you. *So compete with one another in good works.* (emphasis added)

It all depends on how the religious communities begin to institutionalize the culture of inclusiveness realizing that it is truly the divine mystery to allow pluralism in matters of faith and law to exist in human society. What matters ultimately is the common moral responsibility that humans share in order to advance common good.

Notes

1. Joseph Schacht, *An Introduction to Islamic Law* (Oxford: Clarendon Press, 1964), 189–190 discusses procedure in Muslim courts observing: "No action is possible without a claimant.... This principle is limited by the competence of the kadi to take action in matters of public welfare.... It is not compulsory to apply to the kadi, ... as long as no party applies to the kadi he takes no notice."

2. Kent Greenawalt, *Religious Convictions and Political Choice* (New York: Oxford University Press, 1988), 68.

3. It is not an easy task for any conscientious Muslim intellectual in the Muslim world or in the West to undertake this critical task without endangering his/her life. The intolerance exhibited by the religious establishment in some Muslim countries and more recently in Muslim communities in Europe and North America, which feels threatened by the rational assessment of religious texts in their historical context in the universities, has forced these scholars to abandon their religious and moral responsibility to their own community. In some cases these scholars have been forced to go underground and seek asylum in the West. As is well known, both Jewish and Christian academicians have, in the early part of their entry in the academic world, have encountered similar reaction from their respective religious authorities and congregations around the world. For Muslims in general, and their communities in the West in particular, academic study of Islam is a new phenomenon that causes their deep felt insecurities in faith to react strongly against anything that appears to challenge their long-held belief system.

4. Karl-Josef Kuschel, *Abraham: Sign of Hope for Jews, Christians and Muslims* (New York: Continuum, 1995), 190.

5. Mark R. Cohen, *Under Crescent and Cross: The Jews in the Middle Ages* (Princeton: Princeton University Press, 1997), 26; Marcel Simon, *Versus Israel: A Study of Relations Between Christians and Jews in the Roman Empire (AD 135–425)* (New York: Oxford University Press, 1986), especially chapter 3.

6. The Shari'a treated the non-Muslim minorities as a special legal category of *ahl al-dhimma*, giving them a status of "protected minorities." And, even when it discriminated against these minorities, their autonomous status as self-governing community

was well established. On the contrary, there is nothing in the law to guarantee the protection of the life and property of a "dissenter" within the community. A Shi'ite minority was viewed as a "heretical" group by a Sunni majority in power. The situation changed when a Shi'ite dynasty was in power. However, the sheer majority of the Sunni Muslims ruled out the treatment they meted out to the Shi'ite minorities that lived among them. Muslim sources are replete with reports about the execution of the "heretics" (that is, Shi'ite Muslims) who paused a threat to the Sunni governments in power and who openly dissented from the official majority view of Islam. M. G. S. Hodgson, *The Venture of Islam*, 3 vols. (Chicago: University of Chicago Press, 1974) at various points brings out the state policy of the Muslim rule governing its religious minorities. For instance, see: vol. 1, 242–251; 305–308; vol. 2, 536–539; vol. 3, 33–38. The oppressive treatment of Shi'ites continues to this day in a number of Arab and Muslim countries.

7. John Rawls, "The Priority of Right and Ideas of the Good," in *Philosophy and Public Affairs*, Vol. 17 (4), 251–276.

8. John Rawls, "The Priority of Rights and Ideas of the Good," *Philosophy and Public Affairs*, Vol. 17, No. 4, 260, 265.

9. Adam B. Seligman, *The Idea of Civil Society* (New York: Free Press, 1992), Chapters 1 and 2 trace the development of the idea in Europe and the United States. The work is not comparative in any sense and therefore does not deal with similar development in other societies. But, as pointed out in this work, Muslim societies are heir to both biblical and Greek ideas of individual, private and public realms of human activity. Hence, some of the characteristics that are now identified as being consonant with a civil society have been present in all cultures where people had to learn to live in harmony.

10. Michael Walzer, *Thick and Thin: Moral Argument at Home and Abroad* (Notre Dame: University of Notre Dame Press, 1994), x–xi, uses "thick" to designate the detailed reference to the "particularist stories" across different cultures, which also possess "a thin and universalist morality" that they share with different peoples and cultures. The "thickness" and "thinness" of the moral tradition of particular peoples and cultures also lead us to recognize the "maximalist" and the "minimalist" meanings, respectively, in that tradition, with a clear understanding that "minimalist meanings are embedded in the maximal morality, expressed in the same idiom, sharing the same . . . orientation" (3). I have introduced "universal" and "particular" guidance in the Islamic tradition in a similar conceptual framework, where the universal provides the minimalist and thin description of the moral principles; whereas, the particular, provides the maximalist and thick description of culturally integrated moral language that responds to specific purposes.

11. Abdulaziz Sachedina, "Justifications for Violence in Islam," *War and Its Discontents: Pacifism and Quietism in the Abrahamic Traditions*, ed. J. Patout Burns (Washington, D.C.: Georgetown University Press, 1996), 122–160.

12. Benjamin Braude, "Foundation Myths of the *Millet* System," *Christians and Jews in the Ottoman Empire: The Functioning of a Plural Society* (New York: Holmes & Meier Publishers, Inc., 1982), 69.

13. Will Kymlicka, "Two Models of Pluralism and Tolerance," in *Toleration: An Illusive Virtue*, ed. David Heyd (Princeton: Princeton University Press, 1996), 82.

14. Braude, "Foundations," *Christians and Jews*, 69–72.

15. Ibid.

16. Schacht, *Introduction*, 175–176.

17. Ibid.

18. This instruction is part of the famous collection of sermons and letters by 'Ali b. Abi Talib under the title *Nahj al-balagha*. This translation is rendered by William Chittick in *A Shi'ite Anthology* (London: Muhammadi Trust of Great Britain and Northern Ireland, 1980), 69.

10

Dialogue in an Age of Terror

Marc Lynch

The year 2001 began as the Year of the Dialogue of Civilizations at the United Nations, with Secretary General Kofi Annan declaring that "without this dialogue taking place every day among all nations—within and between civilizations, cultures, and groups—no peace can be lasting and no prosperity can be secure."[1] Annan warned that "we should not wait until we are in the thick of conflict to begin this kind of dialogue." That opportunity, tragically, is past. The terrorist attacks of September 11, 2001 put a bitter spin on what had begun as an attempt inspired by Iran's President Mohamed Khatemi, and taken up by the UN, for a global dialogue to prevent a spiral into an avoidable conflict between the West and Islam.[2] Instead, 2001 ended with an escalating confrontation between the United States and Islamism, threatening to bring forward the self-fulfilling prophecy of a "clash of civilizations." The radical Islamism of al-Qaeda, and its seeming rejection of the possibility of peaceful coexistence, seemed a decisive rejoinder to the very idea of a dialogue of civilizations. Was it?

Not necessarily. After a shaky beginning (such as using the term "crusade" and naming the Afghan operation "Infinite Justice"), President George Bush reassured the world that the United States would not pursue a conflict with Islam, calling instead for mainstream Muslims to join in denouncing Osama bin Laden and al-Qaeda. In Bush's initial speech to Congress after September 11, he asserted that "the terrorists practice a fringe form of Islamic extremism that has been rejected by Muslim scholars and the vast majority of Muslim clerics—a fringe movement that perverts the peaceful teachings of Islam." In the same speech, Bush directly addressed "Muslims throughout the world: we respect your faith . . . its teachings are good and peaceful . . . the terrorists are traitors to their own faith, trying, in effect, to hijack Islam itself." Bush warned against attempts to demonize Islam as a whole, and CIA Director George Tenet told Congress that "Islam is neither an enemy nor a threat to the United States."[3]

Many Islamist intellectuals and leaders took up this call, urgently calling for restraint and cooperation to avoid an escalation into a clash of civilizations. A fatwa issued by six prominent moderate Islamists condemning the September 11 attacks as contrary to Islam and calling for the apprehension and punishment of the perpetrators received regrettably limited attention in the West.[4] In the words of Arab League Secretary-General Amr Musa, "in the past, many have regarded [the dialogue of civilizations] almost as a luxury—an 'extra' item on the agenda of international relations. Today, we are paying the price for inadequately dealing with this issue. I propose that this dialogue be given prominence and placed at the top of the global agenda, not as a mere cultural theory but rather as an imminent strategic necessity."[5] Such recognition of the necessity of dialogue suggested that September 11 might have provided a horrific but effective antidote to the skepticism of Fahmi Huwaidi, who in 1996 saw little hope for such a dialogue because "the West sees no need for it and Muslims are not ready for it."[6]

This early potential for a response which brought America and Islam closer together faded in the face of highly unpopular American policies such as its support for Israel's reoccupation of the West Bank, invasions of Afghanistan and Iraq, and increasingly stringent approaches to policing Arab and Muslim communities. For all of Bush's efforts to praise Islam, public opinion polls and public discourse clearly demonstrated rising anti-American sentiments and growing anger, mistrust, and fear. The Pew Global Attitudes Survey in June 2003, for example, showed that "the bottom has fallen out of support for America in most of the Muslim world."[7] As the Council on Foreign Relations task force put it, "there is little doubt that stereotypes of Americans as arrogant, self-indulgent, hypocritical, inattentive, and unwilling or unable to engage in cross-cultural dialogue are pervasive and deep rooted," particularly in the Muslim Middle East.[8] The collapse of Muslim support for the United States, as one author notes, "ironically follows an intensive public diplomacy initiative aimed specifically at the region. How did America's battle for the hearts and minds of Arabs and Muslims wind up alienating the very people Washington was trying to reach?"[9] Such developments suggest a failure of communication, one which in turn suggests the immediate relevance of the critical theory of Jurgen Habermas.

Habermas relates that "since September 11, I have often been asked whether or not, in light of this violent phenomenon, the whole conception of 'communicative action' . . . has been brought into disrepute."[10] Mohammed Khatami faced similar questions about whether the dialogue of civilizations for which he called had ended.[11] Like both Habermas and Khatami, I argue that it has not. On the contrary, Habermas can help to explain the failures of American public diplomacy and of Muslim efforts to reach out to the West. The aftermath of September 11 demonstrates the great relevance of communicative action for world politics, including the immediate emergence of a genuinely global public sphere which struggled to collectively define an appropriate response to terrorism. A report of the Secretary-General of the United Nations argued effectively that "a dialogue of civilizations is not only a necessary answer to terrorism—it is in many ways its nemesis."[12] That many in the West and in the Islamic world alike vehemently deny the possibility of dialogue should no more be taken as definitive than should easy reassurances about the prospects for coexistence. But the appearance of a genuine global public sphere focused on the problem of Islam and its relations with the West suggests at least a possible alternative to escalating confrontation.

September 11 created the potential for a new kind of dialogue by initiating a virtually unprecedented issue-specific global public sphere focused on the question of the relations between Islam and the West.[13] Whereas in the past the dialogue of civilizations had been the domain of experts and partisan advocates, mainly manifested in conferences bringing together cosmopolitan elites, after September 11 their subject became the dominant topic of political debate and public discussion virtually everywhere in the world. These debates involved political leaders and cultural figures, mass publics and elites, intellectuals and religious leaders, private conferences and mass media. As Habermas puts it, the destruction of the World Trade Center "literally took place in front of the 'universal eyewitness' of a global public."[14] The massive, simultaneous demonstrations against the war on Iraq around the world on February 15, 2003 gave political weight to this emergent global public sphere. Iraq aside, one of the primary topics of this global public sphere has been a focused, purposive discussion about the topic of Islam and the West which changed the meaning, the significance, and the potential of the dialogue of civilizations in fundamental ways.

This essay does not seek to prove that dialogue can or will succeed, or test empirical claims about the distribution of opinions on the topic. As a first cut at this problem, it has more limited aims: to demonstrate that the resources, potential, and will to engage in such a dialogue does exist within both Islamist discourse and within the United States. Against hawkish American views which see Islam as uniformly radical and deeply hostile, and against similar views in the Arab-Islamic world which see the United States as an implacable enemy, this essay posits both a demand for and an important potential supply for a meaningful dialogue. It discusses in some detail the intense and important dialogues within the Islamic world about the concept of dialogue and its political possibilities—an intra-Islamic public dialogue which itself merits attention as an international public sphere. Such a dialogue could change the terms of the interaction between Islam and America, in part by breaking the monopoly over representation claimed by—and too often granted to—radicals on either side. Such a dialogue could prove contentious, revealing as many genuine differences as it does commonalities; contrary to the optimism of some enthusiasts, Islamists are not simply Western democrats dressed up in exotic clothing, and a genuine dialogue must take seriously their own views, beliefs, and identities.[15]

The overwhelming power exercised by the United States, and its seeming preference for military solutions, might seem to render problematic any notion of a power-free communicative space. But this should not in itself rule out such a dialogue. Tunisian Islamist Rachid Ghannouchi claims, "Our problem is that we have to deal with the West from a position of psychological and material weakness . . . but I maintain that this unequal and perverse relationship with the West is not fatal."[16] While there is little doubt about the vast inequalities in power, a more parallel feeling of vulnerability and insecurity might level the ground for a meaningful dialogue. Americans obviously felt an unprecedented sense of insecurity after September 11, one for which military campaigns in Afghanistan and Iraq or increased homeland security measures provided only partial relief. Muslims everywhere similarly consider their religion, their civilization, their culture to be under attack. Complicating a recognition of these mutual feelings of insecurity is, as Ken Booth and Tim Dunne put it, not so much "a simple 'clash of civilizations' . . . as a confusion of misunderstandings, crude stereotypes, and parallel absences of self-knowledge."[17] The kind of introspection demanded by many Americans of Islamic societies today is more likely to be forthcoming as part of a reciprocal dialogue, in which both parties open their beliefs, identities, interests, history, and policies to critical scrutiny. The difference in power might be countered by a shared insecurity and a recognition of the need to negotiate the grounds for peaceful coexistence. What is missing is a communicative approach to dialogue.

Is Dialogue Possible?

A demand for dialogue does not, of course, make it possible. What could allow dialogue to flourish in the hostile terrain of terror, force, and mistrust? Public sphere theory often unrealistically assumes the existence of conditions conducive to dialogue—a shared lifeworld, some level of trust, a willingness to set aside identities and power. International politics in general, and relations between the U.S. and the Islamic world in particular, rarely approximate such ideal conditions. The legacies of Orientalism, with its distorting lens shaping Western views of the Islamic world, as well as a mirror image Occidentalism shaping Islamic views of the West, complicated such dialogue even more.[18] As Craig Calhoun put it, after September 11, "the cosmopolitan ideals articulated during the 1990s seem all the more attractive but their realization much less immanent."[19] Does this render public sphere theory inapplicable? It does not. The sheer fact of the existence of fervent attempts to generate dialogue out of fear of the alternatives itself speaks to the remaining potential of a global public sphere.

The extremism of Osama bin Laden and the shocking atrocities of al-Qaeda's terrorism clearly succeeded in convincing many Americans of the impossibility of dialogue: "authentic cultural dialogue can go forward only when the threat of terror is removed," writes Jean Elshtain, dismissing "fundamentalists with whom dialogue is impossible—as a matter of principle, not merely prudence."[20] The American war on terror, and especially the war against Iraq, convinced many Muslims of the same thing. Even Sayla Benhabib finds little in the "nihilism" of al-Qaeda with which to engage in dialogue. Such refusals of dialogue in a real sense grant victory to terrorists, since their violence pointedly destroys trust and spreads fear of the other at moments where that fear might be overcome—and particularly hopes to convince both their own side and the other side that the extremists really do speak for their community.[21] Terror expressly aims at destroying the foundations for peaceful coexistence and reasonable dialogue.[22] This does not, of course, prove the opposite: that in the absence of terror, dialogue would necessarily succeed. But it does provide insight into the strategic rationale of terrorism, and the distinctive challenges this poses to those attempting to resist its iron political logic.

The key, as Benhabib recognizes, lies in the unsettled identity of its participants. In contrast to conventional state to state diplomacy, or even to the democratic deliberations of citizens, the encounter between "Islam" and "America" (or "the West") does not designate any official spokesmen. While it is almost certainly correct to say that the United States has little to discuss with bin Laden, it is almost certainly wrong to say that bin Laden speaks for Islam, or Islamism, or the Islamic world. An international public sphere which rejects exclusive claims to monopolize representation of any group offers a useful defense against such errors. Part of the value of a dialogue of civilizations would be to deny the extremists their desired monopoly on representing Islam—even as a generalized war against "Islamism" or "Islamofascism" plays directly into the hands of the extremists by accepting their claims at face value.

As Tariq Ramadan puts it, "we are opposed to the economic and strategic policies of the West, and this does not mean that the West, in itself, is the enemy. There exist a great number of intellectuals, journalists and researchers who have a genuine concern for understanding and who need to hear, read and refer to an honest and well-thought out discourse."[23] The question of authoritative representation is even more problematic in the case of the Islamic world, which lacks any recognized hierarchy or authoritative spokesman, either politically or religiously. The rise of a new Islamic public sphere over the last decades has led, in Dale Eickelman's words, not to "a homogenization of faith, but rather an intensified, multipolar struggle over people's imaginations—over the symbols and principles of Islam."[24] Politics in the Islamic world often revolves around competing claims to represent authentic Islam and speak on its behalf.[25] Osama bin Laden no more speaks for Islam than Daniel Pipes speaks for America.[26] But bin Laden seeks to speak for Islam, to render his vision authoritative, and his violent actions can be seen as "arguments" towards that end. Neither deeply intolerant voice such as bin Laden's nor more moderate spokesmen can be declared authoritative by outsiders seeking an interlocutor or even by Muslims themselves outside of the process of political argument itself.

Evidence of growing hostility to the United States, and the failure of its attempts to win public support, testify to the need for a more effective international dialogue. Rather than refuse dialogue with Islam because of the existence of Islamic extremists, or snub popular Arabic satellite television stations out of pique at their coverage of Iraq or Afghanistan, the United States might enter into a dialogue aimed at restoring faith with the vast majority of non-extremists and isolating the extremists within their own public spheres. Christopher Ross, self-described American emissary to the Arab street, explains that his mission is to rectify that "Arab and Muslim populations feel that after the end of the cold war, the U.S. turned its back on them, and did not maintain a dialogue."[27] But as Ragheda Dergham, New York correspondent for *al-Hayat*, puts it, "you won't win with words alone. The challenge America faces in reaching out to Arabs and Muslims . . . is to forge a bond of trust with people who have long felt betrayed."[28] The challenge for this essay is more limited: to consider the extent to which there exists the potential for the kind of talk—communicative action—which might help to build such foundations of trust which could shape the terms of future strategic interactions.

The Dialogue of Civilizations as an International Public Sphere

The dialogue of civilizations entered the realm of wide international discussion after the election of Iranian President Mohammed Khatami, in response to the growing appeal of Samuel Huntington's conception of an impending "clash of civilizations" between Islam and the West.[29] As part of his outreach to the West, Khatami appealed in strikingly Habermasian terms for a genuine dialogue which might bridge the dangerously wide gap between the Islamic world and the West. Khatami called for a "moral rationality" in international affairs, to go beyond "unaccountable power" and "to launch a dialogue beyond the predefined confines of power relationships." Khatami's call to "transform the logic of international relations, distancing it from the logic of power," which would "preclude the ascendance of unidirectional relations and political and cultural monologues" suggested a route to global legitimacy grounded in mutual respect and in a global political and cultural dialogue.[30] His proposal generated an extraordinary amount of international discussion and enthusiasm, even when his specific overtures to the United States faltered. Its enthusiasts ranged far beyond the Islamic world—Japan was one of the more active participants—and its participants included a remarkable range of prominent literary, scientific, and political figures. In 1999, the UN General Assembly declared the year 2001 to be the "year of the dialogue among civilizations." UNESCO selected the "dialogue among civilizations" as "a strategic objective" for the period 2002–2007, working with Kofi Annan's personal representative Giandomenico Picco to stage a wide range of events and conferences.[31] A wide range of international conferences and forums brought together representatives of various civilizations, including impressive panels of leading cultural and political figures. This dialogue took place almost entirely among cosmopolitan elites, usually at international conferences, with cultural exploration dominating over political contestation. The products of their efforts—such as the Nicosia declaration—while intellectually engaging, had little direct political significance or engagement.[32] After September 11, their voices were largely drowned out in the outpouring of argument and commentary seeking to impose definitions and perspectives on a suddenly urgent contentious issue.

September 11 and the war over Iraq have generated an historically unique international public sphere in which virtually everyone in the world has been exposed to and has participated in a simultaneous, ongoing debate. But if the global public sphere was new, the issues under debate were not. Arabs and Muslims, deeply concerned about American hegemony after the end of the Cold War—and often taking Samuel Huntington's "clash of civilizations" and Francis Fukuyama's "end of history" as their benchmarks—had been talking about it for a decade. The sheer volume of public discussion about "the clash or the dialogue of civilizations" among Arabs and Muslims commands attention.[33] Almost every Arab public intellectual, as well as politicians such as Amr Musa, Secretary-General of the Arab League, weighed in on the question. The published interventions discussed in this essay alone range from postmodernist philosophers (Mohammed Abed al–Jabiri, Ali Harb, Mohammed Mahfouz) to Marxists (Galal Amin) to liberals (El–Sayyid Yassin, Mohammed Sid Ahmed, Prince

Hassan bin Talal) to Islamist modernists (Abd al-Karim Soroush, Mohammed Khatami, Yusuf al-Qaradawi, Tariq al-Bishri, Tariq Ramadan, Said Bensaid, Abdelwahhab El-Affendi) to Left Islamists (Hassan Hanafi, Fahmi Huwaidi) to Arabists (Burhan Ghalyun, Amer Moussa) to *jihadist* radicals (Ayman al-Zawahiri, Osama bin Laden).[34] Since September 11, the balance between a dialogue and clash of civilizations has been a recurrent theme of Arab public arguments, with a nearly obsessive refrain of the need to prevent bin Laden and Bush from creating an unwanted clash. For example, an *al-Jazeera* special broadcast in October 2001 asked a number of Arabs and Americans whether September 11 would push towards a dialogue or a clash of civilizations, receiving mixed responses amidst worried pessimism.[35] That all of these public intellectuals engaged in public arguments with each other about the concept of a dialogue with the West is itself prima facie evidence of the existence of an issue-specific international public sphere.

The use of "civilizations" even as shorthand for the participants in such a dialogue is problematic, however.[36] Huntington has been widely criticized for his approach to what constitutes a civilization, whether civilizations can act, and so forth. Nevertheless, a self-fulfilling constructivist dynamic has pushed for the definition of global politics along "civilizational" lines, particularly since September 11. Americans have shown an extraordinary willingness to indulge in sweeping generalizations about "Islam" or "Islamic civilization," replete with extensive analysis of the reasons for its failures. Such a reductionist approach fits well with the agenda of radical Islamists, who share the vision of an Islamic world defined exclusively by its religious identity. Osama bin Laden, just as much as Huntington or Pipes, argues for the primacy of religion as a political identity, reserving his fiercest attacks for the "hypocrites" among the Arabs and Muslims who do not prioritize Islamic identity. One of the risks of the "dialogue of civilizations" has always been of accepting that classification of actors, and thereby empowering religious over other potential interlocutors.[37] The "dialogue of civilizations" formulation displaces the large majority of Arabs and Muslims who are not Islamists and accepts an otherwise quite controversial claim on the part of Islamists to speak authentically on their behalf. As Kamal Mahdi asks, "why does the West seek a dialogue with Islam but then talk to the Islamist movement?"[38]

It also assumes the existence of unitary, coherent civilizations—as if there were a single "West" or a single "Islam," or anyone who could authoritatively speak on their behalf. Critics of the concept, including many Islamists, like to point out that Western and Islamic civilization have long been mutually constitutive, emphasizing the "simultaneous and reciprocal formation of Europe and the Islamic Middle East as civilizational units."[39] Ali Harb, for example, accuses those who want to define and defend a single "Western" or "Islamic" civilization of "doing violence to the cultures they claim to champion" (113). Individuals, no less than countries, can contain multiple civilizations—and may well be shaped by an internal dialogue between them. Huntington, as well as bin Laden, postulate pure and pristine civilizations precisely because they observe and fear the opposite.[40] Robert Cox, who takes the concept of civilizations seriously, concludes that "if different civilizations do coexist, the problem of mutual comprehension becomes paramount for the maintenance of world order." To achieve such coexistence, Cox argues, requires finding "means of encouraging popular forces struggling for the entrenchment of human rights in their society without appearing to impose one civilization's norms upon another."[41]

Globalization, including Muslim immigration to the West and Western economic and cultural and political penetration of the Islamic world, has made this interaction ever more intense. As Richard Norton puts it, "The spread of public education and literacy, and the proliferation of information about the world through the modern news media, do not lead to the triumph of any particular interpretation of Islam, but to a growing tendency for Muslims to see themselves as part of a broader global community." Globalization, and its creation of a globally oriented transnational capitalist civilization, cuts across state or cultural boundaries. News media, such as the enormously influential Arab satellite station al-Jazeera, created a platform for intra-Arab and Islamist debates which brought together speakers and audiences not only within the Arab world, but throughout Europe and the United States.

Islamism itself should be seen as part of ongoing dialogues and political struggles within the Islamic world as well as within the wider global public sphere. By tapping in to those ongoing public arguments, rather than only paying attention to those who directly address the West, points of convergence as well as of dissonance, and a different set of interlocutors, might be found. While some—too many—Islamists have turned their project into a means to close down public debate and discourse, others have used Islam as a vehicle for sharp critique.[42] Most of the authors discussed below have themselves fiercely criticized the kinds of closed, intolerant neofundamentalist Islamism associated with bin Laden's network. At the same time, most of these active and engaged intellectuals have little interest in simply being appropriated by American critics of Islam. It is these kinds of voices which might seek a consensus against extremism and intolerance on all sides.

The dialogue here concerns the nature of world order in a world characterized by globalization, American power, and the polarized politics of Islam. Long before September 11, most Arab thinkers placed the dialogue of civilizations in the context of globalization and the end of the Cold War. They commonly positioned the Islamic world between Huntington's clash of civilizations and

Fukuyama's end of history, two interventions which remain points of entry into a common global debate. Globalization, for them, is an unavoidable structural reality which could lead to either conflict or cooperation. A dialogue of civilizations can help to reduce the political tensions produced by globalization and to maximize the possibility of peaceful coexistence. Wide swaths of Arab and Islamic opinion reject the idea that relations with the West are primarily determined by culture or religion. The Sudanese Islamist Abd al-Wahhab al-Affendi argues that Arabs and Muslims should not pursue a dialogue of civilizations as Arabs or Muslims, but rather should insist on a global dialogue about justice, equality, rights.[43] These relations could easily take a Realist form, with civilizations substituting for states in a spiral of hostility and mistrust, but this is neither necessary nor inevitable. Crucially, however, important actors— both in the Islamic world and in the United States—believe that such a conflict is desirable. This means that the most important dialogues, as has become nearly a cliché, are within these regions/actors rather than between them.

Islamist Perspectives

While the dialogue of civilizations received little attention in the United States, except in terms of Khatami's political outreach to restore U.S.-Iranian relations, in the Arab and Islamic world it generated an enormous amount of discussion and debate. Desperate to avoid either a clash of civilizations or submersion within an undifferentiated globalization, Arabs and Islamists seized upon the idea of a dialogue of civilizations as a way of finding a place at the global table. This call for dialogue was controversial in the truest sense of the word, driving a vigorous public debate about its virtues and dangers. Ayatollah Khamenei, Supreme Leader of Iran, forcefully criticized his President's call for dialogue as not only unnecessary and pointless, but as profoundly dangerous. But his rejectionism, as with the wider response by radical Islamists, was laced with the secret fear that it might succeed.

While they disagree among themselves as to the value of dialogue with the United States, Islamists draw on a rich theoretical tradition in their discussions of dialogue (*hiwar*).[44] Indeed, the distinctions drawn in Islamic thought between *hiwar* and other forms of exchange such as *jadal* and *sira'a fikri* echo Habermas's distinction between communicative and strategic action.[45] Tariq al-Bishri distinguishes between "dialogue (*hiwar*)" and "intellectual combat (*al-sira'a al-fikri*)" in his discussion of the possibility of dialogue between Islam and secularism.[46] Said Binsaid insists that Islam requires "a willingness to understand the opinion of others and a disposition towards good relations with them."[47] Islamic political thought has a long and deep history, rooted in the rigors of *tafsir* (interpretation) of the Quran, of considering rules for argumentation in the pursuit of truth through reason.[48] Yusuf al-Qaradawi argues against the radicals that "Islam is a religion of dialogue, and the Quran is at its base a book of dialogue."[49] Egyptian liberal El-Sayyid Yassin attacks secularists who doubt that Islamists can participate in dialogue, pointing to their ongoing internal debates and admirable practices of self-criticism.[50] Many of the problems of the Islamic world, according to Abdelwahab El-Affendi, can be explained by the fact that Islam's normative commitment to a public reason has more often than not been subordinated to politics and the imperatives of power.[51] Abdolkarim Soroush warns that "rational discourse among human beings must not be replaced by emotional harangues," and celebrates a distinctively public reason, a "collective reason [which] is free from such enslavement . . . individual desires and prejudices nearly vanish when reason is made universal."[52] Abd al-Aziz al-Tawijra carefully distinguishes *hiwar* from *dawa* (proselytizing), *munazira* (quarreling), and *mujadila* (argument)—with hiwar reserved for communicative encounters.[53]

Islamists have a generally unrecognized constructivist theory of politics, in which ideas matter and persuasion is a key form of political action. Islamism commands the faithful to engage in *dawa*—an outreach to non-Muslims—as a core tenet of the faith. Islam spreads through persuasion, which entails a strategic orientation with a communicative practice—in other words, Islamists have no intention of questioning their own faith or convictions, but are deeply interested in finding ways to change the minds and hearts of others. Radical Islamists may portray the relations between Islam and the West in purely combative terms, but this can only be maintained by rejecting the basic ontology of Islam itself in favor of a more base Realism. Indeed, even Hassan al-Banna, founder of the Muslim Brotherhood, expressed a strong preference for reconciling political differences through dialogue rather than violence—although Sayyid Qutb's followers among the Brothers in later years despaired of the utility of such dialogue.[54] But Qutb's retreat from reason and insistence on absolute "submission" to God, as well as the tactic of his followers of *takfir* (unilaterally declaring a Muslim to be an apostate for his views or policies, justifying his murder), earned considerable scorn from thinkers such as Yusuf al-Qaradawi and Hassan Hanafi, for whom public argument and the exercise of reason is central to any true Islamic practice. For Hanafi, "defending the rule of reason is the task of our generation"—meaning defense not only from the authoritarian coercion of despotic regimes but also from attempts by Qutb-inspired Islamists to enforce a single, unchallengeable interpretation of Islam.[55]

Yusuf al-Qaradawi, perhaps the most popular and influential Islamist public intellectual today, has long been one of the most outspoken advocates of dialogue as a foundational principle of Islam. He asserts unequivocally that "we—all Muslims—believe in dialogue, because we are commanded to do so by the Shari'a, and the Quran is full of dialogues between the prophets of God and their communities, and between God and his slaves, and even between God and the Devil. . . . We welcome a culture of dialogue instead of a culture of clash whether between civilizations or cultures. . . . Why can't the two civilizations interact and integrate with each other, each profiting from the other, with no supremacy in it?"[56] He takes to task those "extremists [who] pretend that there are no points of agreement between us and the Jews and Christians" for misreading the Islamic position and the word of God. Indeed for Qaradawi, the first indication of extremism is "bigotry and intolerance, which make a person obstinately devoted to his own opinions and prejudices. . . . Such a person does not allow any opportunity for dialogue with other . . . [this] attitude contradicts the consensus of the Islamic community, that what every person says can be totally or partly accepted or rejected."[57] He argues that dialogue can help all believers stand against the enemies of religious faith and the corruption of modern society, pointing to the cooperation between al-Azhar and the Catholic Church on abortion during the 1994 Cairo World Population Conference and the 1995 Beijing Women's Conference. Further, he argues that religions can agree on protecting the weak and seeing justice in the world, although his example—the Palestinian people—suggests that more than dialogue might be needed to achieve consensus.

Cultural or Political Dialogue?

Mohammed Khatami's conception of the dialogue of civilizations eschewed direct political debates for a higher-order attempt to develop some common life-world.[58] Khatami sought to focus the dialogue at a high intellectual and cultural level, arguing against a direct political dialogue before achieving some progress at those more rarified levels. Belying his image as simply a political dove, Khatami states matter-of-factly that "politically, the West aims to govern all corners of the world . . . and it will stop at nothing to achieve its goals and protect its interests. . . . We confront a determined enemy that brings all of its material, military, and informational resources to convince us to surrender."[59] The value of civilizational dialogue in the face of such a threat was to "confront the thought of the opponent by relying on rationality and enlightenment and through offering more powerful and compelling counter arguments" (16). Khatami points to aspects of Western civilization beyond its political quest for domination with which Muslims can and must engage in dialogue: "those who cannot separate the political West from the nonpolitical West are acting against the interests of the nation and the Islamic revolution" (19). Conflicts of interest and political difference does not rule out meaningful dialogue, then, for Khatami.

Mohammed Mahfouz endorses Khatami's call for "not a political dialogue focusing on interests" but rather a higher-order dialogue aimed at establishing the foundations for civilizational coexistence and equality. For Mahfouz, the problem is that the West wants a monologue, not a dialogue, and Arabs and Muslims must find a way to force the West to seriously engage in dialogue rather than lecturing and manipulating (139). Abd al-Aziz Bin Athman al-Tawijra's concept of "dialogue for coexistence" similarly focuses upon the deeper cultural and civilizational issues.[60] After noting that the concept of dialogue has no real legal basis or standing in international law or practice, al-Tawijra notes the deep roots and high status of the concept of hiwar in Islamic thought (13). Dialogue is the guarantor of moderation, tolerance and justice (16). Only through mutual respect and purposive action can a dialogue of civilizations succeed in this spirit (24). He warns against a dialogue which only involves a few thinkers and has no effect on policymakers, against a dialogue tainted by extremists and against a dialogue permeated with a "hegemonic spirit" (24). Other Islamists had less patience for such an abstract dialogue, preferring a direct engagement with the major political differences with the West.

El-Sayyid Yassin epitomizes the elite-centered, intellectualized, and broadly cosmopolitan/liberal approach to the dialogue of civilizations.[61] Emerging from long interaction with the United Nations task force on the dialogue of civilizations, and a regular participant at the many international conferences devoted to the subject, Yassin seeks to transcend political and strategic differences in search of a higher ground, an inter-civilizational zone of agreement: "an attempt after the collapse of the ideological confrontation of the Cold War . . . to build a kind of agreement . . . between the great civilizations of the world in order to form common values, making the basis for the administration of world society . . . in an age of globalization" (85). Yassin accepts the reality of political differences, but sees this as a reason for dialogue, not for abandoning it. And Yassin places considerable responsibility on intellectuals and cultural figures to take the initiative in pushing for such a dialogue.

Dialogue as Persuasion: The Dawa

Islamist notions of dialogue depart dramatically from Habermas's communicative ideal, however, in that the purpose of dialogue is to demonstrate the truth of Islam and to establish a new world order based on its principles—not through conquest but through dialogic reason. Islam demands the interaction of civilizations and not conflict between them, because only through dialogue can other civilizations be persuaded of the truth of Islam.[62] Such a proselytizing approach retains a strategic orientation, for all of its communicative overlay, since the ultimate goal is always to change the other without accepting the possibility of changing one's own beliefs. Charles Hirschkind's anthropological account of dialogues between Islamists and non-Islamists in Egypt, where Islamists politely interrogate non-observant Muslims and attempt to guide them ("Do you believe in God? Well, why do you listen to that music, when you know that the Quran disapproves of it?") richly demonstrates the coercive undertone of outwardly communicative dialogues.[63] For all of its embrace of dialogue as a road to reason, Islamic notions of dialogue must take as their starting point that there is no God but Allah—indeed, Waardenburg describes the belief in God as the "key to the structure of nearly all arguments based on the logic of revelation and faith"—an "argument from the absolute" which provides a boundary for the Islamist acceptance of dialogue.[64] While dialogue can be—indeed must be—communicative in a wide range of ways, and with regard to many issues, it ultimately must remain strategic with regard to the fundamental pillars of faith. Dialogue, al-Tawijra argues, rests on three pillars: belief in God, respect for the ethics of Islam, and the pursuit of the truth (*al-Haqq*).[65] That those three pillars might be in conflict lies beyond the bounds of acceptable argument.

Habermas's distinction between strategic and communicative action is vital here. Even radical Islamists, who are most opposed to dialogue with the West, embrace the idea of dialogue as a form of persuasion, or strategic action. Sayyid Qutb, the Egyptian radical Islamist, argued that the way to deal with hypocrites (those who claim to be Muslims but really aren't) is to "leave their inward state and intentions to God, and carry on Jihad with them by arguments and persuasive means . . . to influence their hearts by the deep penetrating words of God."[66] But such persuasion has little to do with communicative action; instead, dialogue is simply one more weapon in the arsenal of spreading the faith. As Qutb frankly puts it: "Undoubtedly this message does strive through tongue and speech. But when? Only then when people are free to accept this message. . . . But when . . . material influences and impediments may be ruling, there is no recourse but to remove them with force, so that when this message may appeal to the heart and reason of man, they should be free from all such shackles and bonds to pronounce their verdict openheartedly."[67] In other words, while all are free to choose, there is only one correct choice. And where words fail, the use of force is not far behind.

Because contemporary Islamist radicals see the West as an implacable enemy, and as the source of the most pressing threats to Islam, they tend to see dialogue as politically irresponsible and as normatively undesirable. Ayatollah Khamenei rejected Khatami's call for dialogue because, he argued, such an opening would only invite the American enemy to take advantage of Iran's internal divisions and to exploit its dropping its guard. The Wahhabi, or Salafist, strand of radical Islam followed by Osama bin Laden discarded the long tradition of classical Islamic jurisprudence about jihad (and dialogue) in favor of a fierce, intolerant discourse which rejected the very possibility of communicative action—sometimes even with other, non-Salafi Muslims, to say nothing of discourse with the West. Khalid Abou el-Fadl describes this Salafist discourse as enamoured with apologetics "that often descended into moral arrogance" and "was fundamentally centered on power," and which came to "define Islam as the exact antithesis of the West."[68] This strand of Salafism, pushed to prominence within Islamic politics by Saudi money and an aggressive brand of proselytizing, viewed dialogue with the West not only as a threat, therefore, but as worthless. It is from this latter strand of Islamist radicalism that bin Laden's declaration of *jihad* against the United States emerges. While this radicalism remains a minority position within Islamism, and even more so within Islam as a whole, few would deny its ability to dramatically influence political outcomes.

Dialogue and Threats to Islamic Culture

One of the most common objections to a dialogue with the West follows from the fear that Islamic culture will be overwhelmed by the onslaught of globalization and the materialist seductions of Western culture. Jalal Al-e Ahmad's "Westoxication," which deeply influenced the Iranian revolution, offered a withering critique of the Iranian fascination with Western ideas and products. But, in a direct challenge to this widespread and deeply rooted defensive position, Mohammad Khatami argued that "the cultural strategy of a dynamic, vibrant Islamic society cannot be isolation." Khatami calls instead for an open Islamic public sphere as the best defense against Western subversion, which "requires us to allow various, disparate views to engage one another in our society . . . an active, evolving society must be in contact and communication with different, sometimes opposing views."[69] And he forcefully rejects any attempts within Islam to silence free inquiry or the voices of reason: "if, God forbid, some people want to impose their rigid thinking on Islam and call it God's religion—since they lack the intellectual power to confront the opposite side's thinking on its own terms—they resort to fanaticism. This merely harms Islam, without achieving the aims of those people" (16). Or, as Soroush puts it, "only those who lack in ideas need fear the marketplace of ideas."[70] Even the skeptical Hassan Hanafi warns that an internal dialogue must precede a dialogue with the West, but that repressive regimes which criminalize any opposition have rendered such internal dialogue difficult.[71] For these Islamist advocates of dialogue, a genuine and open dialogue, both internal and external, can only strengthen Iranian—and more widely Islamic—societies. Fear of the other is an unworthy position for a strong and confident culture, particularly for a culture which grew and thrived for centuries on the basis of interaction with and integration of other cultures and civilizations.

Tariq Ramadan worries, however, about the "natural seduction" of the Western lifestyle, and equally about the likelihood of a violent reaction by those who find their identities threatened.[72] While such a construction of polar opposites—an Islam threatened by an aggressive West—might be common among those exposed to this challenge, "such is not the position of the majority of intellectuals," who instead of defensiveness against the West emphasize a positive project—"for Islam, not against the West: . . . the assertion of the Muslim universal is not achieved here through the negation of the Western universe, but rather through acknowledgment of plurality" (269). Ramadan insists that "to refute cultural invasion is not . . . tantamount to being anti-Western. It is rather an opposition to the rapport of force and to the will of hegemony of the symbolic universe of the West" (271). What remains to be seen, however, is whether the West can possibly accept any assertion of identity which does not take Western universals as its starting point. Either way, Ramadan insists, a strong Islam must welcome both internal and external dialogues: "One does not protect oneself from one's enemy by concealing from him, and by hiding from oneself, one's defects. Those who consider the West as an enemy feel that any criticism directed at Muslims is a kind of dishonest compromise especially if it is enunciated in the presence of Westerners. . . . Yet to elaborate a critical denunciation in no way means making an 'alliance' with the West. It is before anything else remaining faithful to the Message of Islam."[73]

Mohammed Mahfouz similarly emphasizes the importance of maintaining a strong identity and sense of culture and tradition (*turath*) when engaging in dialogue.[74] Approaching the West from a position of cultural weakness or defensiveness would be tantamount to defeat, since "no people (*shaab*) can achieve its goals if it loses its identity" (110). The real clash he sees is between cultures (*thiqafat*) and not between civilizations (130). Civilization represents a common human achievement, which no culture may claim for itself, while cultures do sharply differ from one another. The great danger for Mahfouz is that Arabs and Muslims will lose their identity, culture, and tradition and thus be defenseless in the face of the Western claim to the mantle of civilization. Mahfouz sees the problem as Western refusal to contemplate genuine coexistence: "all human cultures could easily coexist and work together, if only the West would give up its style of dominating and denying every other civilization" (136). It is the West's desire to dominate the world under a single civilizational which places Islam, like other cultures, at risk (138). Dialogue is the alternative to a conflict of civilizations, and would involve mutual recognition and respect; participation in such a dialogue would "ensure Islam a permanent presence in the era, effective participation in human civilization and a positive role in finding acceptable solutions to the problems which we all face today" (140). Entering into dialogue with the West will require a renaissance of Islamic civilization, if Islam is to survive the encounter without succumbing to domination or followership (140).

In an interesting twist, the Sudanese Islamist Hassan al-Turabi argued in the mid-1980s that the growing strength of Islamist thought made the time ripe for dialogue with the West, pointing out that "in directing the Islamic discourse to the West, the Muslims who are the West's followers are also addressed." For Turabi, Islam should not feel like the weaker party in its dialogue with the West because of its political or economic problems, since it stood on the right side of a "metaphysical conflict" between faith and unbelief.[75] Turabi challenged Islamists to take seriously their own arguments about the superiority of Islam and to engage with the West not as a threatened inferior but from a position of spiritual superiority. By doing so, the Islamic world could freely learn from the technical achievements of the West without fearing for its identity or its soul.

Yet another argument that self-confident and strong cultures have nothing to fear from globalization comes from the Lebanese philosopher Ali Harb, who calls for Islam "to first establish a critical relationship with its self and its concepts," to engage in an internal dialogue without being preoccupied with a dialogue with the West (23). A strong culture need not see globalization as such an imperializing civilization, however; an internally strong and vibrant Islam could relate to the new culture of globalization with confidence and power (101). He warns, however, that this is not optional: those who try to resist globalization through cultural defensiveness will fail, as they have always failed. The relationship between civilizations is not one of conflict, as Huntington (or Hassan Hanafi, for that matter) would have it—it is a relationship of interpenetrating and interacting cultures forming new civilizations (110). Harb rejects efforts to portray Islam and the West as coherent entities clearly divided by a "cultural wall," arguing that the focus on the West displaces critical attention from the far more important internal debates and struggles.[76] Dialogue will fail if its participants only want to make others into copies of themselves (112), but it can succeed on the basis of mutual respect and equality.

Who is empowered to participate in these dialogues? Tariq Ramadan warns against taking Westernized intellectuals as interlocutors, despite their near-complete isolation from their own societies, because "these intellectuals repeat what the West wants to hear." A dialogue which takes these intellectuals as representatives of the Islamic world will create "a dialogue of cultures that [is] truncated and false; it is about inviting the other in order to speak amongst ourselves" (271). Harb writes scathingly about self-appointed elites who set out to defend "authentic" culture from the forces of globalization.[77] But if not these cosmopolitan intellectuals, then who? Neither author would endorse the claim of a bin Laden to speak for Islam. Nor would they accept the authority of traditional Muslim *ulema* (scholars). They, and many others, doubt the right of the organized Islamist movements to speak for wider Islam. Many radical Salafists lack the kind of scholarly and religious credentials which would traditionally have given them a voice in such debates.[78] But the point here is that such questions will only be resolved in the public sphere itself, not through an external appointment. Indeed, one of the virtues of the public sphere approach is precisely that it insists on hearing the voices of all affected actors. Listening to the full range of debates about dialogue with the West would place the position of the radical Islamists in context, important but fiercely contested.[79]

Dialogue as a Mask for Power Politics

The skepticism of many Arab and Islamist intellectuals about dialogue rests upon a deep recognition of the imbalance of power, and a long-nurtured resentment of American policies towards the region. Secular leftists and Arab nationalists often resist dialogue with the West because of a Realist conception of international politics—which contrasts with the more Idealist, or even constructivist, Islamist understanding of world politics. For these skeptics, dialogue is always a mask for the reality of power. Virtually every Arab and Islamist thinker who has addressed the possibility of dialogue with the West emphasizes the importance of mutual respect and equality, and a willingness of both sides to listen and change.

Mohammed Abed al-Jabiri, for example, while describing the concept of "dialogue of civilizations" as "one of the most important issues of the hour, if not the most important," argues that the very focus on Islam, and not on other religions or regions, calls into question the credibility of the concept of a dialogue of civilizations.[80] The dialogue of civilizations only gained importance as a response to the "clash of civilizations" concept, which Jabiri sees in the context of America's search after the collapse of the Soviet Union (6–7) for new enemies against which to define itself in order to maintain its own self-identity. Pointing out its long history of expansion and the incredible diversity of the Muslim world, Jabiri argues that "nobody, not in the West nor in the East, can pretend that Islamic civilization has been closed or has been inclined to conflict or rejection or that it has closed the door to dialogue" (15). Indeed, if anything distinguishes Islamic civilization, it has been its openness to dialogues with other cultures, "an openness to the Other" (16), to the point where Islamic civilization itself is the product of an internal dialogue among cultures which have accepted Islam. Jabiri compares the Islamic style of dialogue with other cultures favorably with the West's approach to other cultures: colonization, invasion, and forcible conversion to Western institutions and ideas (16). Jabari argues for a political, strategic explanation of the West's fixation on Islam as an enemy: "the West is interests, nothing but interests. And any dialogue with it or thought against it which does not depart from that truth will collapse and fall into a confused and irrelevant discourse"(18). The "clash of civilizations" is nothing but a clever phrase to conceal America's pursuit of its interests. But how to respond (19). He warns that the concept "dialogue of civilizations" therefore can never be innocent, and obscures more than it reveals (21): a dialogue about religion, about culture, about civilization only distracts attention from the real clash of interests.

Perhaps the most systematic critique of the possibility of dialogue with the West has been made by Hassan Hanafi, for whom the problem remains Western political domination and "the darkness thrown over human reason." Hanafi argues that "the dialogues between East and West are a curtain to conceal the real economic and military and political conflict . . . the West knows that we continue to be tied to our culture, and they call for a dialogue of civilizations as a way to come closer to us and for us to come closer to them to conceal the hostile dimension . . . all of this conceals the conflict of interests and the desire for hegemony. But that does not mean that dialogue is bad in itself . . . dialogue is part of civil life, and we must listen to the enemy and know his arguments in order to not allow the curtain to conceal the real clash of interests."[81]

According to Hanafi, "a dialogue can only take place between equals."[82] And the current relationship between the West and Islam cannot be one of equals. The Islamic world today faces "an existential historical crisis, which expresses a greater conflict than can be addressed through openness or dialogue."[83] Hanafi sees the calls for "dialogue" as simply another way for the West to undermine and destroy Arab and Islamic culture, integrity, authenticity, and ultimately existence as a civilization (43–45)—and as a mask for the ongoing onslaught of market civilization and Western economic and military power. Indeed, by "softening the sharp edge of conflict between the West and Islam," the dialogue of civilizations will only "smooth the way for other forms of political, economic, and cultural domination."[84] He does not see dialogue as useless, however; indeed, he emphasizes that "dialogue does not mean surrender," as long as it is carried out with a "spirit of resistance."[85] Such a "spirit of resistance" would again leave little room for Habermasian communicative action, however.

For the Egyptian Marxist Galal Amin, the extreme power imbalance renders any talk of dialogue similarly absurd: "if we respond by saying that the need is not for a clash but for a dialogue, we also fall into the trap because the aggression against us can not be solved by dialogue . . . it is useful for them for us to think that dialogue can produce results useful for us (like the Copenhagen group, for example), but what is the value of the dialogue between the fox and the hen? . . . do they really think that the decision makers in the west are still deficient in their understanding of us? . . . why is the dialogue always about how we can adjust to them . . . do we ask them to put their women in *hijab*?"[86]

Even Yusuf al-Qaradawi is not sanguine about dialogue. For all his commitment to the idea that Islam demands dialogue, he remains intensely focused on the ways in which such openness might be exploited by a strategically minded West. At a recent conference at the Egyptian professional associations complex in Cairo, Qaradawi placed the blame for a clash of civilizations on the West, which "seeks to destroy Arab and Islamic civilization" and to keep the Islamic world living in fear of its power.[87] Indeed, he warns that "the cultural and social and intellectual invasion is the most powerful weapon in their war against us now, as we see the pressure they place on us to change our educational curricula and they try to force us to change our laws and they openly and clandestinely intervene in our affairs, because they want to manufacture a generation with a new mentality which serves their interests."

American Views of Dialogue, and the Neoconservative Opportunity

The opportunity for dialogue rests not only on mutual vulnerability, and not only on the emergence of a genuinely global public sphere which has insistently forced leaders and intellectuals to engage in public debate about the relations between Islam and the United States, but also on an often overlooked commonality linking Islamists and the neoconservatives who drive Bush's foreign policy. For both Islamists and neoconservatives, ideas matter. Islamist arguments about the primacy of spreading Islam and purifying the faith and the faithful explicitly rejects theories based on either market incentives or worldly power.[88] Neoconservative arguments about the urgent need for liberal transformation in the Middle East similarly take seriously the power of ideas and normative beliefs.[89] Unlike Realists, who discount the possibility of change, or Liberals, who emphasize instrumental rationality, neoconservatives—though they would hardly admit it—share with Islamists an implicitly constructivist theory of international relations: the belief in the power of ideas, the emphasis on identity, the meaning invested in power, and the aspiration to a normatively legitimate international order.

These commonalities should not mask that for all their agreement on theory, neoconservatives and Islamists have identified one another as enemies, not as potential allies. But "enemies" and "friends" are social constructions which can change.[90] My argument is that those beliefs and identities can best change through public dialogues. But dialogues which retain a strategic orientation— as they largely have to this point—are unlikely to accomplish this goal.

To this point, the neoconservative approach to transformation has rejected dialogue in favor of the overwhelming exercise of power, the demonstration effect of American wealth, and a monologic, strategic form of persuasion.[91] Convinced of the superiority and rightful primacy of American values, the neoconservatives view American power as deeply invested with purpose. Spreading these values—which they present as freedom, capitalism, democracy, and enlightened benevolent American hegemony—is vital to their conception of international relations. They advocate, in William Kristol's words, "a morally grounded foreign policy that seeks aggressively and unapologetically to advance American principles around the world."[92]

But how can such values be spread? Habermas would point to a profound mismatch between neoconservative ends and means, with his core distinction between strategic action, which seeks to manipulate others in the pursuit of self-interest, and communicative action, which seeks consensus and truth. The strategic orientation of neoconservative practice undermines their own goals. Many argue that acceptance of American ideas will follow from the demonstration of American power, with overwhelming military victory forcing opponents to give up their aspirations of resistance.[93] Power will dissuade challengers, while attempts at accomodation—dialogue—will embolden them by suggesting weakness. Or, less delicately, "the way to tame the Arab street is not with appeasement and sweet sensitivity but with raw power and victory."[94] Their object is to change others, not to engage in an open-ended dialogue with, reassure, or accommodate them. Indeed, neoconservatives are radically contemptuous of dialogue, dismissive not only of the views of others but of the very process of discussion. As if approaching dialogue from a position of superiority and adopting a monologic and strategic orientation were not enough, the Bush administration's penchant for issuing threats and for invading other countries—not to mention its cavalier attitudes towards truthfulness—undermines the possibility for dialogue. As the columnist Richard Cohen put it, "That sense of going it alone, of being so big and powerful that even the reluctant must follow, of being so right that persuasion and consultation are merely a waste of time and breath, has been the hallmark of the Bush foreign policy since its inception."[95] This combination renders neoconservatives almost pathologically hostile to any meaningful international public sphere. The intense pro-Israeli and Christian fundamentalist preferences of significant portions of the Bush administration's conservative ruling coalition makes dialogue with Islam, in particular, even less attractive. These attitudes, it hardly bears mentioning, are mirror images of the *jihadist* mentality of some Islamic extremists, who equally claim a privileged access to truth and reject any form of dialogue which does not begin from their premises.[96]

More "liberal" approaches to the Islamic world generally rest on a similarly strategic orientation. American public diplomacy efforts combined advertising (an inherently manipulative approach to changing attitudes); propaganda, some relatively benign (television commercials of happy American Muslims) and some less so (the ill-fated Office of Strategic Communication to disseminate false information to foreign media); and the promotion of moderates who accepted the American terms of debate. None of these approaches took a genuinely communicative approach, or showed any willingness to put American identity, interests, or policies up for discussion. Indeed, the challenging position taken by al-Jazeera and other Arab satellite networks were taken not as an invitation to open political debate, but as evidence of hostility; rather than seriously engage with these popular networks, the Bush administration attempted to threaten and intimidate them, while creating its own alternative, pro-American media outlets (Radio Sawa, Hi! Magazine, a satellite television station).[97] The emphasis on power rather than reason can be seen in the dominant terminology in American debates: "winning the war of ideas"; "the battle for hearts and minds." Such martial metaphors demonstrate a strategic conception of dialogue, aimed at persuasion and manipulation of the other rather than a genuine engagement. As Fahmi Huwaydi dismissively puts it, "the US administration does not think about reviewing its policies but only tries to treat the symptoms without looking at the disease causing them."[98] The Council on Foreign Relations is right to suggest "moderate voices are often not heard over the din of the fanatics. Therefore, U.S. public diplomacy should encourage dialogue with and debate within Islam about the radicals' efforts to hijack Islam's spiritual soul."[99] But this begs the most important question: what kind of dialogue?

Too often, Americans have insisted upon the public performance by Muslims of an acceptable script. Americans demand that Islamists condemn September 11—which, ironically, they hardly needed to demand, given the widespread shock and horror expressed even in bastions of resentment of the United States. But beyond that, the United States looked to aggressively police Muslim public discourse, hyper-sensitive to any signs of "anti-Americanism"—a nebulous category of political and cultural public performance offensive to current American sensibilities. But such forceful policing of Islamic public discourse generated resentment in its own right.[100] As Salah al-din Hafez sarcastically puts it, how are Arabs to react to the argument that the solution to the problems of the world is "to fix our corrupted minds for us if we can't do it ourselves"?[101] An increasingly common formulation of demands for liberal reform, for example, quickly became "we need to reform our educational systems, even if the Americans say so." Faced with demands to endorse American hegemony, many Muslims responded with defensiveness, become more radical rather than more moderate. For example, Yusuf al-Qaradawi, perhaps the most influential Islamist public intellectual today, took a strong and courageous stand against al-Qaeda after September 11, but by late 2002 endorsed *jihad* against an American occupation of Iraq.

Dialogues in Practice

To anticipate a likely critique, the kind of international public dialogues envisioned here are not likely to meet the exalted standards of Habermasian discourse ethics. Nor do they have to. Habermas might call this "weak communicative action," a kind of pre-negotiation in which the participants have only begun the process of reconciling their lifeworlds and establishing the foundations for more focused pragmatic discourses.[102] Undertaking such a dialogue requires a willingness to set aside considerations of power and self-interest which seem quite implausible in today's international order. Helmi Shaarawi points out that "dialogue requires a certain degree of matching power" and warns that a dialogue between the Arab world and the United States today would be hopelessly corrupted by the imbalance of power.[103] As Chris Brown observes, "the problem is that to engage in this kind of dialogue is to undertake a re-evaluation of one's values that inevitably will be painful and with no guarantee that the eventual outcome will be agreeable. Why would those who are comfortable with their values . . . enter into this process in the absence of some compelling reason to think that their situation is untenable?"[104] September 11 perhaps gives such a reason, but only under certain interpretations.

Dialogues might help to dispel unneeded fears and to break unnecessary spirals of conflict. Communicative action, dialogue, can help where "the spiral of violence begins as a spiral of distorted communication that leads through the spiral of uncontrolled reciprocal mistrust, to the breakdown of communication. If violence thus begins with a distortion in communication, after it has erupted it is possible to know what has gone wrong and what needs to be repaired."[105] Of course, where hostility is real, and not the product of misunderstanding—as is the case with bin Laden's extremist views of the necessity for conflict with the West—then better communication will not prevent violence. Some conflicts and hatreds are real, and cannot be talked away. But others are not, and dialogues might help to clarify which are which—an important service in an age of terror, where frightened populations might incline towards assuming the worst about others. As the literature on ethnic conflict, as well as Jervis-inspired work on the security dilemma and attribution errors, amply demonstrates, actors insulated from engagement with others generally have little idea of how those others view them.[106] Virtually all Arabs and Muslims feel threatened by American power, and cannot understand how Americans can fear them. And most Americans fear radical Islam, and can't imagine that others might fear them. Many Americans were genuinely shocked after September 11 to discover how much fear and mistrust of the United States permeated the world. Had they been more engaged in ongoing dialogues with the Islamic world, more might have been aware of the depth and nature of the grievances which animated them.

Great mutual suspicions and fear only increase the importance of Habermas's injunction that such dialogues must begin with an orientation towards mutual understanding rather than towards self-interest. In the report of the Secretary-General, hopes for these dialogues depended on "fully understand[ing] that cultural and religious diversity is a source of strength, not a cause for division and confrontation. The prospects for dialogue will be even better if we understand that the goal of dialogue is not to impose one's viewpoints or even to reach consensus."[107] Fred Dallmayr stresses the importance of the "effort to develop a global or genuinely cosmopolitan model of rational communication along cross-cultural lines; that is, a model which, while recognising the importance of cultural and historical differences, seeks to obviate the danger of an impending 'clash of civilization.'"[108] In Dallmayr's formulation, "the point of such conversation is not to dominate, manipulate, or lecture others 'from on high,' but to take them seriously in their lifeworlds as members of the global community."[109] Susan Buck-Morss takes a similar position: "Islamist discourse cannot be excluded from the global discussion merely because its premises are non-Western."[110] For Bikhuh Parekh, "the point of the dialogue is to deepen mutual understanding, to expand sympathy and imagination, to exchange not only arguments but also sensibilities, to take a critical look at oneself, to build up mutual trust, and to arrive at a more just and balanced view of both the contentious issues and the world in general."[111]

Not just any dialogue will do, however. Louay Safi, for example, warns that "an absolute universalistic stance is incompatible with a meaningful cultural dialogue between the Muslim East and the liberal West, even when the proponents of such a stance truly desire this dialogue . . . the transition from a universalist monologue to a cross-cultural dialogue requires . . . a change in attitude and approach."[112] The experience of some of the more high profile attempts at an American-Islamic dialogue has been less than stellar, in part because of an insufficiently communicative orientation on the part of its participants—on both sides. As Gamil Mattar described his experience at a high profile conference of Arab and American media figures, "many of us participants noticed that from the first session some of the American discussants changed the meeting from dialogue to threats and intimidation . . . the American side always focused on specific accusations which they repeat endlessly as if the goal of the dialogue is to compel the Arab discussant to recognize his weakness and incompetence and lack of Understanding. . . . We hear from the Americans that our schools are bad and our media is bad and our curriculum is bad and encourages extremism and racism and that we do not practice transparency and we hate democracy . . . and so on . . . and never do they admit to any shortcomings of their own."[113]

Or consider an exchange of open letters between a group of conservative American intellectuals and a group of Saudi public figures. Jean Elshtain, one of the principle authors of the American statement, offers a good example of the failure to adopt a communicative approach. While she presents her project as a dialogue, in fact it is a monologue, or at best an internal dialogue with the fixed premises of just war theory. She insists that the principles of the statement "What We're Fighting For" are universal, beyond discussion. While she states that "we sought to begin a dialogue with intellectuals in other countries," (75) the statement offers no room for any such dialogue—the only options are to accept its fundamental principles, or else to be ruled out of the realm of legitimate discussion. Elshtain repeatedly rejects any possibility of dialogue with Islam. She bases this rejection on an equation of Islam with its most radical spokesmen—quoting Osama bin Laden or describing the Taleban as if they stood in for "Islam" as a whole. She asserts with confidence the absence of any internal discussion about September 11 within Islam—an assertion which the evidence in this paper alone roundly disconfirms. In support of her descriptions of Islam, she quotes not a single actual Islamist other than Osama bin Laden.[114] Her near complete ignorance of Islamic politics does not stand in the way of her call for a "just war"—highlighting the dangers of a monologic approach.

This tendency to welcome dialogue while refusing to consider certain kinds of challenges can be seen in the response by Saudi Islamist intellectuals to the American statement of "What We're Fighting For."[115] The Saudi Islamists begin by accepting the invitation to dialogue: "Dialogue, in principle, is a noble endeavor where we can take a good look at our moral foundations and discuss them with the intent of establishing a more just and equitable relationship." Having said, this the Saudis warn against the American approach: "the language of their discourse is the language of power." What kind of dialogue might be better? "It must maintain a tone of respect, clarity, and frankness . . . those participating in it must be willing to accept criticism and correction unflinchingly." But their response itself concentrates on criticizing American policies and defending Islam, accepting little responsibility on the part of the Saudi system. In the end, both the American and the Saudi participants, for all their overt and vocal endorsement of dialogue, share a fundamentally strategic orientation towards dialogue.[116]

Or consider the *Wall Street Journal*'s description of a panel discussion between Bernard Lewis and Hassan Hanafi as a "dialogue of the deaf," concluding that "the cultures of the West and the Islamic world are so far apart that it would seem that even the most basic dialogue . . . is impossible."[117] In response to Hanafi's fairly innocuous comments that "a clash of civilizations is alien to the Muslim world, where we have always championed the dialogue of civilizations" and that "the people who carried out the September 11 attack do not represent Islam, just as the Baader Meinhof doesn't represent Germany," the writer was "ready to weep . . . as he twittered on." Such is dialogue with the thinkers of Islam in the *Wall Street Journal*.

Extremists opposed to dialogue often attempt to silence moderates within their own communities, and to downplay the existence of moderation on the other side. Conditions of conflict, terror, violence, or war empower hardliners to claim a voice monopoly, and an interpretive monopoly, as moderates fall quiet or are ignored. Evangelicals such as Franklin Graham blast Islam as "a very evil and wicked religion."[118] Martin Kramer calls those emphasizing moderate trends in Islam "effectively accomplices to the violence," and the Campus Watch website created by Daniel Pipes expressly labels those offering insufficiently hawkish views on Islam as "apologists for terror."[119] The fear and anger produced by September 11 fueled an appetite for explanations which offered the possibility of an immediate, muscular response. While few publicly endorse Ann Coulter's notorious call for the United States to "invade their countries, kill their leaders, and convert them to Christianity," many do believe that Islam is the problem. Dialogue not only denies such visceral gratification, it directly threatens their own standing as authoritative interlocutors. Extremists on both sides—from Daniel Pipes to Osama bin Laden—contemptuously dismiss dialogue but secretly fear its success. This fear, to be charitable, often rests in their genuine belief in the enmity of the other, which dialogue might conceal until it is too late. They take keen interest in, and make sure to highlight to their own publics, expressions of extremism from the other side.

What is absolutely vital is to recognize that there is no fixed quantity of "extremists" on either side. Hardliners tend to argue that the extremists are the true face of the other, while those open to dialogue tend to claim that extremists represent a minority position. To say that this is an empirical question misses the point, however. Political opinions and identities can and do change, in response to external and internal signals, incentives, and pressures. Adopting a tough stance towards the other will strengthen the position of the hardliners, validate their worldview and their analysis, and likely increase their weight—threatening a self-fulfilling prophecy. On the flip side, a communicative approach can encourage and embolden moderate counterparts, isolating extremists and driving them to the margins. In the case of Iran, for example, Khatami's overtures to the West directly challenged the entrenched power of conservatives, who had every incentive to see the dialogue fail.[120] Americans hostile to Iran similarly criticized the dialogue initiative out of fear that it might soften policy towards a regime they despised. Responding to escalating American rhetoric against Iran, for example, one Iranian official observed that "we hope they will see sense and not use the language of force, because this will have the opposite effect. Certain people [in Iran] think that dialogue is a waste of time, and if the pressure grows too strong, it will strengthen the hand of those against dialogue."[121] The fatal dilemma here, however, is that it is at precisely this moment—of their threatened marginalization—that extremists are most likely to resort to terrorism, to violence, to prevent it.

Such dismissals from the right do not monopolize the public sphere on questions of Islam, of course.[122] Jeremy Rifkin asks, "what if, instead of holding on to every utterance of the extremists . . . we focus on the centre of gravity in the Muslim world and call for a cultural dialogue between Islam and the west?"[123] Extremists oppose dialogue not only on principled grounds, but for eminently strategic reasons: they understand that dialogue could potentially succeed. If a dialogue can reveal a more moderate distribution of opinion on each side to the other, then it might help to break the interpretive monopoly of the hardliners. But their counterparts too often are apologetics for Islam or critiques of American foreign policy which remain devoid of any genuinely communicative engagement with Muslims. Noah Feldmann's enthusiastic *After Jihad* is certainly open to the existence of moderate voices among Islamists, but uses this knowledge to propose an ambitious American foreign policy agenda to transform the Islamic world into Western style democracy, with little pause to ask how these Islamists themselves might think about his proposals.[124]

Conclusion

The events of September 11 paradoxically have made a dialogue between Islam and the West more urgent, more possible, and more real. The eruption of a genuinely global public sphere around this issue presents an opportunity which may or may not be taken. This essay has hopefully shown at least the demand for such dialogue and the existence of a strong current within the

Islamic world already engaged in such a dialogue. The voices calling for dialogue represent a broad cross-section of Islamist opinion, and cannot be dismissed as simply a marginal Westernized elite. The rising profile of new Arab media, particularly satellite television stations such as al-Jazeera, brings these arguments to an ever wider public. As evidenced by the widespread opposition to the American war against Iraq, this pro-dialogue consensus should not be confused with any kind of blanket support for the United States and its policies. But nor should such opposition be mistaken for an immutable hostility. The absence of the conditions widely assumed to be necessary for genuine communicative action, as well as the ability of extremists to sabotage dialogue through acts of violence, should temper any optimism. But the existence of this global public sphere, and the powerful presence of Islamist and American voices open to dialogue, should equally temper any counsel of despair.

Notes

1. Annan speech to Seton Hall University, 6 February 2001, UN document SG/SM/7705.

2. Marc Lynch, "The dialogue of civilizations and international public spheres," *Millennium* 2000.

3. George Tenet, testimony to Senate, February 6, 2002.

4. Fatwa issued September 27, 2001, by Yusuf al-Qaradawi, Tariq al-Bishri, Muhammad al-Awa, Haytham al-Khayyat, Fahmi Huwaidi, and Taha Jabir al-Alwani (English translation at http://www.unc.edu/~kurzman/Qaradawi_et_al.htm).

5. Amre Moussa, "The road to enhanced international dialogue: an Arab perspective," Oxford Centre for Islamic Studies, 9 November 2001.

6. Quoted by Antony Sullivan, "Western and Islamist Leaders Consider 'Dialogues of Cultures and Civilizations,'" *Washington Report on Middle East Affairs*, August 1996.

7. Pew Research Center for People and the Press, *Views of a Changing World*, 2003 (June 3, 2003), 2.

8. Peter Peterson, "Public diplomacy and the war on terrorism," *Foreign Affairs* 81, no. 5 (2002), 75.

9. R. Zaharna, "Winning the second round: American public diplomacy in the Arab and Muslim world," *Foreign Policy in Focus*, June 13, 2003.

10. Giovanni Borradori, *Philosophy in a Time of Terror: Dialogues with Jurgen Habermas and Jacques Derrida* (Chicago: University of Chicago Press, 2003), 35.

11. "Khatami: September 11 Blamed on Lack of Dialogue Among Civilizations." http://www.netiran.com/Htdocs/clippings/FPolitics/020929XXFP01.html.

12. UN General Assembly A/56/523 (2 November 2001), Para. 19.

13. Susan Buck-Morss, *Thinking Past Terror: Islamism and Critical Theory on the Left* (Verso, 2003).

14. Jurgen Habermas, cited in Borradori, *Philosophy in a Time of Terror*, 28.

15. Noah Feldman, *After Jihad* (New York: Farrar, Straus and Giroux, 2003).

16. As quoted by Lisa Anderson, 1998, 25.

17. Ken Booth and Tim Dunne, eds., *Worlds in Collision* (New York: Palgrave Macmillan, 2002).

18. Edward W. Said, *Orientalism* (New York: Vintage, 1979); Edward W. Said, *Covering Islam* (New York: Vintage, 1997); David Little, *American Orientalism* (Charlotte: University of North Carolina Press, 2004); Fred Halliday, "The Politics of Islam, Revisited."

19. Craig Calhoun, "The Class Consciousness of Frequent Travelers." *South Atlantic Quarterly* 101, no. 4 (2002).

20. Jean Elshtain, *Just War Against Terror* (New York: Basic Books, 2004), 45.

21. For example, see David Lake, "Rational extremism," *IO-Dialogue* 2001.

22. Booth and Dunne, *Worlds in Collision*, 10.

23. Tariq Ramadan, *Islam, the West, and the Challenges of Modernity* (Islamic Foundation, 2000), 289–290.

24. Dale F. Eickelman, "Islam and Ethical Pluralism," in Sohail H. Hashmi, ed., *Islamic Political Ethics* (Princeton, 2003).

25. For example, see Dale Eickelman and James Piscatori, *Muslim Politics* (Princeton, 1996); and Salwa Ismail, *Rethinking Islamist Politics* (I. B. Tauris, 2002).

26. Although Bush's recess appointment of Pipes to the board of the United States Institute for Peace, over the objection of American Muslim groups, was seen by many Arabs and Muslims as an official endorsement of Pipes's extremist views.

27. Christopher Ross quoted in *Washington Post*, June 9, 2003.

28. Raghida Dergham, "You won't win with words alone," October 14, 2001.

29. Lynch, "The dialogue of civilizations." For detailed overviews of American relations with the Islamic world in the 1990s, see Shireen Hunter, *The Future of Islam and the West* (CSIS, 1998) and Fawaz Gerges, *America and Political Islam* (Cambridge, 1999).

30. Mohammed Khatami's statement to the Milennium Summit of the United Nations, September 6, 2000 (http://www.un.org/ga/webcast/statements/iran.htm).

31. UN General Assembly document A/56/523 (2 November 2001).

32. For example, see the essays collected in *Dialogue of Civilizations*, edited by Majid Tehranian and David Chappell (I. B. Tauris, 2002), a product of the UN's efforts.

33. For thoughts on the representativeness of these intellectuals, see Peter Mandaville, "What does progressive Islam look like?" *ISIM Newsletter* 12 (June 2003), 34–35.

34. Many of these classifications are problematic and controversial, of course; they are intended purely for heuristic purposes. Suggestions about better labels for these figures are welcome.

35. "American explosions . . . pushing towards dialogue or clash of civilizations?" hosted by Ghassan Bin Jadu, *Al-Jazeera*, 1 October 2001.

36. See Fred Halliday, *Two Hours that Shook the World* (Saqi Books, 2002), for an eloquent dissection of the civilizational approach; and Amartya Sen, "Civilizational distress: Getting the whole world wrong," *New Republic*, 1997.

37. For an overview of thought on this subject, see the essays in Ali Mohammadi, *Islam Encountering Globalization* (New York: Routledge Curzon, 2002).

38. In al-Zaman, 2002.

39. Almut Hofert and Armando Salvatore, eds., *Between Europe and Islam* (Peter Lang, 2000), 14–15.

40. Lisa Wedeen, "Why Huntington, and Bin Laden, Are Wrong," *Middle East Policy* 10, no. 2 (2003), 57.

41. For a thoughtful analysis which takes the civilizational approach seriously, see Robert Cox, *The Political Economy of a Plural World* (Routledge, 2002), especially chapters 8–10, quote at 174 and 186.

42. Akbar Ahmad and Lawrence Rosen, "Islam and Freedom of Thought," *The Chronicle of Higher Education* (November 2001).

43. Abd al-Wahhab al-Affendi on *al-Jazeera*, March 22, 2003, hosted by Khalid al-Hroub.

44. See Dale F. Eickelman, "The Arab 'Street' and the Middle East's Democracy Deficit," *NWC Review* (Autumn 2002) for discussion of the centrality of hiwar for other Islamists not mentioned in this essay, including Mohammed Shahrur (Syria), Fethullah Gulen (Turkey), Nurchomlish Madjid (Indonesia) and Said Binsaid (Morocco). Also see the rich discussion of dialogue in classical Islamic thought in Salah el-Sheikh, "Al-Mujadalah and al-Mujadilah Then and Now: Kalam, Dialectical Argument, and Practical Reason in the Quran," *The Muslim World* 93 (1), January 2003, 1–50.

45. See Michael Fischer and Mehdi Abedi, *Debating Muslims* (University of Wisconsin Press, 1990), for detailed discussion of the role of dialogue in Islamic thought and practice.

46. Tariq al-Bishri, *Al-Hiwar al-Islami al-'Ilmani* (The Islamic-Secularist Dialogue) (Daral-Sharouq, 1996), 43. My translation.

47. Eickelman, "Islam and Ethical Pluralism," 127.

48. For discussion, see Jacques Waardenburg, *Islam: Historical, Social, and Political Perspectives* (New York: de Gruyter, 2002), especially chapter 2, "Faith and Reason in the Argumentation of the Quran." Ahmed Moussalli, *The Islamic Quest for Democracy, Pluralism, and Human Rights* (University Press of Florida, 2001), reviews moderate and radical views over time of these questions.

49. Yusuf al-Qaradawi, "Hiwar ma' al-Gharb" (Dialogue with the West), *Al-Jazeera* program "Sharia and Life," broadcast July 11, 1999.

50. El-Sayyid Yassin, "Ruaya Islamiya lil-Hiwar" (Islamist views of dialogue), *al-Qabas*, 25 July 2002 (my translation).

51. Abdelwahab El-Affendi, "Rationality of Politics and Politics of Rationality," in A. Tamimi and J Esposito, *Islam and Secularism in the Middle East* (NYU Press, 2002), 151–169.

52. Abdolkarim Soroush, *Reason, Freedom, and Democracy in Islam* (translated and edited by M. Sadri and A. Sadri) (Oxford University Press, 2000), 93.

53. Al-Tawijra, *Hiwar*, 15 (my translation).

54. As quoted in Moussalla, 123.

55. See the discussion of Qutb and Hanafi by Shahrough Akhavi, "The dialectic in contemporary Egyptian social thought," *International Journal of Middle Eastern Studies* 29 (1997), 377–401. For more on Hanafi's project, see Yudian Wahyudi, "Arab responses to Hasan Hanafi's Muqqadima fi 'Ilm al-Istighrab," *The Muslim World* 93 (April 2003), 233–248.

56. Yusuf al-Qaradawi, "Al-Hiwar bayn al-Islam wa al-Nasraniya" (Dialogue between Islam and Christianity) *Islam Online*, 2001. My translation.

57. Yusuf al-Qaradawi, "Extremism" (1981), as translated in C. Kurzman, *Liberal Islam* (2002), quote at 199.

58. Lynch, "The dialogue of civilizations."

59. Khatami, *Hope and Challenge*, 13–14.

60. Abd al-Aziz Bin Athman al-Tawijra, *Al-Hiwar Min Ajil al-Ta'ayesh* (Dialogue for Coexistence) (Cairo: Dar al-Sharouq, 1998). My translation.

61. El-Sayyid Yassin, *Hiwar al-Hidarat* (The Dialogue of Civilizations) (Cairo: Merit, 2002). My translation.

62. Al-Tawijra, 23.

63. Charles Hirschkind, "Civic virtue and religious reason: an Islamic counter-public," *Cultural Anthropology* 16 (2001), 3–34.

64. Waardenburg, *Islam*, 53.

65. Al-Tawijra, *Hiwar*, 15 (my translation).

66. Qutb, "Milestones," as translated in *Modernist and Fundamentalist Debates in Islam*, ed. Mansoor Moaddel and Kamran Talattof (New York: Palgrave Macmillan, 2002), 225.

67. Qutb, "Milestones," 232.

68. Khalid Abou el-Fadl, "Islam and the Theology of Violence." See Hamid Algar, *Wahhabism* (Islamic Publications International, 2002), for an unsympathetic discussion of this theology, and Stephen Schwartz, *The Two Faces of Islam* (Anchor: 2003), for an even more unsympathetic expose.

69. Khatami, *Hope and Challenge*, 47.

70. Soroush, *Reason, Freedom and Democracy in Islam* (Oxford, 2002), 102.

71. Hanafi, "Hiwar al-Hidarat bayn al-Mutamar al-Islami wa al-Itihad al-Eurobi" (The Dialogue of Civilizations between the Islamic Conference and the European Union), *al-Zaman*, May 29, 2002. My translation.

72. Tariq Ramadan, *Islam, the West, and the Challenges of Modernity* (The Islamic Foundation, 2001), 269.

73. Ramadan, *Islam, the West, and the Challenges of Modernity*, 289.

74. Mohammed Mahfouz, *Al-Islam, al-Ghurb, wa Hiwar al-Mustaqbal* (Islam, the West, and Dialogue of the Future) (Casablanca: Arab Cultural Center, 2000). My translation.

75. Ahmad S. Moussalli, *The Islamic Quest for Democracy, Pluralism, and Human Rights* (University Press of Florida, 2003), 121, drawing particularly on Turabi's *Tajdid al-Fikr al-Islami* (Renewal of Islamic Thought) and on "Utruhat al-Haraka al-Islamiyya fi Majal al-Hiwar ma'a al-Gharb," *Shu'un al-Awsat* 36 (1994), 70–92.

76. As quoted in Wahyudi, "Arab Responses," *The Muslim World* 93, no. 2 (April 2003), 244.

77. Ali Harb, *Hadith al-Nahayat* (Talk of the Endings) (Casablanca: Arab Cultural Center, 2000). My translation.

78. Quentin Wiktorowicz and John Kaltner, "Killing in the name of Islam," *Middle East Policy* 10 (2), 2003, 76–92.

79. Charles Kurzman, "Bin Laden and other thoroughly modern Muslims," *Contexts* (fall/winter 2002), 13–20. Also see Khalid Abou el-Fadl, "Islam and the Theology of Power," *Middle East Report* 221 (winter 2001), 28–33.

80. Mohammed Abed al-Jabiri, "Hiwar al-Hidarat!" (Dialogue of Civilizations!) *Fikr wa Naqd* 44 (December 2001), 5–22.

81. Hanafi in *al-Rai*, May 7, 2002. My translation.

82. *Al-Ahram*, Feb. 7, 2002.

83. Hassan Hanafi, *Ma al-Ulima* (What is Globalization?) (Beirut: Dar al-Fikr al-Mu'asir, 1999). My translation. Quote from 39.

84. Hassan Hanafi, "Sadamat al-Qua aw Sadamat al-Ruwaya" (Clash of Power or Clash of Vision), *al-Zaman*, 8 September 2002. My translation.

85. Hanafi, "Interview with President Khatami," *al-Zaman*, February 19, 2002. My translation.

86. Galal Amin, '*Ulima al-Qahar* (The triumph of globalization: the United States and the Arabs and Muslims before and after the events of September 11) (Cairo: Dar al-Sharouq, 2002).

87. Report from conference, "Al-Muslimun wa al-Gharb . . . Hiwar aw Saddam?" 10 Sept. 2002. From www.qaradawi.net. My translation.

88. See Carrie Rosefsky-Wickham, *Mobilizing Islam* (New York: Columbia University Press, 2002), for a subtle discussion of "transvaluation" in Islamist mobilization; also see Roxanne Euben, *Enemy in the Mirror* (Princeton, 1999).

89. Marc Lynch, "Critical Kosovo," forthcoming in *Making Sense of IR Theory* (Lynne Rienner, 2004).

90. Alex Wendt, *Social Theory of International Relations*, on the friend-enemy social identities.

91. This apparent irony can be partially explained, of course, from a strictly Realist standpoint: an appeal for power-free dialogue naturally appeals to the weaker party, while a stronger power such as the United States—whatever the ideology of its current leadership—might be expected to have less patience for such artificial equality.

92. William Kristol, "The Axis of Appeasement," *Weekly Standard*, August 26, 2002.

93. Reuel Gerecht, "Losing the Middle East?" *Weekly Standard*, March 9, 2002.

94. Charles Krauthammer, "Victory changes everything," *Washington Post*, November 30, 2001; he credits Martin Kramer with this formulation.

95. Richard Cohen, "But Still Ruffling Feathers," *Washington Post*, June 17, 2003.

96. Roxanne Euben, "The New Manichaeans," *Theory and Event* 5 (4), 2002.

97. Marc Lynch, "Taking Arabs Seriously," *Foreign Affairs* 81, no. 5 (September 2003).

98. Quoted in *al-Arab al-Yom*, May 7. My translation.

99. Peterson, "Public diplomacy."

100. James Scott, *Domination and the Arts of Resistance* (Yale, 1992).

101. Salah al-Din Hafez, "Islah 'Aqoulna al-Fasida!" (Fix Our Corrupted Minds!), *Al-Ahram*, 13 August 2003 (my translation).

102. Lynch, "Why Engage?" *European Journal of International Relations*, 2002.

103. Helmi Shaarawi, "What type of dialogue?" *Al-Ahram Weekly* 615, December 14, 2002.

104. Chris Brown, "Cultural Diversity and international political theory," *Review of International Studies* 26 (2000), 208.

105. Jurgen Habermas, cited in Borradori, *Philosophy in a Time of Terror*, 35.

106. See Harold Saunders, *A Public Peace Process* (New York: Palgrave Macmillan, 2001), for an insightful discussion of these ideas in the context of applied conflict resolution.

107. UN General Assembly A/56/523 (2 November 2001), para. 14.

108. Fred Dallmayr, "Conversations across boundaries: political theory and global diversity," *Millennium* 30, no. 2 (2001), 331–347.

109. Dallmayr, "Conversations," 346.

110. Buck-Morss, *Thinking Past Terror*, 44.

111. B. Parekh, "Terrorism and Intercultural Dialogue," in Ken Booth and Tim Dunne, eds., *Worlds in Collision*, 274.

112. "Overcoming the cultural divide," *American Journal of Islamic Social Sciences* 18, no. 4 (2001); Sayla Benhabib, *The Claims of Culture* (Princeton, 2002).

113. Gamil Mattar, *Al-Ahram*, May 11, 2002 (my translation).

114. Her references include Bin Laden's fatwa, Bernard Lewis, Bassam Tibi, Sohail Hashmi, a statement by Muslim students at Villanova, Saddam Hussein (!), one Muslim website, and a handful of Western scholars and journalists.

115. The text can be found at http://www.americanvalues.org.

116. Al-Qaeda's own response to the American statement is rather more direct: "Why are we fighting and opposing you? The answer is very simple. Because you attack us and continue to attack us." See text of bin Laden's "letter to America," as published in *The Observer*, November 24, 2002.

117. Tunku Varadarajan, "Dialogue With the Deaf," *Wall Street Journal Commentary*, February 21, 2002.

118. Quoted by Nicholas Kristof, "Giving God a Break," *New York Times*, June 10, 2003. See Muqtedar Khan, "Preachers of Bigotry," *Al-Ahram Weekly*, June 9, 2003, for background.

119. http://www.martinkramer.org/pages/899529/, May 19, 2003. Campus Watch can be found at http://www.campus-watch.org/.

120. Geneive Abdo and Jonathon Lyons, *Answering Only to God* (New York: Henry Holt and Co., 2003).

121. Hami-Reza Asefi, quoted by AFP, June 9, 2003.

122. *Boston Review*, April 2003.

123. Jeremy Rifkin, "Dialogue is a necessity," *The Guardian*, November 13, 2001.

124. Feldman, *After Jihad*.

11

Democracy and Its (Muslim) Critics: An Islamic Alternative to Democracy?

Abdelwahab El-Affendi

A ccording to one rather interesting point of view, to ask the question why so many Muslim countries are still undemocratic is a reflection of a serious misconception. To start with, it is based on a conception of democracy that is at once ethnocentric, unrealistic, and reflective of false idealism. (Cantori, 2000) Ethnocentrism is evident in a conception of democracy that posits individualism and secularism as of the essence, and idealizes the parochial American experience of pluralism and individualism. This idealization is false, moreover, since it neglects the deeply elitist nature of American democracy, and rests on a utopian Enlightenment conception of progress and unending ascent to more and more freedom. It is unrealistic because the democracy dreamed up in this theory does not exist in America nor anywhere else, and the advocacy by American policy makers and academics of this "romanticized version of theory and American practice" can be said to resemble "the practice of the Dutch who export Heinekens beer but do not market it or consume it at home." (Cantori, 2000)

In any case, even if the prescriptions of this theory were realistic, they are not appropriate for Muslim societies, which are anti-individualistic and more attached to venerated traditions than future utopias. Muslim societies are corporatist, and the ideal conception of the state there is one that is authoritarian and collectivist. Thus the models for democracy appropriate for these societies must take into account the prevalent values, and not try to impose models based on alien values, especially when the intention is mainly to serve western foreign policy objectives rather than to satisfy the needs of the societies involved. An emerging model of Muslim democracy might not, and need not, conform to western perceptions, but may be an inspiration for new models of democratic polities that may be as viable, if not superior to, western-inspired models. (Cantori, 2000)

Objections to Democracy

One does not have to subscribe to the theses outlined above in order to agree that how one defines democracy and articulates its underlying value system is no doubt crucial to the ongoing debate over whether democracy is suitable for Muslim societies. We will come back to the question of definition in a moment. One major problem with Cantori's analysis, however, is that a huge majority of Muslims appear to prefer democracy to the "authoritarian collectivist" polity he advocates for them. For some radical Islamic theorists, this is precisely why democracy is wrong for Muslims: they do not know what is good for them. The line of thinking advocated by leaders such as Abu'l Ala al-Maududi (1903–1979) and Sayyid Qutb (1904–1966) made the point that present Muslim communities cannot be justifiably described as genuinely Muslim. They are in fact, societies of *jahiliyya* (pre-Islamic barbarism). (Maududi, 1977b, Qutb, 1978) Only the minority of committed and enlightened thinkers and activists who would lead the rest of the ummah back to the right path could be described as Islamic. The combined will of the majority, as it stands today, cannot therefore be deemed as authoritative or legitimate, and it needs to be guided by the enlightened few.

Qutb refused as a matter of principle to discuss the details of the organizational structures of the future ideal Muslim society and how its affairs were going to be managed. These will only emerge when that society comes into existence and could not be speculated about this side of utopia. (Qutb, 1978) Maududi did venture a solution, however, a model which he dubbed a "theo-democracy," as system of rule based on popular sovereignty, but limited by divine law. In this system, the rulers do not initiate legislation, but only implement and enforce divine law. The men of authority, led by the supreme ruler (the Khalifah) will determine what the law is. (Maududu, 1967; Adam, 1983)

One of the groups that are most vehemently opposed to democracy on principle, is Hizb-ut-Tahrir, a small radical party which came to existence in Palestine as a splinter group of the Muslim Brotherhood in 1953. Its leader, Taqiuddin an-Nabhani (1909–1977) advocated a full return to the khilafah system as it had been practiced before its final collapse in Turkey in 1924. In contrast to most other Islamic thinkers who conceived of some form of Islamic democracy, an-Nabhani and his followers rejected democracy without any qualification or reservation.

According to one leading theorist of this group (Zallum, 1995), democracy, which has been promoted by the infidel West in the lands of Islam, is a system of unbelief, with no relation to Islam whatsoever. It contradicts the rules of Islam absolutely: in generalities and particulars, in its source and its basic ideology, in the foundation on which it was established and the ideas and systems it advocates. It is therefore absolutely unlawful for Muslims to accept it, implement it or advocate it. (Zallum, 1995: 5)

According to this author, democracy is a system of rule whereby the people are sovereign, master of their nation and accepting no authority from another source. Legislation and all key decisions must be approved by the people, directly or through representatives. In order for the people to be really master of itself and select its rulers without pressure or coercion, certain freedoms have to be safeguarded for all individuals, including personal freedoms and the freedom of belief, opinion and property. (Zallum, 1995: 5–8) This system originated in the rebellion of the people against monarchs who claimed divine right to rule, and oppressed people on this pretext. As a result of this conflict, a compromise was reached whereby religion would be banished from public life, and the clergy would have no direct political role. The separation of religion and the state is thus integral to this system. (Zallum, 1995: 8–10) In a democracy, all decisions are taken in accordance with the preferences of the majority. Democracy can thus be said to be the rule of the majority. (Zallum, 1995: 10–11)

In real life, however, this utopian system is nowhere observed. To start with, it is impractical for the people as a whole to rule. That is why the ruse of representation was devised by the ruling elite to create the (false) impression that the people rule indirectly. But even according to this imperfect substitute, reality still remains far from the ideal. Those who rule are always elected by a minority of the voters, due to the nature of the voting system. They are also beholden to entrenched interests, in particular the capitalists who finance their election. The parliaments and other institutions are mere rubber stamps to legitimize the will of this dominant rich minority. (Zallum, 1995: 13–19)

However, even in its ideal form, democracy is anathema to Islam. The idea of freedoms on which it is based has been the cause of much corruption on earth. The freedom of possession is at the root of the capitalist system and the greed it has promoted, leading to competition, colonialism and wars. Personal freedoms have also resulted in corruption and social degradation, whereby societies became no different from animal herds in the way in which all moral inhibition over sexual conduct had been abandoned. (Zallum, 1995: 19–24)

It is thus surprising that, in spite of these obvious defects inherent in democratic systems, and the fallacies on which it is based, democratic ideas have attained a disturbing currency in Muslim lands, mainly through willful manipulation by western powers. The latter use their economic, political, technological and cultural edge to disrupt Muslim societies and force alien ideas on them. The motive for this is to destroy Islam, the source of strength of Muslim societies, and thus lay these societies open to foreign influences and manipulation. (Zallum, 1995: 24–30)

Part of this campaign was to transform the educational systems in Muslim lands to bring forth a new generation which knows nothing about Islam, and to use seduction to suggest that there is no contradiction between Islam and western civilization. The truth is that there is a very deep contradiction. The Muslim civilization is based on divine revelation and on the central belief that life must be directed towards fulfilling divine commands. Western civilization, by contrast, is based on utilitarianism, materialism, secularism and individualism. It is devoid of morality or spiritual values, and its ultimate objective is immediate gratification of individual desires. (Zallum, 1995: 39–40) Democracy, the main ideology of this civilization, is anti-Islamic since it is based on secularism, rationalism and supremacy of the human will. In Islam, by contrast, both reason and the human will are subject to revelation, and must submit to the divine will as embodied in Islamic law. Reference in all decisions, public or private, must be made to revelation, which has given clear guidance in all matters, either directly or indirectly. It is divine law that is sovereign in the truly Muslim polity, and it is not possible for the community, even if everyone in it agrees, to change or defy the law. (42–49) The ultimate reference in interpreting the law is the khalifah (caliph), who can defy the majority and even the whole community and follow his own interpretation of the law. In the Muslim state, freedoms are limited by the law, and people cannot believe, think, behave or dispose of their property as they please, but must observe the law in all these matters, and the state has the authority to compel them to observe the law. (Zallum, 1995: 50–60) This shows that democracy is the antithesis of Islamic values, and Muslims are thus forbidden to "adopt it, advocate it, form political parties on its basis, accept it as a worldview, implement it, use it as a basis for constitution, laws, or education." (Zallum, 1995: 61)

This is an unusually categorical and unequivocal rejection of democracy, which is not typical of mainstream Islamic groups. Some objections to democracy by radical Islamic groups, though comparably strong, are more nuanced. According to one representative of the traditionalist *salafi* trend,[1] a distinction needs to be made between democracy as an actual practice, and democracy as a theory, ideology and idea. (al-Faqih, 2001) There are, among the salafi trend, two broad views on democracy in practice. The first regards participation in an existing democratic process categorically unlawful, since it is tantamount to giving legitimacy to systems that do not implement Islamic values. The second, a more cautious one, treats this matter in pragmatic rather than legal terms, arguing that Islamic groups could participate in the electoral process if this could protect them from harassment and help promote Islamic ideas. However, some within this latter camp have argued on the same pragmatic grounds that participation may be unhelpful, since it tends to give legitimacy to oppressive regimes that rig elections and contravene Islamic teachings. (al-Faqih, 2001)

On the theoretical level, there is more consensus among the salafi trends, since all agree that there is a fundamental contradiction between the basis of legitimacy of democratic and Islamic systems. While the Islamic system regards good governance (the right of the community to choose its leaders freely and hold them accountable, etc.) as essential, this is seen only as a means to the end to be pursued by the state, which is the implementation of Islamic teachings. While in a democracy achieving consensus is an end in itself, and the constitution agreed on this basis is the final arbiter in all matters, in the Islamic system the religious text must be the final arbiter regardless of agreed constitutions. Some do agree that constitutions should be respected as interim arrangements provided they do not contravene basic Islamic teachings, but others argue that constitutions could only be legitimate if agreed by all Muslims, which is not practical at present. (al-Faqih, 2001: 6–8) Ideologically, most salafis reject democracy on philosophical grounds, since it is regarded as fundamentally secular, and as it values the democratic consensus above religious teachings. (al-Faqih, 2001: 8) With regards to the particulars of the democratic systems, salafis categorically reject the idea of legislation on the basis of popular will, as for them the only legislation permissible is that which derives from Islamic sources, and this is a matter for competent experts, not the popular will. They also reject such provisions as freedom and equality, since they accept no freedom to break the Law, and do not accept absolute equality between Muslims and non-Muslims or between men and women. With regards to the separation of powers, they do not see this as necessary, and should depend on circumstances (like whether the ruler has the ability to undertake the combined duties). (al-Faqih, 2001: 11–13) Most salafi groups, however, do not object to the employment of democratic methods (elections, accountability of rulers, etc.) provided that these are used within an overall context that accepts the supremacy of the divine law. (al-Faqih, 2001: 15)

Other writers from the radical Islamic tendencies condemn as "pathological" the fascination of some Muslim intellectuals with democracy given that term is so difficult to pin down as to be meaningless. It is a symptom of western cultural hegemony, which has successfully and "systematically destroyed or devalued all non-Western institutions and traditions," and imposed its own values instead. (Siddiqui, 2000) In succumbing to the seductiveness of western values, however, these intellectuals run the danger of endorsing the unwarranted claims of western values to universality and of subscribing to the deliberately marketed illusion that western societies do indeed live up to their democratic ideals. In addition, Muslims endorsing these values are forced on the defensive, since they cannot endorse democratic values wholesale and must express some reservations. This lays them open to the charges of not being really democratic, at which point they lapse into apologetics and make democracy not Islam, the point of discussion. The point is that these intellectuals have permitted themselves to fall victim to western hegemony by uncritically adopting the language of the west, including all its ideological baggage, and thus were handicapped by fighting their battles on territory which has already been conquered by the enemy. The first task that needs to be done is Muslim intellectuals to free themselves from the grip of this dominant language and develop an original discourse based radically on Islamic language and traditions. (Siddiqui, 2000)

Alternative Models: Shura

If democracy is unsuitable for Muslim societies, what are the main features of the authentic Islamic model? The most common counter-proposal put forth is that of Shura (consultation), a term which occurs in two key verses in the Holy Quran. In one verse (3:159), the Prophet is commanded to consult his followers in public matters and treat them with kindness. In the second (43:38), the Muslim community is praised for managing their affairs through consultation. (The term occurs in other verses, but not with similar direct relevance or normative force.) There is a continuing debate among scholars on how essential Shura is for public decision-making in the normative Islamic model. The points were summarized by one writer in the following terms. "Shura is basically a decision making process—consultative decision making—that is considered either obligatory or desirable by Islamic scholars. Those scholars who choose to emphasize the Quaranic verse: 'and consult with them on the matter' (3:159) consider shura as obligatory, but those scholars who emphasize the verse wherein 'those who conduct their affairs by counsel' (43:38) are praised, consider shura as desirable." (Khan, 2001)

Examining historical evidence relating to the way the Muslim community conducted itself during the time of the Prophet does not yield decisive evidence either way. There is one major incident in which the Prophet followed the majority view against his own wisdom (when he accepted advice to fight invaders outside the gates of the city instead of waiting for them inside) and one major incident when he defied the views of the overwhelming majority (when he concluded a treaty seen by his followers as oppressive and unfair with his enemy, Quraysh). Thus while there is agreement that shura is an important value, there is no consensus on how to go about implementing it. In spite of the broad agreement that consultative and consensual governance is the best approach, no consensus has emerged on its obligatoriness. The ulama, in particular, "remain either conservative or ambivalent on the topic. Many of them depend on non-consultative bodies for their livelihood and even their religious prestige and they are in no hurry to deprive themselves of the privileges that non-consultative governments extend to them. Thus in a way they are implicated in the delay in the public recognition that governments in Muslim societies must consult to retain their legitimacy." (Khan, 2001)

One major point raises itself, however. Even supposing that Muslims agree one shura as the norm for Islamic institutions, does this entail wholehearted support for democratisation? Khan is sceptical, given what he regards as three basic differences between shura and democracy. First, shura, unlike democracy, does not permit the modification of foundational texts. And since the interpretation of major foundational texts is a central point of contention at present, this could make it unsuitable for resolving the ongoing conflicts. Second, shura "remains non-binding while democratic processes and laws are binding and can only be reversed through a democratic process." Third, shura as it is understood in dominant Islamic discourse implies that it is the ruler who initiates the process when it suits him, and can determine who to consult and when. This may lead to the exclusion of large sections of the population from the process. By contrast, in a democracy, it is the people who consult among themselves about who will govern and how. In sum, "shura is top-down and democracy bottom-up." (Khan, 2001) The role and scope of shura has been the subject of intense debates in traditional Islamic thought, where the familiar opposition between mandatory and optional shura was repeatedly discussed. According to the opinion of a wide section of traditional ulama, the objective of the command to the Prophet to consult with his followers was primarily to make them feel part of the decision-making process. It is thus a psychological device, not a political institution, since the Prophet is capable of reaching the right decision without consulting anybody. (al-Duri, 1974: 35–37) He is thus free to disregard advice offered, and so is any other Muslim ruler. By contrast, the community must obey its ruler even if it has clear misgivings about his conduct of public affairs. (al-Duri, 1974: 84) This view was in turn contradicted; in their view it would not create a feeling of being party to the decision-making process, but on the contrary, would make them very angry and upset. This meant that the command to consult is simultaneously a command to heed the opinions of those consulted, even if one were to accept the limited objective of shura as a psychological requirement. (al-Duri, 1974: 37–38) Some proponents of this view point to the reports which emphasize the frequency with which the Prophet consulted his community must be deposed without delay. (al-Duri, 1974: 28–29, 52–54)

According to some contemporary views, however, the adoption of shura may not in itself solve the problem of incompatibility between Islam and democracy, since shura is not intrinsically Islamic as is sometimes claimed. The original meaning of the term shura signifies "no more than a procedure of making decisions. It can thus be defined as the procedure of making decisions by consultation and deliberation among those who have an interest in the matter on which a decision is to be taken, or others who can help them to reach such a decision." (Idris, 2001) In this regard, shura "has nothing to do with the kind of matter to be decided upon, or the basis on which those consulted make their decisions, or the decision reached, because it is a mere procedure, a tool you might say, that can be used by any group of people—a gang of robbers, a military junta, an American Senate or a council of Muslim representatives. There is thus nothing in the concept which makes it intrinsically Islamic. And as a matter of fact shoora [sic] in one form or the other was practiced even before Islam." (Idris, 2001) If democracy is broadly understood as to refer to decision taken by the people after deliberation, then it becomes "almost identical" with shoora. This, in turn, suggests that there is "nothing in the primary or extended meaning of democracy which makes it intrinsically Western or secular. If shoora can take a secular form, so can democracy take an Islamic form." If democracy is meant in a sense which makes "the people absolutely supreme, in the sense that they or their representatives are absolutely free to decide with majority vote on any issue, or pass or repeal any laws," then this form of democracy "is the antithesis of Islam because is puts what it calls the people in the place of God; in Islam only God has this absolute power of legislation. Anyone who claims such a right is claiming to be God, and any one who gives him that right is thereby accepting him as God." However, in a democracy where "the right of the people to legislate is limited by what is believed by society to be a higher law to which human law is subordinate and should not therefore violate," then such a democracy can be compatible with Islam, depending "on the nature and scope of the limits, and on what is believed to be a higher law." (Idris, 2001) One of the basic differences between Islam and democracy "is that in Islam it is God's law as expressed in the Qur'an and the Sunna that is the supreme law within the limits of which people have the right to legislate. No one can be a Muslim who makes, or freely accepts, or believes that anyone has the right to make or accept, legislation that is contrary to that Divine law. Example of such violations include the legalization of alcoholic drinks, gambling, homosexuality, usury or interest, and even adoption." It is such possibility of anti-Islamic legislation that some Muslims have in mind when they object to democracy and describe it as un-Islamic. This criticism, however, could also be made of a system based on shura. "A shoora without restriction or a liberal shoora would, however, be as un-Islamic as a liberal or an unconstrained democracy. The problem is with secularism or liberalism, not with democracy, and will not therefore disappear by adoption of shoora instead of democracy."

Shura itself is not the defining feature of the Islamic order. "The proper description of a political system that is based on those principles is that it is Islamic and not shooraic, because shoora is only one component of it." And since Muslim rule is by definition subject to Islamic law, the fact that it is not the ruler who authoritatively determine this law, but the ulama, had always been a check on tyranny. But can a country that abides by the principle of shoora constrained by Islamic values by described as democratic? "Yes, if democracy is broadly defined in terms of decision-making by the people. No, if it is arbitrarily defined in a way that identifies it with the contemporary Western brands of it." (Idris, 2001)

If shura is just one subordinate aspect of the Islamic model according to this view, then it cannot be a defining feature of this model. The defining features have to be sought elsewhere.

Idris's account points to one crucial element, the fact shura has not been invented by Islam, but was practiced in pre-Islamic tribal communities. Numerous accounts exist of how senior tribal leaders in Quraysh met regularly to discuss their political and military campaigns against the Prophet. Determining who could take part in these deliberations was dictated by the status of the person in question, and there are some figures whom it was impossible to exclude. The innovation brought in by Islam was to broaden the scope of shura, since no aristocratic criteria could be applied to exclude any Muslim from offering his opinion on public matters.

Shura in the context of the traditional Islamic political practice did not, therefore, represent a device of convenience for the ruler in order to perfect decision making (in the same way as the owner of a business would today consult with his legal and financial advisors and his aides, but ultimately makes his own decisions). It was in fact a vehicle for political participation. The Prophet and his immediate successors used to consult with their followers specifically to ensure that they were on board with major policy decision. If the leader wanted to go to war, he wanted to ascertain that the bulk of his followers were in agreement with him, and were convinced that the campaign was justified and the way to wage it was the best way. The problem, however, has been that the practice of shura was not institutionalized. Like Athenian democracy, the ad hoc procedure was suitable for a small community like that of Medina. Once the community expanded to span several continents, the procedure proved inadequate. It will be equally inadequate today.

Alternative Models: The Khilafah

According to Hizb-ut-Tahrir, the genuine Islamic alternative system of rule is the khilafah system. This system is fundamentally different from democratic systems and in actual conflict with it. While democracy is a man-made system premised on the sovereignty of the people, the ruling system in Islam is based on divine revelation and supremacy in it is for the shar'ia and not for the people.[2] Democratic systems are bound to honour international borders and the multi-state international systems, as they accept the principle of respect to people's freedom in choosing their systems, laws and rulers. However, the Islamic ruling system, jihad to spread Islam and enforce Muslim unity is a central pillar of foreign policy. The system of khilafah does not recognize existing borders or the independence of one Muslim country from another.

The structure for the "Islamic system" proposed by the Hizb is centered around the khalifah, who is the only person with real authority. While the proposal allows for some other subordinate institutions (executive and other assistants, governors, judges, military leaders, consultative councils and other administrators), their role is entirely dependent on that of the khalifah, who is the final authority in all matters. The khalifah is chosen for life as long as he is able and not known for misconduct, and the people have no right to rebel against him. The only case where it is allowed to disobey the ruler is when his orders contravene God's law. However, this is a questionable exception, since the khalifah is also the only recognized authority on what constitutes the Law. (The Khalifah may be deposed by a special court, but it is one he appoints and controls.) While the formation of political parties is permitted on condition that they be based on Islam as a doctrine and a way of life, no formal opposition is permitted.

While democracy emphasizes compromise solutions, the khilafah system dictates that members of the community must adopt Islamic principles and teachings without question, and reject all that is alien to them. Democracy must therefore be rejected as part of the alien Western civilization which emanates from the capitalist belief of separation of belief from life. Islam has its own rules regarding the rights of the individual and of the *jama'a*, and these rules contrast sharply with the Western notion of freedom and liberties.

In the khilafah system, the principle "sovereignty of shari'a" is put forth in the conjunction with the conception that "authority" is vested in the ummah. The authority of the ummah is operationalised through the election of the Khalifah. The Consultative Council (Majlis al-Shura), which is in turn elected, presents a number of "qualified candidates from among whom one is elected Khalifah. Once the Khalifah is chosen, the power to determine shari'a law is said to devolve on him alone. (An-Nabhani, 1998: 221–222, 240) According to

Hizb-ut-Tahrir's proposed constitution of the Islamic state, once the Khalifah is elected by a majority vote, he can impose his authority by force not only against the minority that did not elect him, but also on the populations of other countries. In fact, it is his duty to do so, since the Muslim ummah can have but one ruler. (Articles 3, 24, 26–29, 33, 34). The Khalifah not only rules on behalf of the ummah, but he "possesses all the authority of the state." (article 35).

One central problem with this vision of the khilafah system is that it contradicts the basic assumptions in the underlying claim that legitimises it, in particular when the claim of sovereignty of the shari'a is vacated by making shari'a subject to the will of the ruler. And while Hizb-ut-Tahrir argues that the Islamic system it advocates is based on divine revelation, the consensus among Muslims is that the khilafah system is grounded primarily in human reason. Only the Shi'a claim that the ruler has been designated by divine revelation, but the Shi'a do not subscribe to the khilafah system as outlined in this model any way. Moreover, the proposed model is eclectic, since it picks up institutions adopted by various dynasties not regarded by ulama as authoritative or normatively binding. (For example, the functions of "associates" [ministers or viziers], which emerged during the Abbasid dynasty, are purely contingent institutions, with only contrived textual validations made in their favour by later theorists). The proposed system also ascribes to some traditional and contingent institutions roles that have never been assigned to them in the past, as when giving the Court of Justice (Mahkamat al-Mazalim) the right to remove the Khalifah. This function had never ocurred to the Abbasid caliphs who established this institution merely with the aim of helping them address individual grievances against state officials.

This model also stipulates for such institutions and practices as elections and formal consultative councils, which are also without precedent in Islamic history and practice. (Taji-Farouki, 1996) Thus the model seems to do what some traditionalist theorists had done: look at existing practices, or practices which are derived from purely contingent and pragmatic considerations, and seek to provide Islamic legitimacy for them. So whatever the merits of this system may be, its claim to being based solely and primarily on Islamic doctrine cannot be sustained.

"Theo-Democracy" or Islamic Constitutionalism

While both Shura and Khilafah remain theoretical constructs as far as modern re-Islamisation projects are concerned, a number of actual experiments with the notion which Maududi called theo-democracy have actually taken place. This notion of combining democracy with the supremacy of shari'a law was first experimented with in Iran during the Constitutional Revolution of 1905–1906. While the constitution vested legislative power in an elected assembly, provisions were introduced for the appointment of a five-man committee of ulama, who were also to be co-opted as members of the assembly, to scrutinize all legislation and ensure its conformity to Shari'a law. This idea was found very appealing by Muhammad Rashid Rida who incorporated it in his proposals for reviving the Khilafah. (Rida, 1925; Enayat, 1982)

Abu'l Ala Maududi's own model, which he dubbed "theo-democracy," is also based on a similar two-tier system, even though he rejects any explicit role for the ulama as arbiters of what the shari'a determines. (Adam, 1983: 117–118) Maududi argues that in an Islamic state, God is sovereign, and no human legislation is permissible, except derivatively or in areas where no explicit Islamic injunctions are known. This entails that divine law should be supreme. Maududi's model suggests that shari'a law can be determined in a straightforward way, the sources being clear enough (Quran, Sunna and their elaborations in traditional jurisprudence) and decisive enough. Any Muslim well versed in the traditions would be able to determine that an Islamic state should consist mainly of the leader (imam, khalifah or amir) and a Shura Council. Both the Khalifah and members of the Shura council should be individuals of high integrity, learning and commitment to shari'a. The ruler is to be selected by the community on the basis of his qualifications, and it is not important how this selection takes place as long as it commands the assent of the community as a whole. The members of the shura council must also be broadly representative. (Adam, 1983: 123–124) It is the leader, however, who is the final arbiter on what the shari'a says. He should consult with members of the shura council and others, but he is not bound by their opinion. (Adam, 1983: 126) However, the council may dismiss the khalifah if it is determined that he was no longer competent to do his job. There is no need, though, for regular elections, and no political parties or formal opposition are to be allowed. (Adam, 1983: 123)

Maududi's position was summarized by one commentator thus: "The legislature or consultative body in the Islamic state in the final analysis, therefore, comes down to a body of pious men with expert competence in the tools and the subject matter of Islamic law, who will work together to understand the shariah, to spell out what it has left unclear or unstated, and to extrapolate from its principles rules to cover what it has not touched at all. This group of men will be at the disposal of the ruler for him to consult, but . . . its opinions are not binding either upon the ruler or the people of the Islamic state. Complete power remains with the ruler who, so long as he is right, may act in disregard of legislative opinion." (Adam, 1983: 126)

Maududi believes that this dispensation reflects the practice in the time of the Righteous Caliphate, the normative model for Islamic political thought and practice. In the Saudi system, which came into existence at about the same time as the Iranian constitutional government, but was itself an absolute monarchy, the claim was also made of following that normative model. The ruler here, however, came to power by force, even though he based his claim to power on the imperative of restoring true Islam and fighting deviation from that model. The ulama, who provided this legitimation and authority, were accorded a leading role in interpreting shari'a and thus endorsing all legislation. However, the monarch could, and often did, overrule the ulama when he so chose. This is of course perfectly in line with Maududi's model, even though he would not explicitly endorse a hereditary absolute monarchy.

A rival model was proposed and implemented by Ayatollah Ruhollah Khomeini (1902–1989) in Iran. Khomeini based his model on Shi'i doctrine, which holds that authority in an Islamic state devolves on an infallible imam authorized and designated specifically by revelation. The Shi'a disagree with the Sunni majority, which holds that the appointment of the ruler is a matter of discretion for the community, and argue that the Prophet had explicitly designated his cousin and son-in-law Ali as successor. Imam Ali then in turn designated his successor, and each imam did the same. The imams, like the Prophet, are infallible, and their judgments are divine in source. There are three major schools of Shi'a, according to the chain of imams chosen.

Theoretically, the Shi'i doctrine resolves the question of public decision-making once and for all. The concept of divine sovereignty is thus operationalized directly, as divine rule is conducted by a divinely inspired imam whose rule is literally God's rule. However, for the main Shi'i sect, the Twelver school, the twelfth and last imam has disappeared in the fourth/ninth century without designating a successor. According to the doctrine, he is supposed to reappear and resume his mission. In the meantime, the community is left without a divinely inspired leader. This leaves it in the same position as the Sunni majority, which has to manage its own affairs as best as it could without the benefit of new divine dispensation.

Khomeini came up with the novel idea that the Shi'i community should follow the Sunni example and appoint its own rulers. Instead of merely waiting for the imam to return, as traditional doctrine counselled, Khomeini argued that a Muslim community cannot remain without a legitimate government, and this government should be run by men of learning. An Islamic government is "neither tyrannical nor absolute, but constitutional." But it is a different kind of constitutional government. "It is not constitutional in the current sense of the word, i.e., based on the approval of laws in accordance with the opinion of the majority. It is constitutional in the sense that the rulers are subject to a certain set of conditions. . . . It is the laws and ordinances of Islam comprising this set of conditions that must be observed. Islamic government may therefore be defined as the rule of divine law over men." (Khomeini, 1981: 55). Such government also differs from other forms of constitutional governments in that the representatives of the people cannot engage in legislation, as legislative power in an Islamic system "belongs exclusively to God Almighty." The law has already been laid down, and the task of government is just to implement and interpret it. (Khomeini, 1981: 55–56) The task of rule in such system devolves therefore on those who know the law. Only two criteria are needed in the ruler. "Since Islamic government is a government of law, knowledge of the law is necessary for the ruler. . . . Knowledge of the law and justice, then, constitute the fundamental qualifications in the view of the Muslims. Other matters have no importance or relevance in this connection." (Khomeini, 59) Any person with these qualifications could, and in fact is duty bound to, assume power. If one faqih exists who has necessary qualifications (probity and superior knowledge of religious law), then he should take steps to form an Islamic government to implement the law. If not, then this becomes the collective duty of all the *fuqaha*. (Khomeini, 1981: 64) If they do, they would have the same full authority as the Prophet and the imams. For even though the Prophet and imams have an unparalleled spiritual status, their role as governors is a role circumscribed by divine law, which it is their task to implement. This role can thus be readily assumed by any suitably qualified person, and the full authority would then devolve on him. (Khomeini, 1981: 62–63) The Iranian constitution of 1979 enshrined this principle of *vilayat al-faqih* (mandate of the jurist) in article five, which stipulated in the time of the absence of the twelfth imam, "in the Islamic Republic of Iran the mandate to rule and leadership of the people are the responsibility of a just, pious jurist aware of the time, brave and with drive and initiative, whom the majority of the people know and accept as their leader." Khomeini was designated as the Leader, and the constitution gave him extensive powers, including appointing key military leaders and members of key institutions like the Council of Guardians. He must also approve candidates for the presidency and can dismiss presidents. However, there was a crucial ambivalence in the constitution, which can be seen even from article five, where popular recognition of the leader was made a necessity. At one level, the constitution endorses the principle of popular sovereignty, and gives crucial roles to elected institutions (parliament, presidency, etc.); it also provides for electoral input in key institutions with veto over these bodies (council of Guardians, the Leader himself, etc.) However, at another level, the role of the faqih leader was made supreme and decisive. This role was further enhanced by constitutional amendments in 1989 which stipulated for the "absolute mandate of the jurists." This rather novel concept gave the leader-jurist the right to overrule explicit Islamic legal provisions in the interest of the Islamic state. A special council, the Expediency Discernment

Council of the System, was set up to undertake the task of determining when provisions of Islamic law can be disregarded. (Articles 111 and 112 of the amended 1989 constitution) This development is very interesting, since it impinges on Khomeini's characterisation of the Islamic state as one where the law is supreme, coupled with affirmation that the divine law had already been laid out and does not need to be elaborated anew, only interpreted and obeyed. For these provisions indicate that the divine law was not as clear-cut as the theory of wilayat al-faqih suggested and, more significantly, it could be overruled by appeal to considerations of (secular) interest.

The Limits of "Islamic" Alternatives

One can find what seems like a consensus among the various lines of thinking which object to democracy on Islamic grounds and seek to promote more authentic alternatives. All these schools of thought claim to be based on the normative model of Medina in the life of the Prophet and his immediate successors. All see the Islamic state as an "Islamic constitutional" polity where Islamic law is supreme. All seem to agree that the establishment of Islamic law is the prerogative of certain privileged and especially qualified individuals (the faqih or the khalifah).

They differ somewhat over the nature of this authority and the extent of its mandate, but there is also a broad consensus here that pious and learned men could be relied on to give authoritative and conclusive determinations of Islamic law.

All seem to agree that a pious and competent ruler must have uncontested authority, even though there is disagreement over whether he should be from among the ulama himself, and to what extent he should consult with the ulama and others when carrying out his duties. Proponents of the khilafah model seem to indicate that the Khalifah must have absolute authority, and need only consult with others at his pleasure. The vilayat al-faqih model is similar in theory, even though in practice the Iranian model enshrines popular sovereignty much more strongly than the model would legitimise, a factor that is central to the current problems the system is enduring. Other "theo-democracy" models tend to give slightly more weight to popular opinion, as does the shura model.

At one level, the perception is that since the primary objective of the state is to implement divine law, the ruler is essentially a Chief Justice who interprets and enforces the law. And since he is selected chiefly on the basis of his erudition, his probity and his deep understanding of the law, he is expected to be the authority on the law. His word in this is final. The state is a court of law, and the "Ruler-Judge" consults with others only to clarify things for himself. Seeking the opinion of others does in no way imply that those consulted share in the ruler's authority. This is a rather narrow conception of the functions of the state, which must be seen as a "conflict resolution mechanism" of a more general nature. It attempts to adjudicate in ongoing conflicts of interests and visions, and tries to reconcile and manage these conflicts. While modern democracies are based on the law, officials have a wider area of discretion within the parameters of the law. It is the same with Islamic states. The early conflicts which erupted in the first decades of Islam did not represent disagreement on matters of law, but of policy. There is, in addition, a basic contradiction between two central presuppositions of all these models, however. At one pole, they seem to be based on the assumption that shari'a law has already been clarified and laid down. All that needs to be done is to implement it. On the other hand, there is the assumption that a supremely pious and learned leader is needed to help the people discover and implement Islamic law. It is not clear why, if the law is already clear, the community needs such a special individual to guide it through its mazes. Nor is it clear why, if there is need for such guidance, the judgment of a single individual should be trusted more than that of a larger group of people.

It becomes quite clear from examining the models themselves (even before examining their practical implementation) that the person in authority will have a wide margin of discretion. This is in fact the very raison d'etre of his function, as he is needed to resolve disputes involving the choice between alternatives. The claim that Islamic law has determined everything is thus immediately put into question. There are actually five simultaneous claims put forth by opponents of democracy among the Islamists. The first is that Islamic teachings encompass every facet of life. The second is that these teachings have already been clearly laid down in such a manner that no one can be left in doubt about what the recommended "Islamic" option is in a specific situation, provided he consults the right sources. Third, that all Islamic teachings could be subsumed under shari'a, or the Law. Fourth, that this Law must be enforced by a public authority, or the state. Fifth, and finally, that public opinion is not a reliable indication when seeking to determine what Islamic law dictates.

None of these claims, except for number 4, can be sustained with reference to Islamic sources. While it is true that Islam requires the individual and community to orient their lives in all its aspects towards pleasing God, this does not entail that very specific instructions were given about how to achieve this in every conceivable situation. This would have left little for human creativity and constrained life unduly. This self-evident logical observation is backed by explicit texts which encourage Muslims to rely on their discretion. There is in fact a Quranic verse forbidding Muslims to ask too many questions of the

Prophet. (Quran, 5:101) There is also a record of an incident when the Prophet became upset because one individual kept asking questions about a command he gave to perform pilgrimage. The Prophet then told the audience to accept his prescriptions as they come, and not risk burdening themselves with additional duties by asking for details.[1] This shows that not only did Islam not make comprehensive prescriptions in even such specifically "religious" acts of worship as pilgrimage, but that the omission was deliberate in order to allow the believers more leeway and freedom to make their input. Not only does Islam not have a rule for every conceivable situation, but it is moreover a fundamental rule of Islam to not have such rules.

This, in turn, makes void the second claim that such rules have already been made explicit and are easily discoverable. For if it is excepted that a wide area of human conduct had been left without explicit rules, then it goes without saying that rules covering every eventuality do not exist, and cannot thus be said to be discoverable. One can say the same about the third claim that Islamic teachings can all be subsumed under legal prescriptions. There are several reasons for this. First, because many of the fundamental teachings of Islam are ethical in character, and not strictly legal, making it difficult to enforce them legally. Secondly, because as mentioned above, these teachings have left a wide room for human discretion. Third, even those teachings which have legal connotations (like the command to be just and fair) also require considerable rational input, as what constitutes fairness in any particular situation is left largely for human reason to determine. The fourth claim regarding the role of public authority in enforcing Islamic teachings is based largely on the past three assumptions, and in particular the claim that all Islamic teachings can be legally reinforced. As those assumptions are shown to be suspect, so this latter claim collapses. This does not mean that no enforceable Islamic laws exist, but Islamic government is not just about law enforcement. It is also about reaching consensus and adjudicating between conflicting, and equally legitimate demands and interests. There are other arguments against this claim, most important among which is the requirement that the ideal Islamic state should be totalitarian. (Maududi, 1967) This claim (and the attempts to enforce it in practice, and with disastrous consequences, by such regimes as the Saudi monarchy, Iranian Islamic Republic and the Taliban Emirate in Afghanistan) is a natural corollary of the two claims that Islam has legally enforceable prescriptions for everything, and is a reductio ad absurdum of these combined claims. Another important point pertains to the way these matters had been approached during the time of the Prophet. It is to be noted that while there are some Islamic teachings pertaining to public social duties, which could and may need to be legally enforced, this has not been the case during the time of the Prophet. For example, such duties as collection of alms and organization of military expeditions, were not imposed by force by the state during the Prophet's lifetime. Quite the reverse in fact, as purely moral sanctions were used. Those refusing to pay their dues or shirking their military duties were punished by being excluded from future expeditions or having their contributions rejected. Of course things changed later, when the state began to enforce these duties. This was perfectly acceptable, but it also shows that those duties have validity independent of this enforcement. In fact, from the Islamic point of view, if an individual had paid his alms or participated in public duties merely to avoid state sanctions, then he would not have fulfilled his religious obligation in performing these tasks.

Finally, the idea that the relevant legal prescriptions can best be determined by certain privileged individuals, and not by the community as a whole, runs into a number of difficulties. This assumption is based on the earlier ones, in particular that clear and specific Islamic prescriptions have already been laid down, needing only to be discovered by those who are qualified. However, if we have established that no such specific guidelines existed in most conceivable cases, and in fact were not meant to exist, then this point cannot be sustained. If a wide area of human activity had been deliberately left open for human discretion, then the question is not one of "experts" discovering or passing legal judgements, but of human beings discharging their ethical duties. The models which shift the responsibility of "experts," namely individuals, in fact do not enable the community to discharge its moral responsibility. For if people were to do no more than follow directions, they could not be said to have acted as moral agents.

Additional problems arise when one tries to determine who these authoritative individuals are. The Iranian constitution is a classical case of circular reasoning in this regard. Departing from the premise that the community needs guidance from an expert who is well versed in the law and also possessing the qualities of knowledge, courage, justice, and piety, it then goes to stipulate that it is the community which determines who this individual is, and whether he possesses the required qualities. But how can the community be trusted to find the right person and elect him when the whole point is that the community cannot be trusted with managing its own affairs without the guidance of this presumed leader? The problem is complicated by the categorical Quranic prescription against a person ascribing to himself (or to anybody else for that matter) qualities such as piety. (Quran, 53:32) By definition, then, a person who puts himself forth as a pious man or commended as such by his fellow men does not fit the bill, and must be disqualified.

The ascription of this role to an individual also negates a central Islamic legal and ethical principle, that of *ijma'* or consensus. The principle of ijma' is considered the most authoritative source of Islamic legislation after the two main sources, the Quran and the Sunna (sayings and practice of the Prophet). It gains even more importance given that, as we have shown above, Islam has left a very wide area of discretion for the community. The importance is even more in case of the political realm, where the endemic disagreements over how to conduct affairs betray an underlying agreement that no definitive prescriptions existed in this area. The Prophet's closest Companions have entered into disputes about how to resolve issues of leadership and conduct of public affairs within hours of the Prophet's death, and the disagreement continues to this day. Even though some of these groups went to war against each other, no one seriously impugned the integrity and sincerity of any of the protagonists. Were there clear and specific instructions pertaining to the area of dispute, no one doubts that those early leaders of the community would have followed them without hesitation. There was thus a genuine difference of opinion over how to go about things. This makes the search for consensus central to resolving these disputes, and makes it essential to search for appropriate mechanisms of dialogue to achieve this consensus.

The argument that an individual or a class of individuals is better placed to resolve matters of dispute than the community as a whole comes into contradiction with another fundamental Islamic tenet: that no priesthood is permitted or can be acceptable. The Quran condemns earlier religious communities for trusting too much in their "priests and monks" to the extent that they have almost treated them as deities beside God. (Quran, 9:31) It makes it clear time and time again that going astray by following the authority of "our masters and nobles" is not an acceptable excuse in the eyes of God. Every individual is responsible for his/her own action, and only they are responsible. (Quran 37: 28–35) (This takes care of Cantori's claim that Islam is collectivist and authoritarian. Nothing is further from the truth, as Islam urges individuals to take full responsibility for their actions and reminds them constantly they will be accountable to God individually.)

The Quranic injunctions against accepting authority (even presumed "religious" authority) unquestioningly shifts moral responsibility squarely on the shoulders of the individual on the one hand, and the community as a whole on the other. It also rules out the prescriptions of the models outlined above as "Islamic alternatives" to democracy. Ascribing "religious authority" to an individual or a class contravenes the most fundamental Islamic tenet of all: the injunction against polytheism. A khalifah or a faqih who puts himself up as an absolute authority in fact claims divine powers for himself. This unacceptable condition can only be negated if the individual in question becomes accountable to the community as a whole. It is not only the fact then, as Idris argues, that a person who claims to legislate without reference to shari'a is a false pretender to divine status. A person who claims to be the final authority on shari'a is also making this false claim. And as history has repeatedly shown, this person who claims to embody divine authority by being the final arbiter on divine law very soon moves to the allied claim that he has the right to put himself above divine law. The example of Ayatollah Khomeini in Iran is the clearest one yet of the nature of this slippery slope. In 1988, Khomeini modified his theory of the mandate of the jurist to argue for the Absolute Mandate of the Jurist. The leader is not only the sole arbiter of what divine law is, but he can, if the need dictates, defy and set aside specific divine injunctions. Since the maintenance of the Islamic state is the highest religious obligation of all (Machiavelli?) then all other injunctions, including prayer, pilgrimage and all other religious duties, must be subsumed under this paramount obligation. This could mean that the jurist-leader can, if he deems fit, suspend all Islamic injunctions (and enforce obligations that negate, even contradict, them) if he deems this necessary to safeguard the interests of the state. Things have gone full circle, and it is now considerations of raison d'etat that are the supreme value in the very secular "Islamic" Republic.

Apart from this glaring anomaly which gives the most crass demands of regime survival a "religious" legitimation, there are several other problems with this vision. To start with, the central role given to the "Islamic state" has no basis in Islamic teachings, which emphasize community (ummah), and make no mention of a state or even public authority. And although it can be argued that the survival of the community is indeed a primary consideration in policy-making, and could justify neglect of some basic obligations, it is also obvious that the community as a whole must be the judge in such matters. Since it has become accepted that the issue is not a legal matter where expertise was needed to determine interest, the original argument which gives a single individual to overrule all others in the name of the law falls by the side.

However, even granting that the idea of an Islamic state is accepted in the terms suggested by the Ayatollah, another question arises: can there be only one Islamic state or many? The underlying assumption is that only one legitimate Islamic state can exist at one time. This requirement is made explicit by the Hizb-ut-Tahrir theorists who argue that once a "proper" Islamic state (i.e. one ruled by a single dictator as prescribed by the Hizb's "constitution") then all other Islamic states lose legitimacy and must submit to the authority of this ruler or risk being subdued by force. This would suggest that the emergence of an Islamic state is a recipe for endless wars, mainly among Muslims. This is not a theoretical question, since in our era several contending "Islamic" states have arisen, starting with the Saudi state at the dawn of the last century. The more enthusiastic followers of King Abdul-Aziz Al Saud (d. 1953) were in fact of the opinion that an Islamic state must conquer the whole Muslim world. The realist king rejected this proposition, but was forced to go to war with his own followers to enforce his view. More recently, the Taliban "Islamic Emirate" in

Afghanistan and the Islamic Republic in Iran followed antagonistic policies. Iran and Saudi Arabia were also at loggerheads. In all of these instances, "ulama" supporting a particular state have justified its pursuit of its own interest (which was in fact the interest of the ruling regime) in religious terms. Saudi ulama justified support for secularist Iraq in its war with Iran, and later legitimized Saudi Arabia's participation in America's war against Iraq. When Iran and Taliban Afghanistan nearly went to war in 2000, both justified their rival claims in religious terms. This makes the concept of interest of the Islamic state so elastic as to be meaningless.

An Islamic Democracy?

If all alternatives suggested to democracy on Islamic terms are found to be untenable, does this mean that democracy remains the only alternative for Muslims? This will depend, of course, on what we mean by democracy. The definition adopted for democracy and the articulation of its underlying value system is crucial to determining this question. The matter is exacerbated by the loaded character of the term "democracy," a term few people use in a neutral or descriptive sense. People tend to conflate the descriptive and prescriptive aspects of the term, which is nearly always deployed in contests over values. (Dahl, 1989)

On the face of it, the definition of democracy should be pretty straightforward affair. Etymologically and historically, the term (from the Greek words for people, *demos*, and rule, *kratia*) emerged to designate a certain form of governance, the rule of the people (or the many), in contrast to rival forms, such as monarchy (rule by one person), oligarchy (rule by the few), plutocracy (rule by the rich) or anarchy (rule by no one). The core idea behind it (that of "a political system in which the members regard one another as political equals, are collectively sovereign, and possessing all the capacities, resources and institutions to govern themselves" (Dahl, 1989) also appears to be simple enough. The fifth century BC famous Athenian leader, Pericles, put it succinctly thus: "Our constitution is called a democracy because power is in the hands not of a minority but of the whole people." (Held, 1996: 16) Put simply, thus, a democracy is a system of government in which all members of the community are permitted to participate in public decision making in some manner found acceptable to all or to the majority.

This says little about the content or direction of such systems, a matter of concern for the system's early and many critics, who included such prominent figures as Plato and Aristotle. For these early critics, democracy had a connotation of "mob rule." The "people" referred to the commoners, even the "rabble," and there was no telling where the whims of the masses could lead the polity. However, from very early on, democracy was associated with a constellation of substantive values, chief among which were liberty, equality, tolerance, public-spiritedness, respect for laws, direct participation and popular sovereignty. Liberty or autonomy is seen by Aristotle as central to the democratic idea, where the ideal is "not being ruled," not by anyone at all if possible, or at least only in alternation." (Held, 1996: 19) This ideal of self-government is closely related to tolerance. Again as Aristotle puts it, a central idea of democracy is "to live as you like" which is the essence of being free, "since its opposite, living not as you like, is the function of one being enslaved." Pericles also emphasizes tolerance as a central quality (and virtue) of the Athenian democracy, where people do not "get into a state" with one's next door neighbor "if he enjoys himself in his own way," and do not even "give him the kind of black looks which . . . hurt people's feelings." (Held, 1996: 16, 19)

The concept did undergo significant changes in the intervening centuries, but the general idea remains the same. According to one contemporary author, democracy is "a mode of decision-making about collectively binding rules and policies over which the people exercise control, and the most democratic arrangement [is] that where all members of the collectivity enjoy effective equal rights to take part in such decision-making directly—one, that is to say, which realizes to the greatest conceivable degree the principles of popular control and equality in its exercise." (Betham, 1995: 55) Democracy as a concept is, therefore, "uncontestable," as it is to be contrasted to systems where people are totally or partially excluded from political participation. In this sense, disputes about the meaning of democracy "which purport to be conceptual disagreements that are really disputes about how much democracy is either desirable or practicable." (Betham, 1995: 55)

It can be a matter of argument whether values such as civic virtue, obedience to the law and to those put in authority, tolerance and liberty are intrinsic to the concept of democracy. Equality certainly appears to be, since it is of the essence of democratic rule to limit privileges that are not based on merit. Liberty is also essential, but as Pericles points out, so is obedience to public authority and the law. While the ideal of democracy is maximum freedom and autonomy, the very concept of rule involves limits on freedoms. On the other hand, the principle of tolerance involves self-imposed limits and restraints on even such spontaneous reactions as showing distaste to other people's private lifestyles.

Held notes that the term democracy is often used as a short for "liberal representative democracy," which is centred, in its contemporary manifestations, around "a cluster of rules and institutions permitting the broadest participation of the majority of citizens in the selection of representatives who alone can make political decisions, that is, decisions affecting the whole community." (Held, 1995) This cluster includes elected government; free and fair elections in which every citizen's vote has an equal weight; a suffrage which embraces all citizens irrespective of distinctions of race, religion, class, sex and so on; freedom of conscience, information and expression on all public matters broadly defined; the right of all adults to oppose their government and stand for office; and associational autonomy—the right to form independent associations including social movements, interest groups and political parties.

For Held democracy "has been conceived as a way of containing the powers of the state and of mediating among competing political projects." It can achieve this because "it holds out the possibility of the entrenchment of a principle of legitimacy based on the one hand, on the political involvement of each and all and, on the other, on a process of decision-making which can mediate differences and distill (by virtue of its adherence to this process) acceptable outcomes." In this regard, democracy can be viewed both as incorporating constitutionalism and the self-imposed limits on the will of the majority, and also as a mechanism for peaceful conflict-resolution between competing interests and visions.

These definitions tend in part to describe ideal-typical situations and in part to normatively endorse practices that have evolved over the years in the West. The description of the institutions and values of late twentieth-century liberal democracy does not in itself carry normative weight, unless coupled with a number of implicit assumptions about values. But the normative component has become inseparable from the term as it is commonly used, so much so that systems which display none of the characteristics enumerated above had for long insisted on calling themselves democratic (e.g. the former Communist regimes of Eastern Europe or the radical dictatorship of Africa and Asia). One reason for this popularity of the concept is, of course, the connotation that democratic systems conform to the magical formula of safeguarding the interests and wishes of the majority while satisfying the basic rights of all. It is this claim that democracy has something for everyone which underlines its normative power. Any definition of democracy must be able to capture this fundamental aspect of the concept.

Another very important element which many theoreticians in the field appear to neglect is the factor of stability. One of modern democracy's most attractive features is its self-corrective capability, which also translates into stability. Governance systems based on broad consent have always existed in history. And this covers not only the classical democracies of Greece and Rome and the Renaissance era republics in Italy and elsewhere, but also the early Muslim state in Medina. However, these systems were characterized by their inherent instability, and their tendency to collapse very quickly into despotism. The reasons for this related first to the absence of international guarantees and second to the presence of violence as a factor in politics. Democracies were most of the time vulnerable to predatory neighbouring states and empires. More often than not, democratic city-states lost their democratic systems when they expanded into empires. In addition, since all members of the political community in the old democracies used to bear arms, disputes often degenerated into violent conflict which brought the system down by favouring generals as opposed to politicians. For this reason, any definition of democracy must incorporate this element of stability.

I am therefore going to venture the following definition: "Democracy is a stable system of governance, which seeks to guarantee the widest possible degree of political participation on equal terms and on the basis of a normatively defensible compromise acceptable to the major players in the political community, a compromise which is also underpinned by a number of enforceable guarantees limiting the powers of government and the shifts which the system may undergo within a predictable range."

The importance of a compromise being normatively based is central, since all government is a compromise based on the balance of power, but it is usually attained by the submission of the weak to the powerful. The democratic compromise seeks to accommodate the values as well as the interests of the parties, so that no one feels aggrieved. The predictability aspect is also important, in spite of the paradoxical requirement that outcomes of the democratic process are not to be fixed in advance. However, all democratic systems are based on written or unwritten constitutions limiting the range of possible outcomes. (Przeworski, 1988)

In what way, then, does a prospective Islamic system differ from democracy so defined? In other words, what Islamic values are in contradiction with the value system underlying the democratic ideal? Certainly not equality, as equality between members of the community is a fundamental Islamic tenet. The Quran and Hadith emphasize that all human beings are equal "as the teeth of the comb," and that no distinction is permissible between human beings on the basis of colour, origin or wealth. Only piety can afford distinction (Quran), and piety is a quality which only God himself can vouch for. It could of course be argued that Islamic doctrine does not grant equality to women and non-Muslims. We do not want to dwell on this issue here, as it had been treated extensively and competently by experts elsewhere. (El-Affendi, 2001) But even granted this was the case, then an Islamic polity could still be seen as compatible with an Athenian-style democracy where only male citizens (Muslims) could participate fully.

Another objection frequently reiterated by Muslim critics of democracy centers on the concept of liberty. A Muslim community, these critics argue, cannot permit unrestricted liberties. Here, one can detect a confusion between liberty and libertarian values. As Pericles emphasized, democracy is not incompatible with the rule of law, discipline and "obedience to those we put in authority." Respecting Islamic law is not, for Muslims, a limit on their liberties. It is a self-imposed limit, and can only make sense if it is a voluntary matter. Thus there is no contradiction whatsoever between the principle of self-government and obedience to the law. If the Muslim community decides to abandon its commitment to Islamic law, then it makes no difference whether this law is observed through coercion or not. (El-Affendi, 1991) Far from being in contradiction with liberty and self-government, Islamic law cannot exist except in a framework of self-government and free adherence to it.

On the other hand, all systems, no mater how coercive they may be, cannot survive without a reasonable level of popular support. And the way to secure such support is to actively seek it. Apart from very restrictive caste systems in ancient times, or overtly oppressive systems of occupation and enslavement, few governments in history have based their legitimacy on principles which excluded the consent of the majority. In fact even caste systems function only when the belief system at their basis acquires mass acquiescence. Thus those who advocate exclusive rule by an upper caste, a religious hierarchy, an aristocracy or a dictatorship of some sort, be it from a monarch, a general, a clique or a holy man, also presuppose popular consent to this principle, either through their ideological inculcation or through political or cultural manipulation. The masses are to be convinced that it is wise or prudent (or divinely decreed) that they should leave governance to their betters. In this regard, therefore, all systems of rule must be "democratic," at least in legitimation, in the sense of being based on the consent of the people. This is emphasized by the fact that even the mechanisms used to impose tyranny have to be democratically managed. In pre-modern times, before states managed to secure what Weber termed the "monopoly of legitimate violence" and rely on specialized professional armies, all able-bodied men were also fighters. Disputes over who has the right to rule were thus resolved roughly according to numbers, since the faction with the biggest fighting force would usually win the day. And although violent conflict, by its very nature, may not always favour numerical superiority, since gifted generals may reverse the odds, the battle for numbers has been crucially important. And this makes it essential to win hearts first. Marc Antony had to wrong-foot Brutus and his faction by an eloquent appeal to the Roman public before the conflict over who should rule the Roman Empire could be resolved on the battlefield. Similarly, even though the faction supporting Imam Ali was on the verge of winning the decisive battle of Siffin (AH 37), one of the most significant in Muslim history, the rival faction succeeded in reversing its fortunes by floating a "compromise proposal" that managed to sow disarray in the other camp. The tactic they used was to lift copies of the Quran on the lances of spears, signaling their acceptance of arbitration according to the Quran. The puritanical followers of Ali made it clear that they were not going to fight against opponents who have agreed to submit to the Quran. Imam Ali, who the Shi'a regard as divinely inspired, and who all Muslims venerate as the last of the Great Caliphs, could do nothing about it. He had to submit to the will of the majority of his followers. Could the lesser men of the models we discussed hope to do otherwise? Does this cast Imam Ali as a democrat? One thing is certain, that the concept of rule as he understood entailed taking the opinions of the majority into account, even if the minority was more vocal and was ready to resort to arms.

We need not dwell much here on the well-known criticisms of democratic practice as imperfect, hypocritical, etc., since these views appear in essence to endorse democracy in principle, and are only concerned that the systems in question were not truly democratic. In any case to argue that democracy is not perfect is not to condemn it as a system, especially given that the criticisms leveled against it (corruption, imbalance in favour of the strong) could be levelled, and with even more justification, against all other systems. And one must add here that all governance is by necessity elitist. In democracy, rival sections of the elite complete amongst each other for popular endorsement. Only a handful of people find the time, the resources and the inclination to compete for office. In other systems, it is also the elite who rule, but competition here takes a different form: war, intrigue, manipulation, etc. The difference is thus mainly in the mechanisms used to establish elite control, not in its fact. In any case, the alternative Islamic systems all appear to espouse some form of elitism. Thus elitist criticism of democracy is irrelevant here.

Similarly, the argument about the popular disenchantment with democracy is not a valid argument, since weak participation may also be an indication that people's concerns are largely allayed. The systems have achieved such a high level of stability and functionality that it becomes largely irrelevant who occupies high office. In crises and when highly contested issues are raised, participation levels also increase. In the final analysis, if people believe political issues were not important enough to bother voting, it is also likely that they will not go to war over them either. And except for those republicans who see political participation as an end in itself, this situation should not present a problem. Certainly not from the perspective of those Muslims who see politics as a means not an end.

In practice, the principle of rule of law does not make popular sovereignty redundant in democracies, and this goes for any law, including law which claims divine origin. Ancient and new theoreticians of Islamic rule assume that a virtuous ruler would be the best guarantee for the upholding of the Law, a task not to be entrusted to mere commoners. In this perception, democracy is understood as mob rule.

Conclusion

The notion that an Islamic community is in essence an ethical enterprise, and that Muslims see their purpose in life in terms of fulfilling their divine obligations has been a central component of the self-perception of Islamic communities across the ages. However, the idea that this ideal could only be achieved within the context of an authoritarian political system which imposes conformity is not equally accepted. The notion of governance as essentially the implementation of divine commands with minimal human discretion runs into numerous difficulties, not least among which is the multiplicity of rival visions. Al-Faqih enumerates at least seven rival salafi tendencies, all opposing democracy, and all claiming religious authority. While the main argument for a unique Islamic system is that it could be directly, clearly and unambiguously derived from Islamic sources, the fact that there are so many different, often contradictory systems claiming Islamic pedigree, puts a big question mark on the fundamental assumption behind this vision. The idea that the basic texts speak so clearly and unambiguously and only need to be interrogated by experts suddenly looks shaky, as the text appears to speak in many tongues and offer conflicting recommendations. The experts need other experts, and in the final instance, some human agency will have to resolve the differences. But the main recommendation of this vision was that it dispensed with this need. We are therefore back where we started.

We have outlined above three main sets of propositions, each claiming to offer the ultimate alternative to a human-based system of governance. Each was found in the end to refer us back to a human arbiter, who not only does not provide a clear and uncontested textual authority for his stance, but has often tended to claim the right to overrule clear and unambiguous divine injunctions. While this presents insurmountable problems at the level of theory, matters have been much worse in practice, whether in past Islamic experience or in contemporary practices.

Most of the objections we have cited to democracy also appear untenable. Presumably, the prescriptions offered by the anti-democracy tendencies are meant for a community made up exclusively of observant Muslims, the only group for which the theorization of Islamists is relevant. And again here we have a paradox. For an observant Muslim community would by definition submit to the Law, and thus does not need an "enforcer" in the shape of an autocrat. By the same token, if the community decides by a large majority not to observe the Law, then it is not clear how one person, in this case the leader, could force them to do so. Thus the efficacy of the ruler in this case would depend on the cooperation of the people, while the main assumption is that the autocrat is needed because the people cannot be trusted. And even if this autocrat was to succeed into intimidating the people into submission, the fact is that this would not be Muslim rule.

One can concede the point that governments need to offer some "leadership" in the sense that they do not follow popular whims. The concept of law also implies holding everyone accountable to a higher moral code than would be justified by mere inclination or pure self-interest. However, this is also the case in democratic societies, as democracies are rule-based systems and not plain anarchy or sheer "mobo-cracy." However, in its liberal variation democracy emphasizes individual autonomy and seeks to minimize, if not eliminate, the role of public authority as an enforcer of morality, especially in the private sphere of personal conduct and economic transactions. Those Muslims who object to democracy on this account object more to liberalism than to democracy, even though modern democracy is essentially liberal.

In sum, it can be argued that an Islamic alternative to liberal democracy is conceivable, even desirable. However, this alternative will inevitably exhibit some of the features we ascribe today to democratic systems. It will certainly not be "authoritarian and corporatist" a la Cantori, and would even more certainly not resemble any of three models discussed above.

Notes

1. According to a report in the authoritative compendiums of Bukhari and Muslim, the Prophet (peace be upon him) said in a sermon: "O people! Allah has prescribed Hajj for you, so you must perform it." A man asked: "Every year, O Prophet of Allah?" The Prophet (peace be upon him) remained silent. When the man repeated it thrice, the Prophet (peace be upon him) said: "Had I said 'yes', it would have become a yearly obligation, and this would have been beyond your power." Then he added: "Leave me alone so long as I leave you alone (i.e. do not pester me with questions about things which I omit and do not mention). Some people who lived before you were destroyed because they asked too many questions and disagreed with their Prophets. So when I command you to do something, you must obey and do it to the best of your power, and if I forbid you from something, then just avoid it." (Bukhari and Muslim)

2. The salafi trend is the self-description of a broad trend more commonly known as "Wahhabi," which is prevalent in Saudi Arabia but also has important pockets of following elsewhere. It is strictly traditionalist, tending towards a more literal interpretation of the original sources and hostile to Sufi and liberal trends. The views of Hizb

ut-Tahrir can be found at any of its numerous websites, in particular, www.khilafah.org. See also an-Nabhani (1998), and Taji-Farouki (1996).

References

Adam, Charles J. (1983) "Maududi and the Islamic State," in John Esposito (ed.) *Voices of Resurgent Islam* (Oxford: Oxford University Press), 99–123.

Algar, Hamid (1981) *Islam and Revolution I: Writings and Declarations of Imam Khomeyni (1941–1980)* (Berkeley: Mizan Press).

An-Nabahni, Taqiuddin (1998) *The Islamic State* (London: Al-Khilafah Publications).

Betham, David, "Liberal Democracy and the Limits of Democratization," in Held (1993), 55–73.

Cantori, Louis J. (2000) "The Limitations of Western Democratic Theory: The Islamic Alternative," a paper presented at the panel "Religion, Islam and Democracy in the Contemporary Middle East," at the Middle East Studies Association's Annual Conference, November 17, 2000, Orlando, FL.

Dahl, Robert (1989) *Democracy and Its Critics* (New Haven: Yale University Press).

Al-Duri, Qahtan (1974) *Al-Shura banya al-Nazariyyah wa'l-Tatbiq* (Baghdad: Matba'at al-Umma).

El-Affendi, Abdelwah (2001) *Rethinking Islam and Modernity: Essays in Honour of Fathi Osman* (Leicester: The Islamic Foundation). (1991) *Who Needs an Islamic State?* (London: Grey Seal).

Enayat, Hamid (1982) *Modern Islamic Political Thought* (London: Macmillan).

Al-Faqih, Saad (2001) "Tahaffuzat al-Salafiyyin 'ala al-Dimiqratiyyah," a paper delivered to the conference on "Misgivings about Democracy in Arab Countries," organized by the Programme for the Study of Democracy in the Arab World, Oxford, August 15, 2001.

Held, David (ed.) (1993) *Prospects for Democracy* (Cambridge: Polity Press). (1995) *Models of Democracy* (Cambridge: Polity Press)

Ibn-Khaldun, Abd al-Rahman ibn Muhammad (1970) *Al-Muqaddimah* (Beirut: Maktabat Lubnan).

Idris, Ja'far Sheikh (2001) "Shoora and Democracy: A Conceptual Analysis," Internet, at Islaam.com (http://www.islaam.com/challenges/shoora and democracy.htm)

Khan, M. A. Muqtedar (2001) "Shura and Democracy," Internet, at: http://www.ijtihad .org/shura.htm

Khomeini, Ayatollah Ruhollah (1981) "Islamic Government," in Algar (1981).

Maududi, Abu'l Ala al- (1967) *Islamic Law and Constitution* (Lahore: Islamic Publications).

———. (1977) *Human Rights and Islam* (Lahore: Islamic Publications Ltd.)

———. (1977b) *Minbaj al-Inqilab al-Islami* (Cairo: Dar al-Ansar).

Przeworski, Adam (1988) "Democracy as a Contingent Outcome of Conflicts," in Jon Elster and Rune Slagstad (eds.) *Constitutionalism and Democracy* (Cambridge: Cambridge University Press, 1988), 61–63.

Qutb, Sayyid (1978) *Ma'alim fi'l-Tariq* (Beirut: IIFSO, 1978).

Rida, Muhammad Rashid (1925) *Al-khilafah aw al-Imamah al-'Uzma* (Cairo: Dar al-Manar).

Siddiqui, Iqbal (2000) "Dangers of 'democratising' Islam and Muslim political discourse," *Crescent International*, June 16–30, 2000.

Taji-Farouki, Suha (1996) "Islamic State Theories and Contemporary Realities," in Sidahmed and Ehteshami (eds.) *Islamic Fundamentalism* (Boulder, Co.: Westview Press).

Zallum, Abdul-Qadim (1995) *Al-Dimiqratiyyah Nizam Kufr* (no publisher or place).

Index

About the Editor and Contributors

Asma Afsaruddin is Associate Professor of Arabic and Islamic Studies at the University of Notre Dame. She taught previously at Harvard University. Her fields of specialization are the religious and political thought of Islam, the Qur'an and *hadith* studies, Islamic intellectual history, and gender studies. She is author of *Excellence and Precedence: Medieval Islamic Discourse on Legitimate Leadership* (E. J. Brill, 2002) and editor or coeditor of two other books. Dr. Afsaruddin is currently serving on the editorial boards of the *Encyclopedia of Medieval Islamic Civilization* (Routledge) and the *Bulletin of the Middle East Studies Association* (Cambridge University Press). She previously served as a consultant for the *Oxford Dictionary of Islam* (2003). Among her current research projects is a specially commissioned monograph on the history of early Muslims and a book manuscript about competing perspectives on *jihad* and martyrdom in premodern and modern Islamic thought. Her research has won funding from the Harry Frank Guggenheim Foundation, among others, and she was recently named Carnegie Scholar for 2005 by the Carnegie Corporation of New York.

Osman Bakar, formerly Professor of Philosophy of Science and Vice President (Academic) at the University of Malaya, is currently Malaysia Chair of Islam in Southeast Asia at the Center for Muslim-Christian Understanding, Edmund A. Walsh School of Foreign Service, Georgetown University. He was educated at London University (1967–1971), where he obtained B.Sc. and M.Sc. degrees specializing in Mathematics. He earned his doctorate in Islamic philosophy from Temple University in Philadelphia (1981–1986). In 1992, he was Fulbright Visiting Scholar in the History of Science department, Harvard University.

Dr. Bakar has published twelve books and more than 120 articles on various aspects of Islamic thought and civilization, particularly Islamic philosophy and science, Sufism, Southeast Asian Islam, contemporary Islam and inter-religious dialogues. Among his books are *Classification of Knowledge in Islam* (Islamic Texts Society, 1998), *Tawhid and Science* (Secretariat for Islamic Philosophy and Science, 1991), *Islam and Confucianism* (University of Malaya Press, 1997) and *Islam and Civilizational Dialogue* (University of Malaya Press, 1997).

Özlem Denli is Research Fellow in the Department of Philosophy at the Norwegian University of Science and Technology. Ms. Denli majored in Political Science and Sociology at Bosphorus University in Istanbul, Turkey. She did postgraduate studies at the University of Oslo and received a Cand.Polit title in the Department of Political Science. Ms. Denli completed the competence-building curriculum of the Norwegian Research Council's Ethics Program in political and normative philosophy, while working as Research Fellow at the Norwegian Institute of Human Rights. She researches in the area of political philosophy, ethics and human rights. She has authored several articles in Turkish, English and Norwegian, including "Between Laicist State Ideology and Modern Public Religion: The Head Cover Controversy in Contemporary Turkey," in *Facilitating Freedom of Religion or Belief: A Deskbook*, ed. Cole Durham Jr., Bahia Tahzib-Lie and Tore Lindholm (Martinus Nijhoff Publishers, 2004) and "Freedom of Religion in Turkey: Laicist Policies and Islamic Challenges," in *Human Rights in Turkey: Policies and Prospects*, ed. Zehra F. Kabasakal Arat (University of Pennsylvania Press, forthcoming).

Abdelwahab El-Affendi is Senior Research Fellow at the Centre for the Study of Democracy, University of Westminster, and coordinator of the Centre's Democracy and Islam Program. He is author of *Turabi's Revolution: Islam and Power in Sudan* (Grey Seal, 1991), *Who Needs an Islamic State?* (Grey Seal, 1991), *Revolution and Political Reform in Sudan* (1995), *Rethinking Islam and Modernity* (2001) and *For a State of Peace: Conflict and the Future of Democracy in Sudan* (2002). Dr. El-Affendi was a member of the core team of authors of the *Arab Human Development Report* (2004) and is a member of the Advisory Board and a contributor to the forthcoming report.

Carolyn Fluehr-Lobban is Professor of Anthropology at Rhode Island College, where she teaches courses in Anthropology and in Islamic, African and Afro-American Studies. At Rhode Island College she has received both the Award for Distinguished Teaching in 1990 and the Award for Distinguished Scholar in 1998. She is author or editor of many books, including *Islamic Societies in Practice* (University Press of Florida, 1994; 2nd edition 2004) and *Islamic Law and Society in the Sudan* (Frank Cass, 1987; Arabic translation 2004). She has published the writings of Egyptian liberal humanist intellectual Muhammad Sa'id al-Ashmawy, translated from Arabic to English in the 1998 publication *Against Islamic Extremism* (University Press of Florida; paperback edition 2001). She is also editor of *Ethics and the Profession of Anthropology: Dialogue for a New Era* (Pennsylvania University Press, 1990; 2nd edition AltaMira, 2003). With Haitian collaborator Asselin Charles, she published in 2000 (Taylor & Francis; paperback edition 2002) the first major work of anthropology by a scholar of African descent, Antenor Firmin's *The Equality of the Human Races*, originally published in French as *De L'egalite des Races Humaines* in 1885. Her latest works include *Race and Identity in the Nile Valley*, coedited with Kharyssa Rhodes (Red Sea Press, 2004), *Race and Racism: An Introduction* (AltaMira, 2005) and *Female Well-being: A Century of Change around the World*, coedited with Janet Billson (Zed Books, 2005).

M. A. Muqtedar Khan is Assistant Professor in the Department of Political Science and International Relations at the University of Delaware. He is Non-resident Fellow at the Brookings Institution. He earned his Ph.D. in International Relations, Political Philosophy and Islamic Political Thought from Georgetown University in May 2000. Dr. Khan was a founding board member of the Center for the Study of Islam & Democracy and is a fellow of the Institute for Social Policy and Understanding. He has been President, Vice President and General Secretary of the Association of Muslim Social Scientists. He is author of *American Muslims: Bridging Faith and Freedom* (Amana, 2002) and *Jihad for Jerusalem: Identity and Strategy in International Relations* (Praeger, 2004). Dr. Khan frequently comments on BBC, CNN, FOX and VOA TV, NPR and other radio and TV networks. His political commentaries appear regularly in newspapers in more than twenty countries. He has also lectured in North America, East Asia, the Middle East and Europe.

Marc Lynch is Associate Professor of Political Science at Williams College. He is author of *State Interests and Public Spheres: The International Politics of Jordan's Identity* (Columbia University Press, 1999). His most recent book, *Voices of the New Arab Public*, was published by Columbia University Press in 2005. Dr. Lynch's research interests focus on the role of deliberation and public spheres in international relations, with a primary empirical emphasis on the Middle East.

Mahgoub El-Tigani Mahmoud is Associate Professor of Sociology at Tennessee State University and Director of the university's Office of International Relations and Programs. He was selected in 2002 and 2005 as one of the Who's Who among America's Teachers. Dr. Mahmoud was cofounder (with Dr. Amin Mekki Medani) of the Sudan Human Rights Organization, Cairo Office. Dr. Mahmoud was its first, and continuing, elected President. He has published, coauthored, and translated in Arabic and English. His works in Arabic include *The Administrative System of the May Dictatorship, African Women: Religion and Governance,* and *A Sudanese Encyclopedia of Criminal Justice.* His works in English include *Sudan Law and International Human Rights Norms* (Edwin Mellen Press, 2002), *Sudanese Thinkers* (Edwin Mellen Press, 2004) and *Human Rights in Africa* (Edwin Mellen Press, 2005), among others. Dr. Mahmoud has also translated from English to Arabic *Nubia, Corridor to Africa* by William Y. Adams; *Islamic Law and Society in the Sudan* by Carolyn Fluehr-Lobban, published in Cairo in 2004; and *Prisoner of the Khalifa* by Charles Neufeld in 2005. Dr. Mahmoud is also founder and editor-in-chief of the bilingual *Sudanese Human Rights Quarterly,* publishing since 1994. Dr. Mahmoud is currently preparing his four-volume work *Encyclopedia of Islamic Criminal Justice,* in Arabic.

Ali Paya is currently Associate Professor of Philosophy and Social Sciences at the National Research Institute for Science Policy, Tehran. He is Visiting Scholar at the Centre for the Study of Democracy, University of Westminster, London. He is author of *University, Scientific Thinking, Innovation, and the Public Sphere* (Tehran: Ministry of Science, Research and Technology, 2005) and *Epistemology and Methodology of Futures Studies* (Tehran: National Research Institute for Science Policy, 2005).

Tariq Ramadan taught Islamic Studies and Philosophy as Professor at Freiburg University in Switzerland for many years. In 2004 he held the posts of Professor of Islamic Studies in the Classics Department and Luce Professor of Religion, Conflict and Peacebuilding at the Kroc Institute, University of Notre Dame. He has authored and co-authored more than twenty books, including *Western Muslims and the Future of Islam* (Oxford University Press, 2004), *Globalization and Muslim Resistances* (2004) and *Islam, the West and the Challenges of Modernity* (Islamic Foundation, 2001).

Abdulaziz Sachedina is Professor of Islamic Studies at the University of Virginia. He has an M.A. and a Ph.D. from the University of Toronto and B.A. degrees from Aligarh Muslim University in India and Ferdowsi University in Iran. He has been Visiting Professor at Wilfrid Laurier, Waterloo and McGill universities in Canada, as well as at Haverford College and the University of Jordan, Amman. He has lectured widely in East Africa, India, Pakistan, Europe and the Middle East. Dr. Sachedina is a core member of the Islamic Roots of Democratic Pluralism Project in the CSIS Preventive Diplomacy Program and a key contributor—along with Rabbi Marc Gopin and the Reverend David Steele—to the program's efforts to link religion to universal human needs and values in the service of peacebuilding. He contributed to *Human Rights and the Conflict of Cultures: Western and Islamic Perspectives on Religious Liberty* (University of South Carolina Press, 1988) and recently published his study *The Islamic Roots of Democratic Pluralism* (Oxford University Press, 2001). Dr. Sachedina's areas of expertise are political Islam, religious conflict resolution through analysis of Islamic legal tradition, Islamic roots of religious and political pluralism and human rights in the Middle East, Pakistan and East Africa.

Tamara Sonn is Kenan Professor of Religion and Professor of Humanities at the College of William and Mary. Dr. Sonn's books include *Between Qur'an and Crown: The Challenge of Political Legitimacy in the Arab World* (Westview, 1990), *Interpreting Islam: Bandali Jawzi's Islamic Intellectual History* (Oxford, 1996), *Islam and the Question of Minorities* (Scholars' Press, 1996), *Comparing Religions through Law: Judaism and Islam* (with J. Neusner; Routledge, 1999), and *Judaism and Islam in Practice* (with J. Neusner and J. Brockopp; Routledge, 2000). She has received grants from the United States Institute of Peace and the American Council of Learned Societies, among others. She is a member of the Board of Directors of the American Council for the Study of Islamic Societies, former Vice President of the Eastern Division of the American Academy of Religion, and Associate Editor of the *Middle East Studies Association Bulletin, Muslim World* and the *American Journal for Islamic Social Science.*